ond chapter approaches the difficult question of the motives of the Evangelist from the angle of his polemics against this or that group. In a third chapter, the approach is the opposite one: what are the causes which the Evangelist tries to defend? The fourth chapter raises and answers the questions of author, date, and place of writing, possible stages in the redaction of the Gospel.

This reading of the Gospel of Mark throws much light on the life and history of the Palestinian church before A.D. 70. Early Christianity comes alive and the Gospel gains depth to a surprising extent. The book is fully documented with references to significant Biblical studies.

ETIENNE TROCMÉ is Professor of New Testament and President of the Université des Sciences Humaines, Strasbourg, where he was formerly Dean of the Faculty of Protestant Theology. He has lectured in Biblical Studies at the University of Oxford; is Fellow of University College, Cambridge; and was Visiting Lecturer at the University of British Columbia in Vancouver. He was educated in France; at the University of Southern California; at the University of Basel, Switzerland; and he holds a doctorate in theology from the University of Strasbourg. He is also author of *Jesus as Seen by His Contemporaries*.

THE FORMATION OF THE GOSPEL
ACCORDING TO MARK

The Formation of the Gospel According to Mark

by
ETIENNE TROCMÉ

Translated by
PAMELA GAUGHAN

THE WESTMINSTER PRESS
Philadelphia

© The Society for Promoting Christian Knowledge, 1975

Translated from the French
La formation de l'Evangile selon Marc, © 1963
Presses Universitaires de France, Paris

Published by The Westminster Press®
Philadelphia, Pennsylvania

PRINTED IN THE UNITED STATES OF AMERICA

Library of Congress Cataloging in Publication Data

Trocmé, Etienne.
    The formation of the Gospel according to Mark.

    Translation of La formation de l'Evangile selon Marc.
    Bibliography: p.
    Includes index.
    1. Bible. N.T. Mark—Criticism, interpretation,
etc. I. Title.
BS2585.2.T7513   226'.3'06   75-15510
ISBN 0-664-20803-7

ANNAE UXORI
DILECTAE

CONTENTS

ABBREVIATIONS

JBL   *The Journal of Biblical Literature* (Philadelphia)

JEH   *The Journal of Ecclesiastical History* (London)

JTS   *The Journal of Theological Studies* (Oxford and London)

RHPR *Revue d'histoire et de philosophie religieuses* (Paris)

RHR   *Revue de l'histoire des religions* (Annales du Musée Guimet) (Paris)

ZNTW *Zeitschrift für die neutestamentliche Wissenschaft und die Kunde der älteren Kirche* (Giessen, then Berlin)

Titles of commentaries and standard works of reference have been abbreviated in the Notes, after their first appearance, e.g.

Blass-Debrunner, *Grammatik* = *G. des neutestamentlichen Griechisch*, 10th edn (Göttingen 1959)

Strack-Billerbeck = *Kommentar zum N.T. aus Talmud und Midrasch*, 6 vols. (Munich 1922–61)

TWNT = *Theologisches Wörterbuch zum Neuen Testament* (Stuttgart 1933–73)

C. E. B. Cranfield, *St Mark* = *The Gospel according to St Mark* (The Cambridge Greek Testament Commentary) (Cambridge 1959)

INTRODUCTION

It is scarcely necessary to say that the author of this study is aware of his numerous predecessors. The making of the Gospel according to Mark has been the subject of many works[1] in the last one hundred and fifty years and to these must of course be added most of the books on the 'synoptic problem', as well as the 'Lives of Jesus', where the question is also discussed. A number of these writings will be examined fairly closely in the following pages. Here we shall confine ourselves to a general observation which we believe is applicable to the vast majority of books and articles dealing with or touching on the question of the origins of the second canonical Gospel.

Most of the interest taken in this question has been for the purpose of supporting one theory or another about the life of Jesus: Mark's dependence on the Gospel according to Matthew (in its canonical form or in an earlier version) has been defended by the members of the traditional school of thought on the subject;[2] the existence of a Proto-Mark or of extensive written sources has been advanced chiefly by liberal critics who were looking in these hypothetical documents for 'the historical Jesus';[3] the accent has been placed on the role of oral tradition in the making of Mark chiefly by theologians who thought any attempt to write a biography of Jesus was useless.[4] Those who have asserted or denied the Paulinism of Mark[5] have usually done so in order to measure the distance separating the Gospel from the events it relates—that is to say, in order to suggest the degree of attention that should be paid to this document by the biographers of Jesus.

This is all very natural, it will be thought. Is not Jesus the central figure of all the Gospels, even in the eyes of the critics most anxious to refute their biographical character? In its

---

[1] See bibliography, pp. 262ff. [2] Cf. below, pp. 8–10 and 11ff.
[3] Cf. below, pp. 21ff. [4] Cf. below, pp. 31ff.
[5] Cf. below, pp. 145ff.

extreme simplicity, Mark cannot even claim to interest the reader by the nobility of its moral teaching, the charm of its stories or the beauty of its theology, as can the Gospels according to Matthew, Luke, or John. Why then should one delve back into its history if not to make sure of the soundness of the information it offers us about the life of Jesus? Such inevitably arid and conjectural research is scarcely worthwhile unless it contributes something to the study of a great subject.

It would be easy to agree with this commonsense view if Gospel criticism had not, in the last forty years, fallen into the habit of searching each Gospel 'pericope' for indications of the life and faith of the early Christians before even looking for those shedding light on Jesus. Whatever one may think of the excesses of certain partisans of Form-criticism, it must be admitted that their methods have permeated to all the schools of exegesis. It is no longer possible today to examine a New Testament text without wondering whether it has not been shaped by the use the first Christians made of it in their cult, their teaching, or their proselytizing well before it was even inserted in any Gospel or Epistle and whether, consequently, it does not tell us something about the Church of the first generation. Besides, it is a long time since the New Testament Epistles were read with no effort to reconstruct, with the help of the indications they contain, the life and faith of the various communities to which they were addressed.

Now it has to be admitted that in studying the Gospels in their final form we do not often imitate the good habit that now prevails in the study of the Epistles or of isolated pericopes. We come close to doing so in the case of John, whose theological thinking is being placed with increasing success in its original setting,[1] but here the mind of the Evangelist and his love of

---

[1] We may mention here simply the masterly works of R. Bultmann, *Das Evangelium des Johannes* (Göttingen 1941) (Kritisch-exegetischer Kommentar über das N.T. begr. v. H. A. W. Meyer, Section 2), with its Supplement of 1957; and of C. H. Dodd, *The Interpretation of the Fourth Gospel* (Cambridge 1953). These two works contain useful bibliographies which can be supplemented by P. H. Ménoud's 'state of the question' in *L'Evangile de Jean d'après les recherches récentes*, 2nd edn (Neuchâtel and Paris 1947), Cahiers théologiques' 3; and 'Les études johanniques de Bultmann à Barrett' in *L'Evangile de Jean: études et problèmes*, s. 1 1958 (Recherches bibliques, III).

mystery will always place a veil between the reader and the church in which the Gospel grew up. In the case of the synoptic Gospels we are far from doing so, although the ground is more promising, since the personalities of their authors are less to the fore. True, it is sought, in order to throw light on their origins, to identify their theological and literary characteristics, then to situate on the map and in the chronology of first century Christianity the place and date at which they and the documents they drew on came into being. But it is almost always a question of fitting the synoptic Gospels and their sources (in the widest sense of the term) into the niches provided by a ready-made theory of the origins of Christianity: the traditional theories inspired by an uncritical reading of Acts and of the *Ecclesiastical History* of Eusebius;[1] theories placing the true birth of Christianity at the time of its entry in the setting of hellenistic syncretism;[2] others postulating the gradual depoliticising of a Christianity that began as a revolutionary movement, etc.[3]

It is not surprising, then, that a number of critics should, in the wake of the late Ernst Lohmeyer,[4] have recently felt the need to return to the study of the synoptic Gospels, concentrating, not on their literary relations nor on the internal structure of the pericopes they contain, but on the theological thought that is implicit in each and has inspired and guided its composition.[5] These scholars believe that their work will lead to a

---

[1] The most recent and satisfying example is to be found in the *Introduction à la Bible sous la direction de A. Robert de A. Feuillet*, vol. II: *Nouveau Testament* (Tournai 1959), in the pages devoted to X. Léon-Dufour to the origins of the synoptic Gospels (pp. 186–94; 222–7; 252–7; 315–20).

[2] The most attractive of these theories today is that of R. Bultmann, who applies it to the synoptic Gospels in his *Geschichte der synoptischen Tradition* 3rd edn (Göttingen 1957). (The 1st edn dates back to 1921.) Our quotations are from the 4th edn (1958), identical with the 3rd. [E.T. *The History of the Synoptic Tradition* (Oxford 1963).]

[3] S. G. F. Brandon, in *The Fall of Jerusalem and the Christian Church* (London 1951, 2nd edn 1957), applies a theory of this type with some success to the determination of the origin of the Gospels (pp. 185–248).

[4] For example in his small book, at the same time provocative and debatable, *Galiläa und Jerusalem* (Göttingen 1936), in which he defended the idea that the Gospel according to Mark, if looked at closely, imposed the theory of the dual origin of Palestinian Christianity.

[5] Let us mention, among the works of some importance, the following:

clearer grasp of what constitutes the originality of each of the
first three Gospels. The result will be a sounder knowledge of the
diversity of Christianity in the first century and, lastly, a
greater subtlety in weighing up the various components of the
evangelical tradition and hence a surer understanding of the
person and work of Jesus.[1] Anyone who is conscious of the
extreme difficulty of interpreting words and stories which
appear to be of the simplest kind but which are fraught with
what is almost an infinity of meanings, will appreciate at its
proper value this patient quest which adds to everything that
has been acquired thanks to Form-criticism.

It might be objected that what our sources tell us about
Christianity in the first century has long been recorded and
there is nothing new to be said on the subject. How could one
hope to change anything in the information we owe to the
Acts and to the Epistles, which come to us direct, by having
recourse to the Gospels, whose testimony as to the milieu in
which they came into being is both involuntary and absolutely
indirect? A first answer is that the direct documents are so
fragmentary and in some cases so tendentious[2] that one is

G. D. Kilpatrick, *The Origins of the Gospel according to St Matthew* (Oxford
1946); K. Stendahl, *The School of St Matthew and its Use of the Old
Testament* (Acta Seminarii Neotestamentici Upsaliensis, xx) (Lund
1954); P. Nepper-Christensen, *Das Matthäusevangelium, ein judenchrist-
liches Evangelium?* (Aarhus 1958); G. Bornkamm, G. Barth and H. J.
Held, *Ueberlieferung und Auslegung im Matthäus-Evangelium* (Wiss. Mono-
graphien z. A. u. N.T., 1) (Neukirchen 1960); W. Marxsen, *Der
Evangelist Markus, Studien zur Redaktionsgeschichte des Evangeliums* (Forschung zur Religion und Literatur des Alten und Neuen Testaments,
ed. R. Bultmann (Göttingen 1956, 2nd edn 1959); J. M. Robinson,
Das Geschichtsverständnis des Markus-Evamgeliums (Abhandlungen zur
Theologie des Alten und Neuen Testaments, ed. W. Eichrodt and O.
Cullman, 30) (Zurich 1956); H. Conzelmann, *Die Mitte der Zeit, Studien
zur Theologie des Lukas* (Beiträge zur historischen Theologie, ed. G.
Ebeling, 17) (Tübingen 1954, 3rd edn 1960). Cf. also the useful
article by X. Léon-Dufour: 'Formgeschichte et Redaktionsgeschichte
des Evangiles synoptiques', in *Recherches de Science Religiouse*, vol. XLVI
(1958), pp. 237–69.

[1] It is significant that one of the members of the new 'school' should be
the author of an excellent book about Jesus, namely: G. Bornkamm,
Jesus von Nazareth (Urbanbücher, 19) (Stuttgart 1956).

[2] We believe we have shown this, after quite a number of others, in the
study on 'Le Livre des Actes et l'histoire' (*Etudes d'histoire et de philo-*

justified in using every means to hand for their amplification and criticism. Besides, the exegesis of the Gospels according to the Form-critical method has already in the past radically transformed our ideas about the first two generations of Christians. It may accordingly be hoped that further results will be achieved in the same direction as we approach these documents today from a rather new angle.

Lastly, many of our ideas about the Jewish background to primitive Christianity have been so shaken by the discoveries at Qumran[1] that some of the most commonly accepted theories about the life and faith of the early Christians threaten to collapse. There are few scholars today who do not feel bound to alter their opinions about the origins of Christianity since they have seen the Dead Sea scrolls.[2] This means that even those who do not think that the religious thought and practices of this sect had any direct influence on Jesus and his successors, are obliged to pose again questions as important for the growth of early Christianity as the development of Christology, the origin of the concept of the Church, the significance of the sacraments, the attitude of the first Christians to the Temple of Jerusalem.[3] In short, one can say that the accounts of the early Christian communities in Palestine have to be thoroughly revised and some serious amendments need to be made to what

---

sophie religieuses; published under the auspices of the Faculty of Protestant Theology of the University of Strasbourg, 45) (Paris 1957), especially in pp. 50ff.

[1] An excellent French translation of all the manuscripts published up to 1959, together with a brilliant presentation of their content and a brief outline of the questions they raise, may be found in A. Dupont-Sommer, *Les écrits esséniens découverts près de la Mer Morte* (Paris 1959). [E.T. 1961.]

[2] It is nevertheless much what R. Bultmann affirms in his preface to the 3rd edn (Tübingen 1958) of his *Theologie des Neuen Testaments*. The celebrated theologian is no doubt right in thinking that the importance of the changes wrought in the interpretation of the New Testament by the Dead Sea scrolls has often been exaggerated. But the scrolls have in fact a much deeper significance for the study of early Christianity than the Mandean texts that so kindled Bultmann's enthusiasm when his system was not yet a hard and fast one.

[3] Cf. for instance: *The Scrolls and the New Testament*, ed. Kr. Stendahl (New York 1957); J. Daniélou, *Les manuscrits de la Mer Morte et les origines du christianisme* (Paris 1957); several articles in *Les manuscrits de la Mer Morte, Colloque de Strasbourg*, 1955 (Paris 1957).

used to be said, until quite recently, about the shift of Christianity over to Hellenism.

Called upon, after the early death of Théo Preiss, to comment on a book that he could have commented on much better himself,[1] the author thought he might associate himself in the present study with the Redaction criticism research referred to above and so take part in the discussions in progress on the history and thought of the first two generations of Christians.

It seemed best to enquire first into the written and oral sources the Evangelist had used—a difficult and rather hazardous task, but one which leads to certain important conclusions regarding the literary activity of this distinctive character who must be acknowledged to have talent as a writer. Whatever may have been said to the contrary, Mark is not the work of a mere compiler. The fact that his language and style are simple and straightforward makes no difference.

Everything inclines us to believe that the writer of Mark composed his Gospel to meet the needs of the Church of his day. It is even plain that he wishes to combat certain ideas and persons whose influence he finds harmful. We shall begin, then, by cataloguing his antipathies before examining the causes he defends. In the course of this twofold enquiry, based on the framework he gives to his Gospel and his choice of material, we shall be led to discuss his chief theological ideas.

A certain number of features observed in the process will then oblige us to reopen a question that is often considered a pointless one, namely: 'Was our canonical Mark preceded by a proto-Mark?' While agreeing that from the literary point of view this hypothesis is chiefly conjecture, we shall endeavour to show that it can nonetheless be defended and that, as presented here, it is more satisfying historically and theologically than the hypothesis of a single edition.

We shall then be in a better position to place the proto-Mark

---

[1] Cf. his posthumous notes on 'Le Fils de l'Homme' in the Montpellier *Etudes théologiques et religieuses*, in particular the early part concerning the synoptic Gospels (26th year, 1951, No. 3). The commentary of Mark that Preiss was to have brought out in the series Commentaire du Nouveau Testament (Neuchâtel 1949ff.) was unfortunately never finished.

and the canonical Mark in the framework of early Christianity. Probable as the current theories appear to be where the place of composition of the canonical Mark is concerned, we shall have to depart from them with regard to the author and date of the canonical Mark and also with regard to the proto-Mark. The hypothesis that will be advanced here as to the source and significance of the last-mentioned will cause some surprise, but we trust that we shall have put forward sufficient arguments in support of it to convince those readers who have remained with us until then. This hypothesis naturally has certain effects on the way we see the Palestinian churches of the first generation and we shall indicate what to our mind are the most important.

It will then be time to ask what Mark contributes to our knowledge of the historical Jesus. Our very rapid conclusion on that point will sum up various hypotheses put forward in the course of this study. It will accordingly be a qualified one—as negative on some points as positive on others. To those who are dissatisfied with one or other of these tendencies our answer is that to be too optimistic or too pessimistic about the possibility of knowing the historical Jesus is to risk moving out of the sphere of history into that of dogma and making the total cognibility or incognibility of the historical Christ an article of faith. We prefer the role of the historian who, less sure of his ground, is content to offer the Christian a limited certainty which can serve, not as an impregnable bulwark, but simply as a buttress, to his faith in Jesus Christ.[1]

---

[1] At the moment of going to press we received T. A. Burkill's important work *Mysterious Revelation: An Examination of the Philosophy of St Mark's Gospel* (Ithaca, N.Y. 1963), which we regret not to have been able to make use of here. [Author's notes to French edn 1963.]

Chapter One

THE EVANGELIST AND HIS
SOURCES

It has never been claimed that Mark was the work of an eye-witness of the ministry of Jesus. Peter, whose authority was invoked very early to strengthen the impact of this Gospel,[1] was, for example, never said to be its author. As the work in question does not present itself as the product of either a divine revelation or an effort of the imagination,[2] but claims to relate real facts dating from a very recent past, it is manifestly based on oral or written information that can be called sources in the wide sense of the term.

Since Augustine let it be understood that the author of Mark was an abridger of Matthew,[3] there have been commentators who have seen in the first canonical Gospel the source of the second. While it may be exaggerated to say, with M. Goguel,[4]

---

[1] As early as the first half of the second century, by Papias and by 'the Elder', whose words the latter quotes (Eusebius, *H.E.* III, 39, 15).

[2] Those who deny the historical existence of Jesus have added nothing constructive to the study of Mark, whether it be Bruno Bauer, *Kritik der evangelischen Geschichte der Synoptiker*, 3 vol. (Leipzig 1841–2); A. Drews, *Das Markus-evangelium als Zeugnis gegen die Geschichtlichkeit Jesu* (Jena 1921, 2nd edn 1928); M. H. Raschke, *Die Werkstatt der Markusevangelisten, eine neue Evangelien-theorie* (Jena 1924); or P. Alfaric, *La plus ancienne vie de Jésus, l'évangile selon Marc* (Paris 1929). It would be a waste of time to refute theories so manifestly based on preconceived and fanciful ideas. Cf. what A. Loisy, *Histoire et mythe à propos de Jésus-Christ* (Paris 1938), pp. 150–72, has to say, with some verve, about the ideas advanced by P. L. Couchoud, *Jésus, le Dieu fait homme* (Paris 1937), pp. 200–30, to explain the making of the Gospel according to Mark.

[3] 'Marcus (Matthaeum) subsecutus tamquam pedisequus et breviator eius videtur'. Augustine, *De consensu evangelistarum*, 1, 2, 4 (Vienna Corpus, vol. XLIII, p. 4, lines 12–13).

[4] *Introduction au Nouveau Testament*, vol. 1 (Paris 1923), p. 55.

that this theory 'prevailed unchallenged until the eighteenth century',[1] it can be said that it only went out of fashion among Protestant exegetes around 1860 and among Catholic exegetes around 1900.[2] It has now been completely dropped: it needs the decisive assurance of an Adolf Schlatter[3] or the paradoxical turn of mind of a Benedictine from across the Channel[4] to go on defending it today.

There is no cause to regret this turn of events, since the theory in question merely complicated still more the already thorny problem of the relationships of the synoptic Gospels to one another. If Mark had used Matthew as its main source, one would find inexplicable both the way in which the author adds to what is related there[5] and his blind passing over of the finest sayings of Jesus that Matthew records.[6] He would have destroyed its noble proportions by amputating it at both ends and removing all trace of the 'five books' into which chapters

[1] Thus Calvin, in the 'Argument' of his *Commentaire sur la concordance ou harmonie composée de . . . S. Matthieu, S. Marc et S. Luc* (Geneva 1561): '. . . Il n'y a nulle apparence à ce que dit S. Hiérome, que l'Evangile de S. Marc est un Epitome, c'est-à-dire un abrégé de celuy de S. Matthieu. . . .' (Quoted from the revised edition in French of the *Commentaires de Jehan Calvin sur le Nouveau Testament*, vol. I (Paris 1854), p. xviii.)

[2] M. J. Lagrange gives an interesting picture of the position of the Catholic critics around 1910 in pages xxxiv–xxxviii of his *Evangile selon saint Marc* (7th edn, Paris 1942 (1st edn 1910)).

[3] The reason he gives for this mistaken choice is the following: 'Für die Worte Jesu hat sich das Urteil unter uns befestigt, dass der Bericht des Matthäus der erste, der des Markus der zweite, daraus abgeleitete sei. Dagegen wird oft der Versuch gemacht, den Bericht über die Worte Jesu von der Erzählung seiner Werke zu trennen und für diesen Teil des Texts Mark voranzustellen. Ich halte diese Trennung nicht für möglich und Matthäus nicht nur in seinen Sprüchen, sondern auch in seiner Erzählung, für das altere Evangelium. . . .' *Erläuterungen zum Neuen Testament*, 1st edn, vol. I (Stuttgart-Calw 1908), p. 311 n.; posthumous edn, vol. II (Stuttgart 1947), p. I, n.

[4] Dom B. C. Butler, *The Originality of St Matthew: A Critique of the Two Documents Hypothesis* (Cambridge 1951). Cf. the sigh his theory draws from X. Léon-Dufour on p. 275 of vol. II of the *Introduction à la Bible* by A. Robert and A. Feuillet.

[5] Some examples are to be found in M. Goguel, *Introduction au N.T.*, vol. I, pp. 416–7.

[6] The whole Sermon on the Mount; Matthew's parables 13.24–30,33, 36–50; 18.23–35; 20.1–16; 21.28–32; 22.1–14; 24.42–51, chap. 25; the community exhortations of 18.10–22.

3—25 of Matthew so visibly fall.[1] He would have weakened its
theological content by leaving out almost all the references to
the Old Testament as well as certain christological texts as
important as Matt. 11.25–30, 14.33, and 16.16ff. In short, a
Mark derived from Matthew would be a wretched 'digest' without head or tail, whose composition would be inexplicable, and
even less explicable its preservation among the canonical texts.

The more recent and widespread theory that Mark is a
summary of the other two Gospels comes up against similar
objections. Formulated for the first time with serious scholar-
ship by J. J. Griesbach in 1789–90,[2] it enjoyed a certain favour
until the middle of the nineteenth century[3] but failed to withstand the polemical fire of the Tübingen school[4] and ended its
career in the arsenal of Catholic criticism.[5] As a theory it is not
worth refuting, any more than that which sees Mark as derived
from Luke alone.[6]

---

[1] We shall return to the comparison between the plan of Mark and that
of Matthew below, pp. 17–19 and 73ff.

[2] In his 'Jena programmes' entitled: *Commentatio qua Marci evangelium
totum Matthaei et Lucae commentariis decerptum esse monstratur.*

[3] Cf. the list of its partisans given by one of its most celebrated defenders,
W. M. L. De Wette, in the introduction to the 3rd edn of his *Kurze
Erklärung der Evangelien des Lukas und Markus* (Kurzgefasstes exegetisches
Handbuch zum N.T.) vol. 1, 2 (Leipzig 1846), p. 3.

[4] The critics of the Tübingen school began indeed by seizing upon this
theory, then current, in order to make of Mark the 'neutral' Gospel
which they believed to have resulted from the shock of the encounter
between Luke and Matthew, diluted forms of the Gospels of Marcion
and of the Hebrews which embodied the spirit of Gentile Christianity
and of Judaeo-Christianity (cf. F. C. A. Schwegler, *Das nachapostolische
Zeitalter in den Hauptmomenten seiner Entwicklung* (Tübingen 1846)).
F. C. Baur, *Kritische Untersuchungen über die kanonischen Evangelien* (Tübingen 1847) already speaks only of the use in Mark of Matthew and of a
proto-Luke, while A. Hilgenfeld, *Das Marcusevangelium* (Leipzig 1854)
refers merely to the use in Mark of Matthew and of Roman traditions.
This is because they were fighting a losing battle against the believers in
the priority of Mark, whose ideas were steadily gaining ground.

[5] H. Pasquier, *La solution du problème synoptique* (Tours 1911). It is true that
shortly afterwards the decree issued on 26 June 1912 by the Pontifical
Biblical Commission placed the composition of Luke after that of Mark,
thus depriving this author of any chance he might have had of imposing
his views.

[6] Maintained by a few isolated critics in the course of the nineteenth
century. Cf. M. Goguel, *Introd. au N.T.*, vol. 1, p. 86.

And so there is no document extant that can be said to be the source of Mark. There is no other solution, then, if we persist in our quest for the documents used by the Evangelist, but to reconstruct them in the mind. This is a delicate operation and calls for more caution than has sometimes been shown in the handling of hypotheses, but it is not necessarily a wasted task, especially if it prompts us to apply our minds rigorously to certain special features of Mark.

The manifold speculations on the part of critics in the last century and a half fall into two categories. One group of critics considers that the author of Mark drew his inspiration from an older Gospel that is often seen as a first version of Matthew.[1] The other group, among whom the author of this study has no hesitation in numbering himself, sees the author of Mark as the inventor of the Gospel as a literary genre. They believe that his 'sources', on whose exact nature they are far from agreeing, did not yet possess the characteristics of this genre: biographical style of the story, fashioned in the mould of a travel chronicle; close association of the sayings of Jesus and the incidents recounted; pre-eminent place assigned to the account of the Passion, although the volume of this section is very much smaller than that of the rest of the work. Before discussing just where we stand among this second group of critics, it is perhaps necessary to look at the main arguments of the first group, who are still numerous, particularly among Catholic scholars.

1
DOES MARK STEM FROM AN EARLIER GOSPEL NO LONGER EXTANT?

This idea seems to date back to G. E. Lessing, the posthumous editor of H. S. Reimarus[2] and to J. S. Semler, who was the first

---

[1] We shall discuss elsewhere certain theories postulating a proto-Mark. Cf. below, pp. 21 ff.

[2] Following the stir created by Lessing's publication in 1774–6 of the 'fragments of the anonymous author of Wolfenbüttel', taken from the unpublished work of the rationalist H. S. Reimarus, cf. A. Schweitzer, *Geschichte der Leben Jesu Forschung*, 2nd edn (Tübingen 1913), pp. 13ff., G. E. Lessing wrote in 1778 his *Neue Hypothese über den Evangelisten als blos menschliche Schriftsteller betrachtet*, which, however, was published only with his posthumous works in 1784.

to attack this author in print.[1] Despite this stormy beginning,
the theory gradually took on substance, especially once J. G.
Eichhorn had undertaken its defence in the last years of the
eighteenth century and the early years of the nineteenth.[2] Its
fortunes remained modest throughout the nineteenth century
but to its influence we have to ascribe various isolated hypotheses formulated towards the beginning of the twentieth
century which it is difficult otherwise to place: those of A.
Resch,[3] Th. Zahn,[4] F. Spitta,[5] E. A. Abbott,[6] for example. Its
success was fleeting; today P. Parker is looked upon as the odd
man out among Protestant critics for his support of the theory
that Mark derives from a proto-Matthew.[7]

On the other hand his belief is shared by a number of
Catholic critics, attracted by the suggestion of an Aramaic
proto-Matthew[8] as the common source of the three synoptic
narratives. We shall confine ourselves here to discussing the
three most elaborate forms of this theory: those of P. Vannutelli, L. Vaganay and L. Cerfaux.

P. Vannutelli began by advancing a daring hypothesis,
ascribing the differences between the synoptic Gospels to the
translation processes resorted to by their authors to render a
Hebrew proto-Matthew in Greek.[9] However free translators

---

[1] J. S. Semler, *Beantwortung der Fragmente eines Ungenannten, insbesondern
vom Zwecke Jesu und seiner Jünger* (Halle 1779).

[2] Cf. in particular his *Einleitung in das Neue Testament*, vol. 1 (Leipzig
1804), p. 353.

[3] *Ausserkanonische Paralleltexte zu den Evangelien*, 3 vols., Leipzig (1893–7)
(Texte u. Untersuchungen, vol. x.1, 2, 3), vol. 1, pp. 7–20 and *passim*.

[4] *Einleitung in das Neue Testament*, 1st edn (Leipzig 1899), vol. 11, pp. 322ff.
3rd edn (Leipzig 1907), vol. 11, pp. 324ff.

[5] *Die synoptische Grundschrift in ihrer Uberlieferung durch das Lucasevangelium*
(Leipzig 1912), in which Spitta presents the fruits of his earlier studies.

[6] *The Fourfold Gospel* (Cambridge 1913–6).

[7] *The Gospel before Mark* (Chicago 1953).

[8] Led by M. J. Lagrange, *Evangile selon Saint Matthieu* (1st edn, Paris
1922, 6th edn 1941), pp. xxxii–xliii. Lagrange refused, however, to
see the Aramaic Matthew as a source of Mark. J. Levie, in *L'Evangile
araméen de saint Mathieu est-il la source de l'évangile de saint Marc?* (Tournai-
Paris 1954), took up and developed these two theories of Lagrange.

[9] *De Evangeliorum origine* (Rome 1923) and several articles, among which
'Les évangiles synoptiques', in the *Revue Biblique*, vol. xxxiv (1925),
pp. 2–53, 321–46, 505–23 and vol. xxxv (1926), pp. 27–39.

may have been in antiquity, one can scarcely believe that their freedom would suffice to explain all the differences between Mark, Matthew, and Luke.[1] In fact the whole system rests on a too literal interpretation of the text of Papias relating to Matthew.[2] But Vannutelli subsequently revised his whole theory[3] and presented Mark as a version, rewritten after Peter's preaching and very much abridged, of the Greek translation of the Aramaic proto-Matthew—a translation differing little from the canonical Matthew. Although less arbitrary than in its original form, this theory is still open to all the objections that can be made to the derivation of Mark from the canonical Matthew. To think that the author of Mark summarized a Gospel almost identical with our Matthew is contrary to all probability, even if it be allowed that the writer drew on some of Peter's reminiscences to complete his 'epitome'.

The ideas advanced by L. Vaganay[4] are much less rigid and deserve more attention, particularly as they have called forth some response from the specialists. Here we shall look only at what concerns us directly. Like Vannutelli, Vaganay sees the source of Mark as a Greek proto-Matthew, translated from the Aramaic; in his view Peter's Roman catechesis furnished a number of 'evocative features' which the author of Mark used to fill out his narrative. What is peculiar to Vaganay is that he postulates as the basis for certain features common to Matthew and Luke alone a small collection of *logia* unknown to Mark. This lessens the difficulty of explaining certain omissions of Mark as compared with Matthew, since the proto-Matthew was also lacking in these passages. It should be noted too that according to Vaganay the *logia* had a firmer structure than the

---

[1] Cf. the biting criticism of M. J. Lagrange, *Ev. Marc*, 7th edn, pp. cxxii–cxxv.

[2] Ματθαῖος . . . Ἑβραῖδι διαλέκτῳ τὰ λόγια συνετάξατο, ἡρμήνευσεν δ' αὐτὰ ὡς ἦν δυνατὸς ἕκαστος (Eusebius, *H.E.*, III. 39. 16). It is just possible here to interpret τὰ λόγια in the sense of 'Gospel', though we would prefer to give it another meaning (cf. below, p. 14). But to read ἕκαστος as 'each of the first three canonical Evangelists' and to restrict their literary activity to the translation of this one document is going much too far.

[3] *Quaestiones de synopticis evangeliis* (Rome 1933)—*Synoptica* (Rome 1936–40).

[4] *Le problème synoptique: une hypothèse de travail* (Bibliothèque de théologie, series III: Théologie biblique . . . , vol. I) (Tournai 1954).

somewhat amorphous collection of texts postulated by the classical 'dual source theory', being, as he believed, divided into five groups corresponding to the five 'books' of the proto-Matthew, which is to say more or less to those of the canonical Matthew—five little addenda to the five chapters of a well-ordered work. The advantages of this theory are considerable in the eyes of anybody who is familiar with the complexity of the problem of the synoptic Gospels.

They are not enough, however, to make the theory accept-able. The arguments Vaganay advances to prove the existence of his proto-Matthew are indeed rather weak. First he looks at ancient tradition,[1] that is to say in the first place the evidence of Papias on the subject of the writings of Mark and Matthew.[2] He establishes in scholarly fashion the meaning of the word λόγια in this passage, that is 'divine pronouncements' or 'oracles' and he shows that the comparison Papias was seeking to make bears on the work of *Peter* and of Matthew. But when he reaches the point when all he has to say is that Papias contrasts the well-ordered collection of the sayings of Jesus composed by Matthew with the disconnected utterances of Peter in his preaching here and there, Vaganay suddenly goes off at a tangent and affirms that the collection due to the first of these apostles is the *Gospel* according to Matthew, or rather, the Aramaic proto-Matthew! He has been led astray, like many others before him, by the words inserted by Eusebius[3] between the two notes, which everything goes to show followed on from one another in Papias. But the interpretation of Eusebius is

---

[1] Ibid. pp. 50–6.

[2] Eusebius, *H.E.* III, 39, 15: καὶ τοῦθ' ὁ πρεσβύτερος ἔλεγεν· Μάρκος μὲν ἑρμηνευτὴς Πέτρου γενόμενος, ὅσα ἐμνημόνευσεν ἀκριβῶς ἔγραψεν, οὐ μέντοι τάξει, τὰ ὑπὸ τοῦ κυρίου ἢ λεχθέντα ἢ πραχθέντα. Οὔτε γὰρ ἤκουσεν τοῦ κυρίου οὔτε παρηκολούθησεν αὐτῷ, ὕστερον δέ, ὡς ἔφην, Πέτρῳ ὃς πρὸς τὰς χρείας ἐποιεῖτε τὰς διδασκαλίας, ἀλλ' οὐχ ὥσπερ σύνταξιν τῶν κυριακῶν ποιούμενος λογίων, ὥστε οὐδὲν ἥμαρτεν Μάρκος οὕτως ἔνια γράψας ὡς ἀπεμνημόνευσεν. Ἑνὸς γὰρ ἐποιήσατο πρόνοιαν, τοῦ μηδὲν ὧν ἤκουσεν παραλιπεῖν ἢ ψεύσασθαί τι ἐν αὐτοῖς.

[3] Ibid., III, 39, 16: ταῦτα μὲν οὖν ἱστόρηται τῷ Παπίᾳ περὶ τοῦ Μάρκου· περὶ δὲ τοῦ Ματθαίου ταῦτ' εἴρηται. Cf. also the end of v. 14 of the same text.
    The Presbyter was speaking of the whole of Mark; Papias was interested only in the transmission of the sayings of Jesus by the apostles Peter (of whom Mark is merely the echo) and Matthew; Eusebius is seeking an explanation of the origins of the canonical Gospels of Matthew and Mark.

in no way binding on us, reflecting as it does the attitudes of a later age, when the fourfold canon was no longer in doubt. This evidence accordingly cannot serve to prove the existence of an Aramaic proto-Matthew.

Vaganay then goes on to a comparative criticism of the synoptic Gospels. The pages he devotes to the 'semitic substratum of the composition' (pp. 78–81) carry no conviction since the few facts advanced can all be explained otherwise than by the existence of an Aramaic proto-Matthew. Thus the 'semitic-looking parataxis', which is peculiar to Luke 6.6 and 23.44, although these verses are to be found in all three synoptic Gospels, is situated in the introductions to passages recast by Luke in a vaguely biblical style;[1] as for the 'impersonal plurals of verbs other than verbs of affirmation', that in Luke 18.33 is not impersonal and comes straight from Mark 10.34 and those in Luke 6.38 and 6.44 come in our opinion from the collection of *logia* which Vaganay, for the purposes of his hypothesis, sees as too small. Lastly, the rare 'aramaisms' in Matthew with no equivalent in Mark seem to be readily explained by the influence of the *logia* (Matt. 5.11; 7.16; 9.17) or by small stylistic changes made by the author of Matthew, sometimes for theological reasons; Matt. 24.36 tones down the rather scandalous character of Mark 13.22 by limiting the Son's ignorance to the exact hour of the Last Judgement, whereas Mark stresses rather the total mystery surrounding the last event in history; Matthew retouches Mark's stumbling sentence in 14.41 by getting rid of two asyndeta; Matt. 27.40 corrects Mark 15.30 by introducing the expression 'Son of Man' and giving the verb σώζειν a less purely material sense.

When he speaks of the 'archaic and schematic character of the content of certain synoptic texts' which he ascribes to the proto-Matthew (pp. 61–78), Vaganay himself agrees that archaism is difficult to discern with accuracy and above all no hasty conclusions should be drawn from its existence. The examples he gives are not at all convincing since they are almost all either common to the three synoptic Gospels, or to two of them, one being Mark, or else to be found in one only,

---

[1] H. J. Cadbury, *The Style and Literary Method of Luke* (Harvard Theological Studies, VI) (Cambridge, Mass. 1920), pp. 105–7.

so that they are easily explained by the priority of Mark and recourse on the part of Matthew and Luke to certain special sources. The archaisms common to Matthew and Luke alone can serve to demonstrate the existence of a proto-Matthew only in so far as they are concerned with other things than the sayings of Jesus, since otherwise they would constitute an argument in favour of a collection of *logia* and not of a 'basic Gospel'. It is a curious thing that they are to be found only in the texts relating to John the Baptist (Matt. 3.1–12;[1] Matt. 11.2–19 and Luke 7.18–35). It is accordingly natural to think of a Baptist document or one about the Baptist which Mark greatly abridged[2] and which Matthew and Luke also knew. Nothing justifies seeing in it a fragment of a proto-Matthew.

As regards the 'schematic' style of writing, by which Vaganay means 'reduced to its essentials', like a 'shorter catechism' (p. 67), its significance is rather different in the narrative passages and in the teachings. As regards the former, Vaganay believes he can trace in Matthew and Luke an austere style, close to that of the proto-Matthew, whereas Mark has added a number of picturesque details culled from the apostle Peter. He backs up his argument with the examination of three major texts: the first multiplication of the loaves, Mark 6.31–44 (pp. 69–70, 71–2); the calming of the tempest, Mark 4.35–41 (pp. 73–4); the healing of the epileptic child, Mark 9.14–29 (pp. 405–25). The analysis is subtle, the conclusions wildly wrong. Vaganay finds it surprising that Matthew and Luke should be briefer than Mark at much the same places but he has to admit himself that several of the picturesque features of Mark are to be found in only one of the other two synoptic Gospels, sometimes Matthew, sometimes Luke. He has thus proved nothing except perhaps that Matthew and Luke approach Mark's narrative with the same desire to tighten it up

---

[1] Of which Vaganay gives an excellent comparative analysis in an excursus, op. cit. pp. 344–60. The other examples given by Vaganay, p. 63, must be rejected, either as coming from the *logia* (texts of the Sermon on the Mount; Matt. 19.28 and Luke 22.30b) or as perfectly explicable by the priority of Mark. (The amendment to Mark 6.3 to be found in Matt. 13.55 and Luke 4.22 is designed to make the accusation of Jesus' compatriots less grossly insulting: cf. p. 131, n. 1 below.)

[2] Cf. pp. 54f. below.

and the same tendency to keep only what is essential.[1] The positive agreements of Matthew and Luke against Mark in the incidents recounted are negligible. In the long story of the epileptic child Vaganay only singles out three as really decisive and in each case it is a matter of a single word, on which Matthew and Luke agree against Mark in a text that contains 133 words in Matthew's version and 124 in Luke's!

The sketchiness of the discourses proves nothing in regard to a proto-Matthew, except perhaps where its original plan, still recognizable in Matthew and Luke, might seem upset in Mark, in which consequently, the other two synoptic authors would not have been able to find it. However, the same facts could be just as well explained if Mark had had knowledge of a current collection of *logia* or of independent traditions which had found a place there subsequently. The harvest is therefore of necessity a poor one, even after an analysis as thorough as that to which Vaganay subjects the 'community discourse' in Mark 9.33–50 and parallels (pp. 361–404). The only possible conclusions are that there is no doubt an Aramaic text with a fairly solid structure behind the discourse in its Marcan form and that Matthew and Luke follow Mark on the whole but have recourse now and then to a different tradition for an isolated saying. This brings us no nearer to a proto-Matthew.

Lastly, Vaganay attaches great importance to the similarity he sees in the plans of the three synoptic Gospels (pp. 57–61). But he goes astray in taking as the basis for comparison the plan of Matthew, whose governing principle must, in his view— one does not quite see why—have been that of the proto-Matthew. This latter must have comprised five sections each relating a group of incidents followed by a discourse. Having posed these premises, Vaganay seeks to find the traces of this plan in Mark and Luke and, in so doing, encounters numerous difficulties, not the least of which is the way in which the words put by Mark into the mouth of Jesus refuse to fit into the suggested framework. Mark indeed has no counterpart to the

---

[1] It may also be, especially in Matthew, that the Evangelist has simply recorded a certain 'wear' suffered by the narrative passages owing to their frequent use for catechetical purposes in the communities. Cf. on this point V. Taylor, *The Formation of the Gospel Tradition*, 2nd edn (London 1935), pp. 121–6 and 202–9.

first two discourses of Matthew: the Sermon on the Mount and
the missionary discourse.[1] Worse still, Mark has a 'discourse'
of considerable proportions which does not figure in the
'official' proto-Matthew and yet greatly exceeds in length the
'legitimate' discourses of 6.8–11 and 9.33–50, namely that of
chap. 7 on purity, which consists of almost 20 verses. By what
right is it refused the privilege of having marked the end of a
section of the proto-Matthew?

It would be better to accept the plain fact: the plan of
Matthew is the work of its author, who saw in the alternating
of narrative and discourse the most elegant way of arranging
the material at his disposal: narratives and discourses from
Mark, discourses and isolated sayings from the *logia* or oral
tradition. Perhaps the version of the *logia* he used presented the
sayings of Jesus in five distinct groups but that does not suffice
to make this document a Gospel which would have served as a
basis for the synoptic Gospels. On the contrary, as has so often
been said since C. Lachmann and C. H. Weiss,[2] it is clear that
the plan of Mark served as a starting point for Matthew and
Luke when it came to arranging their material. There is no
need, therefore, to look elsewhere for the common denominator
of the three synoptic Gospels where the ordering of the material
is concerned. Even supposing that the plan of Mark was
adumbrated in some feature or other of Christian tradition,[3]

---

[1] L. Vaganay in 'L'absence du sermon sur la montagne chez Marc'
(*Revue biblique*, vol. LVIII (1951), pp. 5–46) did try, it is true, to show that
Mark deliberately left out the Sermon on the Mount, but his reasoning
cannot stand up to the evidence of the facts: the break he notes between
Mark 3.19 and 3.20 exists, but it is caused by Mark's incorporation of a
pre-existing list of the Twelve into his account and not by the omission
of the Sermon (cf. p. 29 below). As for the 'missionary discourse' in
Mark, it comprises four verses only, but its brevity is not necessarily
due to the condensing of a long discourse of the kind found in Matt. 10.
It is more likely to be an addition to the list of the Twelve.

[2] Cf. M. Goguel, *Introduction au N.T.*, vol. I, pp. 76–8. The first-mentioned
of these authors published in 1835 in *Theologische Studien und Kritiken*,
1835, pp. 570–90 an article entitled 'De ordine narrationum in evangeliis synopticis' which was reproduced in the preface to vol. II of the 2nd
edn of his *New Testament* (Berlin 1850). The second advanced his idea
for the first time in a book published in Leipzig in 1838 entitled *Die
evangelische Geschichte kritisch und philosophisch bearbeitet*.

[3] Cf. pp. 19–20 and 28–31 below.

it would be rash to assign this role to a 'basic Gospel', whose existence Vaganay's failure to prove his theory makes more problematic than ever.

L. Cerfaux wrote for L. Vaganay's book on the *Synoptic Problem* a flattering preface in which, behind his general agreement, one can sense distinct reservations in regard to the details of the 'working hypotheses' built up by the author. This should cause no surprise: the ideas of L. Cerfaux on the composition of the synoptic Gospels are indeed much less rigid than those of his colleague of Lyons.[1] His Aramaic proto-Matthew bears only a rather remote relation to the canonical Gospels. The suggestion is that it was a 'first large-scale Palestinian systematization' of tradition; this very ancient work, thought L. Cerfaux, was no doubt dealt out, as it were, piecemeal and translated in bits, to which various borrowings from oral tradition were then added. From this mixture (which one would hesitate to call a Greek proto-Matthew), a Gospel was perhaps reconstructed that became our Mark. L. Cerfaux's writing on the gradual emergence of the canonical Gospels by the organization, around various centres of interest, of the elusive material supplied by tradition contains some excellent pages and certain of his ideas on the subject are worth retaining.[2]

But what is a 'basic Gospel' doing in a system so close to those of the Form-critics? True, we are told that it was used by Mark and Matthew, but the impression remains of mere lip-service paid to the decrees of the Pontifical Commission of 1911–2[3] ruling that the oldest Gospel was to be attributed to the apostle Matthew and that it was written in Aramaic and was substantially identical with the canonical Matthew. At most one might ascribe to this proto-Matthew the division of

---

[1] We owe to L. Cerfaux, since 1935, several articles on synoptic questions which have appeared in particular in the *Ephemerides Theologicae Lovanienses* (vol. xii, 1935, pp. 5–27; vol. xv, 1938, pp. 330–7; vol. xxvii, 1951, pp. 368–89; vol. xxviii, 1952, pp. 629–47) and collected in the *Recueil L. Cerfaux: autour des évangiles* (Gembloux 1954), 2 vols. (especially vol. i, pp. 353–485).

[2] Cf. p. 74, n. 3 below.

[3] Especially to that of 19 June 1911, Articles i to v. The Latin text of the decrees of 1911–2 is reproduced in *Introduction à la Bible* by A. Robert and A. Feuillet, vol. ii, pp. 160–2.

the traditional material into four broad biographico-geographical sections which reappear in the three synoptic Gospels: preparation of the ministry (Mark 1.1–13 and par.); Galilean ministry (Mark 1.14 to 9.50 and par.); approach to Jerusalem (Mark 10 and par.); the passion and resurrection (Mark 11 to 16 and par.). But even if we allow the extreme antiquity of this 'attempt at a biographical systematization',[1] it is a far cry from such a traditional arrangement of catechetical texts to a real 'Gospel' that supposedly conformed to this pattern in order to recount in detail numerous sayings and acts of Jesus. To demonstrate the existence of such a Gospel, one would have to prove that the pericopes assigned by the synoptic Gospels to the Jerusalem ministry (Mark 11—13 and par.) had always been joined to the Passion story proper and that the majority of the texts placed by the three Gospels in the second or third section, or even the first half of the fourth section, were not placed there arbitrarily by the Evangelists. In neither case is proof possible, since most of the pericopes have no other localization in time or space than that afforded by their literary setting, and seem to have been transmitted in isolation or in small groups arranged according to their form or subject and not in the chronological or geographical order of the incidents related.[2]

The 'Aramaic Matthew' of L. Cerfaux therefore never existed; so Mark could not possibly have drawn on it, even from afar.[3]

---

[1] L. Cerfaux, *Recueil*, vol. 1, p. 480.

[2] K. L. Schmidt's fine study, *Der Rahmen der Geschichte Jesu, literarkritische Untersuchungen zur ältesten Jesusüberlieferung* (Berlin 1919), has, we believe, established this fact decisively, while admitting the existence of a number of exceptions (e.g. in Mark 6.31—8.26: pp. 181ff.) which bear witness, according to this author, not to the geographical and chronological grouping of the pericopes from very ancient times, but to the historical value of the incidents in question. Cf. also R. Bultmann, *Die Geschichte der synoptischen Tradition*, pp. 338 and 371.

[3] In these circumstances it is rather to be regretted that the ideas of L. Cerfaux and L. Vaganay on this proto-Matthew should be given common credence today by French-speaking Catholic scholars who write for a wide public, namely by X. Léon-Dufour in the *Introduction à la Bible* by Robert and Feuillet, vol. II, pp. 292–3 and by P. Benoît in *La Sainte Bible traduite en français sous la direction de l'Ecole biblique de Jérusalem* (Paris 1956), p. 1284. It should be noted however that these

Another group of critics, mostly 'modernists', maintained that Mark had borrowed its soundest and most probable features from a very old document that had escaped the imposition of a christological superstructure from which, according to them, our canonical Gospels suffer—a sort of Life of Jesus related by eye-witnesses, a Gospel that it would be scarcely necessary to demythologize. This document is often described as a collection of reminiscences of the apostle Peter, received either directly or indirectly by the Evangelist. Some of the partisans of this theory refer to the document as a 'proto-Mark', but it seems preferable to reserve this term for a possible first version of the canonical Gospel.[1] Some of them postulate the existence, side by side with the main source, of other documents of the same type, but of less value, which have been combined by an editor with the first. That makes no difference to the principle underlying all these hypotheses, which is the existence of a proto-Gospel allowing the plain historical truth to be discerned more readily than the canonical Mark.

Though the supporters of the theory that Mark drew on a Gospel of a less theological nature had some predecessors in the nineteenth century,[2] it was only in the twentieth century that their numbers grew, under the influence of W. Wrede's celebrated work on the 'messianic secret' which appeared in 1901.[3] Wrede believed, as is known, that the author of Mark had endeavoured to reconcile the luxuriant christology of his time and milieu with a much more sober tradition which, on the contrary, never gave Jesus the title of Christ. In so doing he

---

theories have opponents among Catholic scholars, who are not all blind defenders of tradition—far from it: thus A. Wikenhauser, *Einleitung in das Neue Testament* (Freiburg-in-Breisgau, 1st edn 1953, 2nd edn 1956); B. de Solages, *Synopse grecque des évangiles, méthode nouvelle pour résoudre le problème synoptique* (Leyden and Toulouse 1959), in particular pp. 1085–6.

[1] We shall revert to this later (pp. 215ff.).

[2] F. Schleiermacher may be considered the first of them, with his article in *Theol. Studien u. Krit.* (1832), pp. 736ff. on the fragments of Papias relating to Mark and Matthew, 'Ueber die Zeugnisse des Papias'. He thought he had found in these fragments an allusion to a collection of stories about Jesus culled from the lips of Peter and presented more simply than in Mark.

[3] W. Wrede, *Das Messiasgeheimnis in den Evangelien, zugleich ein Beitrag zum Verständnis des Markusevangeliums* (Göttingen 1901).

thought that the Evangelist had added to the documents relating to the historical Jesus certain christological affirmations and above all had put into Jesus' mouth numerous utterances forbidding his disciples to make him known as the Messiah while he was still on earth. Jesus, from being simply a prophet, became in Mark a concealed Messiah; the Church had thus not, according to the Evangelist, invented its christology but was simply proclaiming aloud what could only be whispered while Jesus the man was alive. Wrede did not try to reconstruct the documents that Mark had transformed in this way, but one can imagine that other critics, impressed by his theory, sought to do so, while preserving the essence of Mark's biographical outline and picturesque narrative, by cutting out the christological excrescences. It was the only way to restore to Mark the role of principal source of the 'Lives of Jesus' that Wrede was wresting from it after forty years of clear pre-eminence.

Johannes Weiss made the first attempt in 1903[1] with an authority that enabled him to make a considerable advance upon Wrede. He claimed that Peter's reminiscences, which covered the time from the early days of the ministry in Galilee up to and including the passion, were the subject, before the existence of Mark, of a coherent account whose real historical value was not destroyed when it was incorporated in the canonical text, in spite of the writer's minor changes. According to Weiss, it was this document that gave Mark its framework and a large part of its content.

After J. Weiss, Hermann von Soden,[2] and E. Wendling[3] endeavoured, each in his own way, to narrow down the hypothesis further by postulating a second continuous narrative source, less old and less sound than the first. They were followed by Eduard Meyer,[4] who thought he saw underlying Mark a

---

[1] J. Weiss, *Das älteste Evangelium, ein Beitrag zum Verständnis des Markusevangeliums und der ältesten evangelischen Ueberlieferung* (Göttingen 1903).

[2] See in particular his *Urchristliche Literaturgeschichte* (Die Schriften des Neuen Testaments), (Berlin 1905), pp. 71 ff.

[3] *Ur-Marcus, Versuch einer Wiederherstellung der ältesten Mitteilunger über das Leben Jesu* (Tübingen 1905), and *Die Enstehung des Marcusevangeliums, philologische Untersuchungen* (Tübingen 1908). This latter book is much fuller than the former.

[4] *Ursprung und Anfänge des Christentums*, vol. 1 (Stuttgart and Berlin 1924), pp. 121–60.

'disciples' source stemming from the associates of Peter, and a 'Twelve' source, much less elaborate, which fixed the Jerusalem tradition in the state it was in after Peter left the Jewish capital. However, A. Loisy,[1] and B. W. Bacon[2] showed more reserve about the possibility of finding a second 'proto-Gospel' and clung quite firmly, despite the rather vague nature of their hypotheses, to the idea of a 'humble collection of notes which originally recorded the essential facts of the Galilean mission and the messianic venture concentrated on Jerusalem, with its culmination at Golgotha',[3] or of a 'basic summary, no doubt of Petrine origin'.[4] M. Goguel, more cautious, still seeks in a 'co-ordinated source' . . . (which) must have given a general picture of the ministry of Jesus[5] and must rest on Peter's reminiscences, the thread that guided the author of Mark.

But the few recent authors who have proffered any support for the theory of the 'pre-dogmatic proto-Gospel', in the shape of new arguments, do not seem to have inclined towards simplicity. A. T. Cadoux[6] makes Mark a compilation from three previous Gospels, the oldest of which he believed was Palestinian, Petrine, and separated from the death of Jesus by some twelve years only. E. Hirsch[7] postulates only two Gospels as the basis for the compilation of Mark but pushes conjecture to the extreme by stating that the first was written less than a year after the death of Jesus and that the second drew on the first and on a 'Twelve' source document written in Jerusalem

[1] *Les évangiles synoptiques, introduction, traduction et commentaire*, (Ceffonds, vol. I, 1907), *passim*: *L'Evangile selon Marc* (Paris 1912).

[2] *The Beginnings of Gospel Story, a Historico-critical Inquiry into the Sources and Structure of the Gospel according to Mark, with Expository Notes upon the Text for English Readers* (New Haven 1909); *Is Mark a Roman Gospel?* (Cambridge, Mass. 1919) (Harvard Theological Studies, VII); *The Gospel of Mark: its Composition and Date* (New Haven 1925).

[3] A Loisy, *Ev. selon Marc*, p. 19.

[4] B. W. Bacon, *Gospel of Mark*, p. 167.

[5] *Introd. au N.T.*, vol. I, p. 337. The ideas of J. M. C. Crum, *St Mark's Gospel* (Cambridge 1936), are similar. W. Bussmann's *Geschichtsquelle* (Synoptische Studien, Halle 1925–31, 3 vols., vol. I: *Zur Geschichtsquelle*) may also be mentioned here, although its content was rather different and came closer to certain 'proto-Mark' theories.

[6] *The Sources of the Second Gospel* (London 1935).

[7] *Frühgeschichte des Evangeliums*, vol. I (*Das Werden des Markusevangeliums*), (Tübingen 1st edn 1940, 2nd edn 1951).

some time after A.D.60. This latter source he thought had likewise all the appearance of a Gospel, a theory which makes E.
Hirsch rival A. T. Cadoux for audacity. Lastly W. L. Knox,[1]
while he is less venturesome, still postulates two narratives
covering the whole of the ministry of Jesus, including the passion: a 'Twelve' source and an anonymous document which
might have comprised Mark 1.40—3.6, 8.27—9.32, a few
fragments of chapters 8, 11, and 12 and a part of Mark's
Passion story. These two texts co-existed, he believed, with
several small 'tracts' grouping methodically some of Jesus'
words and acts, which adds to the complexity of the theory.

It would be wearisome to describe in detail all the various
forms of a hypothesis whose representatives are few and far
between today, although it had distinct success in the first
quarter of the century. We shall confine ourselves to discussing
the postulate on which the whole system rests. It can be stated
as follows: as early as the first generation of Christians, the
need was felt for a continuous account of the ministry of Jesus.
It is important to grasp the significance of these terms. It is
not enough, to justify the hypothesis in question, to suppose that
Peter related—be it frequently and in public—his memories
of the earthly life of Jesus or that the preachers and catechists of
the first generation illustrated their teachings with brief,
isolated stories about our Lord, or that the converts were
taught, among other religious texts, a brief summary of the
life of Jesus of the kind to be found in Acts 2.22–4, 10.37–42 or
13.23–31; we have to assume the existence of a written document containing a continuous and fairly substantial narrative,
roughly one-quarter of the length of the canonical Mark.[2]

There are certainly passages in Mark whose incoherence is
most readily explained by ascribing it to the use of written
documents: 3.14–16 is probably the best example. Moreover,

---

[1] *The Sources of the Synoptic Gospels,* vol. 1 (*St Mark*), (Cambridge 1953).

[2] Most of the authors whose ideas are discussed here ascribe to this
source (or to each of the sources they believe they can reconstruct)
passages whose total length is equivalent to three to five chapters of
Mark. One isolated scholar, R. O. P. Taylor, in *The Groundwork of the
Gospels* (Oxford 1946), suggests the existence of a sort of official biography of Jesus for use in worship, to which Mark added very little
when setting it down in writing. This is even less probable than the
proto-Matthew theory.

almost all the critics agree that the main lines of the Passion
story were laid down in writing at a very early date.[1] We ourselves do not see any difficulty in supposing that the author of
Mark used certain written texts. But what does appear improbable is that Peter's recollections should have been the subject of a literary composition, even a rudimentary one, at a
time when Peter was either still alive or had just died. The
material sometimes attributed to Peter[2] has little coherence;
Papias makes no mention of such a text;[3] one does not see what
purpose would have been served by such a text in the lives or
history of the first generation of Christians;[4] lastly, neither Paul
nor Luke has any knowledge of such a document, which they
would have been obliged to take account of had it existed.[5]

[1] Cf. for example, V. Taylor, *The Gospel According to St Mark, the Greek
Text with Introduction, Notes and Indexes* (London 1952), pp. 524–6 and
653–64.

[2] This is the case with J. Weiss, B. W. Bacon, M. Goguel, A. T. Cadoux,
E. Hirsch in particular. We shall see below what can be said of the
attribution of a certain number of stories in Mark to Peter.

[3] He suggests only that Mark composed 'his Gospel' after having accompanied Peter during his preaching ministry (cf. Goguel, *Intr. au
N.T.*, vol. I, pp. 125–7). It has sometimes been sought to see in the words
of the Elder quoted by Papias an allusion to a collection of incidents
recounted by Peter and to suggest that Papias misunderstood them.
This overlooks the fact that Papias was able to set those words in a
context, which we can no longer do and that the expression ἢ λεχθέντα
ἢ πραχθέντα applies much better to a Gospel composed partly of 'discourses' than to a collection of memoirs whose purpose would be rather
to relate events. Cf. the text of this fragment of Papias above, p. 14,
n. 2.

[4] The desire to save Peter's memories from oblivion after his death seems
to be the only conceivable motive. It would have been a means of
replacing him as a story-teller. But in all probability that would bring
us to about the year 64 (cf. O. Cullmann, *Saint Pierre, disciple, apôtre,
martyre* (Neuchâtel-Paris 1952), pp. 61–137), that is to say very close
to the likely date of the composition of the canonical Mark, which
most critics place between 65 and 70 (cf. V. Taylor, *St Mark*, pp.
31–2). In these circumstances it would be rash to seek to distinguish
between Mark and a 'collection of Peter's reminiscences' that might
have been its source.

[5] One should certainly not rely too much on this argument. However, it
is striking that Paul, who quotes several times traditional texts relating
to Jesus (Rom. 1.3–4; I Cor. 7.10; 11.23–5; 15.3ff., for example),
should make no reference to stories that can be ascribed to Peter's
memories. As for Luke, his famous prologue (Luke 1.1–4) ascribes to

The 'collection of Peter's memories', or the 'simple Gospel', whose existence is supposed, would have been a story, an account of events. Some of those who accept its existence think then that Mark derives from the *logia*, or from a source presenting primarily the teaching of Jesus, as well as from this collection.[1] This is to affirm that the latter text was distinguished, even more than the canonical Mark, by the few sayings of Jesus it recorded. However, the predominance of narrative in relation to discourse and the fragmentary presentation of the teaching of Jesus in Mark called forth as early as the first century unfavourable reactions which were echoed by Papias in the middle of the second century and resulted in the publication of the 'corrected' Gospels of Matthew and Luke. As, moreover, the Christian Church certainly collected the sayings of Jesus with extreme respect and made very early use of many of them in its teaching,[2] it is difficult to imagine how the author of Mark could have failed, in the face of a purely narrative source, to have the same reaction to his own Gospel as his successors. If he had such a source, he must have considered it too poor in didactic material; why should he have added to it so timidly when he could have used more of the texts furnished by tradition? It is this which seems difficult to explain when one thinks that, independently of one another, Matthew and Luke found roughly the same material to add to Mark by drawing on a body of tradition of which the author of Mark must have known a considerable part. A Mark based on a purely narrative source which he endeavoured to add to would have produced a Matthew or a Luke. Since it did neither

---

eye-witnesses the handing down of the bare facts only and not their systematic setting down in writing, which he seems to suggest was reserved for his own generation. This does not make it absolutely impossible for him to have had knowledge of 'Peter's memoirs' but it does mean that he did not see them as a book comparable to his own and to those he was seeking to replace.

[1] J. Weiss, E. Wendling, A. Loisy, B. W. Bacon, M. Goguel suggest the *logia*. W. L. Knox prefers to speak of small 'tracts' collecting the sayings of Jesus on various subjects.

[2] The most suggestive study in this respect is that of M. Dibelius, *Die Formgeschichte des Evangeliums* (Tübingen 1st edn 1919, 2nd edn 1933, 3rd edn published by G. Bornkamm, with a supplement by G. Iber, 1959). Cf. in particular pp. 8–34 and 234–65 of the 3rd edn. [E.T. *From Tradition to Gospel* (1935).]

one nor the other, it is best to cease speculating about an earlier document and look elsewhere for the explanation of the special features of Mark.

The 'collection of Peter's reminiscences' or 'simple Gospel' whose existence we are asked to accept was, it is suggested, a 'continuous narrative', recounting the course of the ministry of Jesus with reasonable fidelity. On this point the hypothesis seems still more fragile, since the narrative parts of Mark all consist, except for chapters 14—16, of separate anecdotes or, at most, small groups of two or three anecdotes (such as 1.21-39, 2.1—3.6, 4.35—5.43, 6.30-56 and 9.2-29) with extremely precarious links between them.[1] It would accordingly have to be assumed that Mark did away with the chronological and topographical order clearly visible in his source. That would seem most improbable, despite the view of a critic like Loisy that the author of Mark was seeking in this way to mask the political activity of the Messiah Jesus.[2]

Lastly, the critics whose ideas we are refuting see this source as relatively full. They are not thinking like C. H. Dodd[3] of a brief outline of the career of Jesus but of a text with accounts of events as full as those of the canonical Mark. In this document, they suggest, the Passion story formed between one third and one half of the whole—on this point they are roughly in agreement in spite of their differing views about the content of the 'simple Gospel'. In that case, given the close link between the passion and the resurrection in Christian preaching and the decisive importance of the christophany accorded to Peter,[4] it would be necessary to postulate the existence in the source text of a third part devoted to the appearances of the risen Christ and giving a fairly full account of them. The 'simple Gospel' would indeed scarcely have been able to conform to the first two thirds of a kerygmatic scheme or outline such as

---

[1] Cf. K. L. Schmidt, *Rahmen der Geschichte Jesu, passim.*

[2] Cf., for example, A. Loisy, *Evangile selon Marc*, pp. 29ff. More convincing remarks on the political side of the ministry of Jesus are to be found in O. Cullmann, *Dieu et César: le procès de Jésus; Saint Paul et l'Autorité; l'Apocalpyse et l'Etat totalitaire* (Neuchâtel and Paris 1956), pp. 11-53.

[3] C. H. Dodd, 'The Framework of the Gospel Narrative', in *Expository Times* (1932), vol. XLIII, pp. 396-400, reprinted in C. H. Dodd, *New Testament Studies* (Manchester 1953), pp. 1-11.

[4] It is this that the tradition received by Paul places first (1 Cor. 15.5).

that found in Acts 2.22–4 without recording also incidents illustrating the last third (the affirmation of the resurrection) and in particular an account of Christ's appearance to Peter. But we know that the accounts of the appearances of the risen Christ are rare in the New Testament and are late additions and that, in particular, Christ's appearance to Peter is recorded nowhere.[1] If they had had such a 'simple Gospel' at their disposal, the canonical Evangelists, and in the first place Mark, would not have been able to remain so silent on the subject.

It is therefore quite clear that no such document ever existed.

A few authors nevertheless still seek to demonstrate that failing a 'collection of Peter's memories' or a document of the same kind, Mark used a summary account of the life of Jesus. This idea originated with C. H. Dodd,[2] whose authority as a scholar convinced a certain number of English and American critics,[3] as well as some others.[4] It has not been accepted by the majority of specialists, however, even in Great Britain.[5]

The point of departure of this theory is the observance in Mark of groups of pericopes between which there are fairly

---

[1] O. Cullmann, *Saint Pierre*, pp. 51–6, seeks, after many others, to explain this curious silence in the New Testament. We shall return later to the question of the appearances of the risen Christ.

[2] Loc. cit. (cf. p. 27, n. 3, above).

[3] In particular V. Taylor, *Formation of the Gospel Tradition*, 2nd edn pp. 40–1 and *St Mark*, p. 85; H. Branscomb, *The Gospel of Mark* (The Moffatt New Testament Commentary), (London 1937), which however does not cite Dodd expressly; F. C. Grant, *The Earliest Gospel* (New York 1943), p. 51.

[4] Thus X. Léon-Dufour in *Introduction à la Bible* by Robert and Feuillet, II, pp. 221 and 319.

[5] Cf. the implied criticism of this theory in L. Cerfaux, *Recueil*, vol. I, p. 430, and A. M. Farrer, *A Study of St Mark* (London 1951), p. 187; and the explicit criticism by D. E. Nineham, 'The Order of Events in St Mark's Gospel—an examination of Dr Dodd's Hypothesis' in *Studies in the Gospels, Essays in Memory of R. H. Lightfoot*, ed. D. E. Nineham (Oxford 1957), pp. 223–39; and J. M. Robinson, *A New Quest of the Historical Jesus* (Studies in Biblical Theology, 25), (London 1959), pp. 48–50, 56–8, adapted in French and German, *Le kérygme de l'Eglise et le Jésus de l'Histoire* (Geneva 1961), pp. 48–50 and 55–7; *Kerygma und historischer Jesus* (Zurich-Stuttgart 1960), pp. 63–5 and 72–5.

substantial topographical and chronological links, whereas it is difficult to detect any grouping by subject: for example, the section 3.7—6.13. C. H. Dodd sees in this an indication of a pre-existing framework known to Mark which he did not entirely destroy in spite of his preference for grouping the pericopes by subject. Dodd even thinks it is possible to reconstruct this framework by placing end to end the summaries which are found at intervals in the narrative and recognizing in the resulting text the same outline as in Acts 10.37–41 and 13.23–31 in a fuller form. This outline of the ministry of Jesus composed of a little more than twenty verses might have constituted an introduction to the Passion story and have helped Christians to set the stories handed down to them by tradition in the life of Jesus.

This theory has its attractions, since it embodies the main ideas of the form-critical school without coming to a too negative conclusion on the subject of the historic value of Mark. It is fragile, however, since it is difficult to contest that the 'summaries' in Mark were written by the author, even if they contain some older material, such as Mark 1.15 or 3.16–19.[1] In any case C. H. Dodd simplifies his case by confining himself to the summaries in chapters 1 to 6.30, leaving out 4.33–4.[2] However, the summaries to be found in 9.30, 10.1, 10.32, 12.38, which accompany isolated sayings attributed to Jesus by tradition, are quite clearly composed by Mark in order to give his Gospel more coherence. Why whould not the same be true of the earlier ones? Moreover, the continuity that Dodd believes can be detected between the summaries in chapters 1—6, when they are placed end to end, does not extend to the succeeding chapters. This fact gives some cause to doubt the soundness of Dodd's conclusions since the continuity ought to embrace all the passages of a general nature to be found from Mark 1 to Mark 13 if the document whose existence is postu-

---

[1] What was written on this subject in 1933 by H. J. Cadbury, 'The Summaries in Acts', in *The Beginnings of Christianity*, I; *The Acts of the Apostles*, ed. F. J. Jackson and Kirsopp Lake (London 1920–1933), vol. v, p. 393, needs no rectification: 'The summaries . . . represent the latest part of Mark, and specially reveal his editorial motives.'

[2] Whose composition by the author is often contested (thus V. Taylor, *St Mark*, pp. 271–2), wrongly in our view. Cf. p. 160, n. 2, below.

lated was indeed an outline of the ministry of Jesus designed to
serve as an introduction to the passion.

Lastly, it is difficult to see what function such a resumé could
have fulfilled in the life of the churches of the first generation
when it was certainly not a matter of prime concern to give a
setting in time and space to the words of our Lord quoted by
the preachers and teachers of the day. That all dated from a
time 'before' (before the passion and the resurrection) and
was perhaps confused in people's minds, because of its similar
remoteness, with the 'on high' of the glorification. The
authenticity of both was guaranteed by the witness of the
companions of our Lord and formed part of the 'tradition'
they handed down.[1] What point was there in giving a precise
context to what was known to be true? It might even be said
that to set down an account of the ministry of Jesus argues a
certain distrust of the guarantors of tradition and a desire to
criticize it.[2] But an effort of this kind could not possibly have
been made at the very beginning of the Church's existence and
it could not have produced a mere summary; it produced the
Gospels.

It would be wrong to go so far as to deny the soundness of
all the chronological and topographical information contained
in the Gospels. There is no reason why fragmentary, isolated
details, impossible to co-ordinate, should not have survived
in one story or another handed down by tradition.[3] But the
general information, the details co-ordinating the stories or
groups of stories, are certainly secondary and bear the mark of
the Evangelist. And so one cannot lump them all together, as
does C. H. Dodd, as forming a sort of 'emergent Gospel'
very close to the origins of Christianity. At the most one can
imagine that the kerygmatic outline to be found in Acts
2.22–4 sometimes had the relative geographical precision of
Acts 10.37ff. or of Acts 13.31, that is to say, it evoked the

[1] Cf. O. Cullmann's fine article, 'Paradosis et Kyrios, le problème de la
tradition dans le paulinisme', in *Revue d'Hist. et de Philo. religieuses*
(1950), vol. xxx, pp. 12ff., reproduced with certain changes in O.
Cullmann, *La tradition, problème exégétique, historique et théologique* (Neuchâtel-Paris 1953), pp. 11–28.

[2] Cf. below, p. 85.

[3] This is supported by K. L. Schmidt, for example, in *Rahmen der Geschichte Jesu*, pp. 48–54, 208–14, 317.

beginning of the ministry of Jesus in Galilee or the arrival in Jerusalem of a group of Galileans led by him.[1] That is the only outline of the life of Jesus likely to have inspired Mark.

2
IS MARK A MERE COMPILATION?

In rejecting the idea that Mark might have derived from an earlier Gospel which we no longer possess, we were challenging theories on the fringe of what is now the main current of ideas about the New Testament. After forty years of debate, the ideas put forward by the form-critical school[2] still carry weight with most of the Gospel critics, and these theories are scarcely compatible with those which ascribe to the canonical Gospels, and particularly to Mark, sources similar to their own texts. If it is thought that the whole synoptic tradition was first crystallized in separate little units that were gradually grouped around the different themes, there is little room in the chronology and life of the first century of Christianity for a succession of literary works deriving one from another.[3] One is more inclined to consider the composition of Mark as the first attempt to combine the two lines of the tradition relating to Jesus—the words and the narrative. Matthew and Luke would then represent the culmination of this work of compilation.[4] The authors

---

[1] We feel no need to modify the conclusions we reached on this subject in *Le Livre des Actes et l'Histoire*, pp. 207–11, despite the objections of J. M. Robinson, in particular, in *A New Quest*, pp. 58–9 (*Kérygme et Jésus hist.*, p. 56, n. 2), who gives no great credence to the discourses in Acts as the sources of the knowledge of the original kerygma. (Cf. E. Haenchen, *Apg.*, 13th edn (Göttingen 1963), p. 73.

[2] It is scarcely necessary to recall the series of publications which, from 1919 to 1922, marked the emergence of the new school: M. Dibelius, *Die Formgeschichte des Evangeliums* (Tübingen 1919, 3rd edn 1959); K. L. Schmidt, *Der Rahmen der Geschichte Jesu* (Berlin 1919, 2nd edn 1931, 3rd edn 1957, 4th edn 1958); M. Albertz, *Die synoptischen Streitgespräche, ein Beitrag zur Formgeschichte des Urchristentums* (Berlin 1921); G. Bertram, *Die Leidensgeschichte Jesu und der Christuskult, eine formgeschichtliche Untersuchung* (Göttingen 1922).

[3] This is not sufficiently realized by the critics who, while accepting broadly the ideas of the form-critical school, seek to make room in their system for a pre-Gospel prior to the synoptic Gospels. Cf. L. Cerfaux, W. L. Knox, C. H. Dodd (see pp. 18ff. above).

[4] R. Bultmann, *Gesch. der synopt. Tradition*, 4th edn, p. 355ff.

of the canonical Gospels give the appearance of being much
more compilers than original writers.[1]

Somewhat similar ideas on how the stories and utterances
on which the synoptic Gospels were based came into being,
and on the role of the Evangelists, had been put forward by a
number of scholars well before the emergence of the form-
critical school. True, the theory which saw in oral tradition the
common origin of the first three canonical Gospels was very
often formulated in the nineteenth century in a naive version
that was in fact only a substitute for the 'basic Gospel' theory:
hence the theories of J. G. Herder,[2] J. C. L. Gieseler,[3] B. F.
Westcott,[4] G. Wetzel,[5] F. Godet,[6] and numerous Catholic
authors.[7] But various critics had prepared the way more
directly for the new school. F. Schleiermacher[8] with his theory
of 'diegeses'—brief accounts set down early in writing and
which, when put together, produced the synoptic Gospels
opened up the way for D. F. Strauss[9] and his pitiless criticism
of the framework of the Gospel narrative. Strauss studied the
pericopes thus isolated and looked everywhere for the influence
of myths, which he thought often intervened in the oral
transmission of the sayings of Jesus and of incidents recorded
concerning him. His method accordingly foreshadowed that of
the form-critical school, particularly as represented by Bult-

---

[1] M. Dibelius, *Formgeschichte des Evangeliums*, 3rd edn, pp. 2–3.

[2] *Von der Regel der Zusammenstimmung unserer Evangelien* (1797) reproduced
in *Christliche Schriften von Johann Gottfried von Herder*, ed. J. G. Müller,
vol. II (Sämmtliche Werke z. Religion u. Theologie, 12), Vienna-
Prague 1820), pp. 5–60.

[3] *Historisch-kritischer Versuch über die Entstehung und die frühesten Schicksale
der schriftlichen Evangelien* (Leipzig 1818).

[4] *Introduction to the Study of the Gospels*, 1st edn 1860, 6th edn 1882.

[5] *Die synoptischen Evangelien, eine Darstellung und Prüfung der richtigsten
über die Entstehung derselben aufgestellten Hypothesen, mit selbstständigem
Versuch zur Lösung der synoptischen Frage* (Heilbronn 1883).

[6] *Commentaire sur l'évangile de Saint Luc*, 3rd edn (Paris 1888–9), vol. I,
pp. 36–41 and 60–71; cf. also his *Introduction au Nouveau Testament* (Paris
and Neuchâtel 1893–1908), vol. II: *Les évangiles synoptiques*.

[7] M. Goguel, *Introd. au N.T.*, vol. I, p. 64, gives a convenient list of these.

[8] Study entitled 'Kritischer Versuch über die Schriften des Lucas',
published in Berlin in 1845 in his posthumous *Einleitung in das Neue
Testament, Sämtliche Werke*, I. 8), pub. by Wolde.

[9] *Das Leben Jesu* (Tübingen 1835–6).

mann and Bertram. But his excessively radical conclusions and the rudimentary nature of his literary criticism did harm to his reputation as a scholar and prevented his contribution to New Testament studies from bearing its full fruit.

It can be said, however, that many subsequent scholars accorded a larger place to oral tradition in the description they gave of how the material gathered together in the synoptic Gospels came into being. More characteristic in this respect than the isolated efforts of C. Holsten,[1] or C. Veit,[2] are the numerous pages devoted to the development of the pre-evangelical tradition by J. Weiss in a semi-popular work published at the beginning of the twentieth century.[3] The works of J. Wellhausen on the Gospel according to Mark,[4] placing the accent as they do on oral tradition and on Mark's almost exclusive authorship of the framework of his Gospel, also prepared the way for the form-critical school, which in any case did no more than apply to the New Testament the method that had long been used by H. Gunkel and his disciples[5] for the Old.

However this may be, it was the group of works published in Germany in the years 1919–22 that was decisive in directing the study of the first three Gospels, and particularly of Mark, towards the analysis of the pre-literary forms of the tradition, and the recognition of the profound influence exerted on it by the life and faith of the first Christians. These same publications transformed the picture that was then current of the Evangelists as clever manipulators of 'sources' or eye-witness

---

[1] *Die drei ursprünglich noch ungeschriebenen Evangelien* (Karlsruhe 1883); *Die synoptischen Evangelien* (Heidelberg 1886).

[2] *Die synoptischen Parallelen und ein alter Versuch ihrer Enträthselung mit neuer Begründung* (Gütersloh 1897).

[3] *Die Schriften des Neuen Testaments neu übersetzt und für die Gegenwart erklärt* . . . hgg. *von Johannes Weiss* (Göttingen 1st edn 1906, 2nd edn 1907), vol. 1: *Die drei älteren Evangelien. Die Apostelgeschichte*, pp. 37ff. (of the 2nd edn).

[4] J. Wellhausen, *Das Evangelium Marci übersetzt und erklärt* (Berlin 1903, 2nd edn 1909). *Einleitung in die drei ersten Evangelien* (Berlin 1905, 2nd edn 1911).

[5] As R. Bultmann admits very frankly in *Geschichte der synopt. Tradition*, 4th edn, p. 3. With regard to what the form-critical school owes to its predecessors, see E. Fascher, *Die formgeschichtliche Methode, eine Darstellung und Kritik. Zugleich ein Beitrag zur Geschichte des synoptischen Problems* (Giessen 1924), pp. 4–51.

accounts into one of them as compilers from a many-faceted 'tradition'. To realize the innovation that this meant, it is enough to compare the commentaries, both quite conservative, of Mark by M. J. Lagrange in 1910[1] and by V. Taylor in 1952,[2] whose very full introductions allow the authors to expound in detail their ideas about the sources of the Gospel. While the first-mentioned stresses the complete dependence of Mark on Peter, as an eye-witness of the whole ministry of Jesus, and his dignity as an author, the latter stresses the great diversity of the traditional material collected by Mark after its use in the teaching and preaching of the Church, as well as the extreme discretion of the modifications and additions made by the Evangelist to the materials at his disposal.

Concerned as we are with the making of Mark's Gospel, we shall not undertake a detailed inventory of the traditions that preceded it as form-criticism enables us to glimpse them. We shall merely outline them and note in passing the facts that this method does not explain adequately. In so doing, we shall adopt the order followed by R. Bultmann in his *History of the Synoptic Tradition*. He groups the material forming part of the synoptic tradition empirically, in categories that are more readily usable than those proposed by Dibelius in his *From Tradition to Gospel*. In particular the inclusion among the 'sayings' of accounts of incidents where the words spoken by Jesus constitute the point of the story—Bultmann's 'apophthegms'—is both justified and useful.

Among these we find in the first place the controversies and the scholastic dialogues of Jesus ('Streit- und Schulgespräche'), about which almost everything has been said by M. Albertz.[3] Mark has two small collections of such sayings (2.1—3.6, and 11.27–33 together with 12.13–40), in addition to a few isolated examples (3.22–30; 7.1–13; 8.11–13; 10.2–12; 10.17–27): a fifth of the Gospel, or almost as much as the Passion story. Matthew and Luke, although their Gospels are much longer, add few texts of this kind and most of them are brief. On the other hand, they abound in utterances by Jesus against the

---

[1] M. J. Lagrange, *Ev. Marc.* Cf. in particular pp. cviii–cxxii of the 7th edn 1942.

[2] V. Taylor, *St Mark.* Cf. especially pp. 67–104.

[3] M. Albertz, *Die synopt. Streitgespräche* (Berlin 1921).

leaders of the Jewish people,[1] which is an indication of a more complete break with Judaism. As these little discussions have many parallels in rabbinic literature, it must be recognized that most of them go back to the oldest Palestinian community, which was still rooted in the Jewish environment.[2] There is thus little point in speculating whether the two collections of controversial sayings, composed by putting together a number of isolated incidents, took this form before Mark or were given it by him.[3] In any case, the incidents are grouped methodically and not chronologically. Besides it is not certain that the same conclusion should be drawn for both collections, one of which could have been compiled by the Evangelist on the model of the other: the same number of controversies (five), the same counter-attack by Jesus on the occasion of the last of them, the same allusion to the Pharisees' obscure allies the 'Herodians' (3.6 and 12.13) never mentioned elsewhere except in Matt. 22.17, which took them from Mark. Whereas W. L. Knox considers the first collection only as pre-Mark,[4] we would give

---

[1] Ibid., pp. 110–7. This contrast does not apply to the magisterial sayings, of which Mark gives only three (9.38–40; 10.35–45; 11.20–5), whereas Luke and Matthew add several others.

[2] R. Bultmann, *Gesch. der syn. Trad.*, 4th edn pp. 42–9.

[3] While M. Albertz, op. cit. pp. 5 and 35–6, is categorically of the opinion that both collections are pre-Mark, and M. Dibelius, *Formgeschichte des Evang.*, 3rd edn p. 220, rejects that view, though less firmly, in the case of 2.1—3.6, V. Taylor, *St Mark*, pp. 91–2 and 101, opts for their composition by the author of Mark at a time earlier than the writing of the Gospel. He believes that this theory reconciles the arguments in favour of a pre-Gospel origin (completeness of the collections in themselves, unsatisfactory insertion into Mark's plan, theological orientation slightly different from that of the rest of the Gospel) and those which plead in favour of their composition by Mark (very much the language and style of Mark). One can admire this harmonious compromise; it is more difficult to support it.

[4] *Sources of the Synoptic Gospels*, 1, pp. 8–16 and 85–92. This author simply accepts the arguments advanced by M. Albertz on the subject of the first collection, that is to say above all the unsatisfactory insertion of the passage in the plan of Mark (3.6 he finds is 'left in the air') and the non-eschatological use of the term 'Son of Man' in 2.10 and 2.28. These arguments seem weak. They merely prove that the Evangelist sought to isolate in the first part of his Gospel certain pericopes whose ideas had a special significance for him. We shall see later with what intention he seems to have done this (pp. 83 and 184ff. below). The

preference to the second, where the language differs indeed just as little from the rest of the Gospel as in 2.1 to 3.6 but where the rabbinic undertone is much more perceptible and the feeling of rupture between Judaism and Christianity emerges less strongly.[1] In any event, the controversies and scholastic sayings recorded by Mark reached him via the church tradition where they served apologetic and catechetical ends. Everything points to the fact that the Evangelist accorded them his special favour.

The 'biographical apophthegms'[2] form a less distinct cate-

comparison made by W. L. Knox between Mark 1.40–5 and 2.1ff. (pp. 8–9) is a judicious one, but reveals only the editorial work of the Evangelist, who wished to show Jesus as observant of the Law at the moment when he is about to relate the daring affirmations of the 'Son of Man'. As for the objections put forward by Knox (pp. 85–92) to the earlier origin of the collection in chap. 12, they consist essentially in denying the passages 12.1–12, 28–34, 35–7 the honour of being called 'controversies' (which no critic calls them except D. Daube, loc. cit. in n. 1 below). We shall accordingly describe these two collections as 'scholastic', which does not prevent them from having existed in a collection of 'debates led by Jesus' pre-dating Mark. It will be noted lastly that Matthew respects the collection in chap. 12 of Mark but not that in chap. 2.

[1] If this collection is taken out of the context in which Mark placed it (in particular if it is separated from the cleansing of the Temple, the parable of the husbandmen and perhaps Mark 12.35ff.), one can hear in it the echo of the life and faith of a community very comfortable in its Judaism and simply seeking to impose its spiritual and intellectual authority on other groups. With regard to the rabbinic undertone of the collection, D. Daube recently presented (*The New Testament and Rabbinic Judaism* (London 1956), pp. 174–87) some interesting rabbinic parallels that would enable the collection of debates in Mark 12 to be regarded as a group of four 'standard questions' corresponding to haggadic categories—and even perhaps to the questions of the four sons in the liturgy of the night of the Passover. This is very suggestive and a little venturesome. One can agree that a fairly 'rabbinicized' Church might have published quite early, following the scholastic customs of the surrounding community, a small collection of brief arguments showing how its Master triumphed over every conceivable objection. One cannot follow D. Daube when he endeavours (op. cit. p. 183) to read the parable of the husbandmen as the Christian substitute for the blessing that precedes the questions of the four sons in the liturgy for the night of the Passover.

[2] R. Bultmann, op. cit., pp. 26–38 and 58–64 of the 4th edn, from which we quote.

gory, characterized by their extreme conciseness and the abstract, idealized feeling of the scene related. In certain cases the sayings of Jesus are relatively independent of the narrative framework (Mark 3.34–5 and 6.4); elsewhere they derive their meaning only from the framework (Mark 12.41–4 and 14.3–9). As a rule they are placed at the end of the passage in question, which clearly brings out their importance. One can find many parallels to these 'biographical apophthegms' in the anecdotes related about certain rabbis by various '*midrashim*' and treatises of the Talmud.[1] In most cases there is no doubt of the Palestinian origin of these stories any more than of their use as illustrations by preachers. It would not seem that any collection of them existed, like that of the debates. R. Bultmann classifies in this category Mark 1.16–20; 2.14; 3.20–1; 3.31–5; 6.16; 7.24–31 (much retouched); 10.13–16; 11.15–19; 12.41–4; 13.1–2; 14.3–9. He traces in the two other synoptic Gospels, especially Luke, roughly the same number of stories of the same kind not to be found in Mark, to whom one cannot therefore ascribe a special preference for this kind of text, even if it can be thought that the list of them given above needs adding to a little.[2]

Among the sayings proper, R. Bultmann distinguishes in the first place three categories that are rather difficult to define precisely: the '*logia*' or wisdom sayings; the prophetic and apocalyptic sayings; the legal sayings and church rules. We shall not dwell here on what Mark may have derived from tradition in this sphere.[3] It is enough to say two things. The

---

[1] Cf. H. L. Strack and P. Billerbeck, *Kommentar zum Neuen Testament aus Talmud und Midrasch* (Munich 1922–58), vols. I and II ad loc.

[2] It seems to us possible to detect in Mark 8.13–15 and 9.36–7, beneath the touches added by Mark, two 'biographical apophthegms' of the normal type. In the first place the indication is given by the fact that the remainder of the pericope (8.16–21), which is visibly in Mark's style, is linked to the scene described in vv. 13–14 but not to the words of Jesus in v. 15, with which it overlaps, Mark not having dared to leave the latter out. In the second case the passage has a counterpart in Mark 10.13–16 but the point is different (attitude to children instead of example set by children) and it is very likely that the episode is not due to Mark but served as an introduction to the collection of sayings of Jesus which continues to the end of chap. 9. The apophthegm in this case was not transmitted in isolation but is nonetheless pre-Marcan (in reply to R. Bultmann, op. cit. pp. 160–1).

[3] Cf. Bultmann's long discussion of this, op. cit. pp. 73–161.

first concerns the state in which tradition handed down these words to Mark: in oral form, no doubt, and in no special order. The Evangelist might therefore simply have drawn on his memory in order to fit a few of the sayings of Jesus into his text from time to time. There are, however, in Mark several small collections of sayings of Jesus belonging to these three categories: 4.21–5, 8.35–7 belong to the first; 13.5–27, 13.30–7 to the second; 7.14–23, 9.35–50 to the third. Even if Mark retouched or added to one or other of them, it is probable that these groupings are in the main older than the Gospel and were constituted for catechetical purposes. The similarity of the subjects of several sayings was conducive to their grouping and memorization was facilitated by mnemonic devices such as the series of key-words.[1]

The second thing to be pointed out is the small number of these three types of sayings of Jesus to be found in Mark by comparison with Matthew and Luke. True, it cannot be said that Mark had at his disposal exactly the same material as Matthew and Luke, that is to say a form of the *logia*.[2] But if we

---

[1] The most striking case is to be found in Mark 9.35–50, with the words ἐν (ἐπὶ) τῷ ὀνόματι in vv. 37, 38, 39, 41; παιδία (or μικροί) in vv. 36, 37, 42; βάλλειν (or ἐκβάλλειν) in vv. 38, 42, 45, 47; σκανδαλίζεσθαι in vv. 42, 43, 45, 47; πῦρ in vv. 43, 48, 49; ἅλας in vv. 49 and 50. With R. Bultmann, op. cit. pp. 160–1 and V. Taylor, *St Mark*, pp. 408–10, we must see in this very primitive chain of words an indication of composition for catechetical purposes. M. Black, *An Aramaic Approach to the Gospels and Acts* (Oxford 2nd edn 1954 (1st edn 1946)), pp. 127–8, even believes it possible to detect, at least beneath Mark 9.38–48, a series of Aramaic alliterations which the translator could render only very imperfectly in Greek. L. Vaganay, *Probl. synopt.*, pp. 361–404, analyses the structure of this speech in depth, going back to an Aramaic original built up on a series of key-words. In any case its composition pre-dates Mark and was designed to meet the needs of oral catechizing.

[2] As we know, the dependence of Mark or otherwise on the *logia*, the second source common to Matthew and Luke, was a much debated question before the influence of the form-critical school became more general. (A convenient list of the holders of both views is to be found in M. Goguel, *Introd. au N.T.*, vol. 1, p. 98, which should be corrected, however, in regard to the position of A. Harnack and B. Streeter, who are much less inclined to believe in the use of the *logia* by Mark than Goguel suggests). It has become pointless today because it is recognized that the traditions passed on by the Christians of the first century on the subject of Jesus were both relatively fixed in form and very widespread,

think of tradition as an abundant source which fed all catechetical teaching and from which preaching drew part of its
content, it becomes likely that the author of Mark knew many
more sayings of Jesus of the three types in question than he
used. His ignorance is particularly improbable when it comes
to the pronouncements and sayings on the subject of the Law
and of discipline, given the highly moral character the catechism always possessed, if we are to rely on appearances.[1]
It must therefore be supposed that the Evangelist made a
choice among the sayings of Jesus known to him. As Matthew
and Luke made no similar choice, one is led to ask what the
significance of Mark's choice may have been.[2]

R. Bultmann makes the 'I'-sayings a fourth category of the
sayings of our Lord preserved by tradition.[3] Many of them,
however, do not appear to have had any independent existence
in tradition, which makes it rather artificial to group them in
this way. However, some of them were doubtless handed down
in isolation, before being placed by the Evangelist (or by the

---

which explains at the same time the similarities and the differences
between certain sayings recorded in Mark and their equivalent in
Matthew and Luke. We shall not go so far as to contest the existence of
the *logia* as a second source of Matthew and Luke, however, like A. M.
Farrer ('On Dispensing with Q', in *Studies in the Gospels, Essays in
Memory of R. H. Lightfoot*, ed. D. E. Nineham (Oxford 1957), pp.
55–8), who prefers the hypothesis that Matthew used Mark and
tradition and that Luke used Mark and Matthew. In our view it has
to be concluded that Matthew and Luke had access to a body of tradition perhaps not yet in existence or not widely known when Mark was
written and which was placed under the patronage of the apostle
Matthew.

[1] Cf. the numerous hortatory passages in the epistles of Paul and the
deutero-Pauline writings, the Epistle of James, the Sermon on the
Mount, the ethical colouring given by Luke to part of the Gospel
tradition, the *Didache*, etc. A. Seeberg's theory, *Der Katechismus der
Urchristenheit* (Leipzig 1903), according to which the sayings of Jesus on
moral questions were collected very early to form the 'ethical section'
of a catechism accepted by all the churches, no doubt goes too far. But
it reflects the tendency, as old as Christianity itself, to base moral
teaching on the authority of Jesus by quoting his own words as often as
possible. There is no reason why it should have been otherwise in the
community to which the author of Mark belonged.

[2] Cf. below, pp. 45 and 84f.

[3] R. Bultmann, op. cit. pp. 161–79.

compiler of some small earlier collection) in an arbitrary context. There are two groups of this type in Mark: those where Jesus himself speaks in the first person and those where he speaks of the suffering and resurrection of the Son of Man. To the first group belong Mark 2.17, 8.34 and 9.37, whereas Mark 1.38 is part of a note written by the author. This type of saying, more numerous in Matthew and Luke than in Mark, does not seem to have interested the author of Mark particularly.[1]

On the other hand, the sayings of Jesus about the suffering and resurrection of the Son of Man had a special importance for the author of the Gospel,[2] as is shown by the place of honour he gives to the prophecy of the passion, repeated three times in similar versions, perhaps deriving from the same traditional archetype (8.31; 9.31; 10.33–4). To this prophecy must be added Mark 9.9–12 and perhaps 10.45, which bear the signs of having been transmitted separately from their present context. Remembering too the allusions in Mark 14.21 and 14.41, one is tempted to seek the origin of these texts in a stereotyped statement of faith of the nature of 1 Cor. 15.3–4, that is to say including a reference to the 'Scriptures' whose prophecies Jesus had fulfilled; or, better still, in some '*pêshêr*' of Isa. 53.[3] The accumulation of terms applicable to the

---

[1] These are often sayings in which Jesus speaks of his 'coming'. Their growing number (still modest in Matthew and Luke but large in John) may be due to the growing influence of the idea of the pre-existence of Christ. But it would be wrong to cast suspicion on all these pronouncements on the grounds that many of them seem of late date, as R. Bultmann does, op. cit. p. 168. The argument could be turned round the other way: since several of these sayings have all the appearance of authenticity (those in Mark in particular), one could say that they all go back to Jesus himself. It seems wiser to accept the principle of selection.

[2] We shall revert to this point several times. Here we are simply reviewing the texts rapidly from the point of view of their origin.

[3] The interpretation by Jesus and the first Christians of the Servant Song in Isa. 52.13—53.12 as a prophecy of the ministry of Jesus has been many times discussed because, no doubt, of the small number of express quotations of this text to be found in the New Testament, particularly in the synoptic Gospels. Cf. on this point R. Bultmann, *Theologie des Neuen Testaments*, (3rd edn, Tübingen 1958), pp. 32–3 and 53–4, who is convinced that this interpretation is of later date; cf. also two authors who, on the contrary, attribute it to Jesus: J. Jeremias.

Scriptures and to their explanation is indeed striking in these
few passages; διδάσκειν[1] in 8.31, 9.31; δεῖ, of the necessary
fulfilment of the eschatological prophecies,[2] in 8.31, 9.11;
γέγραπται in 9.12–13, 14.21; ἦλθεν ἡ ὥρα in the sense of the
application of God's plan announced by the prophets, in
14.41. As for the expression 'Son of Man', whatever its exact
significance may be in Mark, it is certain that it was used by the
original Palestinian church.[3] There again, consequently, the
Evangelist has used and interpreted Palestinian traditions.

Before leaving the subject of the 'I'-sayings it should be
noted that of the passages in the synoptic Gospels where the
risen Christ speaks of himself (e.g. Matt. 28.18–20 and Matt.

---

art. παῖς θεοῦ, in the *TWNT*, vol. v, pp. 653–713 (in particular pp.
698ff.); O. Cullmann, *Christologie du Nouveau Testament* (Neuchâtel-
Paris 1958), pp. 48–73. On the question of the literary influence of
Isa. 53 on Christian writings of the first century sound comments are
to be found in C. H. Dodd, *According to the Scriptures, the Substructures of
New Testament Theology* (London 1952), pp. 92–4, and above all in
H. W. Wolff, *Jesaja im Urchristentum*, 3rd edn (Berlin 1952) (1st edn
Bethel-bei-Bielefeld 1942). It may be asked whether the influence at
once obscure and general of this passage of Isaiah might not be due to
the existence of a very ancient commentary, comparable to the *pesharim*
found at Qumran, containing an 'up-to-date' commentary of various
prophetic texts (cf. the translation given of most of the fragments of
this type already published by A. Dupont-Sommer, *Les écrits esséniens
découverts près de la Mer Morte*, pp. 267–90). The bizarre features of this
hypothetical commentary might perhaps explain why it was never
translated into Greek although it influenced the whole Christian
tradition and served as a screen between it and the Biblical text.

[1] Cf. H. Rengstorf, art. διδάσκω in the *TWNT*, vol. II, pp. 138–50,
especially pp. 141–3 and 147–50.

[2] Cf. W. Grundmann, art. δεῖ in the *TWNT*, vol. II, pp. 21–5.

[3] In contrast to R. Reitzenstein, *Das iranische Erlösungsmysterium* (1921),
pp. 117–31, who believes in the influence of the gnostic myth of the
redeeming man on the messianic consciousness of Jesus, R. Bultmann,
Gesch, d. syn. Trad., 4th edn p. 145 and 163n. and *Theol. d. N.T.*,
3rd edn pp. 30–2 and 52, thinks that the title of 'Son of Man' came to
Jesus through Jewish apocalyptic channels and had no personal
significance for him, but that the early community very quickly applied
this title to its Lord. In any case, therefore, the 'sayings of Jesus' about
the Son of Man are very ancient; moreover, the disuse into which this
christological title fell in the later Church (in spite of Paul and Irenaeus:
cf. O. Cullmann, *Christologie du N.T.*, pp. 143–56 and 164–5) makes it
impossible to suppose that the words concerning the Son of Man came
into being after the first generation of Christians.

18.20) not one is to be found in Mark. R. Bultmann is inclined to include in the list he gives of them[1] two texts from Mark: 8.34b and 3.35. But he has himself to admit that the first of them could perfectly well date back to the historical Jesus.[2] As for the second, supposing that it has to be separated from 3.31–4, it is quite absurd to assert that it is not authentic without advancing the slightest proof, since it contains no trace of enhanced Christology, no allusion to the passion or the resurrection, no anti-judaism or Greek ideas.[3] This absence in Mark of words spoken by the risen Christ about himself is partly bound up with the absence of any account of Christ's appearances. But even if this be taken into account, it is still surprising in a document containing so many allusions to the resurrection and in which the life of the Church is referred to, in 9.33–50, for example. Should we see in this a consequence of the fact that many of these sayings come from the Greek-speaking churches and not from the oldest Palestinian tradition? In that case Matthew and Luke would have had access to a more highly evolved and more hellenized tradition than their predecessor Mark.

The fifth and last category of sayings of Jesus, as classified by R. Bultmann, comprises the 'parables and related texts'.[4] This, as all agree, is a typically Jewish form of discourse, much used by the rabbis and by Jesus. Even though certain parables in the synoptic Gospels may come from the ambient Judaism

---

[1] *Gesch. d. syn. Trad.*, 4th edn pp. 169–79.

[2] Particularly as R. Bultmann, in his Supplement to the 3rd edn of his *Gesch. d. syn. Trad.*, p. 25, supports the very pleasing interpretation of these words by E. Dinkler, 'Jesu Wort zum Kreuztrag' in *Neutestamentliche Studien für Rudolf Bultmann zu seinem siebzigsten Geburtstag am 20 August 1954* (Berlin 1954), (Beihefte zur Zeitschr. f. die neutestamentliche Wissenschaft, 21), pp. 110–29.

[3] It is only too clear that R. Bultmann is ruled here—consciously or unconsciously—by the desire to reject any text that could support the theory that Jesus founded any kind of community. It is therefore gratifying to see that in his *Theol. d. N.T.*, 3rd edn pp. 8–9, he no longer denies the authenticity of Mark 3.35, although he still insists on making an absolute distinction between the 'group of disciples' and anything which could foreshadow a Church—religious order or sect. This change of opinion would be worth recording in the Supplement to the next edition of the *Gesch. d. syn. Trad.*

[4] *Gesch. d. syn. Trad.*, 4th edn pp. 179–222.

or be a product of the first Christian Church,[1] Mark certainly used Palestinian traditions formed at a very early date for the few parables he records: the three parables in Mark 4, that in Mark 12.1–12, the two in Mark 13 (vv. 28–9 and 34), to which may be added images like those in 2.19, 2.21–2, 4.21–2, 9.49. This is still true even if it be admitted that the use of the parables of Jesus by the primitive Church in its ethical teaching often distorted their meaning[2] since this distortion must have occurred right at the start. The author of Mark grouped some of these texts together in his chapter 4, but it is doubtful whether they were grouped beforehand, since their grouping is loose[3] and they are very closely linked to the context in which they are placed by the author.[4] Our view is rather that these parables were known to Mark separately[5] or, at most, that he had access

[1] Ibid., pp. 219–22. Thus W. G. Kuemmel, 'Das Gleichnis von den bösen Weingärtnern (Mark 12.1–9)', in *Aux sources de la tradition chrétienne, mélanges offerts à M. Maurice Goguel à l'occasion de son soixante-dixième anniversaire* (Neuchâtel-Paris 1950), pp. 120–31, brings sound arguments to support the theory that interprets this parable as the creation of the primitive Church. In our view, however, C. H. Dodd, *The Parables of the Kingdom*, 2nd edn (London 1961), pp. 96ff., and J. Jeremias, *Die Gleichnisse Jesu* (Zürich 1947, 5th edn Göttingen 1958), pp. 45–9, are right in postulating an authentic form more or less obscured by later allegorization.

[2] J. Jeremias, op. cit. pp. 15–58, gives an excellent account of the paraenetic use of the parables of Jesus and the effect this had on their form and content.

[3] One long parable, that of the sower, is followed by at least one interpretation (4.3–9 and 4.10–12 or 4.13–20) alongside two other very short ones which are rather obscure and could have been explained with great advantage (4.26–9 and 4.30–2). A group of sayings which looks like a conclusion is placed in the middle of the collection (vv. 21–5). The form of the three parables differs greatly, even if one compares the two last, which have more resemblance to one another, but which begin in a much less uniform way (vv. 26 and 30) than the parables in the corresponding chapter of Matthew (Matt. 13.24,31,33, 44,45,47).

[4] This group of parables marks the transition from public teaching in the face of opponents (Mark 3.20–35) to semi-public teaching in the midst of a group of sympathizers (4.35—5.43). In each case, Mark gives some examples of the attitude of Jesus: two controversies, three parables, three (or four) miracles. It is thus that one can explain this small collection of parables. Cf. also pp. 188–90 below.

[5] In opposition to many authors, including Ch. Masson, *Les paraboles de Marc 4, avec une introduction à l'explication des évangiles* (Neuchâtel-Paris

to a general collection of them from which he made a strict selection.

However this may be, it is striking that Mark should contain so few parables. It is most unlikely that he could have known only so few as ten, since Jesus often taught in parables and the early community based its moral teaching on the parables of our Lord. Whatever the form in which the tradition came to the author of Mark it must be supposed that he made a choice among all the '*meshalim*' known to him. We shall be enquiring later into the reasons for this selection, which is surprising in a man who must surely have had the greatest respect for all the teaching of Jesus.[1]

At the conclusion of this rapid review of the tradition from which Mark drew the sayings of Jesus he recorded, one may make the following remarks:

(*a*) All the components of this sort that have gone into Mark are of Palestinian origin and very early, with a few exceptions only (like 7.2–4, 7.21–3 and 10.10–12). Unlike Matthew and Luke, Mark contains few words of anathema against the Jewish leaders but instead accounts of arguments with them: this is a sign of a less complete separation of the Church and the Synagogue. Mark contains few 'I'-sayings, which indicates a less developed Christology than in the succeeding Gospels.

(*b*) These 'sayings of Jesus' used by Mark were handed on to him separately, except for a collection of controversies (corresponding roughly to Mark 11.27–33 and 12.13–34) and a few small groups of words of a wisdom, apocalyptic, or 'canonical' nature.[2] The Evangelist's work consisted partly in arranging this heterogeneous material.

(*c*) For all the 'sayings of Jesus' taken over by Mark it is

---

1945) (Cahiers théologiques, 11), pp. 49–54; J. Jeremias, op. cit., p. 8, n. and p. 59; W. L. Knox, *Sources of the Synoptic Gospels*, 1, pp. 35–8. All the critics who favour the theory of the small collection pre-dating Mark are obliged to admit that the author of Mark made many changes in this document, but they do not succeed in making it homogeneous, even when they have eliminated the corrections and additions.

[1] Cf. pp. 84–6 below.

[2] The word is used here in the sense of 'canon' in 'canon law'.

relatively easy to imagine their function in the early Church:
preaching, catechism, exhortation, controversy, exegesis.

(*d*) Lastly, it is clear that the author of Mark made a certain
selection among the 'sayings of Jesus' handed on to him by
tradition. For certain kinds of sayings he chose to reproduce all
those he knew, perhaps even increasing their number by giving
to others the form he preferred—thus the controversies and
sayings on the subject of the passion of the Son of Man. For
other kinds the Evangelist used the material handed down by
tradition without seeking to be exhaustive but also, it would
seem, without rejecting a great deal: this is the case with the
'biographical apophthegms' and the passages where Jesus in
his earthly life speaks of himself in the first person. Towards all
the other kinds of saying deriving from tradition the Evangelist's attitude is one of reserve and he retains only a small number in his Gospel. This can be seen in the case of the scholastic
discussions, the *logia*, the prophetic and apocalyptic utterances,
the 'canonical' pronouncements, perhaps the passages where
the risen Christ speaks of himself, and certainly the parables.

The points made in (*b*) and (*d*) are particularly important
because they imply an active attitude on the part of the
author of Mark to tradition, which was after all his only source
for the words of Jesus.

If we now turn to those texts of Mark that have not yet been
examined, we may group them, with R. Bultmann,[1] under the
heading 'narrative material' and distinguish two main types
of story: the miracle stories and the 'stories and legends',
whose origin does not seem to be the same.

The miracle stories[2] number about fifteen in Mark if we do
not count among them either the controversies or the apoph-

---

[1] R. Bultmann, *Gesch. d. syn. Trad.*, pp. 223–346.

[2] In addition to the very rewarding pages devoted to these accounts by
R. Bultmann, op. cit. pp. 223–60, the following may be consulted:
A. Fridrichsen, *Le problème du miracle dans le christianisme primitif* (Stras-
bourg 1925) (Etudes d'historie et de philosophie religieuses, XII);
O. Perels, *Die Wunderüberlieferung der Synoptiker in ihrem Verhältnis zur
Wortüberlieferung* (Stuttgart 1934); A. Richardson, *The Miracle-Stories
of the Gospels* (London 1941); J. Kallas, *The Significance of the Synoptic
Miracles* (London 1961).

thegms which include a miraculous act on the part of Jesus (2.1–12; 3.1–6; 7.24–30), or the author's summaries of his healing and exorcizing activities (1.32–4; 1.39; 3.10–12; 6.54–6). Of this total, five are acts violating the laws of nature (4.35–41; 6.35–44; 6.45–52; 8.1–10; 11.12–14,20–2), three are exorcisms (1.23–8; 5.1–20; 9.14–29), six are healing the sick (1.29–31; 1.40–5; 5.25–34; 7.31–7; 8.22–6; 10.46–52) and there is one raising of the dead (5.21–4,35–43). This classification probably corresponds more to our modern mentality than to that of the Evangelist, for whom the miracles are apparently either miracles performed by the spoken word, where the accent is on the power of Jesus[1] or miracles performed by physical contact, where the accent is on his loving kindness.[2] The former show the triumph of Jesus over the forces of evil, masters of fallen creation; the latter have the sentimental aura that modern people tend to see in all acts of healing, including exorcisms. It would in any case be wrong to lay too much emphasis on these categories, which do not correspond to any arrangement of his text by the Evangelist but to categories implicit in tradition or in his own mind.

The miracle stories are roughly as numerous in Mark as the controversies, and they occupy a similar space in the text, that is to say about one fifth, the same amount as the Passion story. It can be said, then, that the Evangelist welcomes them and this is the more apparent since the other two synoptic Gospels, although much longer, add nothing to the volume of the miracles related by Mark, which greatly lessens the relative importance of this type of pericope in their texts. In Luke one can even speak of a reduction in volume of the miracle stories since he leaves out five of those contained in Mark (Mark 6.45–52; 7.31–7; 8.1–10; 8.22–6; 11.12–14,20–2), plus one of the 'biographical apophthegms' that includes a miracle, and replaces them only by four 'apophthegms' of this type (Luke

---

[1] First the three exorcisms and then the stories of the stilling of the storm (4.35–41), the blind man of Jericho (10.46–52) and the barren fig tree (11.12–14, 20–2).

[2] Five of the six healings, the raising of the daughter of Jairus, the two miracles of the loaves (6.35–44 and 8.1–10) and the walking on the sea (6.45–52) where the miracle is performed to extract the disciples from a difficult situation (cf. vv. 48a and 51a). On the subject of these two aspects of the miracles of Jesus cf. Acts 10.38.

7.1–10; 13.10–17; 14.1–6; 17.11–19), one composite story that is more of an 'apophthegm' with a legendary prolongation than a miracle story (the miraculous draught of fishes in Luke 5.1–11) and the account of one raising from the dead (the son of the widow of Nain, in Luke 7.11–17). In Matthew three of the miracles related by Mark are missing (Mark 1.23–8; 7.31–7; 8.22–6) but there are two others[1] not in Mark (Matt. 9.27–31 and 9.32–4); one of Mark's accounts (6.45–52) is added to in the shape of an unsuccessful miracle story that has more the appearance of a preacher's embellishment (Matt. 14.28–31: Peter venturing to walk on the water); a legend bordering on a biographical apophthegm contains the promise of a miracle (Matt. 17.24–7) and a biographical apophthegm including a healing makes its appearance (Matt. 8.5–13, the centurion of Capernaum, = Luke 7.1–10). In short, we must conclude that here, too, the space given to miracle stories has been reduced, especially if we bear in mind the abridgement in Matthew of the narrative passages of Mark.[2] This does not mean, of course, that the authors of Matthew and Luke had less liking for the miraculous than the author of Mark. The many editorial summaries in both Gospels which refer to the very numerous acts of healing performed by Jesus and the miraculous features of their accounts of the childhood and resurrection of Christ suffice to prove the contrary. But it is clear that Matthew and Luke have not the same love as Mark of miracle stories as a literary genre.

These stories, as the exegetes of the form-critical school have shown,[3] are cast in a fairly constant mould: the *critical nature of the situation* is first stressed whether it be a threat to Jesus himself (Mark 1.23–4; 4.37; 5.2–5; 5.27–8; 11.12), or the misfortune of the person or persons for whom the miracle is to be performed (1.30a; 5.23,25–6,35; 6.35,48; 8.1–3; 9.17–18, 20–2a); then *the case is presented to Jesus* and his intervention

---

[1] R. Bultmann, *Gesch. d. syn. Trad.*, p. 226, regards these two as being composed by Matthew, on the model of Matt. 12.22–4 and 20.29–34, in order to illustrate Matt. 11.5. This is probably going too far.

[2] Thus Mark 5.1–20 is reduced to the nine verses of Matt. 9.18–26; Mark 6.30–44 to the nine verses of Matt. 14.13–21; Mark 9.14–29 to the eight verses of Matt. 17.14–21; etc. Cf. G. Bornkamm, G. Barth and H. J. Held, *Ueberlieferung . . .*, pp. 155ff.

[3] Cf. for example R. Bultmann, op. cit. pp. 236–41.

sought,[1] sometimes in imperious or sceptical terms by the person concerned or, more often, his friends or family (1.30b; 1.40; 4.38; 5.23b; 6.36; 7.32; 8.4; 8.22; 9.22b–24; 10.46–51); the *performance of the miracle* is then related, very soberly and as a rule with no descriptive accompaniment (1.25–6; 1.31a; 1.41–2; 4.39; 5.29,34; 5.40–1; 6.41–2; 6.48–51; 8.6–8a; 9.25–7; 10.52; 11.14) but sometimes in considerable detail (5.8–13a; 7.33–5; 8.23–5); a *concrete detail* sometimes testifies to the reality of the miracle (1.31; 5.13b; 5.30-2; 5.42a,43b; 6.43; 7.35; 8.8b; 9.27; 10.52; 11.20); lastly, in most of the accounts, *the crowd*, scornful or indifferent before the miracle, sometimes held back during the performance of the act but informed of it immediately, against the wishes of Jesus, expresses fear or astonishment (1.27–8; 1.44–5; 4.41; 5.14–20; 5.37–40, 42b–43a; 7.36–7; 8.26; 9.25a,26b). Thus they are stories based on a narrative outline plan of an extremely simple kind—in a word they are popular tales, obeying the instinctive laws that govern that genre almost anywhere in the world.

It is difficult to express an opinion on the exact origin of these fifteen or so passages in Mark. The parallels that can be found to most of them in the Old Testament and rabbinic texts, in Greek literature or in Egyptian or Buddhist tradition,[2] far from suggesting borrowings, prove only that they are not literary texts bearing the imprint of the author's style and personality, but anonymous tales told with rudimentary means and consequently subject to the influence of the degenerate literary themes that formed the common fund of popular culture in the Middle East of two thousand years ago.

Can one, with R. Bultmann,[3] ascribe a hellenistic origin to most of these accounts, arguing that they give a 'mythical' picture of Jesus whereas the *logia*, a Palestinian document, show him in the more probable guise of a preacher of the end of the world and a master of wisdom? True, there are great

---

[1] In the accounts of exorcisms, on the contrary, 'the unclean spirit' seeks to avoid Jesus' intervention which he foresees: 1.24; 5.6–7; 9.20. Cf. an interesting study of these passages by O. Bauernfeind, *Die Worte der Dämonen im Markus-Evangelium* (Stuttgart 1927).

[2] R. Bultmann, op. cit. pp. 247–53, gives a list of the best-known of these parallels.

[3] Ibid. p. 256.

differences between the Jewish accounts of miracles ascribed to rabbis and Mark's accounts, where the person of the healer is thrown much more sharply into relief.[1] But might not this be due to the fact that Jesus was not like other rabbis (Mark 1.22), the present writer is naive enough to suggest. Besides, once separated from the christological retouching that must be ascribed to the Evangelist in several cases, do these stories contain anything but a description of isolated events that caught popular imagination in some districts of Galilee and created around the principal actor in them an aura as bright as it is confused—neither very Jewish, nor very Greek, but simply, perhaps . . . animistic? Lastly, it would be strange, if hellenistic Christianity had added to the number of miracles, that it should have stopped doing so immediately after the composition of Mark. If that were so, how could one explain that there are fewer such accounts in Luke, a typically hellenistic Gospel, without abandoning the theory of R. Bultmann? It is much more probable that Mark used Palestinian stories. His successors, more marked by Hellenism than he, rid the texts of their most grossly material features and generalized their import with the help of summaries, but added scarcely anything for want of any new source of information.

To speak of Palestinian stories, however, is not enough. Is there cause to think that these stories were used, before Mark, in the churches of Palestine or elsewhere, to serve various practical or theological purposes? In other words, can one see them as forming part of the church tradition, in the same way as the 'sayings of Jesus'? Critics have sometimes said so,[2]

---

[1] M. Dibelius, *Formgesch. d. Evang.* 3rd edn, pp. 148–9.

[2] For example by A. E. J. Rawlinson, *St Mark, with Introduction, Commentary and Additional Notes* (London 1925) (Westminster Commentaries), p. xiii; A. Richardson, *Miracle Stories of the Gospels*, p. 1; H. Riesenfeld, *The Gospel Tradition and its Beginnings, a Study in the Limits of 'Formgeschichte'* (London 1957), pp. 8–10 and 26–7. This latter critic goes so far as to ascribe to Jesus not only the performance of miracles but even the intention of making the relating of them by his disciples one of the foundations of the 'Gospel' (on the basis of Mark 14.3–9 in particular). This rather venturesome hypothesis rests on the affirmation of the symbolic character of all the miracles of Jesus, which are to be compared to the symbolic acts of the Old Testament prophets. This is to place too little stress on the miraculous nature of the acts of Jesus, their nature as manifestations of power, which makes them in the eyes

but always rather hesitantly, comparing these stories to the various forms of the sayings of Jesus, about which there can be no doubt. But while the form and content of the sayings strongly suggest a specific 'Sitz im Leben', the accounts of the miracles collected by Mark do not readily lend themselves to such a hypothesis. Their relatively large number, the wealth of concrete and somewhat irrelevant detail some of them contain,[1] the great ambiguity of the theological and christological content of certain of them[2] make it impossible to see them as documents 'received' for the purpose of expressing the faith and moral teaching of a church, even at a time close to its origin. Although they conform to a common plan, these stories have not the polish, the sobriety or the doctrinal soundness of the 'controversies' or the 'biographical apophthegms'. They are for the most part 'untamed' documents, if we may be allowed the expression, whose 'domestication' is barely begun in Mark.[3]

---

of Mark something quite other than symbolic acts (in the Old Testament sense) similar to that of the woman of Bethany or of John the Baptist on the day of the baptism (Mark 1.9–11). The tradition handed down must surely have contained a few accounts of symbolic acts, among which should be classed, no doubt, those of Jesus at the Last Supper (Mark 14.22–4), but that is no proof of a pre-Marcan tradition of miracle stories.

[1] On this point, cf. V. Taylor, *St Mark*, where he explains the accounts of several miracles and makes some very pertinent remarks. It is clear that Matthew was particularly struck by the verbosity of Mark's stories, so that he abridged them considerably (cf. p. 47, n. 2, above). Luke, for his part, being a good story-teller, liked the stories for their picturesqueness and merely eliminated the passages in bad taste: H. J. Cadbury, *The Style and Literary Method of Luke* (Cambridge, Mass. 1920) (Harvard Theo. Studies, VI), *passim*.

[2] Cf. V. Taylor, op. cit., pp. 143–4. One might cite, for example, the strange dialogues between Jesus and the 'unclean spirits' in Mark 1.23–5 and 5.7–13, where one can glimpse the idea that Jesus and the demons somehow belong to the same world (cf. Mark 3.22!); the crudeness of the conception of Jesus' power in the story of the woman with the issue of blood; the small number of references to God and of calls to give thanks to him (5.19; 6.41; 8.6; 9.29); etc.

[3] This domestication is brought about primarily by their editorial setting: cf. for example the introduction of the theme of the mission in 5.18–20, which T. A. Burkill ('Concerning Mark 5.7 and 5.18–20', in *Studia Theologica*, vol. XI (1957), pp. 159–66) does not seem to us to have succeeded in joining to the preceding account of the incident; it is clearly an editorial touch. In Matthew and Luke, this domestication

A few of them only, to judge by their schematic structure and their christological classicism, might pass for borrowings from the official tradition of the primitive Church: 1.29–31, 8.1–9, 10.46–52. But in the case of two of these texts it may well be that they are of Marcan origin[1] or else that they were exceptionally sober accounts.

If we reject the idea that the stories of the miracles collected by Mark come from the tradition 'received' from the Palestinian church, should we see in them a transcription of eyewitness accounts whose authority would have been sufficient for the Evangelist to have accepted it without question? As we know, the apostle Peter has often been suggested as the main source of information drawn on by the author of Mark, especially where the stories are concerned. As we have already shown, it was not thanks to any written collection of 'Peter's memoirs'.[2] But it might have been thanks to stories told by the apostle or another of the disciples either in the presence of the Evangelist[3] or even expressly for his benefit. We know so little

---

goes much further and can be sensed even in the stories themselves (cf. the attenuation by the two latter Evangelists of difficult verses such as Mark 1.43, 4.39, 5.29), except where they preferred to leave out the passage as unusable (cf. p. 47 above).

[1] This may be asked in particular about the second multiplication of the loaves (Mark 8.1–10), which seems to be modelled on the first account, with the omission of some unnecessary details and which, as we shall see, is probably intended to serve a specific purpose in Mark (cf. p. 180 below). The story of the healing of Peter's mother-in-law (1.29–31) might be an editorial note based on a simple reminiscence, designed to show from the outset that Jesus used his miracle-working powers, which had just been revealed (1.23ff.), to help his own followers as well as people in the crowd and that he exercised them in private as well as in public. As for the restoring of his sight to Bartimaeus, this is a noble confession of faith on the part of a blind clairvoyant and the miracle plays a very small part; it is tempting to see in it a 'biographical apophthegm' whose point is the confession of Bartimaeus and not a pronouncement by Jesus. In that case it would derive from the official church tradition.

[2] Cf. pp. 21ff. above.

[3] It is in this way that the beginning of the note by Papias about Mark as the interpreter of Peter has often been understood (cf. p. 14, n. 2 above). That is the theory of M. J. Lagrange, for example, *Ev. Marc*, 7th edn, pp. cix–cxiii, and of V. Taylor, *St Mark*, p. 80. The latter

of the disciples of Jesus and of their religious ideas in particular[1] that this possibility cannot be absolutely ruled out. It does not seem very probable, however, so sharp is the contrast between the accounts of the miracles, with their rather crude theology and their sensational rather than edifying character[2] and the 'sayings of Jesus' which formed the basis of the church tradition handed on and authenticated by the disciples.

It is preferable to trace these tales back to popular memory, to be distinguished, in our view, from the memory of the organized Christian community which shaped the 'traditions'.[3] Though we know so little of the ministry of Jesus, it is clear that it was marked by considerable popular success, at least for a time.[4] It would not be surprising if in various places people should have remembered the prodigies performed by this

---

admits (pp. 140–5) that the miracle stories in Mark are far from being simply noted down from eye-witness accounts by Peter and believes that there is a number of legendary additions. One does not quite see how this combination could have occurred—perhaps in the mind of Peter, since according to V. Taylor, the author of Mark is definitely John Mark, Peter's collaborator, and so his knowledge of the miracles did not come from the general church tradition. Taylor's theory is very close to that of Lagrange and differs from it only in its different concept of the miracle and its smaller esteem for the memory of the Prince of the Apostles.

[1] These men of fairly modest origin, provincials with no great education (Acts 4.13), were probably not absolutely orthodox in their Jewish theology; they were perhaps attracted by miracles as modern crowds are by sensation. But what one can vaguely sense of their theological and christological ideas is worth more than the ideas underlying the accounts of the miracles in Mark (cf. for example, O. Cullmann, *Saint Pierre*, pp. 57–60).

[2] Cf. M. Dibelius, *Formgesch. d. Evang.*, 3rd edn, pp. 75–88.

[3] J. Wellhausen, *Einleitung in die drei ersten Evangelien* (Berlin 1905), pp. 52–3, at the same time recognized the popular origin of Mark's stories, where the voice of authoritative eye-witnesses is scarcely to be heard, and made the mistake of confusing this 'vox populi' with the official tradition of the earliest Church as revealed in 'the sayings of Jesus'.

[4] Even an author who, like G. Bornkamm, *Jesus of Nazareth* (Stuttgart 1956) (Urban-Bücher, 19), pp. 49–141, while not believing that the popularity of Jesus was always unchallenged, admits that it was real. Ch. Guignebert, *Jésus* (Paris 1933) (L'Evolution de l'humanité, 29) is clearly indulging in excessive scepticism when he reduces the career of Jesus to a succession of failures which excited no public attention.

unusual preacher, even though they had not belonged to the circle of his most ardent admirers. Events like those related in Mark 4.35—5.43, like that of the first multiplication of the loaves, like those of the healing of the sick in 7.32–7, 8.22–7, 9.14–29, were no doubt the subject of excited gossip among the village folk of north-east Galilee.[1] That is how they collected their touches of legend and folklore while keeping the vivid and sometimes earthy quality that still strikes us today. They reflect the religious ideas of small groups of people living on the border of Jewish Palestine and Syria, in an area undergoing hellenization following the founding of the 'Greek' cities of Caesarea Philippi, Bethsaida Julias and Tiberias.[2] To explain their formation it is not necessary to pose the hypothesis of a Galilean Christianity separate from the church of Jerusalem and just as old.[3] It is enough to suppose that the works of Jesus were witnessed by people other than the disciples and made a mark on them.

The problem posed by the introduction of these stories into the Gospel is a more arduous one. How could a Christian

[1] Mark 1—9 contains some thirteen to fifteen of the accounts of miracles in the Gospel and places them in Galilee or on its northern and eastern borders, especially on the shores of Lake Tiberias. True, the place where most of these incidents are situated is due to the author, and is known to be artificial. But before we ascribe to the Evangelist any theological or symbolical intention, it might be asked whether it does not reflect, in addition to history, the source of the material he used. We shall revert (see p. 249 below) to the question of the meaning the author gave to 'Galilee' in his Gospel, but it should be stressed here that the miracle stories give much more the impression of a 'lakeside collection' from Capernaum or Bethsaida than of a Galilean collection. The Evangelist seems to have sought to introduce into material which did not lend itself very well to the purpose the idea of a ministry pursued by Jesus throughout the whole of Galilee (1.14; 1.39; 7.31; 9.30).

[2] Cf. G. Dalman, *Les itinéraires de Jésus: topographie des Evangiles*, Fr. trans., J. Marty (Paris 1930), pp. 215ff.

[3] The theory of E. Lohmeyer (*Galiläa und Jerusalem* (Göttingen 1936)) on this subject has been accepted only by a minority of critics, amongst whom one of the most recent and individual is L. E. Elliott-Binns, *Galilean Christianity* (London 1956) (Studies in Biblical Theology, 16). It represents one of the most ingenious attempts ever made to explain the duplication of the accounts of the appearances of the risen Christ and the respective roles of Peter and James (cf. Acts 12.17; 15; 21.18ff.; 1 Cor. 9.5; Gal. 1.18—2.14), but it is nevertheless fragile, although some of the points made are usable: cf. pp. 248ff., below.

author be so bold as to place such unorthodox documents on the same footing as the tradition 'received' from Jerusalem? How did he even know of them, since they did not come from his habitual source, the church authorities? These questions seem to us highly important. More than the accurate replies that we shall endeavour to make to them, these questions are among the keys to the interpretation of Mark. Any theory about the origin of Mark's Gospel which evades or ignores them is bound to be weakened. But as soon as one admits their importance one is obliged to see the author of Mark as much more than a mere compiler of traditions. Whatever his identity may have been,[1] he sought his information outside his own milieu and perhaps far from where he lived,[2] and he must have had overriding reasons for juxtaposing documents of recognized authority and others that were both new and surprising. In short, he did what a writer, and indeed an audacious writer, can be expected to do.

The narrative passages of Mark also comprise, if we continue to follow R. Bultmann's classification, three sections very different from one another: the 'stories and legends' of chapters 1—13, the Passion story and the announcement of the resurrection. The first of these categories[3] has no great unity. It includes, in addition to the passages where John the Baptist is the principal figure (Mark 1.1–8 and 6.17–29), the accounts of the baptism and the temptation (Mark 1.9–13), those of the confession of Peter (Mark 8.27–30), the transfiguration (Mark 9.2–8) and the entry into Jerusalem (Mark 11.1–10).

The second of the passages relating to John the Baptist

---

[1] Cf. pp. 257ff. below.

[2] Documents as unliterary as the miracle stories in Mark spread only slowly and occasionally beyond the limits of the social and linguistic group from which they derive. Since the time between their origin and their inclusion in the Gospel according to Mark must have been at most forty years, the most probable hypothesis is that they were collected at their place of origin by the Evangelist or by some member of his circle. If true this would be the more remarkable when it is remembered that Luke, in spite of his claims to be a historian, scarcely sought the information that served as the basis for Luke and Acts anywhere except where his ministry led him or beyond the frontiers of the Christian Church (Cf. the author's *Livre des Actes et l'histoire*, pp. 79–80).

[3] R. Bultmann, *Gesch. d. syn. Trad.*, pp. 261–81 and 328–9.

(6.17–29) is a case apart; it is a legend at once naive and highly coloured, without the slightest Christian flavour, which is probably not due even to the followers of the Baptist, since the accent is so strongly on the picturesque and sensational details, to the detriment of the religious significance.[1] This text needs to be compared to the miracle stories, whose origins it shares. It is a popular Galilean tale designed to show to what depths of immorality the Tetrarch—a hellenizer and collaborator—had sunk. The author of Mark could not resist the pleasure of reproducing it once he had discovered it—perhaps by chance. Matthew and Luke toned down and abridged this somewhat scandalous story (Matt. 14.3–12; Luke 3.19–20). Once again the author of Mark appears in the light of a daring author and one who was not tied exclusively to the church tradition.

The first of the passages relating to John the Baptist (1.1–8) is, for all its conciseness, highly complex. But it seems certain that here the Evangelist presents a sort of summary of the ministry of John the Baptist, condensing as much as possible what church tradition related about him: two commentaries on prophetic texts (Matt. 3.1–6 and Luke 3.1–6; Matt. 11.7–11 and Luke 7.24–8); and a certain number of exhortations and prophecies ascribed to him (Matt. 3.7–12; Luke 3.7–18). By abridging these texts, the author of Mark christianized them more than either Matthew or Luke was to do[2] and also, more than they, reduced John the Baptist's role to that of a forerunner to Jesus.[3] Even if Christian tradition concerning John

---

[1] A comparison with the account of the passion is instructive in this respect. Whereas in chapters 14—16 our attention is constantly brought back to Jesus, in chap. 6 John the Baptist shares the stage with Herod and his harem: Flaubert, to whom it did not occur to write a story about the last days of Jesus, must have sensed this.

[2] By associating the quotation from Mal. 3.1 with the announcement of the coming of 'one mightier than I', which makes of God's words a promise made to Jesus and no longer to Israel, and by transforming the eschatological 'baptism' with 'the Holy Ghost and with fire' (Matt. 3.11 and Luke 3.17) into 'baptism with the Holy Ghost' (Mark 1.8).

[3] By placing Mark 1.1 before the passage about John the Baptist, which makes the latter take his place in 'the Gospel of Jesus Christ' (whatever the meaning of this expression may be: cf. for example W. Marxsen, *Der Ev. Markus*, pp. 87–8); by quoting only those words of John the Baptist concerning the One who was coming after him.

the Baptist comes from the Baptist's disciples, there is no special reason to think that the author of Mark derived it from them directly. He received the content of the eight verses in question from his church but he has made of them quite a refined literary composition.[1]

The accounts of the baptism and the temptation (Mark 1.9–13) raise very difficult problems of a number of kinds,[2] whose solution may be facilitated by a comparison with the account of the transfiguration in Mark 9.2–8.[3] The baptism and the transfiguration are indeed only the narrative framework in which the voice from heaven is heard (1.11 and 9.7); the words pronounced in each case are very similar, they come at the end of each passage and they are the only words pronounced by a voice from heaven in Mark's Gospel. Moreover, there are similarities in the two contexts; temptation by Satan (8.32–33 corresponds to 1.12–13), allusion to John the Baptist (1.4–9 and 9.11–13). It will be noted also that the 'six days' in Mark 9.2 and the 'forty days' of Mark 1.13 are to be found side by side in Exod. 24.16–18. In these circumstances ought we to suppose that the church tradition handed on to the author of Mark a more or less embroidered and mythologized

---

[1] E. Lohmeyer, *Das Evangelium des Markus* (Kritisch-exegetischer Kommentar über das Neue Testament, 1.2), (Göttingen 1937, with a Supplement published in 1951), pp. 9ff., has demonstrated how Mark 1.4–8 is in the eyes of the Evangelist the fulfilment of the prophecies of 1.2–3. However, he has not properly grasped that Mark builds up a chiasmus in which vv. 4–6 are a commentary on v. 3, as in Matt. 3.16 and Luke 3.1–6, whereas vv. 7 and 8 echo v. 2, which is a 'christianizing' innovation.

[2] Apart from the various commentaries ad. loc. the following may be consulted: W. E. Flemington, *The New Testament Doctrine of Baptism* (London 1948), pp. 25ff.; O. Cullmann, *Christologie du N.T.*, pp. 60–1; M. A. Chevallier, *Le Messie et l'Esprit dans le Bas-Judaïsme et dans le christianisme primitif* (Paris 1958) (Etudes d'hist. et de philo. relig., vol. 49), pp. 57–67.

[3] On this text, still more difficult than the preceding one and interpreted in widely differing ways, cf. for example G. Boobyer, *St Mark and the Transfiguration Story* (Edinburgh 1942); H. Riesenfeld, *Jésus transfiguré, l'arrière plan du récit évangélique de la Transfiguration de Notre Seigneur* (Copenhagen 1947) (Acta Semin. Neotest. Upsal., 16); H. Baltensweiler, *Die Verklärung Jesu, historisches Ereignis und synoptische Berichte* (Zurich 1959) (Abhandl. z. Theol. d. A. u. N.T., 33). Cf. also pp. 168–70 below.

version of the theme:[1] 'As God spoke to Jesus on the day of his baptism to enable him to resist Satan, he spoke to the 'pillars' to give them strength to remain wholly faithful to the teaching of their master'?[2] The Evangelist would in that case have cut up this text and twisted it to fit in to his plan, but there is an echo of the tradition juxtaposing the two voices from heaven to be found in 2 Peter 1.16f.[3]

Peter's confession (Mark 8.27–9), which should be read in conjunction with Mark 6.14–16, which reproduces it in part for editorial reasons,[4] has practically no narrative framework. It might be a 'scholastic discourse' deprived by Mark of its point, namely the words of praise spoken by Jesus to Peter, which have been preserved in Matt. 16.17–19.[5] True, the

---

[1] The rabbinic theme of the *Bath Qol*, the echo of the divine voice that man can hear without danger, is inspired by the desire to get rid of anthropomorphisms but in fact results frequently in objectivizing— and hence in mythologizing—the act of revelation (cf. Strack–Billerbeck, I, pp. 125–32). It certainly had an influence on the accounts of the baptism and the transfiguration.

[2] The Peter, James, and John may have been, in the tradition drawn on by Mark, not those of Mark 5.37 (= Peter and the sons of Zebedee) but those of Gal. 2.9, that is to say the heads of the church of Jerusalem about the year 44, among whom was James the brother of our Lord. The second voice from heaven established their authority in the Church.

[3] 2 Pet. 1.17 refers to a revelation that came to Jesus Christ by a voice from heaven proclaiming his divine fidelity; it is very probable that this was an allusion to the baptism. 2 Pet. 1.18 relates to a subsequent occasion (the verb of v. 17 is an aorist participle indicating a fact anterior to the main verb) consisting in a revelation to the disciples by a voice speaking in the same terms as the first (the καί should be translated with ταύτην τὴν φωνήν in the sense of 'it is also'); this was the transfiguration. There is nothing to justify seeing in it the resurrection (v. 17) followed by a christophany (v. 18) because this would necessitate interpreting the transfiguration as an ante-dated christophany. Widespread though it may be, this theory is debatable, as has been shown, despite the great distance that separates their individual conclusions, by G. H. Boobyer, *St Mark and the Transfig. Story*, pp. 11–16; H. Riesenfeld, *Jésus transfiguré*, p. 293 and H. Baltensweiler, *Die Verklärung Jesu*, pp. 91–5.

[4] Cf. p. 82 below.

[5] On this point one must agree with R. Bultmann, *Gesch. d. syn. Trad.*, pp. 276–7, rather than with E. Lohmeyer, *Das Ev. des Markus*, pp. 161–2, who has to admit that Mark would be a work unique of its kind if it had to be considered, as he believes, as a complete traditional text. But one cannot follow R. Bultmann when he asserts that it is an account

mutilation was an audacious one, but it fits in with the general
attitude of Mark to Peter[1] and is no more daring than the cuts
made earlier in the tradition relating to John the Baptist.
What makes it probable is the abrupt ending of the pericope
in Mark 8.30 and the visibly editorial character of the arrangement of verses which follows in vv. 31ff.[2] The reprimand to
Peter which one finds here (vv. 32–3) replaces in the Evangelist's eyes the words of praise, which he leaves out for reasons of
expediency. What justified the substitution is that in both cases
the words were spoken by Jesus about Peter.

Lastly, the account of the entry into Jerusalem (Mark
11.1–10), with its appearance of legend (cf. in particular
vv. 2–6), brings to mind a fragment of a *midrash* on Zechariah
9.9,[3] and is followed in vv. 9–10 be a double response borrowed
from the Jewish worship in the synagogue or more probably
from Christian worship.[4] This arrangement for liturgical
purposes, no doubt pre-dating Mark, reflects here the Evangelist's desire to set against the corrupt cult of the temple (Mark
11.15–19) a purer form of worship, practised by the disciples
of Jesus alone and full of eschatological fervour.[5] Once again

---

of a christophany embodying the conferring of supreme authority on
Peter. The influence of pre-existing dogma is so visible here that it is
difficult to take this theory seriously: for the transfiguration perhaps,
but scarcely for this rather pedantic conversation!

[1] Cf. below pp. 81ff.

[2] We have detected: a fragment of a commentary on Isa. 53 in v. 31; a
fragment of a narrative framework surrounding the two voices from
heaven in vv. 32–3 (?); various isolated sayings in vv. 34ff. We cannot
agree with O. Cullmann, *Saint Pierre*, pp. 156–7, when he says that vv.
31–3 form 'the natural sequel to the story' in vv. 27–30. What is striking,
on the contrary, when one reads this text is the abrupt way the mind is
made to jump from v. 29 to v. 31; the extremely anti-petrine character
the whole would have if v. 33 were its traditional conclusion; the
pointlessness of vv. 27–8 if v. 29 is only the introduction to vv. 31–3.

[3] One might also think of Gen. 49.10–12, although the episode related in
Mark 11.1ff. seems to have a less direct link with this last-mentioned
text.

[4] Antiphonal texts of the same kind are to be found in the Revelation of
Saint John (1.5b–6; 1.7; 5.8–14; 7.9–14; etc.), in other passages of the
New Testament (e.g. 1 Cor. 16.22–4), in the *Didache* (chap. 9 and in
particular chap. 10), etc.

[5] On the attitude of the author of Mark to the Temple and its cult, cf. pp.
101–7 below.

we see the author of Mark intervening actively to arrange and shape his traditional material. This does not mean that the solemn entry of Jesus into Jerusalem was not a historical event, but the memory of it has been preserved very indirectly under the combined influence of a prophetic text to which it seemed to correspond and of the needs of the cult.

The result of our rapid review of the 'stories and legends' of Mark 1—13 is at once simple and surprising. These passages do indeed derive from the church tradition, except for 6.17–29, to which the same origin must be attributed as to the miracle stories. But they all have to be linked to various categories of 'sayings'. They are either commentaries on Scripture (1.2–6; 11.1ff.), scholastic discourses (8.27–9), prophetic words of John the Baptist (1.7–8), words from heaven (1.9–13 and 8.32–3; 9.2–8) or, lastly, liturgical texts (11.9–10). If, then, the Passion story, to which we shall be returning later, be excepted, the church tradition contained no stories legendary or otherwise. This is a measure, once again, of the novelty of the work undertaken by the author of Mark.

The Passion story (Mark 14 and 15), as has been said a hundred times since K. L. Schmidt,[1] has a much more solid topographical and chronological framework than the rest of the Gospel. Rather unexpectedly, R. Bultmann draws from this fact the conclusion that C. H. Dodd reached on the subject of the summaries in Mark 1—6:[2] the framework, he suggests, existed separately at a very early date and it is by filling it in gradually, drawing partly on pre-existing tradition, that he arrived at the existing text.[3] But one cannot see very clearly for what purpose such a document would have come into being and been used as a peg on which to hang the various little

---

[1] *Rahmen der Gesch. Jesu*, pp. 303–9.

[2] Cf. pp. 28–31 above.

[3] R. Bultmann, *Gesch. d. syn. Trad.*, pp. 297–308. This 'very brief . . . account' (p. 301) related, he suggests, the arrest, the double condemnation, the way to Golgotha, the crucifixion and the death of Christ. J. Finegan, *Die Ueberlieferung der Leidens-und Auferstehungsgeschichten Jesu* (Giessen 1934) (Beihefte zur Zeitschr. f. d. N.T. Wissenschaft, 15) arrives at much the same conclusions as Bultmann, as does J. Jeremias, *Die Abendmahlsworte Jesu*, 3rd edn (Göttingen 1960), pp. 83–90. V. Taylor, *St Mark*, pp. 653–64, proposes a similar solution.

anecdotes 'received'.[1] Aware of the weaknesses of this theory of Bultmann, M. Dibelius and G. Bertram have sought to find a 'Sitz im leben' for the whole of the Passion story, if not in its canonical form, at least in a fairly full version. The former[2] is struck by the numerous apologetic touches (eye-witness accounts, recourse to scriptural evidence) and sees preaching, in particular apologetic preaching, as the ground in which the seed of the story was sown. But the idea is not a very convincing one, considering the length of the text, which would not make it easy to handle in preaching, whatever we imagine the eloquence of the earliest Christians to have been. As for G. Bertram,[3] he sees the liturgical worship of Jesus by the primitive community as the agency that shaped a document in which the supernatural figure of the Hero constantly occupies the place of honour and greatly exceeds the stature simply of a martyr. This theory, once stripped of its numerous conclusions as to detail which spoil it by going too far, seems acceptable. But it is still far too vague, since G. Bertram does not endeavour anywhere to define in concrete terms the kind of liturgical framework he has in mind.

Here we may welcome two recent hypotheses which seek to remedy this deficiency and to show that the Passion story had a specific place in the Christian cult of the first generation. The first of them is somewhat compromised by the context in which it is placed by its author, P. Carrington, but it appears quite sensible, at least in its main lines.[4] The evangelical account of

---

[1] The dependence on the kerygma suggested by R. Bultmann, op. cit., pp. 297–8, does not appear well established since the 'very brief . . . account' would have said nothing, this author believes, about the resurrection, which is the 'point' of the whole 'kerygma'.

[2] M. Dibelius, *Formgesch. des Evang.*, 2nd edn. (1933) and 3rd edn (1959), pp. 178ff. The first edition of this work (1919) contained only a few brief remarks in which the author stressed the unity of the Passion story, except for the anointing at Bethany (pp. 57–8). Cf. also his article entitled 'Das historische Problem der Leidensgeschichte', in *ZNTW*, vol. xxx (1931), pp. 193ff., and reprinted in the collection *Botschaft und Geschichte* (Tübingen 1953), pp. 248–57.

[3] G. Bertram, *Die Leidensgesch. Jesu u. d. Christuskult* (Göttingen 1922).

[4] P. Carrington, *The Primitive Christian Calendar, a Study in the Making of the Marcan Gospel*, vol. i: *Introduction and Text* (Cambridge 1952), proposes a rather daring theory for the structure of Mark which, according to him, consists of a collection of texts placed in the order of

the Passion, he believes, in particular in Mark, was put together as the *'megillah'*, or scroll for reading aloud in public, that was used by the primitive Church for the Christian Easter. The book of Esther, probably written for the Jewish feast of 'Purim' at which it is read every year,[1] provides an interesting parallel. It could even be supposed that it was in order to propagate the Christian Easter in the churches, some of which were hesitant,[2] that this text was translated into Greek and perhaps added to a little.[3]

The second hypothesis, more complex and probably too specific, is accompanied by a large number of observations showing great insight into the form of the Passion stories, which is sufficient to make it promising.[4] Its author, G. Schille, thinks that it was the annual commemoration in Jerusalem of Good Friday and Easter that made it necessary to crystallize the memories of the passion. This crystallization, the author believes, took place around three poles: an 'anamnesis' of the last night of Jesus, probably combined with an annual 'agape' (Mark 14.18–72); a liturgy connected with the Jewish three hours of prayer, for the annual commemoration of the crucifixion (Mark 15.2–41); an Easter morning liturgy, possibly

the liturgical year as the Galilean church took it over from Judaism. But he admits that the account of the passion does not fit into his plan and must have been a separate document whose limits are rather vaguely indicated: 13.1—16.8, of which the 'original core', this author thinks, was 14.3—15.41 or 15.47 (cf. in particular pp. 75–89 and 204–27).

[1] Cf. for example A. Lods, *Histoire de la littérature hébraïque et juive depuis les origines jusqu'à la ruine de l'Etat juif* (A.D. 135) (Paris 1950) (Bibliothèque historique), pp. 793–807.

[2] In particular in the churches subject to the influence of Paul: cf. Rom. 14.5–6; Gal. 4.10–11; Col. 2.16–17, and P. Carrington, op. cit., pp. 38–44.

[3] Certain of the passages relating to Peter could have been added at this time to reinforce the authority of this text among the most hesitant communities: for example, 14.12–16, 14.27–31, 14.37–9, 14.54, 14.66–72 (all of which go back no doubt to Peter's eye-witness account). More than guaranteeing the authenticity of the account, then, Peter would be giving authority for the ecclesiastical practice which it implicitly defends.

[4] G. Schille, 'Das Leiden des Herrn: die evangelische Passionstradition und ihr Sitz im Leben', in *Zeitschr. für Theologie u. Kirche*, 52nd year (1955), pp. 161–205.

including a visit to the tomb of Jesus (Mark 15.42—16.8). These three components, it is suggested, were 'dovetailed together into a continuous narrative even before the addition of the specifically Marcan features, with the help of a few editorial passages such as 14.1–2, 14.10–11, 14.17, 15.1.

This theory contains too much conjecture to be accepted unreservedly, but it has the advantage of carrying through to a conclusion an enquiry which form-criticism had so far undertaken only superficially. It accounts for the numerous chronological and topographical indications, as well as for the dramatic features, by the needs of the liturgy and sets the origin of the Passion story in the living worship of the church of Jerusalem, whose primacy thus finds an additional explanation.[1] Our personal conclusion, therefore, lies half-way between the theories of Carrington and Schille: the Passion story which Mark used was the 'canonical' text that was read out at Jerusalem in the course of the liturgy which, on the occasion of the Jewish Passover, and perhaps also of other annual pilgrimages, commemorated the suffering, death, and resurrection of Jesus Christ; but it entered the Gospel in a slightly amplified Greek version, designed to establish the celebration of this feast in the non-Palestinian Churches.[2]

The only feature of Mark 1—13 which bears any relationship to this document is the story of the entry into Jerusalem in chapter 11.1–10.[3] The implicit influence of the Old Testament, the combination of dramatic and liturgical features (especially in vv. 7–10), the curious parallelism of 11.1–6 and 14.12–16, are so many points of comparison between this passage and the Passion story. Of the two, this latter is in our view the older,

---

[1] It is not only as the place of residence of the 'pillars' (Gal. 1.18—2.10) or of the 'Twelve' (Acts 1—5), as the centre of authority in the Church (Gal. 2.12–13; Acts 15), as the religious capital of Judaism and the great place of pilgrimage for the Jews (Acts 21.23–7; 22.17), that Jerusalem held a certain fascination for Paul. It is also, one may think, because on the occasion of some great Jewish pilgrimages cults dedicated to the commemoration of the passion were celebrated there, which would be a decisive factor in the eyes of the Apostle of the Gentiles (cf. for instance 1 Cor. 2.1ff.). It would seem less explicable otherwise that Paul should have had such a keen desire to make his visits to Jerusalem coincide with one or other of the Jewish feasts (cf. Acts 18.20–2; 20.16).

[2] Cf. pp. 232–3 below.   [3] Cf. p. 58 above.

since it always—or in any case very early—contained the curious account of the preparations for the Last Supper.[1] The combination of this text with the passage in Zech. 9.9, which had come about already before Mark's gospel was written, produced in our view, the liturgical text used by the author of Mark (in Mark 11.1–10).

R. Bultmann places Mark 16.1–8 in a last category of narrative passages, the 'Easter stories', alongside several other texts of Matthew and Luke.[2] It would seem, however, that this passage forms the natural conclusion to the great liturgical story of Mark 14—15:[3] after the long enumeration of the sufferings

---

[1] The earlier date of Mark 14.12–16, which is often contested by the opponents of the paschal character of the Last Supper because of the references to the Passover in vv. 12, 14b, and 16 (cf. for example R. Bultmann, *Gesch. d. syn. Trad.*, pp. 283–4 and 286–7) is also challenged by some of those who, like ourselves, believe in its paschal character. Thus J. Jeremias, *Die Abendmahlsworte Jesu*, 3rd edn, pp. 86–7, judges this passage to be of late origin because of the strange chronology of v. 12, which places the sacrifice of the paschal lamb on 15 Nisan, whereas this rite always took place the day before (cf. Jeremias, op. cit. pp. 11–12). But this difficulty does not seem insuperable, since Strack–Billerbeck, vol. II, pp. 812–15, have shown that the rabbis sometimes fixed 'the first day of unleavened bread' on 14 Nisan. Besides, it is strange to reject five verses to save four or five words that could have been inserted there by the Evangelist (cf. p. 231 below), whereas these verses form an introduction that the remainder cannot well do without if one regards it with Carrington and Schille, as a liturgical text of some length in which the chronological and topographical indications played an important part (cf. G. Schille, op. cit., pp. 195–8, who, however, rejects Mark 14.12–16 without sound reasons: pp. 201–2). Indeed, without these verses, the Last Supper would have no context either in time or space, whereas all the following episodes are located with precision. Besides, Jesus and his disciples, and also the primitive Church, perhaps celebrated their Passover on a date fixed by a sectarian calendar (cf. A. Jaubert, *La date de la Cène: calendrier biblique et liturgie chrétienne* (Paris 1957) (Etudes bibliques), in particular pp. 79–136), quite different from the official calendar we know from the rabbis. It is therefore rash to draw too many conclusions from the obscurities of Mark's chronology, which perhaps only reflect a complex situation.

[2] R. Bultmann, *Gesch. d. syn. Trad.*, pp. 308–16.

[3] G. Schille, op. cit. pp. 182–3, rightly stresses the close link between 16.1–8 and the last verses of chapter 15. On the other hand, he is not convincing when he says that 15.2–41 was originally separate from

undergone by Christ, the community founded on belief in the resurrection cannot forgo an allusion to Jesus' victory over death, but the allusion to it is enough, since hundreds can testify to that triumphant event[1] and the Church lives in the calm certainty of the glorification of the Master in the sight of God.[2] Thus one might say that the source of Mark 14—15 came to its end in 16.8.

It remains to explain the absence in Mark of any real 'Easter story'. It would not seem to be due to accident or to censorship,[3] in spite of all the arguments that critics have put forward in favour of that hypothesis.[4] The idea that the original document was accidentally mutilated or that a heart attack carried off the author reed in hand are imaginative suppositions in the naive mode. Though less naive, the theory that the strange break in the narrative at 16.8 was due to the scissors of some ecclesiastical censor is no less imaginative. One might

---

15.42ff.: neither the confession of the centurion nor the enumeration of the women present at Golgotha forms a conclusion even to a liturgy; as for the chronological indication in v. 42 ('when even was come'), far from marking a new beginning, it merely follows on from those in 15.25,33,34, which mark the passage of time in the story of the crucifixion.

[1] Cf. 1 Cor. 15.5–8, where the main point is the large number of witnesses: 'above five hundred brethren at once, of whom the greater part remain unto this present. . . . ' No matter if the women say nothing (16.8), the news will spread nevertheless!

[2] The assembly had just been reminded of Jesus' answer to the High Priest (14.62). In its amazing audacity, it was enough.

[3] We are firmer on this point today than in our earlier *Livre des Actes et l'histoire*, p. 47, n. 2, which does not reject this hypothesis outright.

[4] Among the partisans of the mutilation theory are H. B. Swete, *The Gospel According to St Mark* (London 1898, 3rd edn 1909), pp. ciii–cxiii; M. Goguel, *Introd. au N.T.*, vol. 1, pp. 292–7; R. Bultmann, *Gesch. d. syn. Trad.*, p. 309; J. Schniewind, *Das Evangelium nach Markus* 4th edn (Göttingen 1947), pp. 205–6; W. L. Knox, 'The Ending of Mark's Gospel' in *Harvard Theological Review*, vol. xxxv (1942), pp. 13–23; V. Taylor, *St Mark*, pp. 609–10. It is clear that verses 16.9–20 of the 'received' text are a later addition since most of the witnesses to the text earlier than the fifth century make no mention of them, but they are nevertheless old, since Irenaeus quotes one of these verses and attributes it definitely to Mark 'at the end of his Gospel' (*Adv. Haer.*, III 10.6). It is thus as early as the second century that Mark was found incomplete and it was sought to replace the 'missing' passage.

perhaps support it if the other Gospels agreed in their accounts of the appearances of the risen Christ, since it could be supposed that there was an orthodox version of this chapter which the original Mark had departed from. But we know that there is no uniformity in this respect between Matthew, Luke, and John and that in addition the 'official' list of Christ's appearances to be found in I Cor. 15.5ff. does not correspond at all to the accounts of the three Evangelists.[1]

The chief reason for the absence of any paschal narrative in Mark is supplied moreover by the very confusion of the tradition. If thirty or forty years after the composition of the list in I Cor. 15.5ff. Evangelists as careful as the authors of Matthew and Luke not to neglect anything of the tradition were unable to relate more than one of the five or six christophanies enumerated in the official text, if they were reduced to doing so with the help of meagre, posterior, and very divergent accounts,[2] if, in order to fill in such a vague outline they were

---

[1] The explanation of the mutilation of Mark that considers it a consequence of the rivalry between the tradition of the Galilean christophanies (Matthew) and the Jerusalem tradition (Luke) is pure fantasy. This would mean that while leaving Matthew and Luke intact, 'editors' in both camps bore down on Mark in order to bring it into line with their respective ideas about the resurrection; the resulting versions of Mark 16 were so numerous, it is suggested, that the disheartened copyists gave up trying to choose between them and took refuge in omission. The author of this odd hypothesis is B. W. Bacon, *The Gospel of Mark*, pp. 187–203.

[2] The appearance of Christ to the 'Eleven' (to the 'Twelve', according to I Cor. 15.5) is the only one of the list which the Gospels relate: Matt. 28.16–20 and Luke 24.36–53; cf. Acts 1.14 and John 20.19–23. But it is placed and related very differently in Matthew and Luke. Although it is possible to recognize in both the two basic features of all the accounts of christophanies (hesitating recognition of our Lord by the disciples and instructions given by the risen Christ), according to C. H. Dodd, 'The Appearances of the Risen Christ: An Essay in Form-Criticism of the Gospels', in *Studies in the Gospels* . . . , ed. D. E. Nineham, pp. 9–35), they are expressed in quite different terms in the two Gospels. It does not seem possible to trace them back to an early common tradition, except perhaps for the expression: ἕως τῆς συντελείας τοῦ αἰῶνος (Matt. 28.20) and: ἕως ἐσχάτου τῆς γῆς (Acts 1.8), for which the same Aramaic original is just conceivable (עַד־עָלַם?) But this is only a saying of Jesus, which could have been transmitted outside the context in which the Evangelists place it.

forced to resort to editorial devices[1] and to 'legends' which are poetical but whose origin is obscure[2]—the only possible explanation of these strange facts is that *the church tradition contained no accounts of appearances of the risen Christ.*

This conclusion may seem surprising, but there is really nothing astonishing about it. The christophanies—individual or collective religious experiences—were personal encounters with the Almighty, which people were probably no more inclined to recount than it was the custom to describe the person of God in the theophanies of the Old Testament or than it was deemed possible for man to see the 'face' of Yahweh.[3] Moreover, the appearances of the risen Christ served more to impose the authority of those to whom he appeared[4] than to establish the reality of the resurrection of Jesus.[5] There was accordingly no need to relate them; it was enough for them to

[1] An appendix to the story of the empty tomb adding to it an appearance of Christ to the women (Matt. 28.9–10); an allusion to the appearance of Christ to Simon Peter (Luke 24.34).

[2] The story of the disciples on the road to Emmaus (Luke 24.13–35), with which one can compare, from the literary point of view, the appearance on the shores of Lake Tiberias (John 21.1ff.). On these two stories, seen from the angle of their form, cf. the pertinent remarks of C. H. Dodd, op. cit., pp. 13–15.

[3] Exod. 33.18–23 and 1 Kings 19.13. Cf. E. Jacob, *Théologie de l'Ancien Testament* (Neuchâtel-Paris 1955) (Manuels et précis de Théologie), pp. 62–3. However Israelite thought may have evolved on this point, it had reached the certainty, well before the Christian era, that God could neither be seen nor described.

[4] Cf. 1 Cor. 9.1 and the apologetic purpose in Acts of the three accounts of the appearance of Christ to Paul (Acts 9.1ff., 22.5ff., 26.12ff.): Luke is seeking to establish the authority of Paul and not to prove the resurrection.

[5] In 1 Cor. 15 the resurrection of Jesus is not really at issue; Paul's adversaries were apparently merely refuting the resurrection of Christians. The quotation from a traditional document that Paul places at the beginning of his discussion of the subject is designed in his mind to stress the close link between the forgiveness of sins and the resurrection of Jesus (cf. vv. 3 and 17) and consequently the serious religious risk that lies in undermining the certainty of the latter by rejecting the whole notion of resurrection. Paul regards the christophanies not as proof of the resurrection of Jesus but as a demonstration of the saving character of the death-resurrection nexus, as the revelation of the one gospel to those who are to carry it throughout the world (vv. 9–11).

be enumerated in the official list of the christophanies.[1] Consequently, Mark was merely conforming to custom and adhering to the substance of the tradition when he abstained from relating any of the appearances of the risen Christ. Matthew and Luke, Gospels of a more highly evolved type, were subjected to pressure on the part of the churches, where witnesses were becoming rare and where the growing historicalization of Jesus' ministry was producing the accounts of his childhood. They either took the first steps or recorded the first steps taken towards the formation of the accounts of the 'major' christophanies which are to be found in later Christian literature.[2]

The absence in Mark of any appearance of the risen Christ is explained, accordingly, chiefly by the great respect the Evangelist had for the content and spirit of the tradition. But that is not enough to explain the awkward abruptness of Mark 16.8 as the conclusion of the Gospel. It has rightly been stressed that none of the other pericopes in Mark ends so abruptly on a γάρ[3] and that the second-last word, ἐφοβοῦντο, is too obviously the justification of the silence preserved by the women in spite of the angel's commands for it to be passed off as a subtle conclusion designed to end the Gospel on a 'numinous' note.[4] The author of Mark is usually more skilful than that, even if his literary pretensions are modest.[5] It is accordingly probable that this ending is not his. In the eyes of the present writer it must be the work of an editor more slavishly faithful than he to the

---

[1] Hence Paul's insistence on adding his own name to those of the others to whom Christ appeared (1 Cor. 9.1–6; 15.8–11), the list of whom was probably complete before he came on the scene. Cf. J. Héring, *La première épitre de saint Paul aux Corinthiens* (Paris–Neuchâtel 1949) (Commentaire du N.T., VII), pp. 133–7.

[2] Thus, the appearance to Peter, of which Peter's gospel must have contained an account similar, perhaps, to that of John 21: cf. L. Vaganay, *L'évangile de Pierre* (Paris 1932) (Etudes bibliques) and C. Maurer, 'Petrusevangelium', in E. Hennecke, *Neutestamentliche Apokryphen in deutscher Uebersetzung*, 3rd edn ed. W. Schneemelcher, vol. 1 (Tübingen 1959), pp. 118–24, or the appearance to James, recorded in the Gospel of the Hebrews (P. Vielhauer, in E. Hennecke, op. cit. pp. 104–8).

[3] W. L. Knox, loc. cit.

[4] R. Bultmann, *Gesch. d. syn. Trad.*, p. 309, n.

[5] Cf. pp. 70ff. below.

letter of the church tradition, who perhaps added an appendix to the Gospel without worrying too much about fitting it into the original version of Mark. We shall return to this point later in an endeavour to set limits to this addition and to determine the circumstances that led to its insertion at the end of the original text.[1]

3
THE AUTHOR OF MARK – A WRITER

One of the main results of the above enquiry into the sources of Mark is the repeated observations of the Evangelist's attempts to collect, sort out, and arrange his material. The author of Mark appears to have had a certain individuality and to have taken some freedom with church tradition. It is accordingly difficult to see him simply as an echo of the Church in whose midst he was writing.[2] But ought we on these grounds to recognize him as a writer with a literary personality? There are several objections to taking that view.

The first is the complete absence of refinement that characterizes Mark's language. This is not the place to go once more over the ground trodden by so many scholars on the subject of the vocabulary and syntax of this Gospel.[3] Where the vocabulary is

---

[1] Cf. pp. 215ff. below.

[2] R. Bultmann himself (op. cit. pp. 370ff.) recognizes the great novelty of what the Evangelist set out to do, namely, in this author's view, to combine the hellenistic kerygma relating to Christ (in particular, that is, the 'myth of Christ' that we know from Phil. 2.6ff. or Rom. 3.24) with the tradition about the life of Jesus. But he does not enquire into the reason for this innovation that proved so decisive for Christian thinking and, in short, he evades the problem of the origin of the Gospel as a literary genre. This weakens his historical analysis, which is of far less value than his literary study of the synoptic Gospels.

[3] Cf. in particular J. C. Hawkins, *Horae synopticae, Contributions to the Study of the Synoptic Problem* (Oxford 1st edn 1899, 2nd edn 1909), pp. 9–12 and 93–122; H. B. Swete, *The Gospel Acc. to Saint Mark*, pp. xlivff.; C. H. Turner, 'Marcan Usage', several articles in the *JTS*, vols. xxv (1924) to xxix (1928); J. C. Doudna, *The Greek of the Gospel of Mark* (Philadelphia 1961); the tables of R. Morgenthaler, *Statistik des neutestamentlichen Wortschatzes* (Zurich and Frankfurt 1958), in particular pp. 66–157. Among the commentaries of Mark more recent than that of Swete, the most interesting on this question are those of M. J. Lagrange, 7th edn, pp. lxvii–lxxv and V. Taylor, pp. 44–52. Useful indications are also to be found in all the Introductions to the

concerned, it is enough to note that it is neither very poor nor very rich,[1] that there are few words in it not to be found in the rest of the New Testament,[2] whereas words unknown in pre-Christian Greek are proportionately more frequent in Mark than in the other books of the New Testament,[3] and that it contains more diminutives, Aramaic or Hebrew words, and transcriptions of Latin words than the other New Testament books.[4]

N.T. (for example in M. Goguel, vol. I, pp. 348–52 and over the name of X. Léon-Dufour in Robert and Feuillet, *Introduction à la Bible*, vol. II, pp. 197–201), as well as in various grammars of New Testament Greek (e.g. in J. Moulton, *A Grammar of New Testament Greek*, vol. I, 3rd edn (Edinburgh 1908), vol. II 1929, and in A. Debrunner, *Friedrich Blass' Grammatik des neutestamentlichen Griechisch*, 10th edn (Göttingen 1959).

[1] 1345 different words in a text numbering 11,242 words, which means a far richer vocabulary than John, slightly richer than that of Matthew (1691 different words in a text of 18,305 words) but a little smaller than that of Luke (2055 in a text of 19,428) and distinctly poorer than that of Hebrews (1038 in a text of 4,951). These figures are taken from R. Morgenthaler, op. cit., p. 164 and need to be interpreted bearing in mind that the longer a text the fewer new words appear after the early pages.

[2] 79 words out of 1345, whereas Luke has 250 out of 2055. Cf. H. B. Swete, *Gospel Acc. to St Mark*, 3rd edn, pp. xlivff.

[3] 46 words, as compared with the 320 found in the New Testament. Paul alone (132 new words in a vocabulary of 2648 words, that is to say twice as many as Mark) has a higher proportion of 'Christian' words, whereas I Peter, with 18 new words in a vocabulary of 545 words has roughly the same as Mark. Unlike these authors and the Epistle to the Hebrews, the author of Mark uses few words peculiar to the Septuagint (31 in Mark as compared to 93 in Paul, 26 in I Peter and 29 in Hebrews); in this respect he does not exceed either Luke (50 'septuagintal' words out of 2055) or Acts (44 out of 2038) or James (12 out of 560) and exceeds only by very little Matthew (33 out of 1691) and Revelation (17 out of 916). If, therefore, the author of Mark gives room in his vocabulary to the 'Canaan dialect' of the Church of his day, it is a dialect that has nothing to do with Scripture—a jargon used by preachers rather than theologians. These figures are taken from R. Morgenthaler, op. cit. pp. 164 and 175–6.

[4] Cf., where the diminutives are concerned, C. H. Turner, op. cit. vol. XXIX, pp. 349–52 and, as regards foreign words, R. Morgenthaler, op. cit. pp. 162–3, whose table clearly shows, on the contrary, Mark's small liking for translations of Latin words. He writes κεντυρίων where Matthew and Luke write ἑκατοντάρχης.

The sensible conclusion to be drawn from all these facts is that Mark's vocabulary derives, like that of all the canonical Gospels, from the hellenistic 'koine', slightly modified by Christian usage, at least in religious matters. Unlike Paul, John, and Luke, whose strong personality or, in the case of the last-mentioned, love of literary effect, caused them to leave their own mark on the Christian 'koine', the author of Mark was content to use the vocabulary current in his milieu.

His syntax also presents certain peculiarities, all to be explained by the influence of the spoken language, or of Aramaic:[1] partial substitution for the classic imperfect of a periphrastic imperfect formed with the aid of the auxiliary verb εἰμί followed by a present participle; numerous participles in apposition to the subject (5.25–7); grossly improper use of the indicative after a subordinating conjunction followed by the particle ἄν; frequent use of cumulative double negation, sign of a rather awkward attempt at emphasis; misuse of the historic present, to be explained grammatically at once by the influence of Aramaic and by that of the spoken language; large numbers of verbs in the third person plural, equivalent to the impersonal use of 'one'—a turn of phrase which Matthew and Luke have corrected in each case and where an Aramaic influence is probable; use of ἤρξαντο as an auxiliary verb followed by an infinitive, corrected almost everywhere in Matthew and Luke; for connection between sentences parataxis with καὶ is very frequent, whilst δέ is in proportion twice as infrequent as in Matthew and Luke; asyndeton is not uncommon, when it is normally deplored by the Greeks; as for anacoluthon, it is the mark of a popular style and disappears almost entirely in Matthew and Luke.

If the language of Mark is that of the Greek spoken in the milieu where the Gospel was written, is the originality of the Evangelist to be sought in his style?[2] It would not seem so either. Indeed the main feature of Mark's style is its rusticity. The author of Mark did not set his own imprint to any great extent on the material he received from the 'doctors' of his

---

[1] This is excellently discussed in V. Taylor, *St Mark*, pp. 45–52, to which we refer the reader once and for all.

[2] M. Zerwick, *Untersuchungen zum Marcus-Stil, ein Beitrag zur stilistischen Durcharbeitung des Neuen Testaments* (Rome 1937).

church and the Galilean story-tellers. From being rhythmic and structured when he reproduces something gleaned from church tradition (for example, 4.3–9; 9.35–50), it becomes much more colloquial and picturesque in the miracle stories or scenes of similar origin (for instance in chapter 5; 6.17–29; 9.14–29). But that is no reason to exclaim at the versatility of his literary genius! The author of Mark can only introduce variety when it is present in advance: he reproduces the story of the multiplication of the loaves with very little change, except that he tries to emphasize its importance and succeeds only in losing its picturesqueness (compare 6.34–44 and 8.1–10); he pours two accounts of healing into exactly the same mould (7.32–7 and 8.22–6); he arranges the accounts of the controversies as tradition had arranged them before him (compare chapters 2 and 12). He is sometimes wordy (6.17–29) and has a liking for repetitions.[1] In spite of this wealth of verbiage, he is far from being always clear;[2] moreover his obscurity is just as unfortunate in the passages where he is endeavouring to be brief.[3]

Lastly, the framework he builds around the various texts he uses is an extremely discrete one, which is contrary to the tradition of his time; it consists chiefly of very short 'summaries' which generalize about the stories and teachings taken over

[1] M. J. Lagrange, *Ev. Marc*, pp. lxxii–lxxv, who sets out to prove that Mark was not guilty of repetition, is nevertheless obliged to admit that some of the Evangelist's expressions 'are rather tautologous' (2.25b; 3.26b; 4.2; 4.5a; 5.15b; 7.15a; 7.21a; 7.33a; 9.2b; 14.1; 14.43a; 15.26a). The point could not be better made.

[2] There is one good illustration of the kind of obscurity Mark did not find it easy to avoid: in the dialogue between Jesus and the Gadarene inhabited by an unclean spirit there are seven exchanges of words in which the speaker is never clearly indicated (except in the first and, implicitly, in the sixth) nor is the alternation of speakers respected (the second and third are spoken by the same person and the fourth, fifth, and sixth also). One has to read this passage twice in order to follow the very awkwardly presented dialogue (5.7–13).

[3] Thus in 6.10 the expression is so concise as to appear at first sight: 'In what place soever ye enter into an house, there abide till ye depart from that place.' It is only on examining the text more closely and comparing it with its parallels in Matt. 10.11 and Luke 9.4 that one grasps the meaning, which is that the missionaries are exhorted not to go from house to house for hospitality when they are staying in a town.

from church tradition and popular memory.[1] But there is no introduction in which the author explains his purpose and method, as Luke does, or else, like John, the theological back-cloth against which he intends to set his Gospel.[2] This extreme restraint is not without its strength, since it lets the stories and words make their own impact on the reader. But it would seem to be due to the poverty of the Evangelist's literary art rather than (as with Paul and John) to the superiority of a mind freed from the usual stylistic conventions of the day.

The point is thus settled: the author of Mark was a clumsy writer unworthy of mention in any history of literature. But that is not the real issue. What is important to understand is the real reason for the surprising prestige Mark's Gospel enjoyed among the second generation of Christians. Why did Matthew and Luke accept Mark as their guide and chief source when the author had no overriding authority,[3] when they had at their disposal a vast fund of church tradition on which Mark had drawn to a limited extent and made use of with great freedom, and when they obviously realized all the faults of Mark's text, to judge by the numerous corrections they made when they

[1] As we said earlier, these 'summaries' have to be regarded as being composed by Mark.

[2] True, as J. M. Robinson, *Das Geschichtsverständnis des Markus-Evangeliums* (Zurich 1956) (Abhandl. z. Theol. des A. u. N. Testaments, 30), pp. 11–33, has shown, Mark 1.1–13 forms a theological prologue to the Gospel which announces the theme of the whole work. But besides consisting of a rearrangement of traditional material where the author's style is barely perceptible, this passage is clearly not a 'foreword' to the Gospel proper, like John 1.1–18, but is already a part of it (Mark 1.1). The Evangelist says nothing in it either of his own purpose or of God's purpose, but begins straight away to relate God's works, without any reference back.

[3] Peter's authority, to which Papias refers, is a little remote. Some decades earlier it must have been more remote still, since the tendency in Christian thought has certainly not been to dim it. (The growing radiance of Peter's memory was further enhanced vis-à-vis that of Matthew and John, by the strengthening of his links with Mark. Conversely, Mark, in the clearer affirmation of his dependence on Peter, found the apostolic backing needed to withstand competition from the other Gospels.) It is accordingly most improbable that the authors of Matthew and Luke should have been impressed, in their attitude to Mark, by the authority of Peter.

took it over? They must have found in Mark features attractive enough to draw them to the work or make them overlook its literary weaknesses. The stories related by Mark which did not stem from church tradition certainly enhanced the prestige of this first Gospel, but more still its order, which Matthew and Luke both preserved, each in his own way.[1] The author of Mark must have appeared to them above all as an organizer of material who had produced a coherent literary work from the chaos of tradition.

The testimony of the Presbyter concerning Mark, as Papias recorded it, shows that the question of the *order* of the Gospel accounts was highly important in the first half of the second century.[2] The appearance of the Gospel according to John had doubtless come as a challenge to the presentation of the life of Jesus in the synoptic Gospels and the Presbyter was echoing the slight condescension with which the little evangelists of the past were regarded in the Asian circles attached to the Johannine tradition. But it is not very likely that the circles in which the Gospels of Matthew and Luke were written would have been as severe towards the order of Mark. On the contrary, they must have had great respect for it, since they did not rid themselves of it as John did. One might even go a step further and find it symptomatic that the Presbyter should have attacked Mark alone, whereas in fact John is in conflict

[1] Matthew, by accentuating the distinction between narrative and discourse and yielding to a certain inclination towards methodical classification, which made him break up the narrative by inserting long passages of Jesus' sayings (e.g. the Sermon in chapters 5—7) and move certain of Mark's stories to bring them nearer to others with which he thought they had an affinity (cf. chapters 8—9 combining the miracles and controversies from chapters 1, 2, 4, 5, and 10 of Mark); Luke, by preserving the intimate mixture of narrative and discourse that he had found in Mark and inserting the additional material that tradition had to offer in two long passages which he placed at the points where Mark's geography allowed the most latitude (Luke 6.20—8.3 and 9.51—18.14). In each case the fundamental intention was to respect the order of Mark while adding many other ingredients derived from elsewhere and totally lacking in coherence.

[2] Eusebius, *H.E.*, III. 39. 15 (cf. text, p. 13, n. 2 above). We share the view of many critics (thus L. Vaganay, *Prob. synopt.*, pp. 51–3) that it is important to distinguish between the testimony of the Presbyter, which forms the first sentence of this text, and the commentary of Papias, which comprises all the rest.

with the whole synoptic tradition.[1] In this person's eyes, Mark was no doubt responsible for that tradition's 'lack of order', which is to say, in fact, its clinging to a wrong chronological and geographical plan.

But is the plan of Mark, on which Matthew and Luke are based, really a literary creation that would earn for its author the recognition as a writer that his language and style certainly do not deserve? We have explained earlier[2] the objections to ascribing a pre-Marcan origin to this plan, whose historical soundness is confined to a few general facts common to John and to the synoptic Gospels: Jesus carried out his ministry in Galilee, at Jerusalem and nearby places; his baptism by John the Baptist preceded the beginning of his public career which culminated in his crucifixion at Jerusalem.[3] But is this order in Mark, which must be ascribed to the author alone and which

---

[1] It is not our intention here to take sides in the discussion between critics, of long duration now, on the question of the literary relationship of John to the synoptic Gospels and John's attitude to them (cf. on this point Ph. Menoud, *L'évangile de Jean d'après les recherches récentes*, 2nd edn, pp. 27–9 and 'Les études johanniques de Bultmann à Barrett', in *L'Evangile de Jean, études et problèmes*, pp. 18–20). In any case it is unlikely that the author of John could have been unaware of the synoptic tradition. Since he followed it at a considerable distance, it may be assumed that he accepted it with reservations.

[2] Cf. pp. 17ff. and 28ff. above.

[3] It seems, for example, that in searching chapters 6—8 of Mark for indications of a 'Galilean crisis' which saw Jesus abandon his public preaching and all activity whatsoever in Galilee, M. Goguel (cf. for example, *Jésus*, 2nd edn (Paris 1950), pp. 281–317) greatly overestimates the historical value of Mark's plan, which, incidentally, he believes, most improbably, to pre-date Mark. The comparisons he makes with John 6 are much more indicative of the theological significance the Church attributed to the multiplication of the loaves than of the importance of the events surrounding it for the life of Jesus. The same objections may be made to H. Clavier, 'La multiplication des pains dans le Ministère de Jésus', in *Studia evangelica, Papers presented to the International Congress on 'the Four Gospels in 1957' held at Christ Church, Oxford, 1957* (Berlin 1959) (Texte u. Untersuchungenzur Geschichte der altchristlichen Literatur, vol. 73), pp. 441–57, where the first part of his study is concerned. But in the second part he justly stresses the implicit theological significance that Mark, and later Matthew, saw in this episode, as does also L. Cerfaux, 'La section des pains (Mark 6.31—8.26; Matt. 14.13—16.12', in the *Synoptische Studien* presented to A. Wilkenhauser (Munich 1954), vol. I, pp. 471–85.

was transmitted to Matthew and Luke, a coherent plan? Is the Gospel anything more than a collection of texts isolated or grouped with others for reasons too unimportant to enquire into? Opinions are greatly divided on this point.

Certain critics are very sceptical about the possibility of tracing a plan in Mark. A. Loisy[1] speaks of the 'confusion' that reigns in chapters 1—10, of the 'accumulation of reminiscences, if, indeed, they are all reminiscences, whose arrangement is not governed by any strict principle of history or logic but by mere analogy, or by editorial considerations which one would need to ascertain'. In regard to chapters 11—16, he allows that the material has been arranged to fit into a chronological framework which, though historically arbitrary, is a strict one. As for R. Bultmann, he asserts that 'Mark has not yet sufficient mastery over his material to be able to fit it into a plan' and he does not discern any break in the Gospel apart from Peter's confession in 8.27ff.[2]

Without being as negative, other critics have shown themselves very cautious. M. J. Lagrange, for example,[3] sees only four sections in Mark: the introduction (1.1–13), the gospel of the Kingdom (1.14—8.26), the preparation of the future gospel (8.27—13.37), the 'great act' (chapters 14—16). A. E. J. Rawlinson[4] is even more cautious and vague: as far as one can see, he recognizes a first part that extends from 1.1—8.26, a second from 8.27—12.44, and a third from 13.1—16.8.[5]

---

[1] *L'évangile selon Marc* (Paris 1912), p. 9.

[2] R. Bultmann, *Gesch. d. syn. Trad.*, p. 375; 'Mark ist eben noch nicht in dem Masse Herr über den Stoff geworden, dass er eine Gliederung wagen konnte.' Less derogatory, S. E. Johnson, *Gospel According to St Mark* (New York 1960), sees no obvious break except at 8.27 and compares Mark to 'an oriental rug in which many patterns cross one another'.

[3] *Ev. Marc*, pp. lxii–lxvi. It has to be admitted that Lagrange detects within the three latter sections 'a progression in the relations of Jesus with his friends and his enemies, in changing geographical settings'. But, he explains, 'that does not make it possible to speak of subdivisions corresponding to specific themes' (p. lxv).

[4] *St Mark*, pp. ix and 110.

[5] This comparison between Mark 13 and the Passion story, which assumes a break at 12.44, seems surprising. It is nevertheless defended, with much more explicit arguments, by R. H. Lightfoot, *The Gospel Message of St Mark* (Oxford 1950), pp. 48–59, to whose ideas we shall return later (p. 228 below).

This more or less radical scepticism is not entirely arbitrary when one remembers the extreme discretion with which the Evangelist marks any liaisons, transitions, or breaks that he may wish to make in his text.[1] It nevertheless appears excessive to the majority of specialists, who usually endeavour to describe the plan of Mark in more detail.[2]

These attempts are not always successful. That of M. Goguel lacks balance, being slanted too much towards the biographical use of Mark.[3] After the introduction, this great French critic distinguishes four parts: the Galilean ministry and preaching to the crowds (1.14—8.26); teaching to the disciples alone (8.27—10.52); ministry in Jerusalem (11.1—13.37); the Passion story (chapters 14—16). To lessen the impression of onesidedness given by the considerable volume of the first part (almost half the Gospel), M. Goguel subdivides it into eight rather arbitrarily defined and very unequal sections. The whole rests on the hypothesis of a correspondence between the plan of Mark and the actual course of the ministry of Jesus; there is thus very little to be gleaned from it. The same can be

---

[1] His 'summaries' are less developed than in Luke-Acts, where they quite clearly mark stages in the narrative (H. J. Cadbury, *The Style and Literary Method of Luke*, pp. 108–11; id., in *Beginnings of Christianity*, I, vol. 5, pp. 392–402; M. Dibelius, 'Stilkritisches zur Apostelgeschichte', in *Eucharisterion für H. Gunkel* (Göttingen 1923), vol. II, pp. 34–6 and in M. Dibelius, *Aufsätze zur Apostelgeschichte herausgegeben von Heinrich Greeven* (Göttingen 1951) (Forschungen z. Religion u. Literatur des A.u.N. Testaments, new series, 42, pp. 15–17). Mark's pericopes almost always begin with a καὶ which marks the break, whereas Matthew and Luke begin their sections much more often with the more emphatic δέ. If we confine ourselves to the pericopes indicated in the edition by F. J. A. Hort and B. F. Westcott, 80 out of 88 begin with καὶ in Mark as compared with 38 out of 159 in Matthew and 53 out of 145 in Luke; on the other hand 6 only have δέ as the second word in Mark, as compared with 54 in Matthew and 83 in Luke (J. C. Hawkins, *Horae synopticae*, 2nd edn, p. 151).

[2] Even when they show no definite preference for a particular type of plan, like W. Grundmann, *Das Evangelium nach Markus* (Berlin 1959), pp. 12–15, who regards the order of Mark as depending at once on geographical and on catechetical considerations.

[3] M. Goguel, *L'évangile de Marc dans ses rapports avec ceux de Matthieu et de Luc* (Paris 1909) (Bibliothèque de l'école pratique des hautes-études, section des sciences religieuses, vol. 22), pp. 23ff.; id., *Introd. au N.T.*, vol. I, pp. 282ff.

said of other attempts based on this false premise. That of
B. H. Branscomb is very close to that of M. Goguel, with the
difference that he does not try to subdivide the first part
(except 2.1—3.6) and hints without conviction at a combination of the two following parts.¹ Others are founded on
Mark's geography, which makes them even less satisfactory,
since they overlook the sharp break that separates the Passion
story from all that goes before and do not account for the confused geography of chapters 3—10.² Among the believers in
this plan may be mentioned J. Wellhausen,³ who distinguishes
three parts in Mark after the introduction 1.1–13: chapters
1—5 (region of Capernaum); 6—10 (withdrawal from Galilee
and approach to Jerusalem); 11—16 (Jerusalem). E. Kloster-
mann⁴ accepts Wellhausen's division except that he distinguishes
a separate conclusion (15.40—16.8) forming a counterpart

---

¹ H. B. Branscomb, *Gospel of Mark*, pp. ix–xii and xxvi–xxix.
² It is doubtful whether Mark saw the departure of Jesus from Galilee as
a decisive event marking a turning-point in his narrative. He is interested essentially in the numerous departures of Jesus for various places in
Galilee (1.35ff.; 1.45; 6.1; 6.7); on the frontiers of that province (3.7;
3.13; 4.1; 4.35; 5.17–18; 6.31–2; 6.46; 8.10; 8.13; 9.30) and in—or
to—the neighbouring areas (5.1; 6.45; 7.24; 7.31; 8.22; 8.27; 9.2;
10.1). The topographical confusion resulting from these many departures in chapters 3—10 matters little to him since it serves his purpose of
showing Jesus always on the move (cf. p. 149ff. below). It is Luke, with
his acute sense of the progression of the story of salvation who is the
first to be embarrassed by the deep thrusts into pagan territory ascribed
to Jesus quite innocently in Mark 5—9 and accordingly places on them
an interpretation scarcely guessed at by the author of Mark, namely
that they anticipated the mission to the Gentiles. Such an anticipation
seeming unthinkable to him, he omits Mark 6.45—8.26 and locates
Peter's confession by implication at Bethsaida (Luke 9.10 and 9.18), a
place situated at the entrance to Galilee, thus making the ministry of
Jesus before his journey up to Jerusalem appear exclusively Galilean
(cf. for example B. W. Bacon, 'Le témoignage de Luc sur lui-même'
in *RHPR*, vol. III (1928), p. 224, and E. Trocmé, *Act. et l'hist.*, pp. 45–6,
which we would correct here simply by a more qualified judgement of
the intentions of the author of Mark: what Luke thought he saw underlying Mark 6.45—8.26 was scarcely there at all. One can, therefore, trace
a geographical plan in Luke-Acts, but not in Mark.
³ *Einleitung in die drei ersten Evangelien* (Berlin 1905), pp. 45ff.
⁴ *Das Markusevangelium*, 3rd edn (Tübingen 1936) (Handbuch z. N.T.,
3), p. 1.

to the introduction. C. G. Montefiore[1] shows originality in suggesting the following plan: prelude (1.1–13); ministry in Galilee and the territory of Philip (1.14—7.23); round journey in the north (7.24—9.50); approach to Jerusalem (10.1–52); ministry in Jerusalem (chapters 11—13); passion and resurrection (14.1—16.20). While this has the merit of not 'submerging' the story of the passion, the breaks suggested between 7.23 and 7.24 and between 9.50 and 10.1 are very arbitrary and do not even succeed in marking out sections of approximately equal length.

Other attempts have been made recently in an entirely different direction. It has been sought to investigate the text of Mark carefully for any indications that might serve to reconstruct a plan in the author's mind, however surprising that plan might appear to 'modern' minds. While this principle is a good one, it is difficult to put into practice and likely to produce fragile theories. Such is the case with A. Farrer's paradoxical attempt.[2] He takes as his starting-point the distribution of the accounts of healings (in which he includes the resurrection of Jesus) in Mark and on that foundation he builds up a complex structure with numerous underlying correspondences between pericopes and groups of pericopes according to a 'rhythm' that is sometimes 'alternating', sometimes 'cyclical'. The somewhat distraught reader finally learns (p. 154) that Mark can be divided into a 'little Gospel' (chapters 1—6) comprising two 'double cycles' (1.1—3.12 and 3.13—6.56); a 'continuation of the little Gospel' which brings the train of thought on to the time separating the resurrection of Jesus from the end of the world (7.1—9.1); lastly a 'fulfilment of the little Gospel' (9.2—16.8), also subdivided into two 'double cycles' (9.2—13.2 and 13.3—16.8), which relate the fulfilment of the prophecies contained in chapters 1—6.

This bewildering theory contains certain ingenious observations but one turns from it with relief to that of P. Carrington[3] which, while one cannot accept it, seems at least more sensible.

---

[1] *The Synoptic Gospels, edited with an Introduction and Commentary*, 2nd edn (London 1927), pp. xvi–xviii.

[2] *A Study in St Mark*, pp. 1–181. Farrer incidentally retracted a number of his hypotheses in his book *St Matthew and St Mark* (London 1954).

[3] *The Primitive Christian Calendar*, vol. i, pp. 77 and *passim*.

This critic bases himself on the Jewish and Christian liturgical calendars of antiquity and on the chapter divisions of the principal early manuscripts of Mark (the Codex Vaticanus on the one hand and the weight of testimony regarding the Greek text and the Latin versions on the other), in order to put forward the hypothesis that Mark is a collection of texts for each Sunday of the year. Originating in Galilee on the model of the Jewish calendar, this collection, he suggests, was originally composed of seven groups of seven pericopes extending to the end of chapter 13: 1.1–37 (Autumn); 1.38—3.6 (Winter); 3.7—6.6 (Spring); 6.7–29, plus the Passion texts, from 13.1—16.8 (Lent and Easter Eve); 6.30—7.37 (the season of Easter); 8.1—9.1 (the season of Pentecost); 9.2—10.45 (Summer); 10.46—12.44 (Feast of Tabernacles). This plan, the critic believes, was overlaid by another for liturgical purposes when Mark was adapted for use in the church of Rome and to the Julian calendar. In our view, if it is no longer discernible, it is because it never existed and because the liturgical subdivisions whose traces are to be found in the early manuscripts of Mark all date from well after the first century. Superimposed on a text with which they had nothing to do, these 'plans' merely reflect the liturgical gropings of the third and fourth centuries.

Are all these unfruitful attempts an indication that Mark has no plan and that it is a waste of time to persist in looking for one? This is not our view for a number of scholars subdivide Mark's Gospel in more or less the same way and there are good reasons for thinking that this way corresponds to the author's intentions. Among them may be mentioned G. Wohlenberg,[1] K. L. Schmidt,[2] E. Lohmeyer,[3] X. Léon-Dufour,[4] V. Taylor,[5] A. Kuby,[6] C. E. B. Cranfield.[7] In spite of their differences of

[1] *Das Evangelium des Markus* (Leipzig 1910) (Kommentar zum N.T., hgg. von Th. Zahn, vol. 2), pp. vii–x and 29–31.

[2] *Rahmen der Geschichte Jesu*, pp. xi–xvi.

[3] *Das Evangelium des Markus*, pp. 5–6, 8–9, 70–1, 121–2, 160–1, 227–8, 287–8.

[4] In his article on 'Les évangiles synoptiques' in *Introd. à la Bible* by Robert and Feuillet, vol. II, pp. 208–13.

[5] *Gospel Acc. to St Mark*, pp. 105–13.

[6] 'Zur Konzeption des Markus-Evangeliums' in *ZNTW*, vol. 49 (1958), pp. 52–64.

[7] *The Gospel According to Saint Mark, an Introduction and Commentary* (Cambridge 1959), pp. 13–14.

detail, it can be said that these authors agree on the essentials. All subdivide Mark into six large sections of approximately equal length which some of them divide again into two groups of three, with the break after 8.21 (Kuby), or after 8.30 (Léon-Dufour).[1] These six sections are as follows:

SECTION 1: 1.1 or 1.14 to 3.6 or 3.19. Verses 1.1–13 are counted in some cases as forming part of a section and in others as forming an introduction to the Gospel as a whole.[2]

SECTION 2: 3.7 or 3.20 to 6.6, 6.13, or 6.29. The uncertainty as to where this section ends is due chiefly to the exceptional nature of the account of the death of John the Baptist in 6.17–29.

SECTION 3: 6.7, 6.14, or 6.30 to 8.21, 8.26, or 8.30. The hinge here is the confession of Peter (8.27–30), so that this episode may be attached to Section 3 or Section 4 as desired.

SECTION 4: 8.22, 8.27, or 8.31 to 10.45 or 10.52. The healing of the blind man Bartimaeus (10.46–52) is difficult to place in the plan owing to its isolation.

SECTION 5: 10.46 or 11.1 to 13.37.

SECTION 6: 14.1 to 16.8.[3]

The titles given by the various critics to the foregoing sections differ considerably and reveal very different conceptions of Mark, some stressing the historical character of the text, others regarding it as a work of theology with practically no historical intention. This being so, the similarity in the plans suggested by these authors is all the more striking. Even if it is not possible to define with precision the limits set by the Evangelist to each

---

[1] Riesenfeld, 'Tradition und Redaktion in Markusevangelium', in *Neutestamentliche Studien für Rudolf Bultmann*, pp. 157–64, distinguishes three parts after the break, which he places between 8.26 and 8.27, but he does not appear to have thought of subdividing anything before 8.26.

[2] K. L. Schmidt divides this section into three distinct parts (op. cit., pp. xi–xii): 1.1–13; 1.14–45; 2.1—3.6.

[3] C. E. B. Cranfield (op. cit., p. 14) would like to make 16.1–8 a separate section, constituting the key to the whole book, but his arguments are not convincing.

section—supposing that such limits existed—it would seem reasonable to think that this sub-division of his subject-matter was what was in the mind of the author of Mark. There are indeed in the text several indications of its early date.

True, G. Wohlenberg[1] and E. Lohmeyer[2] are trying to be too systematic when they seek to divide the whole subject-matter of Mark into groups of seven pericopes (according to the former) or of three (according to the latter), which exactly fit into the six sections. The triple nature of certain groups of texts is difficult to deny: the *threefold* prophecy of the passion (8.31; 9.31; 10.32–4) forms the backbone of the section following the confession of Peter; the ministry in Jerusalem is presented in *three* successive aspects (acts in 11.1–26; public discussions in 11.27—12.40; private teaching from 12.41 to 13.37); the Evangelist chose *three* parables to illustrate Jesus' teaching to the people (4.1–34) and *three* miracles to demonstrate his power (4.35—5.43): (the healing of the woman with an issue of blood, coming as it does in the middle of the story of the daughter of Jairus, is part of that story) etc. But the few remarks that can be made on the subject do not take us very far in our knowledge of the structure of Mark.

What is more revealing is the way in which the pericopes situated at the joins between the sections are linked to one another. The beginning of each section is echoed in its last verses and these in turn may be closely linked to the section that follows. The success of John the Baptist in drawing all the people of Judea to him is echoed by the obviously greater and more sensational success of Jesus (1.4–5 and 3.7–12), likewise in a place apart (ἐν τῇ ἐρήμῳ in 1.4; ἀνεχώρησεν in 3.7) and at the water's edge (the Jordan in 1.5 and the 'sea' in 3.7), in which we also find again the theme of falling down before Jesus suggested in 1.7 (cf. 3.11) and that of the transcendent spirit that takes hold of men (1.8 and 3.11–12). These correspondences suggest that the first section extends from 1.1 to 3.12.

Section 2 seems to be composed of two groups of three (parables: 4.1–34; miracles: 4.35—5.43), surrounded by two passages relating to Jesus' relatives (3.20–35 and 6.1–6), themselves accompanied by two texts concerning the Twelve

[1] Op. cit., p. 31.   [2] Op. cit., pp. 8–9.

(3.13–19 and 6.7–13). The Evangelist's intention here is obviously to place these latter in contrast to the family of Jesus.[1] The frame for the third section seems to be formed by the repetition in 8.27–30 of all the essentials of 6.14–16. As for the fourth section, whose internal structure is so evident (the three prophecies of the passion in 8.31, 9.31, and 10.33–4), its external frame is to be sought, it would seem, in the two healings of the blind in 8.22–6 and 10.46–52, the only ones of their kind in Mark. The author may have wished to contrast the difficulty of the first with the extreme rapidity of the second in order to symbolize how greatly the teaching of Jesus from 8.31 to 10.45 had 'opened the eyes' of his disciples. To assign 8.27–30 to section 3 and 8.22–6 to section 4 causes a slight overlapping, but this seems a very small difficulty which simply bears witness to the writer's undoubted clumsiness, torn as he is between his desire to make the first prophecy of the passion follow Peter's confession and his endeavour to respect the topographical indications of 8.22 and 8.27, which he no doubt derived from his sources.

In the fifth section, a distinct symmetry is to be observed between 11.1–25 and 13.1–37: 13.33–7 echoes 11.1–10, with its theme of the 'Triumphal Entry'; the 'parable' of the fig-tree (13.28–9) corresponds to 11.12–14,20–25; verses 13.14–26 bear quite a distinct resemblance to 11.15–19. Lastly, there is certainly a parallel between the anointing at Bethany (14.3–9) and the episode of the women going to the tomb (16.1–8). In short, the Evangelist, who likes to 'sandwich' some of his stories,[2] has used a similar—and just as elementary—literary technique to mark the limits of the various sections of his book and to call the reader's attention to the main ideas contained in each. Such contrivances would have been unworthy of a trained writer. But at Mark's level, which is that of the first gropings of a religious literature designed for a public with

---

[1] Cf. p. 134 below.

[2] It is frequent in Mark for a story to be related in two parts, between which comes a passage relating to some quite different episode. In such a case, even if the conection between the two is not clear, Mark endeavours to explain one with the help of the other. Examples are: 3.20–21,31–5 and 3.22–30; 5.21–4,35–43 and 5.25–34; 11.12–14,20–5 and 11.15–19; 14.1–2,10–11 and 14.3–9; 14.54,66–72 and 14.55–65.

little education, their use reveals a desire for order and clarity which is the mark of a writer aware of his methods.

This conclusion would be strengthened if it could be shown that the sections thus defined are each of them dominated by one or two important ideas and that they mark stages in the life of Jesus only in order better to illustrate certain ideas that are dear to the Evangelist. In the sixth section everything is clear: there is only one theme, the passion of Christ, which no man can share but which is the source of salvation for all. In the case of the preceding sections which, unlike the sixth, are not derived fully formed from tradition, there is more cause for hesitation.[1] But there does seem to be an acceptable solution as soon as we turn our attention to the groups of people sketched in by the author[2] around the person of Jesus: the disciples,[3] the crowd ὁ ὄχλος almost everywhere), the leaders of the Jewish people (scribes, Pharisees, 'Herodians', High Priests, elders). It might be said indeed that, in Mark 1—13, the activities of Jesus can be summed up as drawing the people away from their bad shepherds and giving them new leaders in the persons of the disciples he is training for the purpose. It so happens that the five sections of this text mark stages in this undertaking.

The first (1.1—3.12) is devoted to the call to the disciples and to the people and the break with the previous leaders of the Jewish nation. Vv. 3.6–7 sum up fairly well the message of this part: absolute hostility of the leaders of the people; Jesus, followed by his disciples, leaves the towns and villages of Galilee and their synagogues and withdraws to the shores of

---

[1] Although agreeing on the limits of the various sections, the authors who defend the plan we are discussing here differ entirely on the titles to be given to the first five.

[2] Cf. R. Bultmann, *Gesch. d. syn. Trad.*, pp. 336–7.

[3] Whom Mark also sometimes calls 'the Twelve' (3.14,16; 4.10; 6.7; 9.35; 10.32,41; 11.11; several passages in chapter 14). This name came to him from tradition, like the term μαθητής, applicable to a less well-defined group. But the Evangelist uses one or other with skill, as it serves his purpose (cf. pp. 176ff. below). It is accordingly impossible to use the change from one to the other as evidence for distinguishing two sources of Mark, one referring to 'the disciples' and the other to 'the Twelve', as E. Meyer does, *Ursprung und Anfänge des Christentums*, (vol. I, Stuttgart-Berlin 1921), pp. 133–47. That would only be feasible if Mark had reproduced mechanically the contents of the documents he used.

the 'sea' where he attracts a great crowd. The second section (3.13—6.13) stresses strongly the privileges conferred by Jesus on the Twelve, his new family, within the group thus gathered together. The third (6.14—8.29) places the accent on the role of 'shepherds' that the disciples must learn to play in regard to the crowd thus deprived of other leaders; Peter's confession appears to conclude this part with the suggestion that the 'disciples' are all those who confess that Jesus is the Christ.[1] The fourth section (8.22—10.52) shows that the disciples, and in particular the Twelve (9.35; 10.32,41) and their most out-standing representatives, like Peter (8.32–3; 9.2–5; 10.28) or the sons of Zebedee (9.2,38; 10.35–41), have a long apprentice-ship of faith and renunciation to serve before this mission can be properly accomplished.[2] Lastly, the fifth section (11.1—13.37) offers the disciples the prospect of participation in the eschatological triumph of their Master over the bad shepherds of Israel of whom they are implicitly told to beware until that time comes.

And so the considerations that guided the author of Mark in his effort to arrange the material composing his book were of an ecclesiastical order. It was the desire to define as precisely as possible the place and mission of the Christian Church and of its leaders in the society in which he lived that provided the Evangelist with the themes around which to group the stories and sayings of Jesus he derived from tradition and popular memory. We shall look later in much greater detail at the definition he gives of the Church's place and mission and the circumstances which led him to do so.[3] But here and now it can be said that the birth of the literary genre of the Gospel, that great mystery of Christian literature of the first century, has thus quite a natural explanation. The man who wrote Mark was

---

[1] It would seem also that the presence of a second account of the multipli-cation of the loaves in this section (8.1–10) should be interpreted as an indication of a relaxation of the monopoly of the Twelve. Cf. pp.179–81 below.

[2] What the disciples are not allowed to say, according to 8.30, at a time when Jesus has just effected a difficult healing of a blind man (8.22–6), the blind beggar himself proclaims in 10.46–52 and is healed with a word. This is a strong affirmation of the value of preaching by example, by *imitatio Christi* (cf. 10.28–30).

[3] Cf. pp. 158 and 248ff. below.

neither a more or less passive compiler of material derived from tradition, nor a keen mind seeking stylistic effect, nor a brilliant theologian for whom the Gospel was first and foremost an opportunity to expound his christology[1] but an audacious Christian whose strong convictions about the life of the Church of his day prompted him to confront tradition and those who transmitted it with a statement of the real ecclesiological intentions of Jesus. His book is an appeal to history against the institution which had, in his view, deviated from the true tradition whose custodian it was.[2]

His appeal is made by three means: by choosing, among the material offered by tradition, the parts that would best serve his purpose; by adding to this a certain number of popular tales concerning John the Baptist and above all Jesus; and by placing the whole in an artificial framework designed to bring out its ecclesiological significance. If this arrangement of his material turns out to be almost biographical, it is because the tradition, whose supreme authority the Evangelist was seeking to shake, referred constantly to the man Jesus, whom the author, for want of any structured doctrine on the Holy Spirit, was unable to offset with the risen Christ, as Paul could do and did.[3] In order to break the hold of 'the sayings of Jesus', therefore, the author of Mark resorted to a semi-biographical presentation of Jesus and his real intentions. There is nothing to be gained, we believe, in denying the new and personal nature of the decisive contribution he thus made to the formation of a Christian literature.[4]

[1] These three definitions apply to the three canonical authors who followed the lead of Mark: 'Matthew', 'Luke' and 'John'.

[2] One must of course not yield to the romantic notion of Mark as an individual standing alone against a group. The individual in this case is the spokesman of a minority just as convinced as the majority of the community character necessary to Christian life.

[3] For the elementary nature of Mark's pneumatology cf. p. 188, n. 1 below and E. Schweizer, art. πνεῦμα in *TWNT*, vol. VI, pp. 394–401.

[4] The reasons why one has to reject the hypotheses that see in the framework of Mark a piece of literature pre-dating the Gospel and stemming from the kerygma, to which it formed the introduction, have been stated earlier (pp. 27ff.). It is not possible either to agree with G. Schille, 'Bemerkungen zur Formgeschichte des Evangeliums: Rahmen und Aufbau des Markus-Evangeliums' in *New Testament Studies*, vol. IV (1957–8), pp. 1–24, when he tries to show that the plan of Mark

reproduced the 'agreed outline', filled out by the author with the help of the esoteric 'teaching' given by the Church to its catechumens and of other material. The 'outline' in question (cf. Phil. 2.6–11; Heb. 5.5,7–10; 1 Tim. 3.16) has indeed no parallel in the Gospel except for the first half describing Christ's abasement. The same objection is to be levelled at O. A. Piper, 'The Origin of the Gospel Pattern', in *JBL*, vol. LXXVIII (1959), pp. 115–24, who sees in the 'proclamation of Jesus by the apostles' the origin of the plan of the Gospels and the criterion for the selection of the episodes they relate. As for the solution suggested by H. Riesenfeld, *Trad. u. Red. im Markusevangelium*, loc. cit., who sees in Mark's plan a rather awkward combination of a pre-existing geographical plan and a dogmatic plan centred on 8.27–30, it seems to us to give too little weight to the Evangelist's contribution to the ordering of the material in the Gospel. H. Schlier recently presented at the third study day of German Catholic New Testament specialists (Würzburg, 5–8 March 1959) a paper entitled 'Aufbau von Mk. 1.1—8.26', in which he distinguishes three sections (1.16—3.6; 3.7—6.6a; 6.6b—8.26) in this part of the Gospel and centres each of them on a practical theme fairly close to those we suggest here. One may hope, with R. Schnackenburg, in his report on the meeting in question (*Biblische Zeitschrift*, vol. III of the new series (1959), p. 298) that this paper will soon be published.

Chapter Two

THE AVERSIONS DISPLAYED BY
THE EVANGELIST

In the preceding chapter we have seen that the author of Mark
shows a tendency to non-conformism and a lively desire to win
his readers over to his ideas about the Church. These two traits,
we concluded, largely explain the literary structure of his book.
But they do not of course suffice to account for the intellectual
and spiritual content of the Gospel or to build up an idea of the
personality of the man who wrote it. To gain this insight we
must study Mark more closely in order to bring out several
major theological and ecclesiological lines of thought.
True, these lines of thought must have been present in the
main in the pre-Marcan tradition,[1] but the Evangelist,
who made his choice among the material offered by tradition,
at least accepted them. They all reflect, therefore, his own
general way of thinking and are of interest to us for that
reason.

As the author does not give his Gospel any systematic or
visibly partisan character, it is a little difficult at first sight to
grasp the personality and the thought that lie behind the text.
For this reason it will be wise to begin with what emerges most
clearly and look at the people and ideas that the author detests.
Is this a too narrow approach? Possibly, but when we have
seen what aversions the Evangelist displays, we shall be able to
grasp more clearly where his sympathies lie and what his hopes
are for the Church he has undertaken to serve. In this way we
shall be better able to understand the climate in which he lived
and the trend of his religious thought.

---

[1] Cf. pp. 36–45 above.

1

CRITICISMS OF NON-CHRISTIANS

When the author of Mark chose among the material offered by
tradition a certain number of texts which show Jesus in
conflict with one or other groups of people, or intellectual or
spiritual attitudes, it is legitimate to think that he harboured
an aversion for the people or ideas the Master was combating.
Otherwise he could easily have left out those episodes or sayings,
as he did so many others. He could at least have toned down
their language or placed them in a neutral context. When he
does not take either of these ways of escape, he reveals his own
hostility to the opponents of Jesus and their ideas.

It is commonly thought that, according to the Gospels, the
worst enemies of Jesus were the Pharisees, who are shown only
in the most unpleasant light. This, many claim,[1] is most unjust,
since it is unlikely that the religious élite of Israel would have
been systematically hostile to the rabbi of Nazareth, whose
ideas were similar to their own on numerous points. But the
prejudice can be explained, it is suggested, by the growing
rivalry, in the latter two-thirds of the first century, between the
Pharisees, as leaders of the synagogues, and the Christian
preachers who were seeking more and more to found competing
communities.

If we examine the Gospel according to Mark more closely,
we have to make some amendments to this theory, which is
valid above all for Matthew. Mark does not make the Pharisees
the chief adversaries of Jesus, although he treats them rather
harshly. Perhaps this relative moderation should be interpreted
as an indication of the book's early date.

What are the facts? Mark uses the word *Φαρισαῖος* only
twelve times, that is to say, in absolute as well as in relative
terms, slightly less often than John and much less often than
Matthew and Luke.[2] These references are unequally distri-

---

[1] Cf. for example A. Réville, *Jésus de Nazareth* (Paris 1906), vol I, p. 119;
M. Goguel, *Jesus*, 2nd edn (Paris 1950), pp. 274–6; G. Bornkamm,
Jesus von Nazareth, pp. 88–9; A. Tricot in *Introduction à la Bible* ... by A.
Robert and A. Feuillet, vol. II (Tournai 1959), p. 72. On the other hand,
the almost entire historicity of the Gospel accounts of the disputes
between Jesus and Pharisees is upheld by W. Beilner, *Christus und die
Pharisaer* (Vienna 1959), but he is not very convincing.

[2] That is to say one word in 937 in Mark, one in 811 in John (19 times);

buted: five in the first section (2.16,18,18,24; 3.6), where they leave their mark on four successive pericopes; none in the second section, or in the sixth and last section;[1] five references in the third section, in two groups (7.1,3,5, and 8.11,15); the fourth and fifth sections contain one isolated reference each (10.2 and 12.13). The Pharisees are presented by Mark as almost exclusively Galilean opponents of Jesus. Outside Galilee they play a much less noticeable part (10.2 and 12.13), which is not the case in any of the other Gospels.[2]

This curious localization of the brushes between Jesus and the Pharisees might derive from tradition, since that is the source of all the passages in Mark where they are mentioned.[3] But almost everywhere the Pharisees are referred to at the beginning or end of the passages in question, that is to say at the points where the author may have been most tempted to retouch his material. Considering the general tendency of the Evangelists to refer frequently to the Pharisees, we can therefore allow that Mark introduced their name several times where the tradition referred to other adversaries[4] or mentioned no names. Thus it is the author who chose to locate the conflicts between Jesus and the Pharisees outside Jerusalem and more particularly in Galilee.

On the other hand, Mark never shows the Pharisees as a

---

one in 720 in Luke (27 times); one in 631 in Matthew (29 times). These figures are calculated on the basis of R. Morgenthaler, *Statistik*, pp. 152 and 164.

[1] For the limits and subjects of these sections see pp. 79ff. above.

[2] Matthew gives considerable space to the Pharisees in chapters 22 and 23, set in Jerusalem; Luke has most references to the Pharisees in chapters 11—19, that is to say during the 'journey to Jerusalem'; John makes no mention of the Pharisees except in Jerusalem. The difference between Mark and these other authors would be even more striking if, in Mark 10.2, one were to opt for the Western text, which omits the reference to the Pharisees. This reference would then be explained as a later borrowing by the copyists from Matt. 19.3.

[3] Cf. pp. 34ff. above.

[4] It is curious to note that Mark scarcely ever refers to the Pharisees alone but almost always in association with some other group which might perhaps have been the only one traditionally cited (2.18; 3.6; 7.1,3,5; 8.15; 12.13); elsewhere the author of Mark refers to a special category of Pharisees, in a rather awkward way that could well be ascribed to him (2.16; 2.18).

group of leaders whose decisions direct the lives of the Jewish
people, whereas the other Evangelists all do so more or less.
When they want to go into action against Jesus, the Pharisees
run for help to the 'Herodians' (3.6); when they come to ask
Jesus embarrassing questions, they may be *sent* by the Jewish
authorities (12.13) or *brought* by the latter's representatives
(7.1 suggests this). Whenever they appear on the scene they
behave as worthy citizens who take a high moral line and are
shocked by the disrespect shown in public by Jesus and his
followers for the rules they hold most sacred. The political
problem itself is posed by them only from the point of view of
'conscientious objection' to paying taxes, that is to say from
the individual angle (12.14). Once only Mark hints that their
religious attitude comprised an apocalyptic element (8.11),
which is brought out better in the other synoptic Gospels
(Matt. 12.38ff.; Luke 17.20ff.).

The portrait painted in Mark of the Pharisees thus avoids
certain exaggerated traits and improbabilities that distort
the picture of them in the other Gospels. It is nonetheless
defective and tendentious, since, wherever he mentions them
in his book, the author of Mark reduces the role of this highly
important group[1] to that of a mere Galilean union for the defence of individual morality. Let us then neither praise too
highly his historical objectivity in this respect, nor yet ascribe
to him any too violently polemical intentions. It is wiser to
suppose that he reflects more or less unconsciously the state of
relations between the Church for which he is writing and the
Pharisees. The situation was no longer what it has been when
the tradition began to take shape, but it did not present the
critical and pressing character to which Matthew and John
were to bear witness later. Given the central role the Pharisees
are known to have played in the synagogues of the day,[2] this
observation might quite naturally be interpreted as meaning
that the problem of relations between the Christians and the
synagogues, non-existent at first but becoming a burning

---

[1] Cf. for example E. Schürer, *Geschichte des jüdischen Volks im Zeitalter Jesu
Christi*, 3rd–4th edn (Leipzig 1909), vol. II, pp. 388–406; R. T. Herford, *Les Pharisiens* (Paris 1928), *passim*; Ch. Guignebert, *Le monde juif
vers le temps de Jésus* (Paris 1935), pp. 213–20.

[2] M. Simon, *Les sectes juives au temps de Jésus* (Paris 1960), p. 31.

question when the religious life of Judaism fell back on these local assemblies after the destruction of the Temple, was beginning to emerge at the time the author of Mark was writing.

Alongside the Pharisees, Mark sometimes refers to 'Herod' or the 'Herodians' (3.6; 8.15; 12.13). The juxtaposition is surprising, whatever the precise meaning one attaches to these names.[1] Was this highly respectable party compromising itself by associating with the despised group of politicians who collaborated with the occupying power? Some critics are loud in proclaiming the improbability of this assumption,[2] while others, on the contrary, point to the amazing alliances that political or religious hatreds have sometimes produced.[3] There seems little point in discussing the question. What is more important is to understand why Mark stressed this association, which he certainly felt to be an incongruous one, even if one of his sources alluded to it.[4]

It is possible in the first place that he may have been prompted

---

[1] It is generally accepted that they were notables won over to the Herodian dynasty (H. H. Rowley, 'The Herodians in the Gospels', in *JTS*, vol. XLI (1940), pp. 14–27). But certain critics maintain that they were more probably officials of the Tetrarch: thus, for example, C. G. Montefiore, *The Synoptic Gospels*, vol. I, p. 83 and W. Grundmann, *Ev. nach Markus*, pp. 73–4. It is difficult to come down on one side or the other.

[2] Thus E. Lohmeyer, *Ev. des Mk.*, p. 67. But cf. also the warning against excessive scepticism in this matter given by B. W. Bacon, *The Gospel of Mark, its composition and date* (New Haven 1925), pp. 74–6.

[3] V. Taylor, *St Mark*, p. 224.

[4] In Mark 12.13–17 the collusion between the Pharisees and the Herodians is much less marked than in 3.6. The text suggests, rather, that they were two groups of antagonists between whom Jesus was obliged to weave his way carefully in order not to attract the hostility of either. The scene is certainly reduced to its bare essentials and is one of the controversy dialogues that Mark no doubt received ready-made from the church tradition and altered very little (cf. pp. 34–36 above). The reference to the Herodians is necessary to give the passage balance and is a natural one in a group of stories presenting in succession the principal Jewish parties. Unlike the reference in Mark 3.6, it is repeated in Matthew (22.16), so that it is very unlikely to have been introduced by Mark. One might even wonder whether its presence in the tradition might not have suggested to Mark the rather obscure allusions in 3.6 and 8.15.

to it by the political situation established fleetingly in Palestine towards the year 40. Agrippa I, grandson of Herod the Great, is known to have been counting, around that date, even more than his uncle Herod Antipas had done, on the Jews (and even the Pharisees) in order to win back for himself his grandfather's kingdom, over which he reigned a short time only, however, until his early death in 44.[1] This pro-Pharisee policy led him even to persecute the church of Jerusalem (Acts 12.1ff.). The Palestinian Christians of the day could easily conceive, therefore, of collusion between the Pharisees and the partisans of the Herodian dynasty.[2]

This fact is not enough, however, to explain Mark's insistence on the point. It would seem certain that the Evangelist was seeking to cast suspicion on the sincerity of the Pharisees by associating them with such unsavoury circles as those of the Herodian dynasty and its supporters. The extraordinary story in Mark 6.17–29 is designed to spoil the reputation for moral uprightness enjoyed by those who set themselves up as the defenders of morality, much more than to incite Christians to resentment against the family of Herod. The means used by the author of Mark to denounce the hypocrisy of the Pharisees are thus much less direct than those of Matthew (chap. 23) or of Luke (numerous isolated sayings in chapters 11ff.), both of which are very brutal. Should it not be deduced that the author of Mark still hoped for at least a partial conversion of the Pharisees? While he attacks them, he does not do so too roughly and suggests that the danger for them is that of succumbing to evil influences. In short, he invites them again indirectly to mend their ways.

The author of Mark does not use 'Herod' merely to compromise the Pharisees, however. Like the latter, 'Herod' becomes, thanks to a rather arbitrary stylization, the typical example of an attitude hostile to Jesus and his followers. Along-

---

[1] Cf. in particular B. W. Bacon in *JBL*, xxxix (1920), pp. 102ff. and *Gospel of Mark*, pp. 74–6.

[2] By giving the Tetrarch Herod Antipas, in 6.14,22,25,26,27, the title of 'king', which is so obviously exaggerated that in the parallel texts Luke changes it (cf. Luke 3.19 and 9.7) and Matthew keeps it only once (Matt. 14.9), Mark shows a certain tendency to project the image of the reign of Agrippa I on to the much more modest reality of that of the Tetrarch Antipas.

side the ineradicable mistrust of the moralists, he incarnates, it would seem, the sterile curiosity of the immoral man, who refuses personally to repent despite his liking for the man sent from God. Verse 8.15 shows that this symmetry is intentional, even if here it only reproduces a tradition.[1] Indeed, since Mark at least preserves the association of the Pharisees and of 'Herod' (which Matt. 16.6 and Luke 12.11 do not) and uses this curious *logion* as the key to the section 6.14—8.29, to judge by the commentary he gives on it in 8.17–21, where he refers to the two principal episodes of those chapters, one must suppose that Mark saw this comic opera ruler as typifying the worst kind of spiritual turpitude, whereas the Pharisees symbolized for him the extreme of strait-laced respectability.[2]

It has often been pointed out that there is no expression in Mark of hostility to the Romans or to the representatives of their domination. Even if one hesitates to draw from this conclusions as extreme as those of some critics,[3] it must be regarded as due to more than pure chance. For manifestly apologetic reasons, as little attention is drawn to the Roman authorities as possible, in Mark and in the other Gospels, in the account of the trial of Jesus.[4] Mark even avoids any reference to the well-known brutality of the Roman yoke, unlike Luke (13.1ff.; 20.20) and John (11.48); in addition, he always refers to Pilate in his individual capacity and never mentions his official position, which may be only due to negligence,[5] but appears

---

[1] As V. Taylor thinks, for example, *St Mark*, p. 365.

[2] The 'Herodians', on the other hand, appear in Mark solely as the representatives of political opportunism or even, one might say, of the secret police. The only purpose they serve in Mark is that of making the Pharisees suspect.

[3] Cf. for example S. G. F. Brandon, *Fall of Jerusalem*, pp. 185–205.

[4] Cf. for example M. Goguel, 'Juifs et Romains dans l'histoire de la Passion', in *RHR*, LXII (1910), pp. 165–82 and 295–322; *Jésus*, 2nd edn, pp. 392–3; Hans Lietzmann, 'Der Prozess Jesu', in *Sitzungsberichte der Berliner Akademie, Phil. hist. Klasse*, XIV (1931), pp. 11–12; J. Isaac, *Jésus et Israël*, 2nd edn (Paris 1959), pp. 449ff.; P. Winter, *On the Trial of Jesus* (Berlin 1960), pp. 52–3, 55–7; T. A. Burkill, 'The Trial of Jesus' in *Vigiliae christianae*, vol. XII (1958), pp. 1–18.

[5] Matthew and Luke, who pay more attention than the author of Mark to the form of their stories, both state the office held by Pilate: Matthew (27.2,11,14,15,21,27 and 28.14) gives him the title of ἡγεμών; Luke

rather to be deliberate, if we remember that the only Roman functionary whose title is recorded in Mark is the one who fore-shadows the good-will of the Roman authorities towards the Christian evangelists, namely the centurion converted by the sight of the death of Jesus (15.39, 44–5). Nowhere, either, does Mark see in Pilate the example of a spiritual attitude, as is the case in Matthew (the coward: 27.24) and John (the sceptic: 18.38). For him this figure derived from tradition is of passing interest only and he does not seek, as he does for 'Herod', to accentuate his role.

The Sadducees, to whom Matthew and Luke–Acts attach some importance, are referred to only once, in a passage in which Jesus is shown treating them rather harshly (Mark 12.18–27). Here again, it must be admitted, this is a piece of information derived from church tradition, which Mark re-corded, while paying little attention to its details. As, however, on the other hand, Mark devotes considerable space to the ἀρχιερεῖς,[1] it can be seen that he is not interested in the priests as a party or a theological school (in spite of the help given him by the tradition in referring here to the Sadducees) but simply as the wielders of power. The Church for which he was writing cannot, therefore, have had the same rivalry with the Sadducees as with the Pharisees or the same debates as with the 'scribes'.

These last-mentioned (γραμματεῖς) indeed play a particularly important part in Mark. They are mentioned more often than in the other Gospels[2] and appear in each section as the leaders

---

states at the beginning of his Gospel that he was 'governing' (ἡγεμονεύω) Judaea (3.1) and calls him indirectly ἡγεμών (20.20 and 23.1). John, while giving Pilate no title, is much more explicit than Mark about his powers and describes him as seated in the 'hall of judgement' (18.28,33; 19.9), where he has the sole power of life and death over Jesus (18.31 and 19.10), whereas in Mark the hall, or praetorium, is simply the scene of the flagellation (Mark 15.16) and Pilate is a slave to custom who merely executes the wishes of the crowd (Mark 15.6–15).

[1] Cf. pp. 99–101 below.

[2] 21 references in Mark as compared with none in John, 14 in Luke and 22 in Matthew, which are much longer Gospels. The use of νομικός (unknown in Mark) in one place in Matthew and six times in Luke does not restore the balance. On the subject of γραμματεύς and νομικός, cf. the articles by J. Jeremias in *TWNT*, vol. I, pp. 477ff. and vol. IV, pp. 1080ff.

of the opposition to Jesus and to his teaching. From the beginning[1] their prestige is undermined by the innovating action of
Jesus (1.22); it is with them that Jesus has his first controversy
(2.6) and it is they[2] who level against him the formidable
charge of collusion with Beelzebub (3.22). It is with them that
the disciples come into conflict as soon as the Master leaves
them (9.14). It is they too[3] whom Jesus ridicules in public at
Jerusalem (12.35–7) before denouncing their hypocrisy (12.38–
40). True, Mark is no more severe where the scribes are concerned than Luke (cf. Luke 11.45–52) and Matthew (cf. Matt.
23.1–36). But in Mark they are presented as a more organized
and omnipresent group than in the other two synoptic Gospels.

Luke, indeed, makes a fairly clear distinction between the
γραμματεῖς, members of the Sanhedrin of Jerusalem, or at least
holders of a certain administrative power,[4] and the νομικοί,
whose function was to comment on and teach the Law.[5]
The result is a less strong impression of mass opposition to Jesus
than we feel on the part of the scribes in Mark. Matthew uses
the term νομικός once only, as an adjective, it would seem

---

[1] Matthew, who alone keeps the term γραμματεύς in the parallel text,
hides it away in 7.29, after the Sermon on the Mount, and thus de-
tracts from its impact.

[2] In Matt. 12.24 this calumny is laid at the door of the Pharisees, in
Luke 11.15 it is attributed to some of the people in the crowd. Was it
thought that Mark went too far in accusing the scribes?

[3] In the parallel texts the scribes are dealt with rather less harshly:
In Matt. 22.41—23.2 the Pharisees are the main target of the attack by
Jesus and the scribes are reproved only in the second *logion*; in Luke
20.41–7 the opinion Jesus is refuting is not attributed to the scribes;
they are merely being questioned about it.

[4] In Luke 6.6ff., the γραμματεῖς play alongside the Pharisees a part
comparable to that of the Herodians in the parallel passage of Mark
3.1–6. In Luke 20.46–7 it is their social attitude that is criticized and not
their teaching, which, on the contrary, is the subject of Luke's reproaches to the νομικοί in 11.45ff. It will be recalled that the only place
where the word γραμματεύς is used in the New Testament to designate a
non-Jewish functionary is in the sequel to the treatise addressed to
Theophilus, in Acts 19.35.

[5] The use of γραμματεύς in Luke 11.53—a verse whose text is doubtful,
it is true, since the Western variant gives νομικός—and the parallelism
of 6.7 and 14.1–3 militate against insisting too much on this distinction
which, however, is emphasized by the term νομοδιδάσκαλος, used twice
(Luke 5.17 and Acts 5.34), in an attempt at elegance, it would seem.

(22.35), in a sentence where he wishes to stress that the person thus described belongs to the party of the Pharisees (cf. 22.34, 41) and is hostile to Jesus (πειράζων αὐτόν:22.35). The term is thus intended to suggest an amateur lawyer who is a mere spokesman for the Pharisees. Matthew has obviously some respect for the office of the γραμματεῖς (23.2–3) and even, it seems, makes certain references to the scribes of the Christian Church (13.52; 23.34; cf. 7.29). He keeps only a small number of the references made to them in Mark in the Passion story (Matt. 26.57 and 27.41) and, when he relates their intrigues or denounces their love of honours he always associates them with the Pharisees or the 'high priests'.[1] Not in Matthew either, consequently, do the scribes take first place among the enemies of Jesus as a group specially to be feared.

In Mark, on the contrary, their hostility leads rapidly to a very violent conflict (3.22) which goes on practically without interruption. There is the very quiet scene of Mark 12.28–34, it will be objected, but it concerns one scribe only, whose question to Jesus, moreover, is presented as bordering on insolence (12.34). It is followed by two short passages where the scribes are attacked en bloc with exceptional vigour (12.35ff.). This juxtaposition gives weight to the mutual satisfaction with one another expressed by Jesus and the scribe in 12.28–34. In the eyes of the author of Mark, the scribes are among the instigators[2] of the concerted offensive on the part of the various Jewish groups against Jesus at Jerusalem (11.27–12.37) and it is they whom the Master chooses to crush when he embarks on his counter-attack. One only of them rallied in time to the winning side and thus escaped the judgement that fell on the group as a whole: he was the exception that proved the rule.

---

[1] Matthew mentions the scribes (or 'one of them' or 'certain of them') only five times (7.29; 8.19; 9.3; 13.52; 17.10), whereas Mark does so nine times (1.22; 2.6; 3.22; 9.11,14; 12.28,32,35,38). Of these five cases there is not one where the scribes display hostility to Jesus or where Jesus attacks them. Of the nine corresponding cases in Mark, the scribes attack Jesus three times and are twice challenged by him.

[2] Enumerated in 11.27. It will be noted that Matthew (21.23) leaves the scribes out of this list as he also does at the end of the series of controversies (22.34–46).

Are these ideas peculiar to Mark? Or do they derive rather from the church tradition? In our opinion they can be ascribed to the Evangelist, who seems to have received from the Church of his day a collection of controversies[1] recording the triumph of Jesus successively over the members of the Sanhedrin (11.27–33), the Pharisees, and the 'Herodians' (12.13–17), the Sadducees (12.18–27) and ending[2] with the 'conversion' of a scribe astounded by his authority (12.28–34). The meaning of this ordering of the text is clear: it is an appeal to the honest scribes to leave their authorities and organized parties in order to recognize the superiority of Jesus as an interpreter of Scripture and a representative of the best rabbinic tradition.[3] It was a society for which Christianity represented a new party within Judaism which brought these four short passages together for the purposes of propaganda among the Jewish intellectual élite. But by placing this group of stories just after the purification of the Temple and associating it with the stern parable of the husbandmen (12.1–12), by following it up with the saying on the subject of the Son of David (12.35–7), Mark changes its internal balance and gives it a much more unfavourable turn. The Jewish institutions and everything in society that supported them are the subject of his severe condemnation, which falls above all on the group least ill-judged by the church tradition, namely the scribes. The Evangelist has ceased to expect anything from these intellectuals whom it had once been hoped to win over to the cause of Jesus Christ. The scribe of verses 12.28–34 who is 'not far from the Kingdom of God' interests him only as the representative of a few rare lawyers attracted by the Christian faith or converted to it but unable to convince their fellows or to bring the gospel to the mass of

---

[1] Cf. pp. 34–36 above.

[2] Verse 12.34 concludes somewhat solemnly, which means that the introduction to vv. 35–7 is a little laboured. There is no definite conclusion, either in v. 37 or in v. 40, or even in v. 44, which has no connection with the controversies but merely points the lesson to be drawn from vv. 41ff.

[3] This explains, in our view, the fact that the scribe replies to Jesus' quotations from Scripture with one or two others of his own (Deut. 4.35; 1 Sam. 15.22) in order to confirm and prolong the thought of his partner in the discussion. The teaching of Jesus fits smoothly into the tradition represented by those of the scribes most influenced by the great prophets of Israel.

the people.¹ It might even be thought that Mark preserved the text referring to this person because of the slightly derogatory allusion to the cult of burnt offerings (12.33), which brought grist to his mill, since it undermined the prestige of the Temple at Jerusalem.²

The same intention no doubt explains why twice (3.22 and 7.1) the author of Mark makes the scribes attacking Jesus come from Jerusalem.³ Jerusalem being the seat of the council of the 'high priests, scribes and elders' who were to send Jesus to his death (8.31; 11.27; 14.43–53; 15.1), these adversaries from the capital appear in the light of official representatives of tyrannical religious authorities. Thus, indirectly, doubt is cast on their sincerity and disinterestedness. In this way Mark shows how deep his hostility to the scribes goes and at the same time gives evidence of a decidedly autonomous attitude in the face of a religious 'centralism' of which it is not certain that the Judaism of his day had the monopoly.⁴

But Mark's insistence on the conflict between Jesus and the scribes has a wider significance. For the Evangelist, the scribes are theologians rather than interpreters of Scripture. Nowhere, except in 12.32–3, does he place a biblical quotation in their mouths. On the contrary, he takes a malicious delight in quoting texts that contradict or undermine their opinions

---

¹ 'The people', who had remained in the background since 11.18 (11.32; 12.12), reappear in 12.38 to hear 'gladly' the severe judgement passed by Jesus on the scribes, who clearly do not have their ear. The scribe of Mark 12.28–34 plays in this Gospel somewhat the same part as Nicodemus in John: half-converted, this διδάσκαλος τοῦ Ἰσραήλ (John 3.10) is capable only of a timid and useless plea in favour of Jesus before the Sanhedrin (John 7.50–2) and of taking part in his burial (John 19.38–42), but not of bearing witness to his resurrection.

² See pp. 103ff. below.

³ This detail is worthy of note above all if one agrees with D. Daube, *The N.T. and Rabb. Jud.*, pp. 210–2, that in the Tannaitic epoch the scribes ('sopherim') were humble village schoolmasters to be distinguished clearly from the 'maschnim' and 'hakhamim' who were the real scholars.

⁴ As is known, there is some reason to suppose that the church of Jerusalem claimed the right to control the other Christian churches until the revolt of A.D. 66. Cf. for example M. Goguel, *L'Egl. prim.*, pp. 28–36, 167–8; O. Cullmann, *Saint Pierre*, pp. 28ff. and 201ff.; S. G. F. Brandon, *The Fall of Jerusalem*, 2nd edn, pp. 20–1, 26ff.

(7.6–7; 7.10; 9.12; 12.36). The weapons with which the scribes combat Jesus are their tradition of casuistry (7.5), their messianic ideas (9.11; 12.35) and their concept of the honour of God (2.6–7; 3.22; 14.64). In short it is their theological thinking that Mark reproaches with departing from the Scriptures on which it was in principle founded. As the Evangelist has little to propose in place of the ideas he rejects, one may legitimately ascribe to him a certain anti-intellectualism which, while essentially outward-looking, may also have coloured his judgement of the emergent Christian theology of his day.[1]

Another group of opponents of Jesus, which is of some importance in Mark,[2] is that of the ἀρχιερεῖς. We are familiar with the numerous discussions arising out of the Evangelists' use of this plural for men who, in the majority of cases, cannot be 'high priests' in the strict sense, even if we allow that all the holders of that office retained their title after they laid it down.[3] It is generally thought that the Christian writers, like Josephus also, who writes ἀρχιερεῖς in cases where he cannot be referring to real high priests[4] were following here popular usage in the first century of our era. But that usage is unknown to us and the texts do little to enlighten us: in daily life was this title given to the members of the Sanhedrin belonging to the great priestly families and thus possible future high priests[5] or was it only

---

[1] Cf. pp. 111–9 below.

[2] They are mentioned fourteen times (without counting eight references to the High Priest in 2.26 and in vv. 47, 53, 54, 60, 61, 63, 66 of chap. 14), that is to say slightly more often, proportionately, than in Matthew (eighteen times, plus seven references to the High Priest) and distinctly more than Luke (twelve times, plus three references to the High Priest) and John (ten times, plus eleven references to the High Priest).

[3] Although in principle a High Priest was appointed for life, the Romans and the Herodians deposed a large number of them, certain of whom continued to play an important role at Jerusalem after their fall from favour: thus Annas, deposed in the year 15 of our era but much consulted during and after the trial of Jesus (John 18.13,24; Acts 4.6), indeed so much so that in Luke-Acts he is given the title of ἀρχιερεύς (Luke 3.2 and Acts 4.6).

[4] For example in *B.J.*, II. xiv–xvii, *passim*.

[5] E. Schürer, *Geschichte des jüdischen Volkes im Zeitalter Jesu Chrisit*, 4th edn, vol. II, pp. 274ff.; Ch. Guignebert, *Le monde juif vers le temps de Jésus*, p. 77.

given to the holders of the highest office in the priesthood at a particular time?[1] However this may be, the earliest of the writers in question, the author of Mark, may have distorted this vague popular usage which he adopted.

If we keep to the text of the Gospel, who are these ἀρχιερεῖς in his eyes? Their role in the cult is not mentioned anywhere,[2] although their links with Jerusalem[3] and with the Temple[4] emerge very clearly. On the other hand, Mark presents them as the authorities chiefly responsible for keeping order in the sanctuary and its vicinity (11.18, 27–8; 14.1,10,43; 15.1–3, 10–11). Their activity in this sphere is not confined to taking part in the meetings of the Sanhedrin for the purposes of deliberation or judgement.[5] It includes outside action comparable to that of our modern police officer—recording a denunciation (14.10), presenting a suspect and the file concerning him to the competent judge (15.1–3,10), handling a crowd (15.11), directing an execution (15.31). It is, moreover, when they are performing these functions that the ἀρχιερεῖς, who are almost always associated with other groups, are mentioned alone (14.10; 15.3,10–11) or else made to stand out from the others: οἱ ἀρχιερεῖς μετὰ τῶν. . . .[6]

In short, in the Evangelist's eyes, the ἀρχιερεῖς are a sort of

---

[1] J. Jeremias, *Jerusalem zur Zeit Jesu*, 2nd edn (Göttingen 1958), II, pp. 33ff. is the principal defender of this theory, which seems to us the most probable, although it is less commonly accepted than the preceding one.

[2] Two passages in Mark only (1.44 and 2.26) refer to the functions assigned to the priesthood under Mosaic law. Both contain the word ἱερεύς which occurs nowhere else in the Gospel.

[3] The ἀρχιερεῖς are always located in Jerusalem, although this is only implicit in 8.31.

[4] In 11.18,27, the ἀρχιερεῖς are in the first ranks of the defenders of the Temple against the brutal attack by Jesus.

[5] This is not the place to discuss the delicate question of the trial of Jesus and the part played in it by the Sanhedrin. For this see J. Blinzler, *Der Prozess Jesu* . . . , 3rd edn (Regensburg 1960), pp. 95ff.; P. Winter, *On the Trial of Jesus* (Berlin 1960), pp. 20–30, 135–48. The term 'judgement' is used here solely to express the idea that emerges from Mark of the role of the Sanhedrin in the trial and condemnation of Jesus.

[6] This expression is to be found only in 15.1 and 15.31, that is to say in the passages that speak of action by the Jewish authorities directed towards outside people.

executive college forming the core of the Sanhedrin without being identical with it (14.55), and enforcing its decisions. It is tempting to think that he takes the title of these people to mean 'ruling priests'. Where he presents them as the bitter opponents of Jesus, he is accordingly giving an inkling of his hostility towards the police powers exercised by the priests of Jerusalem. It is the voice of a church, which no doubt suffered from those powers, which Mark lets us hear rather more clearly than the later Evangelists.[1]

While he is hostile to the masters of the Temple of Jerusalem, is the author of Mark hostile to the Temple as an institution? And, if so, is he also hostile to the sacrificial cult? It would seem possible to reply to the second question in the negative. True, Mark is not interested in the sacrifices and other offerings prescribed by the Mosaic law: he scarcely mentions them,[2] which shows the unimportant part they played in the piety of his church. Moreover, on two occasions he places them in opposition to the two most important rules of the law, namely to honour one's parents (7.9–13) and to love God and one's neighbour (12.32–4). But a certain indifference to the sacrificial cult is nothing very unusual in primitive Christianity or in the Judaism of the day[3] and the two passages referred to are in no

---

[1] It is important in this case not to exaggerate the differences between the four canonical Gospels. Let us note simply that in addition to the less frequent use of the plural ἀρχιερεῖς, the other synoptic Gospels differ from Mark by the greater rarity of the passages where this group is mentioned alone: three in Matthew (26.14; 27.6; 28.11), one only in Luke (23.4, in a verse where they are associated with the ὄχλοι).

[2] The vocabulary of the sacrificial cult is used only rarely in Mark: θυσιαστήριον does not appear at all; θυσία only once (12.33), accompanied by ὁλοκαύτωμα, which is rare in the New Testament; δῶρον is found only once, to translate κορβᾶν (7.11); προσφορά is not found at all and προσφέρειν is used only once in its ritual sense (1.44); etc. Luke is as reserved in this respect as Mark; Matthew rather less (six times θυσιαστήριον; nine times δῶρον; three or four times προσφέρειν in the ritual sense).

[3] It is striking for example that the fidelity of the early Christians to Judaism and the Temple should be recorded in Acts without any reference to their participation in sacrifices. Luke did not hesitate, however, to describe the Temple ritual (cf. Luke 1.5ff.; 2.22ff.; Acts 21.23ff.). It is also well known that Judaism at the beginning of the Christian era was in process of evolving the new structures (synagogues, rabbinic schools, brotherhoods) that would enable it one day to survive

way arguing against the rites prescribed by the Pentateuch. The first criticizes a custom whose relations with ritual offerings were quite remote,[1] whereas the second merely takes up the theme of the Israelite prophets, whose indignation was directed much more against the unworthiness of the people who offered the sacrifices than against the practice itself,[2] in its principle at least.

Far from launching out into attacks against the offering of sacrifices for the purposes of the cult, Mark accepts this practice without questioning its validity. When he refers to the rules regarding the showbread (2.26), he seems to regard keeping them as a matter of course, since he feels himself obliged to plead the state of hunger in which David and his followers found themselves in order to justify their breaking of them. The cleansed leper is told by Jesus to go and make the offerings prescribed in Leviticus (Lev. 14.1–32), which included sacrifices (Mark 1.44); Mark relates the incident without the slightest reservation regarding the value of these rites. Similarly, he makes no criticism of the faithful putting offerings in the boxes at the Temple; on the contrary he relates pertinently the praise the widow earned from Jesus for her heroic fulfilment of this obligation (12.41–4). Lastly, there is nothing in the account of the cleansing of the Temple to make one suppose that Jesus

---

the destruction of the Temple but which in the meantime were detracting from the importance of ritual sacrifice in the religious life of Israel. Cf. for example, Ch. Guignebert, *Le monde juif vers le temps de Jésus* (Paris 1935) (L'évolution de l'humanité), pp. 103–4, 237–8; M. Simon, *Les sectes juives au temps de Jésus* (Paris 1960) (Mythes et religions), pp. 63–4, 90.

[1] It was in fact a case of a vow which preserved property from the claims of an importunate third party without obliging the owner to hand it over to the Temple for the purposes of the cult. Cf. Strack–Billerbeck, vol. I, pp. 711ff.; C. G. Montefiore, *The Synoptic Gospels*, 2nd edn (London 1927), vol. I, p. 148.

[2] Cf. for example A. Neher, *L'essence du prophétisme* (Paris 1955), pp. 293–304; E. Jacob, *Théologie de l'Ancien Testament* (Neuchâtel-Paris 1955), pp. 193–4, whose moderate conclusion seems the wise one; R. Vuilleumier, *La tradition cultuelle d'Israël dans la prophétie d'Amos et d'Osée* (Neuchâtel-Paris 1960), *passim*. The classical theory that the prophets were inclined towards a religion without sacrifices is expounded, for example, in A. Lods *Les prophètes d'Israël et les débuts du Judaïsme* (Paris 1935) pp. 74–7 [E.T. 1937]. It can be regarded as no longer current.

was attacking either physically or verbally the cult of sacrifice itself (Mark 11.15–19). The expression οἶκος προσευχῆς in verse 17 should not be taken out of its context and interpreted as the expression of a preference for a cult of the synagogue type. The only significance that can be attributed to it, assuming that is at all emphasized, is that of alluding to the final conversion of the nations, seen as a gigantic pilgrimage to the 'Mountain of Yahweh' and consecrated by the participation of the Gentiles in the eschatological Temple.[1]

Does this mean that Mark accepts the Temple with the same easy indifference as he accepts the rite of sacrifice? It would not seem so. There are certain indications, on the contrary, that the sanctuary of Jerusalem roused his disapproval. It is striking, for example, that the part of the Gospel where almost all the incidents take place in the Temple (11.11—13.2) should be placed between the cleansing of the Temple (11.15–17) and the prophecy of its destruction (13.1–2) and that it should consist of a long series of denunciations, controversies, and manifestations of hostility. Being very ill-disposed towards the rulers of the sanctuary, the Evangelist makes no attempt to distinguish between them and the institution over which they rule by recalling a glorious past now trodden underfoot by a decadent generation, or by painting the glorious future ahead of the Temple if it freed itself from a disastrous yoke. The Temple is not 'God's house' (11.17); it is merely the residence of the Jewish leaders (14.49), the place where they tolerate no

---

[1] The text of Isaiah partially quoted by Jesus mentions indeed the burnt offerings and sacrifices that the 'sons of the stranger' will make on the great day when Yahweh invites them into his 'house of prayer'. By truncating this quotation, Matthew (21.13) and Luke (19.46) (who in addition changes the verb) shift the accent on to the words οἶκος προσευχῆς and mask the reference to Isaiah and eschatology: it is in those Gospels that Jesus appears to contrast the cult of sacrifice at Jerusalem with the ideal of a more spiritual cult resembling the offices of the synagogues. It is accordingly impossible to agree with E. Lohmeyer (*Ev. des Markus*, pp. 236–7) when he believes he sees in Mark 11.17 the 'attitude of the Galilean layman who, living far from the cultural centre of the Jewish faith, honours the Temple simply as the highest synagogue'. On the other hand, he is quite right to stress here the allusion to the eschatological call to the nations. This second interpretation is scarcely compatible with the first: one has to choose between the two. Cf. also E. Lohmeyer, *Evangelium und Kultus* (Göttingen 1942).

other authority than their own (11.18–28; 12.1–12). In a word, it is nothing but 'a den of thieves', the place where a group of malefactors hide away the fruits of their crimes (cf. 12.40) and expect to escape the consequences of their acts.[1] Even its splendour is suspect (13.1–2), as well as its good material organization (11.15–16).

Is there any hope, according to Mark, that things will change and the Temple will one day be devoted to the service of God? None at all: the magnificent edifice is doomed to total destruction (13.1–2), together with the surrounding country, when the sacrilege shall have reached its height.[2] Even the

---

[1] The expression σπήλαιον λῃστῶν has been understood in various ways, which are discussed by W. Grundmann, *Ev. nach Markus*, vol. II, p. 232. Apart from the one we adopt here, the only other that seems worthy of attention is that which E. Lohmeyer rejects as useless (*Ev. des Markus*, p. 236) while admitting that it has a grain of probability: these words, it is suggested, are an allusion to the excessive prices charged by the merchants in the Temple to the pilgrims for their wares. This may be a secondary explanation of the choice of the words σπήλαιον λῃστῶν by Jesus or the Evangelist, but they are designed above all to recall Jer. 7.11 and its context and to denounce the Temple as the refuge whose existence allows its occupants to commit the worst abuses without fear of consequences. This hideout of brigands is moreover destined to call down the wrath of God and to be utterly destroyed (Jer. 7.12–14).

[2] This would seem to be the only meaning of the celebrated saying in Mark 13.14 linking the final θλᾶψις to the coming of the 'abomination of desolation', 'standing where it ought not'. In the light, perhaps, of some threat by the Romans (like Caligula's plan in A.D. 39–40 to have his statue set up there, as suggested by O. Pfleiderer, *Das Urchristentum, seine Schriften und Lehren*, 2nd edn (Berlin 1902), vol. I, pp. 380–4, followed by numerous other critics), the Evangelist suggests here a comparison with Dan. 9.27, 11.31, 12.11, which refer to the profanation of the sanctuary by Antiochus Epiphanes in B.C. 167. But although a little further on (v. 19) he quotes Dan. 12.1, it is doubtful whether he sees the 'affliction' prophesied by Jesus as reproducing that announced in the book of Daniel. In Mark it is not a question of a long period of war and oppression but of a sudden and relatively brief catastrophe (cf. v. 18) that is to strike Judaea. The Evangelist is no doubt thinking of another flood, a great earthquake, or some other natural disaster sent suddenly by God to destroy the Temple and of which the disciples will be warned by the presence in the Temple of an abomination, at once a 'thing' (τὸ βδέλυγμα) and a person (ἑστηκότα, a grammatically misplaced masculine to which attention is drawn by the words ὁ ἀναγινώσκων νοείτω). It might be the Anti-Christ, as suggested in a tradition going back to the exegetes of the second century and as a com-

mountain on which it stands will be razed to the ground[1]

parison with 2 Thess. 2 and Rev. 13.1ff. would also suggest; but Mark 13.21–2, by introducing a time of waiting between the 'tribulation' and the end of the world in which he places the rise of false Christs and false prophets, makes that solution difficult to accept. The most probable theory is that Mark 13.14 applies to the erection of a *statue* in the Temple. No doubt the Evangelist did not know who was to commit this supreme sacrilege, but he may have imagined that one day the abhorred would go to those lengths, or at least would permit it, like Aaron in the desert (Exod. 32) or like certain priests in the days of Antiochus Epiphanes (1 Macc. 1.45,52; 4.42–3). Hence the brutality of the punishment that shall be inflicted by God on these rebels and their people in that day.

These difficult verses of Mark 13.14ff. have been so much discussed that we cannot refute here all the theories that differ from our own. A very useful 'Note on the History of Interpretation of the *ΒΔΕΛΥΓΜΑ ΕΡΗΜΩΣΕΩΣ* is to be found in G. R. Beasley-Murray, *A Commentary on Mark Thirteen* (London 1957), pp. 59–72, and B. Rigaux, '*ΒΔΕΛΥΓΜΑ ΤΗΣ ΕΡΗΜΩΣΕΩΣ* Mark 13.14, Matt. 24.25', in *Biblica*, vol. XL (1959), pp. 675–83, also contains some interesting remarks. As for the question of the authenticity of the words that Mark puts here into the mouth of Jesus and of the sources drawn on by the Evangelist, we shall venture to pass over them here, since our sole purpose is to ascertain the ideas of the author of Mark, whether or not he invented them or merely passed them on.

[1] It would seem necessary, indeed, to interpret Mark 11.13–14,20–3 in this sense. There is an obvious relationship between the mysterious episode of the barren fig-tree and that of the cleansing of the Temple (11.15–19) which is sandwiched into it. Whatever meaning is to be attributed to Jesus' attitude to the tree (real hunger? symbolic gesture? distorted parable?), it is clear that the curse cast on it and its miraculous effectiveness are designed in Mark to explain the significance of the brutal cleansing of the Temple. Christian exegesis, from Victor of Antioch, the first commentator on Mark whose work we know, repeats many times that they turn the cleansing of the Temple into a prophecy of the ruin of Jerusalem. If we examine the parable of the fig-tree closely, it is suggested, we see that its barrenness represents that of the Temple, whch might still have passed for temporary (ὁ γὰρ καιρὸς οὐκ ἦν σύκων), but which has become manifest and permanent at the time of Jesus' action. It is not a question of destruction, since the dead tree remains standing, but of the end of all hope of reform: the Temple will never produce any fruits again!

But it would seem to be a question of the destruction of the Temple in verses 22–3. The Evangelist uses a saying of Jesus about the power of faith (cf. Matt. 17.20 and Luke 17.6) and, by placing it on the road from Bethany to Jerusalem, gives a precise location to the 'mountain' referred to: the Mount of Olives, it is often said by the commentators and those who claim to locate the eschatological coming of Christ there can only be impostors (13.21–2). Jesus' gesture in purifying the Temple (11.15–16), therefore, does not fore-shadow its reform but preludes its final destruction.

So much fury on the part of a man who accepts the cult of sacrifice is somewhat surprising. Even if it is in line with the thinking of Jesus,[1] it implies the existence, in the community for which the Evangelist is writing, of violent feeling against the Temple of Jerusalem. The climate must have been very far from that of the markedly 'temple-centred' account in Acts 1—5. Were ideas similar to those of the speech of Stephen in Acts 7 (cf. above all Acts 7.44–50) cultivated there? This would seem difficult to deny if we accept M. Simon's con-vincing interpretation of Stephen's ideas about the Temple.[2]

(thus M. J. Lagrange, pp. 299–300; A. E. J. Rawlinson, p. 158; E. Lohmeyer, p. 239, n. 2; C. E. B. Cranfield, *Saint Mark*, p. 361; W. Grundmann, p. 234). This seems very doubtful; it is much more likely that the Evangelist places Jesus on the Mount of Olives, from where he can see both the Dead Sea and Mount Zion and puts into his mouth words relating to the latter, the only one which interests him here. According to him, Jesus said at that time that the day would come when one of the disciples would have faith enough to raze to the ground with a word the hill of the Temple, thus performing a much more amazing action than his own cleansing of the Temple (cf. Matt. 21.21). The unleashing of God's wrath against the Temple thus depends on the faith of Christians—expressed in prayer, Mark hastens to add (11.24–5), to avoid any confusion between this power of faith and a mere magical force. According to Mark, then, Jesus is not shown as the one who would bring about the destruction of the Temple; he is content to announce it as a coming event (13.1–2), as the work of God's wrath (13.14ff.), which the faith of any Christian would make possible (11.22–3). Thus it is explained why Mark charged with bearing false witness the people who accused Jesus of having said that he would destroy and rebuild the Temple himself (14.57–9; cf. 15.29). There is nevertheless a certain difference in tone between these two last-mentioned passages and the texts of chapters 11 and 13. S. G. F. Brandon, *Fall of Jerusalem*, pp. 37–40 and 201–2, is right not to wish to pass over these divergences, even if his conclusions are not entirely satisfying. We shall return to this point below (p. 227).

[1] It is not easy to reconstruct Jesus' ideas on the subject of the Temple. A well-balanced exposition is to be found, for example, in M. Goguel, *Jésus*, 2nd edn (Paris 1950), pp. 325–33.

[2] M. Simon, 'Saint Stephen and the Jerusalem Temple' in *JEH*, vol. II (1951), pp. 127–42; id., *St Stephen and the Hellenists in the Primitive*

In that case, one would expect Mark, like Acts 7.44–50, to contrast the idolatrous cult of the Temple with the legitimate cult following on from that celebrated in the desert in the 'Tabernacle of Witness': a cult reduced to its essence and linked, not to a place fixed once and for all, but to the ever-changing places where the people assembled. We shall see later whether that is indeed the case.[1]

2

IMPLIED CRITICISMS OF CHRISTIANS

By adopting such a decided attitude on the subject of the Temple, the author of Mark was in opposition to a large section of the primitive Church, the majority, perhaps, for whom the sanctuary at Jerusalem had a place in their religious thinking and piety.[2] There is nothing surprising in that, since we have

---

Church (London-New York-Toronto 1958), pp. 50–8. We are hesitant in following this author, however, when he ascribes to Stephen a radically anti-sacrificial attitude (op. cit. pp. 49–50) on the basis of the quotation from Amos 5.25–7 in Acts 7.42–3 and of the absence of any reference in the speech in Acts 7 to non-idolatrous sacrifices. Despite the support of H. J. Schoeps, *Theologie und Geschichte des Judenchristentums* (Tübingen 1949), pp. 221ff., and 442ff., this theory seems to have insufficient foundation: the argument from silence is weak and the quotation from Amos seems designed solely to stress the long history of revolt among the Jews. We continue to think, with F. Overbeck, *Kurze Erklärung der Apostelgeschichte* (Leipzig 1870), p. 111, n. 2, 'that the speaker is objecting to the Temple building and not the Temple cult. This latter . . . he may have seen as subsisting without the idea underlying the building of the Temple of the setting up of an οἶκος θεοῦ. On the other hand, we agree with M. Simon, op. cit., pp. 39–40, as opposed to F. Overbeck, op. cit. pp. 90–5 and E. Haenchen, *Die Apostelgeschichte*, 3rd edn (12th edn of the Krit. exeg. Kommentar), (Göttingen 1959), pp. 238–41 (who incidentally wrongly lists Overbeck among the opponents of his theory, p. 240), when he accepts, with the majority of critics, the existence of a written source for Acts 7.2–50.

[1] Cf. p. 197 below.

[2] In addition to Acts 2—5, which certainly brings us an authentic echo of the positive attitude adopted by the church of Jerusalem to the Temple in the earliest days (E. Trocmé, *Le Livre des Actes et l'histoire*, pp. 102–3 and 194–7), we should recall the very large place occupied by the sanctuary throughout the writing of Luke; cf., for example, H. Conzelmann, *Die Mitte der Zeit, Studien zur Theologie des Lukas*, 3rd edn, pp. 68–71 and 153–4; R. Morgenthaler, *Die lukanische Geschichtsschreibung als Zeugnis: Gestalt und Gehalt der Kunst des Lukas* (Zurich 1949), vol. I, pp. 163ff.; and in the Fourth Gospel, where Jesus is frequently

already noted the independent mind and combative spirit of this innovator vis-à-vis the church tradition and its custodians.[1] But that is an additional reason for asking whether the Evangelist, when he attacks one or other Jewish adversary of Jesus, is not also criticizing certain Christians of his day whose attitude he thinks comparable to that of the opponents in question. This seems to be the case with the two principal groups referred to above, namely the Pharisees and the scribes.

The Pharisees are reproached by the author of Mark, not very violently, with their narrow-minded respectability and the fact that their naive and malicious reactions play into the hands of the scribes, the 'Herodians', and other shrewd people.[2] In addition to the Pharisees who were the contemporaries of Jesus, he is also thinking, as we have seen, of those that the communities for which he is writing may have encountered. He reproves these opponents for their attitude to fasting (2.16ff.) to the Sabbath (2.23ff.; 3.1–6), to ritual purification practices (7.1ff.), to the seeking for signs from heaven (8.11–12), to divorce (10.2ff.) and to the Roman authorities (12.13). Now all these questions had been the subject of controversy within the Christian Church in the course of the half century that followed its foundation. There are definite indications of this, even if we cannot be very certain about the identity of the opposing parties or the significance of their disputes.[3] Although

---

represented in the Temple (2.13–22; 5.14ff.; 7.14—8.59; 10.22–39; 18.20). For it to have played, after its destruction, such an important part in these two thoughtful works, the Temple must long have continued to enjoy the respect and interest of many churches, even among the Gentile-Christian churches which had cut themselves off from Judaism. It will be recalled, too, that Matt. 17.24–7 (the story of the tribute money) seems to have been handed down by a church that still paid taxes to the Temple while knowing it was free not to do so. That is another sign, of a practical order this time, of the great prestige the sanctuary of Jerusalem still enjoyed among many Christians, even after the year 70.

[1] Cf. pp. 40ff. above.
[2] Cf. pp. 88–91 above.
[3] Where fasting is concerned, Mark 2.20 and par. certainly constitute a justification in the eyes of the Evangelists for Christian fasting in the face of the attacks of certain more radical brethren. With regard to the Sabbath, it is enough to cite Col. 2.16, and no doubt Rom. 14.5–6, to show that its observation provoked discussion among Christians.

he does not actually enter into discussion with Christians of other views, the author of Mark states on all these points the ideas he believes to be most consistent with the teaching of Jesus and rejects implicitly the other points of view existing in Christian circles, particularly those descending from, or in sympathy with, the Pharisees.

By relating the conflicts he believed Jesus to have had with the Pharisees, the Evangelist is thus simultaneously combating a Christianity contaminated by rabbinic tradition in the matter of moral teaching and by a somewhat naively apocalyptic eschatology. He reproaches Christians indirectly for their acceptance of the practices and ideas current in Pharisaic Judaism. These are the thrusts of a Gentile Christian at Judaeo-Christianity, it will no doubt be said. A closer examination shows, however, that things are not quite as beautifully simple as that, as we have already seen in connection with the Temple, which Mark condemns although he does not attack the sacrificial cult. It would seem rather that these are the reproaches made by a man who cannot readily be labelled,[1]

The problem of ritual purity is well known to have caused tension among the churches with congregations of mixed Jewish and pagan origin (cf. Gal. 2.11ff., for example). The over-anxious seeking for signs of the end of the world was the cause of many illusions, aberrations, and warnings in the various Christian circles of the day (cf. for example Mark 13.4–6 and par.; Rev. 13.11–18). On the subject of divorce, the change made by Matthew in the *logia* of Jesus (Matt. 5.31–2 and 19.3–9) implies profound divergences between the discipline of the church for which that Gospel was written and the communities for which Mark and Luke were written. As for the attitude of Christians to the Roman authorities, it seems to have been, around the year 70, less uniformly one of obedience than one would think from reading the New Testament, where Paul's anti-revolutionary point of view prevailed. Cf. on this point S. G. F. Brandon, *The Fall of Jerusalem*, whose ideas are highly intelligent, if sometimes carried rather too far.

[1] This we shall endeavour to do later (pp. 248–59). Let it simply be said here that where he is at his most radical on the subject of the Mosaic Law or tradition the author of Mark appears to be reproducing Jesus' actual words (e.g. in 7.9ff. and in 10.2–9). On the other hand, where he adds to an authentic saying or elucidates it, one sometimes has the impression that he is reducing its import somewhat in order to make use of it as an argument in a controversy between Judaeo-christians. Thus he underlines the great radicalism of 2.18–20 by adding the independent *logion* of vv. 21–2 but, when he adds the words ἐν ἐκείνῃ τῇ ἡμέρᾳ at the end of v. 20 he is defending the Christian fast (on Good Friday?

to some Jewish-Christians anxious not to break with their Jewish background, and fearful of drawing the practical conclusions of their faith in Jesus Christ.

It is to this group that the warnings contained in Mark 8.14–21 (a passage where most critics see the hand of the Evangelist especially plainly and where one must therefore expect to find an expression of his personal antipathies or at least those of his Church) are directly addressed.[1] This application of the text to the contemporaries of Mark is the more easily possible since the people with whom Jesus is talking are not specifically designated, even by the collective title of 'disciples', although it is clearly the group that surrounded the Master on the occasion of the multiplication of the loaves (vv. 19–20). The Evangelist uses an authentic saying of Jesus, whose exact meaning escapes us[2] and which he interprets slightly differently from Matthew and Luke[3] in order to denounce the attitude of Christians who behave like Pharisees or 'Herods' towards Jesus. The narrow-mindedness and the unhealthy apocalyptic tastes of some of them, combined with the spiritual flabbiness

every Friday?) against those who believe in more frequent fasting (cf. Matt. 9.15 and Luke 5.35), whereas Jesus was probably only thinking of his disciples' sorrow after he left them. Similarly, the explanations the author adds in 7.17–23 to the foregoing words of Jesus surely have a hellenistic ring; but the last words of v. 19 reduce Jesus' very bold assertions (v. 15) to the mere removal of the distinction between clean and unclean food, that is to say to the level of the (so typically Jewish Christian) vision of Peter in Acts 10.9–16. Again, in Mark 10.10–12 the Evangelist uses an independent *logion* to give to a saying of Jesus with a very general purpose (v. 9) a somewhat restrictive legal interpretation designed apparently to cover cases where the spouse who had not taken the initiative in seeking divorce found himself released from his or her obligations and achieving it thanks to a broad definition of adultery. Here again we may detect a touch of hellenism (equality of sexes in the matter of divorce) but we are some distance away from the elastic and at the same time firm practice recommended by Paul to the non-Jewish Christians (1 Cor. 7.10–16) and closer to the judaizing legalism of Matt. 5.32 and 19.9 (which Mark nevertheless opposes, by not allowing Christians to take the initiative in divorce).

[1] Cf. for example E. Lohmeyer, *Ev. des Mk.*, pp. 157–8; V. Taylor, *St Mark*, pp. 363–8; W. Grundmann, *Ev. nach Mk.*, pp. 162–4.

[2] R. Bultmann, *Gesch. d. syn. Trad.*, pp. 139 and 158.

[3] Matthew 16.12 sees in the 'leaven of the Pharisees and of the Sadducees' (16.6: note the replacement of Herod by a Jewish party) the doctrine of

of others, makes them all too stupid to grasp the most obvious truths (Mark 8.17–18). They all think themselves poor and withdraw into themselves, fearing that they may die of starvation if they venture to share their 'bread' with people from outside. By a slightly rhetorical reminder of the multiplication of the loaves, Mark sweeps away the fears of his Christian brethren and draws their attention to the miraculous powers of Jesus which enable his followers to share everything they have with the crowd and to emerge better off than before (8.19–20). Then, with very striking emphasis, Mark concludes with the words 'How is it that ye do not understand?' (8.21), directed at his own contemporaries at least as much as at those of Jesus.

Apart from the isolated people whose rank prevents them from being really converted (the 'Herods'), the Evangelist is thus attacking here groups of Christians whose vain legalistic scruples, together with a naive messianic belief, prevent them from turning to the mass of the people and admitting to the Church all those who are drawn towards it by the gospel, or who would be so drawn if it were preached to them. It is impossible not to think of certain sectarian aspects of the church of Jerusalem which can be sensed behind Acts 1—5, though Luke introduces there his missionary outlook and his concept of the victorious gospel.[1] Could it be this community, or those to which its tradition was handed down that the author of Mark is attacking here and, on the rebound, in the passages where he brings the Pharisees on to the scene? It is not at all impossible.

Are we to understand that, in the same way, the Evangelist is attacking indirectly the emergent Christian theology of his day when he shows Jesus in conflict with the scribes?[2] It would seem so, on condition that this hypothesis is not pushed too far: more even than the Pharisees, the scribes are for the author of Mark the real adversaries of Jesus.[3] But he seems to delight in drawing attention to certain debates between the Master and

---

these two groups; Luke 12.1 speaks of the Pharisees only and takes 'leaven' to mean 'hypocrisy'.

[1] As we believe we have shown in E. Trocmé, *Le Livre des Actes et l'histoire*, pp. 196–200.

[2] Cf. pp. 94ff. above.

[3] Moreover, Mark, if the special case of Mark 12.28–34 is excepted, does not appear to have known any Christian scribes like those known to Matthew (Matt. 13.52; 23.34; cf. 7.29).

the Jewish scribes because they concern points that have been much discussed in the churches of the first two generations and the views of Jesus are also his own.

In Mark, the scribes sometimes enter into conflict with Jesus over the healings he effects. Leaving out the story related in 2.1–12, where the dispute is not concerned with the healing and behind which one can discern nothing which could provoke a discussion among Christians,[1] we come to the violent dialogue of 3.22–30, where Jesus appears, not as an occasional wonder-worker, but as a very active exorcizer. Otherwise, the accusation of being possessed by Beelzebub (v. 22) would be difficult to explain, especially in the forceful sense imposed by the proximity of ἐξέστη in v. 21 and the brief commentary in v. 30. The first Christians were not as enterprising in this direction. Apart from Peter,[2] the Book of Acts presents as exorcizers only Philip (8.7) and Paul (16.16–18; 19.12–16). Moreover, as we saw earlier,[3] the miracle stories made a rather late appearance in the 'tradition', at the instigation of the author of Mark. One is thus led to suppose that the latter belonged to a group more addicted to miracle-working than the first church of Jerusalem. In the author's eyes, the warning in Mark 3.29 was addressed just as much to certain Christians who were hostile to a constant quest for healings as to the Jewish non-believers. For him, blasphemy against the Holy Ghost is contrasted not with blasphemy against the Son of Man (Matt. 12.31–2; Luke 12.10), which would confine it to the past, but with all other kinds of blasphemy. Thus, whoever accuses a Christian exorcist moved by the Holy Spirit of being moved by the Devil is doomed to perdition, like the calumniators of the exorcizer Jesus. They that have ears to hear, let them hear!—even in the Church.

The existence of a group of Christians among whom healings were rare and who were somewhat despised by the author of Mark is confirmed by several features of the curious story in

---

[1] But where there is perhaps an effort to justify the miracle-working of Jesus in the face of Jewish critics of the type recorded in Mark 3.22.

[2] In Acts 5.16. Even so, the reference is in a summary which is certainly deliberately embellished by Luke and has little historical value. Peter was known as a healer much more than as an exorcizer (Acts 3.1ff.; 9.32–43).

[3] Cf. pp. 45–54 above.

Mark 9.14–29. The Evangelist stresses here the inability of the disciples (Peter, James, and John excepted) to perform an exorcism (vv. 18, 28). In the absence of their Master, who had gone up into the mountain of the transfiguration, these men had been unable to do anything for the patient brought to them—they had succeeded only in entering into a discussion with the scribes (v. 14), a surprising detail that Matthew (17.14) and Luke (9.37) left out. Clearly, the author of Mark supposes that they were discussing the legitimacy of exorcism, or its methods. At the end of the same story, Mark differs again from the other two synoptic Gospels by a much more practical conclusion than theirs (v. 29) but which, nevertheless, is far from clear.[1] The only plausible way of explaining this saying on the subject of prayer is to compare it to the discussion with the scribes in verse 14 and to see in it an editorial touch[2] directed against Christians more concerned to establish in the eyes of Judaism the legitimacy of the exorcisms performed by Jesus or of all other exorcisms performed in Jesus' name than to respond to the urgent appeals made to them for healings that Jesus was no longer there to perform. It is an invitation to follow by prayer in the footsteps of Jesus the healer rather than waste time in vain discussions. If the Church were to disregard this exhortation, it would be placing itself in as ridiculous a situation as the disciples Jesus found when he came down from the mountain of the transfiguration; it would deserve the exclamation of Jesus in 9.19.

Another subject of dispute between Jesus and the scribes in Mark is that of ritual purity, so keenly discussed by Christians in apostolic times (cf. Acts 10.1—11.18; Gal. 2.11ff.). Chapter 7 of Mark refers to the risk of impurity incurred in the eyes of the scribes and the Pharisees by those of the disciples who neglected the ablutions practised before eating by the most

---

[1] E. Lohmeyer, *Ev. des Markus*, pp. 189–90, rightly stresses that prayer is not an uncommon healer's recipe, when it is a case of healing an especially serious disease. He concludes that Jesus' reply is deliberately obscure and aims at concealing his occult power. This is an elegant way out of a difficulty, but still not a very satisfying one.

[2] E. Lohmeyer, op. cit., p. 189, notes that it is not the usual final 'chorus' to miracle stories but an intimate talk between Jesus and his disciples, comparable to those which often follow his public statements.

zealous Jews.[1] He also ascribes to Jesus a devastating reply (vv. 6–8) of which the essential part is a quotation from Isaiah interpreted as an irrevocable condemnation of 'the commandments of men' on which the partisans of ritual ablutions relied.[2]

---

[1] The construction of 7.2 is strange and was always thought to be so, if one can judge by the variant in codex Alexandrinus, Bezae, purpureus, Freerianus, etc. (τινάς ... ἐσθίοντας instead of τινάς ... ὅτι ... ἐσθίουσιν). Here we have a case of prolepsis of the subject of the noun clause concerning which it matters little whether it is a semitism (as, after J. Wellhausen, with suitable qualifications, several specialists in the language of the Gospels would have us believe, among them M. Black, *An Aramaic Approach to the Gospels and Acts*, 2nd edn, pp. 36–8), or not (Blass–Debrunner, *Grammatik*, p. 305). What is important is to translate the expression correctly, not as 'Seeing certain disciples eating' or 'who were eating', as most translators and commentators erroneously do, thus introducing again the rejected variant and accentuating the fortuitous character of the observation by the Pharisees and the scribes, but by 'Seeing that certain of the disciples ate' (with J. Weiss, *Die Schriften des N.T.*, 2nd edn (Göttingen 1907), vol. I, p. 133; *la Version Synodale*; A. E. J. Rawlinson, *St Mark*, p. 91; B. H. Branscomb, *Gospel of Mark*, p. 119. E. Lohmeyer gives a literal translation fairly similar to this in his *Ev. des Mk.* ad loc.). This second translation has the advantage of stressing, as does Mark himself, that the disciples concerned were in the habit of eating with soiled hands and that their opponents had been able to observe them at their leisure. If it were a chance occurrence, there would be no gathering of scribes and Pharisees come from a distance (v. 1); Mark would not use the plural to say that the disciples ate their bread (v. 2); that suggests several meals, since the normal expression is in the singular (v. 5); the accusers would not assert that the disciples περιπατοῦσιν incorrectly, which would imply that their whole lives were lived in disregard of the accepted moral standards.

Since there is the question of permanent behaviour, the τινὲς τῶν μαθητῶν of v. 2 cannot be the few men encountered by chance by the opponents of Jesus; *these are those of the disciples who have rejected tradition*, the group of the emancipated. The formulation of the question put to Jesus in v. 5 has made no change in the situation, in spite of what Lagrange says in his *Ev. Marc*, 7th edn, p. 79; he does not wish to recognize that v. 2 introduces a distinction between the disciples of Jesus. The impression of v. 5 cannot cancel out the precision of v. 2, which it does not contradict in the least.

[2] The text of Isaiah to which Jesus is referring is Isa. 29.13, quoted in a slightly corrupt form, similar to that of the Septuagint version. This form is more suited to the context of the original oracle but it would be going too far to assert that the passage was inserted by the Evangelist, since the Hebrew, with its reference to the cult 'of the lips', was also suited to another text denouncing the attachment of importance to the

In order to defend the hot heads among his disciples, the Master does not seek to excuse them, as he does in Mark 2.23ff., in order to save all his followers from an attack of this kind. He asserts loudly that his followers are faithful to God's law, which their critics on the other hand are breaking seriously by clinging to 'tradition'. Even if this scene is historical,[1] it is certain that the Evangelist when writing it was thinking of the debates on this point between certain Christian churches and the Jewish upholders of the oral Law, but also of the controversies that had sometimes raged between Christians in this matter of ritual purity. To his brethren in the faith still clinging to their respect for tradition on this point, the Evangelist replies that the Master condemns them. The harshness of this attack shows the depth of his animosity against these conservatives and their ideas.

In 2.15–17, Mark broaches the question of uncleanness contracted by partaking of meals with people living on the fringe of the Law. There again the scribes reprove Jesus and his disciples for their neglect of ritual cleanliness. Here too one cannot help feeling that the Evangelist is thinking of the attacks on the Palestinian church launched by certain Jews and of the disputes between Christians on the subject of the attitude to adopt towards eating with Gentiles. A curious little feature, moreover, seems to confirm that interpretation: the reference in 2.15 to the presence of numerous disciples who followed

---

purity of food one is about to consume. What is more likely is that the author of Mark added to a very brief quotation from Isa. 29.13 (attributed traditionally to Jesus and faithfully modelled in 7.6 on the Hebrew), with the help of a phrase which formed the usual continuation in Greek of Isa. 29.13. Indeed this phrase was being used separately in the Greek-speaking churches from the first generation in order to describe the taboos regarding food and the other rules of ritual purity (cf. Col. 2.22). In addition, it seemed to give a definition of the 'early tradition' (ἐντάλματα ἀνθρώπων) and its introduction by the Evangelist following the half-verse quoted from Isaiah was very natural.

[1] As we think with the majority of critics, despite the arguments to the contrary evolved by R. Bultmann, *Gesch. d. syn. Tradition*, pp. 15–16, who nevertheless admits the Palestinian origin of the text. Of his ideas we can adopt that of a possible link between this story and the controversies carried on in or by the Palestinian church on the subject of the relations between the Law and the tradition.

Jesus. This is the first time that the word μαθητής is used and
that we are given the idea of a large group of people accompanying Jesus.[1] A more skilful writer might have chosen a less
surprising place to introduce this word and this idea. But
however clumsily it is done, the Evangelist's choice of a passage
concerning a meal shared with 'sinners' is significant. It is
designed to stress the fact that Jesus did not act alone and that
his disciples, from this time on, acquired with him their habit
of sharing meals with all kinds of people in order to facilitate
the Master's call to them (v. 17). This attitude is the direct
opposite of that of certain Palestinian Christians and in
particular of the people 'that came from James' (Gal. 2.12).
By putting it forward, the author of Mark is thus contesting
indirectly the views of such Christians as these, whose presence
we can feel behind the persons of the 'scribes of the Pharisees'
referred to in v. 16.

Lastly, the opposition between Jesus and the scribes, in Mark,
is sometimes set in the context of eschatological and messianic
expectation. In these passages too we see the Evangelist's
hostility rebound from the Jewish doctors on to certain Christian circles he abhorred. This transfer is not obvious in 9.11-13,
where Jesus, in reply to a question by Peter, James, and John
referring to a doctrine taught by the scribes, identifies, in rather
mysterious terms, John the Baptist with Elijah *redivivus* as
announced in Mal. 4.5-6 (LXX 3.23-4). It is nevertheless
present in this text if we can trust to two indications. The first
concerns the identification of John the Baptist with Elijah.
The views of the Christians of the day on this point were indeed

---

[1] It is our belief, and that of most recent commentators (thus Rawlinson,
Lohmeyer, V. Taylor, Grundmann, Cranfield, ad. loc.) that the proper
text is that of B and that the words ἦσαν γὰρ πολλοί, καὶ ἠκολούθουν αὐτῷ at
the end of v. 15 apply to the disciples who are mentioned just before.
The καὶ here is perhaps the equivalent of a relative pronoun (H. Pernot,
Etudes sur la langue des évangiles (Paris 1927), p. 196. One can therefore
translate, as the Jerusalem Bible does: 'for there were many who
followed him'. But it is wiser probably to translate literally: 'for these
were numerous and followed him'. That translation preserves better
the meaning of ἀκολουθεῖν, which does not signify only that the disciples
had gathered around Jesus but more specifically that they followed him
everywhere and conducted themselves as he did (cf. G. Kittel, art.
ἀκολουθέω in *TWNT*, vol. I, pp. 213-15).

far from being unanimous: 'Johannine' circles were categorically opposed to this identification (cf. John 1.21); in the
church for which Matthew was written the idea was favoured,
although not imposed on those who did not accept it;[1] elsewhere certain people, among whom there may have been
disciples of Jesus, preferred to reserve for him the honour of
being Elijah *redivivus*.[2] By introducing a *logion* where Jesus
identifies John the Baptist with this eschatological personage,
Mark is thus contradicting certain Christians as well as criticizing the spiritual blindness of the scribes, whose thinking is
imprisoned in a too rigid apocalyptic framework. There would
perhaps be no cause for comparing the two groups the Evangelist is opposing here, were it not for a second indication that
encourages us to do so. Mark puts the doctrine of the scribes
concerning Elijah *redivivus* into the mouths of Peter, James, and
John, whose inability to understand Jesus' teaching he has just
stressed (9.10; cf. 8.32 and 9.5–6), and suggests that the three
disciples had sought in Jewish speculations an argument with
which to contradict their Master. It is as though the author of
Mark wished to insinuate that in paying too much attention to
the ideas of the γραμματεῖς, certain Christians were deviating
from the real teaching of Jesus.

In Mark 12.35–7, the Evangelist must certainly have been
thinking of some group of his Christian brethren when he relates Jesus' sharp attack on a messianic idea attributed to the
scribes—that of the Messiah, Son of David.[3] Indeed the Davidic

---

[1] This would seem to be the meaning to be attributed to Matt. 11.15,
with its curious restriction: εἰ θέλετε δέξασθαι . . . . An authentic *logion*
must have been qualified in this way, in a church that accepted its
teaching, out of regard for the reservations of certain of the members
of that church about the idea it expressed.

[2] Cf. Mark 6.15 and par.; Mark 8.28 and par. We have discussed these
two texts in pp. 57–8 above.

[3] The arguments we shall advance in support of this idea are further
strengthened if it be accepted, as suggested in pp. 34–36 and 96–98
above, that the author of Mark added this *logion* to a collection of
controversies he had received from the church tradition in order to
prevent this little set of sayings from appearing too conciliatory,
especially towards the scribes. By accentuating the rather timid anti-
judaism of this collection, the Evangelist is showing his disagreement
with the communities and people who had shaped the tradition and is
accusing them implicitly of collusion with the scribes.

descent of Jesus was accepted by the very earliest Church[1]
and no doubt corresponded to a family tradition whose
historical authenticity is far from certain but which must have
been unchallenged at the time.[2] In reproducing this *logion*,[3]

[1] Cf. the widespread occurrence of this idea in the books of the New
Testament, which have sometimes received it from earlier church
tradition: this is surely the case with Rom. 1.3, which is certainly
quoting a very early christological confession (O. Michel, *Der Brief an
die Römer* (Göttingen 1955), pp. 30–1; it is no doubt also the case where
the insertion of David in the genealogies of Matt. 1.1–17 and Luke
3.23–38 is concerned. The most convincing argument is that drawn
from the absolutely general use, from the earliest Christian times, of
the title of 'Christ' to designate Jesus—indeed in Paul it has almost
become a proper name, very often joined to the name of Jesus as a sort
of personal appellation and replaced as a title by κύριος. The Old
Testament contains only one text that quite distinctly identifies the
Anointed with the House of David (Ps. 89.20ff.), but two texts from
around the Christian era show that at that time it was common to call
the 'Messiah' the Davidic King who was expected to come at the end
of the world: an Essene text (IV Q. Ben. Patr., 1. 3–4) commenting on
Gen. 49.10 and a Pharisaic text (Pss. Solomon, 17.23–36) inspired by
Isa. 11 and Isa. 49 (cf. M. A. Chevallier, *L'Esprit et le Messie dans le Bas
Judaisme et le Nouveau Testament* (Paris 1958), pp. 12ff.). Considering the
growing interpenetration at that time of the various traditional eschato-
logies (of which the most striking example is the 'messianism' of Qumran: cf. A. S. Van der Woude, *Die messianischen Vorstellungen der Gemeinde
von Qumran* (Assen 1957)), it is legitimate to think that in calling their
humble Master 'Christ', rather than giving him a title more suited
to his person, such as 'Prophet' or 'Servant', the founders of the
Christian Church must have considered his Davidic descent as established beyond question. Otherwise, since Jesus, as a layman, could not
in any case be accepted as a 'Messiah of Aaron', another title would
surely have prevailed over that of 'Messiah'.

[2] Cf. the pertinent remarks on this subject by O. Cullmann, *Christologie
du Nouveau Testament* (Neuchâtel-Paris 1958), pp. 110–12.

[3] Which we believe to be authentic, despite the objections put forward to
this theory by certain critics, such as W. Bousset, *Kyrios Christos*, 3rd
edn (Göttingen 1926), p. 43; R. Bultmann, *Gesch. d. syn. Trad.*, pp.
144–6; B. H. Branscomb, *Gospel of Mark*, pp. 224–5. It will be noted
that J. Weiss, *Die Schriften des N.T.*, vol. I, 3rd edn (Göttingen 1917),
p. 189, is not among these objectors (despite what V. Taylor says,
St Mark, p. 493), and that many commentators hesitate to pronounce
definitely against its authenticity: thus A. Loisy, *L'évangile selon Marc*,
p. 358; E. Klostermann, *Das Markusevangelium*, 3rd edn (Tübingen
1936), p. 129; C. G. Montefiore, *The Synoptic Gospels*, 2nd edn (London

the author of Mark was thus consciously contradicting an idea derived from the Christian communities and very probably used by them for apologetic purposes in arguing with the Jewish theologians who denied that Jesus was the Messiah. Rather than endeavouring awkwardly to prove to the scribes that Jesus, in spite of certain appearances, was indeed the Christ, since he descended from David, he preferred, as Jesus did himself, to denounce the false learning of these self-styled 'doctors' with no real knowledge of the Scriptures. In this way the Evangelist was dissociating himself, not from a naive faith in the 'Son of David',[1] but from the apologetic subtleties derived from it by certain spokesmen of the Christian community who were far too exclusively concerned for his liking with defending the new faith vis-à-vis the intellectual élite of Judaism.

1927), vol. I, pp. 288–9. On the other hand, J. Wellhausen, *Einleitung in die drei ersten Evangelien* (Berlin 1905), p. 93; A. E. J. Rawlinson, *St Mark*, pp. 173–5; E. Lohmeyer, *Das Evang. des Mk.*, pp. 262–3; V. Taylor, *St Mark*, pp. 490–3; C. E. B. Cranfield, *St Mark*, pp. 380–3; W. Grundmann, *Ev. nach Mk.*, pp. 253–5, bring telling arguments to support the authenticity of this *logion*.

The most convincing of these arguments are the following: 1. If it were not authentic, it could only have been invented by an erring group of Christians who rejected the idea of the Davidic descent of Jesus (in the physical or legal sense) and whose spokesman Mark would need to have been; but Mark does not seem to wish to argue about the Davidic descent of Jesus (10.48–9; 11.10); he is attacking the scribes and, through them, certain Christians and their behaviour. 2. The style of this text, so concise yet pregnant with meaning, is not at all that of Christian polemic or teaching, which are much more explicit; on the contrary, it bears the mark of Jesus himself (cf. Luke 7.22–3, for example).

[1] On the contrary, since Mark relates with some gratification the incident of the blind beggar who welcomed Jesus as he went out of Jericho (10.46–52), calling him 'Son of David', and the cries of the crowd as they strewed branches of trees in the path of Jesus and proclaimed 'the kingdom of our father David', which the entry of Jesus into Jerusalem was bringing closer (11.10). Perhaps he saw in the title of 'Son of David' given to Jesus a Judaean habit that only became dangerous when it was made the subject of elaborate theological argument. The theory of E. Lohmeyer, *Gottesknecht u. Davidsohn* (1945), (Symbolae Bibl. Upsal. vol. 5), pp. 6ff., who seeks the origin of this title in the christology of the Galilean Church seems untenable.

3
EXPLICIT CRITICISMS OF CHRISTIANS

The author of Mark displays the same reserve, moreover, in regard to any christological speculation likely to turn the leaders of the Churches aside from their real task, which he sees above all as missionary and pastoral.[1] This can be sensed in several of the passages where Jesus is speaking to his disciples and the scribes do not play the same part as in those texts we have just discussed. For example, the warning against 'false Christs' given by Jesus in 13.5–6,21–3 is directed not so much at the simple faithful as at Christians holding leading positions in the community, at the 'porters', commanded to watch at the door (13.33–7) and who may seek to add to the teaching of Jesus himself about the coming of the Son of Man (13.23,31) or to prepare the fine confession of faith that they and their brethren will make to their persecutors, rather than relying solely on the instant help of the Holy Ghost (13.11). It is definitely against the elaboration of a christology and an eschatology designed to serve as guarantees for the community that Jesus, according to Mark, is warning his most intimate disciples (13.3), condemning it as a source of error and inaction.[2]

In rather the same way we see Jesus, in Mark 9.38–41, warning his disciples against the temptation to build up for their own benefit a christological monopoly that would lessen the influence and spread of the Christian community and, worse still, keep certain 'little ones' from salvation (9.42). The discussion centres indeed in these verses on the use of the name of Jesus by those who have not known the Master and been

---

[1] We shall see later (pp. 149ff.) that the Evangelist has a certain distrust of any too elaborate christology and favours a christology of awe and active fidelity.

[2] With F. Busch, *Zum Verständnis der synoptischen Eschatologie, Markus 13 neu untersucht* (Gütersloh 1938); E. Lohmeyer, *Ev. des Mk.*, pp. 285–7; R. H. Lightfoot, *Gospel Message of St Mark*, pp. 48ff.; W. Marxsen, *Der Ev. Markus* (Göttingen 1956), pp. 101–28, and many others, we believe that it is important to recognize the hand of the Evangelist in the arrangement of the material that went into this chapter 13, whatever one may think of its likely sources. Consequently we must see in this chapter as a whole a message which is essentially that of the rest of Mark and has a certain coherence, but which does not exhaust the meaning of the separate *logia* that have gone into its making.

taught by him and who may consequently 'speak evil' of him (cf. 1 Cor. 12.3). As they are alone in knowing and confessing Jesus, the disciples also claim the exclusive right to speak in public in his name. The Master, on the contrary, firmly stresses the decisive importance of *action* inspired by faith in him, however rudimentary that faith may be (vv. 39–41): such action, whether it be a successful healing[1] or a simple kindness, is sufficient guarantee against the abuses that the disciples, in their exclusive orthodoxy, fear. The real danger lies in the attitude of these defenders of Jesus' honour. They are in danger of condemning the humble faithful and hence themselves to eternal damnation (v. 42). A resounding lesson in christological liberalism, which the author of Mark was certainly directing at adversaries in high places in the churches of his day![2]

Lastly, the same intention would seem to underly the celebrated passage of Mark 8.27—9.1. We have already said[3] why we believe, with R. Bultmann, that the Evangelist omitted the conclusion of a 'scholastic dialogue' in which Peter's confession was followed by the Master's praise addressed to his good disciple (cf. Matt. 16.17–19). What follows this amputated dialogue in Mark is a highly artificial collection of *logia* whose arrangement clearly reveals the underlying intention. The 'scholastic dialogue' used by the author of Mark was plainly seeking to state the correct christology as opposed to various questionable definitions of the person of Jesus. In accordance with current doctrine among the first generation of Christians,[4]

---

[1] It is a miracle performed which, according to Mark, guarantees the faith of the healer. A person who used the name of Jesus simply as a magic formula would suffer the unhappy fate of the sons of Sceva, related maliciously in Acts 19.13–16.

[2] Many commentators agree in recognizing the pre-Marcan nature of the composite collection of *logia* on which Mark 9.33–50 is based, in particular in verses 38–42 (cf. for example V. Taylor, *St Mark*, pp. 401ff., in particular pp. 408–10; cf. also p. 38, n. 1 above). But that does not preclude a certain amount of retouching by the author of Mark who wished to turn some of these sayings to his own ends. In any case, he preserved the collection, whereas Matthew (18.1–9) left out the passage contained in Mark 9.38–41 and Luke (9.46–50) left out everything after Mark 9.40. Thus these two Evangelists omitted the most striking feature of Mark's text, namely the suggestive juxtaposition of Mark 9.38–41 and Mark 9.42, which accentuates the severity of Jesus' reply to John.

[3] Cf. pp. 57–59 above.   [4] Cf. p. 118, n. 1 above.

it gave preference to the title of 'Christ', whose adaptability was well suited to the striking originality of the ministry of the Nazarene. The author of Mark made no attempt to challenge this original basic choice,[1] which dated no doubt from before the crucifixion.[2] He simply sought, by substituting other *logia* for the original ending of the 'scholastic dialogue', to show the inadequacies and dangers of an attitude centred on defending this christological orthodoxy and seeking above all to keep the ear of those experts in messianic doctrine, the Jewish authorities.

The author of Mark stresses in the first place that the recognition of Jesus as the Messiah constitutes only one part of the 'gospel', which must be preached in its entirety. The disciples are not entitled to speak of their Master without saying also that he was rejected by the Jerusalem authorities and put to death, and then rose again.[3] If they were to disobey

---

[1] Mark 1.1 shows plainly, if there were need to do so, that the author believes in Jesus 'Christ' and wishes to make it clear.

[2] We see no convincing reason to reject the historicity of the essential substance of the scene related in Mark 8.27–9, in spite of the arguments of R. Bultmann, *Gesch. d. syn. Trad.*, pp. 275–8, whom, moreover, few critics follow on this point. There are three indications in favour of its historicity: the reference to Caesarea Philippi, which there could be no reason to invent; the fact that the three titles with which that of 'Christ' is contrasted could scarcely have been applied to Jesus after he had been put to death, since they would have lost all their point (Who would be interested in spirits of the dead who died again?); lastly, the disciple's belief in Jesus as the Messiah before the end of his life on earth is implied in the episode in Mark 10.35–40, where the naive request of the sons of Zebedee has every chance of being historical, considering its down-to-earth realism and the humility of Jesus' reply (10.40; cf. 13.32).

[3] This, we believe, is the meaning of Mark 8.30 and of the first words of v. 32, with which this verse should be contrasted (μηδενὶ λέγωσιν . . . παρρησίᾳ τὸν λόγον ἐλάλει). It may be an authentic saying of Jesus but it does not constitute a reply to Peter's confession, as we have seen. It therefore seems difficult to make it one of the grounds for ascribing to Jesus a strong repugnance (A. Merx, *Die vier kanonischen Evangelien nach ihrem ältesten bekannten Text* . . . (Berlin 1897–1911), vol. 11.2, pp. 81–90; J. Héring, *Le Royaume de Dieu et sa venue*, 2nd edn (Neuchâtel 1959), pp. 122–7), or a distinct reserve (O. Cullmann, *Christologie du N.T.*, pp. 105–7) where the title of Messiah is concerned. In fact Mark 8.30 is linked above all to v. 31 and may have been originally, with it, the recollection of a permanent ban by Jesus during his life on earth on any

this command, they would prove that they were ashamed of Jesus and his teaching (Mark 8.38). Besides, the Evangelist adds, they would be showing that their desire was above all to win the good graces of the 'world' (8.36–8), that they are afraid to risk their lives for him who died in obedience to God (8.34–5), in short that in their too human cowardice they remain the tools of Satan (8.33). The violence of this collection of sayings of Jesus derives to a large extent from the way in which the author has grouped and presented the materials on which he drew.[1] It would therefore seem obvious here that he was attacking Christians whose concept of the Christian mission revolted him and whom he believed guilty of not preaching the whole of the gospel and being too cautious in speaking of the fate that Jesus suffered.

The idea is roughly the same and the editorial processes comparable in the passage immediately following (Mark 9.2–13). To an episode drawn from tradition,[2] in which certain

---

tendency by the disciples to add to the preaching of the coming of the Kingdom and of repentance (1.14–15; 6.12) any statements whatsoever about the person of their Master, whose real role they did not yet know. It is the author of Mark who joined this passage to 8.27–9 and followed it by the first words of v. 32, which assimilates the words of Jesus to the 'whole Gospel'. He has thus reduced 8.30 to a specific prohibition of christological preaching too concerned with scriptural demonstration or verbal exactitude, contrasting it with the preaching of the 'whole word', which laid great emphasis on the passion (cf. the pertinent remarks on the subject of this contrast by E. Percy, *Die Botschaft Jesu, eine traditionskritische und exegetische Untersuchung* (Lund 1953), pp. 227–31 and 299, from whom we differ however on many points in the analysis of this text.

[1] Cf. the preceding note on the subject of vv. 27–32a. It is moreover probable, considering the clumsiness of the beginning of v. 33, that the Evangelist himself inserted the words καὶ ἰδὼν τοὺς μαθητάς in order to underline the public nature of the rebuke to Peter. It was again the author who joined vv. 34ff. to those preceding them, thus suggesting a comparison between the bad preaching of the disciples and the denials of cowards seeking to escape martyrdom. It was he, lastly, who joined 9.1 to 8.34–8 and in so doing gave this obscure *logion* a mercilessly ironic twist: 'Among those here present there are cowards who would never be willing to die before the end of the world, who avoid taking risks so that they may be alive to see the great Day come!' The disciples these words were directed at could scarcely have been spoken to more harshly.

[2] Cf. pp. 56–7 above.

disciples received an extraordinary revelation, the Evangelist adds a command to tell nobody (9.9), followed by a picture of the sufferings and resurrection of the Son of Man composed of several separate *logia* (9.10–13). Here again it is much less a question of the institution of a 'messianic secret' which has been far too much discussed in the past sixty years[1] than of a

---

[1] The celebrated book by W. Wrede, *Das Messiasgeheimnis* . . . is an interesting attempt to elucidate the ideas of the author of Mark in the matter of christology and the way they influenced his literary work on the traditional material he used, which did not contain them. But it rests on a postulate that can only be described as absurd, namely that in Mark, wherever Jesus enjoins silence on anybody (demon, sick person, disciple) about any subject, whenever he teaches his disciples in private, whenever his disciples fail to understand, it is an indication of the author's own literary work, designed to impose on rebellious sources the strict theory that Jesus concealed throughout his life that he was the Messiah. In fact all these cases are very different from one another: in some places the passages are drawn from tradition, in others they are editorial notes; in some episodes the silence imposed is a question of the technique of the healer, in others it is a matter of the aim of the mission; some again simply reflect the presence of a group of disciples around Jesus and some are connected with the mystery surrounding the person of the Messiah. We must therefore beware of trying to fit all this heterogeneous material into a single theory—even a more cautious one than that of Wrede. This seems sufficient reason for rejecting the formula of M. Dibelius, *Formgeschichte d. Evang.*, p. 232 ('Mark . . . a book of secret epiphanies'), the theory of H. J. Ebeling, *Das Messiasgeheimnis und die Botschaft des Marcus-Evangelisten* (Berlin 1939): the healings, even accompanied by commands for silence, serve to reveal the victorious lordship of Jesus, whereas men's lack of understanding, the theory of the parables and the injunctions of 8.30 and 9.9 evoke the mystery of the person of the Revealer: it is not very clear, but the author gives a good synopsis in pp. 1–113 of his book of the discussion provoked around 1939 by Wrede's ideas; and that of E. Percy, *Die Botschaft Jesu*, pp. 271–99 and J. B. Tyson, 'The Blindness of the Disciples in Mark', in *JBL*, LXXX (1961), pp. 261ff.: the Messianic secret superimposes on an existing messianic tradition surrounding the earthly Jesus a more Pauline interpretation of the dead and risen Christ. The same objection can be made to hypotheses like that of V. Taylor, *St Mark*, pp. 122–4 (who traces the messianic secret he sees everywhere in Mark to Jesus himself) or of E. Sjöberg, *Der verborgene Menschensohn in den Evangelien* (Lund 1955): a Marcan theory in part, the messianic secret is nevertheless implied in the life of Jesus before the passion; it is lifted as the passion story progresses to reveal in him the hidden Son of Man, the key to God's plan of salvation. We prefer, for our part, to explain separately or in small groups texts as different as

reminder of the incomplete and outmoded character of any christology that left aside the suffering, death, and resurrection of Jesus and passed over the deadly part played in this tragedy by the Jewish authorities, represented here by the scribes. Once again the author of Mark is directing sharp thrusts at certain leaders of the Church of his day, whom he accuses of wasting their time in vain contemplation (9.5–6) instead of facing the real problems posed for the Christian community by its encounter with people from outside (9.14ff.).

The church leaders thus attacked are easy to identify since, in each of the episodes we have just cited, the disciple or disciples reprimanded by Jesus are named and they are all personages relatively well known in the early days of the Christian community: Peter (Mark 8.29,32,33; 9.2,5–6; 13.3), John (9.2,38; 13.3), James (9.2 and 13.3) and Andrew (13.3). True the words spoken by Jesus in these few texts are not addressed to these four alone; the 'disciples' (8.27–31,33,34; 9.14), 'the Twelve' (9.35), 'the crowd' (8.34; 9.14), 'all' (13.37) are also mentioned among the Master's hearers, or at least as those to whom his teaching must finally be brought. On the other hand it might be claimed that the three or four chief disciples are cited here merely for the purposes of historicity, out of mechanical respect for tradition or simply as typical of certain spiritual attitudes. But these explanations, while partially sound, leave no room for the author's intervention and the intentions he might have had. Can we see his hand in the distribution and presentation of the references to the principal disciples in his Gospel (including those we have not yet mentioned)? It would seem so, and also that in these passages one can sense a distinct reserve on the part of the author of Mark towards these illustrious founders of the Church, whose importance he nevertheless does not contest.

This mixture of deference and reserve is perceptible above all in the way in which the author of Mark speaks of Simon Peter. He recognizes the decisive part played by this disciple throughout the ministry of Jesus. Of all the people mentioned

those Wrede grouped together: hence our explanation of Mark 9.2–13 by comparison with only one other passage, Mark 8.27ff.

in the Gospel it is Peter who is mentioned most often, if we except Jesus;[1] he is frequently mentioned alone and almost always first when he is in company with other disciples;[2] he occupies a specially important place in several essential passages in Mark: the second half of chap. 1 (beginning of Jesus' public ministry), the end of chap. 8 and the beginning of chap. 9 (discourse at Caesarea Philippi and the transfiguration) and lastly the second half of chap. 14 (at Gethsemane and in the courtyard of the High Priest). It is easy to understand, therefore, that serious critics refuse to countenance any suggestion of 'anti-petrinism' on the part of Mark.[3]

And yet, we find in Mark a tendency to detract from the pre-eminence tradition accorded to Peter and to emphasize certain details of a nature to dim a little of the reputation of the 'Prince of the Apostles'—details which the other synoptic Gospels pass over or avoid underlining. True, there is no detracting from the special role of Peter in the Passion story, but the reputation of the man who fell asleep at Gethsemane when Jesus had told him to keep watch, then denied his master in the court-yard of the High Priest does not emerge enhanced from this long series of defections. On the other hand, it is clear that in chapters 1—13 the author of Mark is endeavouring to suggest the existence of a small group of intimate disciples rather than to stress the pre-eminence of Peter. A curious detail that has not always been pointed out is that he mentions

[1] Peter's name is mentioned nineteen times in Mark (3.16; 5.37; 8.29,32, 33; 9.2,5; 10.28; 11.21; 13.3; 14.29,33,37,54,66,67,70,72; 16.7) as compared with twenty-three times in Matthew and eighteen in Luke: in addition, Peter is mentioned seven times under the name of Simon (1.16,16,29,30,36; 3.16; 14.37), which occurs five times in Matthew and twelve times in Luke. One can say, then, that considering the length of the three Gospels, Mark mentions the Prince of the Apostles slightly more often than Matthew and Luke and that Peter is the person most on the scene, since John the Baptist, who comes next in order, is mentioned by name only sixteen times.

[2] The most striking example of the priority of Peter is his presence at the head of the list of the 'Twelve' (3.16). The only exceptions to this rule are to be found in 8.33 and 16.7, where the disciples are mentioned before Peter but where the effect is rather one of bringing out the latter's exceptional role.

[3] This is the case with M. Goguel, *L'Eglise primitive* (Paris 1947), p. 191 and with O. Cullmann, *Saint Pierre*, pp. 19–20.

Andrew, the brother of Simon, and the two sons of Zebedee much more often than Matthew and Luke do,[1] which has the effect of making Peter less important in relation to the other disciples than is the case in the other two Gospels.[2] This may be an editorial touch reflecting the Evangelist's intentions; and if so it would reveal a certain reserve in regard to Peter, or else some mechanical reproduction of the traditional material which would mean that the author of Mark was not specially interested in the primacy of Peter[3]—an idea which, on the contrary, Matthew and Luke are prepared to accept, leaving out most of the references to Andrew, James, and John, who have lost interest for them. It is difficult to choose between these two hypotheses, which are almost equally probable.[4]

---

[1] Mark mentions Andrew four times (1.16,29; 3.18; 13.3), whereas he is mentioned only twice in Matthew and once in Luke; he mentions ten times James, son of Zebedee, (1.19,29; 3.17,17; 5.37; 9.2; 10.35,41; 13.3; 14.33), who is mentioned three times in Matthew and five in Luke; ten times also John, son of Zebedee (1.19,29; 3.17; 5.37; 9.2,38; 10.35,41; 13.3; 14.33), who is mentioned three times in Matthew and seven times in Luke.

[2] In Matthew the two names of Peter are mentioned twenty-eight times in all, whereas Andrew is mentioned twice, James the son of Zebedee three times, John the son of Zebedee also three times and Judas five times. In Luke we find a total of thirty references to Peter by name, whereas Andrew is mentioned once, James the son of Zebedee five times, John the son of Zebedee seven times and Judas four times. In Mark we find the same disciples mentioned respectively twenty-six, four, ten, ten, and three times; if we take Mark 1—13, the figures are sixteen, four, nine, nine, and one.

[3] This is the conclusion reached by H. Strathmann, 'Die Stellung des Petrus in der Urkirche: zur Frühgeschichte des Wortes an Petrus, Matt. 16. 17bis, 19', in *Zeitschrift für systematische Theologie* (1943), pp. 223ff.

[4] One can indeed detect two divergent trends in the documents left by the first generation of Christians. According to one, best represented by Gal. 2.1ff., the mother community in Jerusalem was led from a very early time by three 'pillars'—James, Peter, and John. These are not necessarily the same as the three intimates of Jesus we find in Mark (the James of Galatians is probably the brother of Jesus and not the son of Zebedee) but the existence of this group may have influenced the tradition and favoured the perpetuation of stories in which Jesus granted special favours to three of his disciples. According to the other and more widespread opinion, Peter is from the outset the leader of the new Church: cf. Gal. 1.18 and the traditions concerning Peter which

But it is obvious that the author of Mark, while mentioning Peter often, is not seeking to advance his claims to pre-eminence in the Church. At the best, he notes that pre-eminence; at worst he reminds his readers of its limitations, without challenging its legitimacy.

If we look rather more closely at the passages in Mark where Peter receives an especially significant call or revelation, we see that the apostle of the circumcision is never *the only beneficiary* of an act on the part of Jesus or of God, as is sometimes the case in Matthew (16.17ff.) and in Luke (5.1–11). Even if he is mentioned first, Peter receives, in Mark, only what some of his companions also receive: thus his calling by Jesus (1.16–20), his naming among the Twelve and receiving of a surname,[1] his admission to the bedside of the daughter of Jairus (5.37), the invitation to the mountain of the transfiguration (9.2), the eschatological revelation (13.3) and the watch at Gethsemane (14.33). It would be difficult to suggest more clearly that Peter has no monopoly of any function or revelation, despite the importance of his role in the community.

There are, nevertheless, in Mark 1—13, passages where Peter is represented alone with Jesus and where one might see his superiority in relation to the other disciples affirmed. In fact, these passages do not help at all to enhance his reputation.

Luke used in writing Acts 1—5 and 8—12. Such a situation could not but foster stories and sayings where Peter was to the fore. These two major trends in our documentation are difficult to reconcile historically but are probably to be explained by the unstable organization of the Christian community in its first few years of existence (cf. on this point, for example, the pages devoted by M. Goguel to the ministries in his book, *L'Eglise primitive* (Paris 1947), pp. 110ff.). The author of Mark may therefore simply have echoed a tradition that was not yet uniform or else he may have sought to stem the progress of the second trend, so clearly victorious in Matthew and Luke, by making numerous references in his text to the group of intimates and its various members.

[1] True, Simon is mentioned first in the list of the Twelve and has the honour of being given a surname by Jesus (3.16). But unlike what is related in Matthew and Luke, James and John are received immediately after him and are also given a surname, as though the Evangelist wanted to show that they were practically as important as Peter (3.17). In addition, Peter is not called πρῶτος, as in Matt. 10.2. Lastly, it will be noted that Peter's surname is not explained (as it is in Matt. 16.18) whereas that given to the sons of Zebedee is (3.17).

In Mark 1.29–31 he does not even have the honour of receiving Jesus in his own house, as in the parallel texts of Matt. 8.14–15 and Luke 4.38–9: the house he shares with Andrew is invaded by the whole group of Jesus' followers and his only 'privilege' is that of being the sick woman's son-in-law. In Mark 10.28 and 11.21 he acts as spokesman for the disciples in putting questions to Jesus. But he shares this role with John (Mark 9.38) and does not emerge from it with any particular glory, since Matt. 21.20 places the words of Mark 11.21 in the mouths of 'the disciples' (there is no parallel in Luke). Lastly, in the three other texts (1.36; 8.29–33; 9.5), where Mark 1—13 mentions him alone, Peter is presented in such an unfavourable light that Matthew and Luke felt bound to suppress or tone down the anti-petrine thrust by the author of Mark: in Mark 1.36 'Simon and they that were with him' (the Evangelist does not wish to call them disciples) tried to tie Jesus down to his function of healer, an attempt that Luke 4.42 ascribes to 'the people' and which Matthew does not mention; in Mark 8.29–33 Peter earns only reprimands in his two appearances, whereas Matt. 16.16 accords him in the first case at least the praise and promises with which we are familiar, while Luke (9.20ff.) prefers to omit the second reference and its consequences; lastly, in Mark 9.6, the fear shown by Peter on the mount of the transfiguration is stressed with scant sympathy in a sentence that Matthew preferred to leave out and which Luke (9.33) abridged and toned down.

We are accordingly entitled to conclude that the author of Mark is not a very enthusiastic defender of the rights of Simon Peter and even occasionally gives an inkling of his reservations regarding a leader of the Church whose great authority he nevertheless accepts.

It would be wrong to go so far as to ascribe to the Evangelist the desire to place some other one of the Twelve in the forefront, as, for example, one of the intimate disciples of whom he speaks on various occasions. Andrew is still for him the insignificant character that he is throughout the earliest Christian tradition. As for the sons of Zebedee, they are certainly given a surname, like Peter (Mark 3.17) and are mentioned a considerable number of times in Mark's Gospel, but aside even from the stern reply to John in Mark 9.38ff., they are treated so

harshly in Mark 10.35ff. that Matthew preferred to ascribe
their request to their mother (Matt. 20.20ff.) and Luke decided
to omit the whole episode, of which there is incidentally a rough
equivalent in Luke 9.51–5. The author of Mark is accordingly
practically as reserved towards the sons of Zebedee as towards
Peter.

If the author of Mark is ill-disposed towards Peter and the sons
of Zebedee, could it be because he prefers to them that other
great leader of the primitive Church who seems to have sup-
planted them quite rapidly in Jerusalem,[1] James, the brother
of Jesus? Obviously not, since Mark does not contain the
slightest trace of any bias in favour of this James. He is mentioned only once, first in a list of four brothers of Jesus whom his
countrymen knew so well that they found it impossible to take
Jesus' mission seriously (Mark 6.3). This one allusion is not a
direct criticism but it carries slightly unflattering undertones.
James is put back in his place as one of the family of Jesus and
his personality is scarcely touched upon. In addition, this family

[1] Cf. certain texts like Gal. 1.19 where Paul, coming only a few years
after his conversion to see Peter in Jerusalem, feels the need to visit only
one other member of the community, James, the Lord's brother; Gal.
2.9, where the James mentioned first among the 'pillars' is no doubt
also the Lord's brother; Gal. 2.12, which bears witness to the authority
of James outside Jerusalem, even over Peter; Acts 12.17, where Peter's
last act in fleeing from Jerusalem is to have 'James and the brethren'
warned, which shows the consideration that was due to the Lord's
brother by that date; Acts 21.18, etc. It is difficult to combine these
various pieces of evidence, and they have given rise to various hypotheses, the most reasonable of which seems to be that of O. Cullmann,
Saint Pierre, pp. 28ff., who distinguishes a first period when Peter was
at the head of the church of Jerusalem (although James had already
a relatively high position in the community) and a second period where
James took over the leadership of the Christians in Jerusalem while
Peter led the Judaeo-Christian mission from city to city. At the most
one might be inclined to think that the historical reality must have
been rather more complex and less harmonious than this rather legalistic picture would have us believe. Was Peter never tempted to regain
his ascendancy in Jerusalem after he had lost it? Could there not have
been at certain times two rival communities in the Jewish capital?
That cannot be ruled out, even if we agree that O. Cullmann's theory
gives an accurate idea of the general course of events.

is not distinguished by any exceptional characteristic[1] and it seems inconceivable to their friends and acquaintances that these people could have produced a prophet and miracle-worker. It would not seem either that Jesus was supported in any way by his family in the trials he had to endure at the hands of his compatriots. Otherwise Mark would at least have mentioned the family house where the Master would have found refuge and performed some miracles (cf. 1.29–34) or would have excepted the mother, brother, and sisters of Jesus from the accusations of unbelief (6.6) and disrespect (6.4) he makes against the people of Nazareth. Worse still, the Evangelist even makes Jesus say that he is unhonoured as a prophet in his own country, 'among his own kin' (ἐν τοῖς συγγενεῦσιν αὐτοῦ and 'in his own house' (καὶ ἐν τῇ οἰκίᾳ αὐτοῦ). A common proverb, one might say. But it is significant that the parallel texts in Matt. 13.57, Luke 4.24 and John 4.44 (cf., however, John 7.5) make no reference to the family and that Luke 4.24 and John 4.44 make no reference to the house either. Here we have a text where the author of Mark is deliberately attacking James and the whole of Jesus' family, from which he does not dissociate him.

---

[1] Except that there is no father, since Jesus is described as 'the son of Mary', an expression that is found nowhere else in the New Testament and which, in Jewish usage, suggested inevitably the addition 'and of father unknown'. The variant 'the son of the carpenter and of Mary', to which a certain number of MSS in minuscule testify (fam. 13,33, 472, etc.) and also a few old versions (it., a few vg. MSS, a few boh. MSS), supported as regards the first part by P 45 and indirectly by Origen, *Contra Celsum* 6.36, when he says: οὐδαμοῦ τῶν ἐν ταῖς ἐκκλησίαις φερομένων εὐαγγελίων τέκτων αὐτὸς ὁ Ἰησοῦς ἀναγέγραπται, is not strongly enough corroborated to be preferred to the reading of all the great uncials and derives certainly from the parallel in Matthew (13.5), in which Gospel it is due to the desire to refute the calumnies regarding Mary's virtue (cf. Matt. 1.18–25). On this point one can agree with E. Lohmeyer, *Ev. des Mk.*, p. 110; B. H. Branscomb, *Gosp. of Mark*, pp. 99–101; C. E. B. Cranfield, *St Mark*, pp. 194–5, rather than with E. Klostermann, *Das Mkev.*, p. 55; V. Taylor, *St Mark*, pp. 299–300; W. Grundmann, *Ev. nach Mk.*, pp. 120–1, the embarrassed defenders of the wrong variant out of a desire not to ascribe to the author of Mark belief in the virgin birth or a freedom of language that shocks them. There is nothing for it, however, but to opt for the second alternative, it would seem, thereby judging the force of the Evangelist's animosity towards the family of Jesus.

The attack is even plainer in the other passage of Mark concerning the family of Jesus (3.20–1,31–5). True, the second part of the text, of which exact parallels are to be found in Matt. 12.46–50 and Luke 8.19–21 (cf. Luke 11.27–8), certainly derives from the earliest tradition, from which the Evangelist simply took it over.[1] But a few details of style in this second part, the content of the first and, above all, the context in which Mark places both, have no equivalent in Matthew and Luke and give an inkling of distinct hostility towards the mother and brothers of Jesus. A combination of texts which is at first sight fairly harmless reveals, on closer examination, the hand of an author passionately antagonistic to our Lord's family and hence to James.

The few details of style which embarrassed Matthew and Luke are the following: In Mark 3.31 the mother and brothers of Jesus, arriving at the place where Jesus is, stay outside and have him called (ἔξω στήκοντες ἀπέστειλαν πρὸς αὐτὸν καλοῦντες αὐτόν) with the assurance of people certain of their authority; Matthew says (12.46) that they 'stood without, desiring to speak with him' (εἰστήκεισαν ἔξω ζητοῦντες αὐτῷ λαλῆσαι) as is fitting for the humble relatives of a great man who have come from their village to visit him without an appointment; Luke 8.19 states merely that the crowd prevented them from reaching Jesus (οὐκ ἠδύναντο συντυχεῖν αὐτῷ διὰ τὸν ὄχλον) whereas they had come to see him (παρεγένετο . . . πρὸς αὐτὸν ἡ μήτηρ καὶ οἱ ἀδελφοὶ αὐτοῦ), which has not the edifying note of Matthew's version but tones down appreciably the sentence in Mark. In Mark 3.32 Jesus is told that his mother and brothers are looking for him (ζητοῦσίν σε), which, having regard to v. 31, means more or less that they are asking him to come outside to see them. Matt. 12.47, which is incidentally perhaps only an interpolation,[2] says merely that they desire to speak with him

---

[1] All the critics agree on this point, even if they do not agree entirely as to the content of this tradition, built up around vv. 31–4 according to M. Dibelius, *Formgesch. des Evang.*, pp. 43–4, 60–1; or constructed on the basis of v. 35, according to R. Bultmann, *Gesch. d. syn. Trad.*, pp. 28–9; or composed of the two pieces put together by Mark (vv. 31–4 and v. 35) as V. Taylor, *St Mark*, would have it (p. 245).

[2] This verse, which reproduces almost word for word the preceding verse, is missing in B ℵ* and in some of the earliest versions. Its late

(ζητοῦντές σοι λαλῆσαι); Luke 8.20 arrives at the same result, writing that they wish to see him (ἰδεῖν θέλοντές σε); in addition, both place the emphasis on the presence of the family of Jesus (main verb) rather than on their intentions (participles in apposition with the subject of the main verb), whereas in Mark the intentions (main verb) count more than the presence, which is simply indicated by an adverb. Lastly in Mark 3.34, Jesus says that his real family consists of those sitting about him (τοὺς περὶ αὐτὸν κύκλῳ καθημένους . . .)—that is to say almost anybody, since the disciples are not mentioned in proximity— and gives it to be understood that by gathering around to listen to him people are obeying God's will (v. 35). Matt. 12.49, rejecting this vague definition so wounding for the family of Jesus, ascribed to Jesus a gesture designating his disciples as his mother and the brethren; as for Luke (8.21), he chose to omit all reference to a gesture on the part of Jesus and to change his words a little so as to give the title of 'my mother and my brethren' to those 'who hear the word of God and do it' (οἱ τὸν λόγον τοῦ θεοῦ ἀκούοντες καὶ ποιοῦντες). In both cases a minimum of tried perseverance and obedience is required in order to take the place of Jesus' natural family, whereas in Mark Jesus seems to deprive his family of any rights over him without even troubling to find proper substitutes for them.

The first part of the passage in Mark that interests us here (3.20–1) has no parallel in Matthew or Luke, whereas in Mark it determines the interpretation of 3.31–5. It is not very likely that these two verses ever had a separate existence, whatever one may believe about their exact origin.[1] In omitting them, consequently, Matthew and Luke were not simply leaving out

---

introduction might be explained by the influence of Mark and Luke and above all by the desire to clarify an episode abbreviated too much by Matthew, who was very prone to abridging texts he found in Mark (cf. M. Goguel, *Introd. au N.T.*, vol. i, pp. 416–7).

[1] Thus, according to R. Bultmann, *Gesch. d. syn. Trad.*, p. 28, v. 20 is due to the Evangelist, whereas v. 21 is the beginning of vv. 31–5; according to M. Dibelius, *Formgesch d. Evang.*, pp. 33–4, vv. 20 and 21 are both by the author. V. Taylor, *St Mark*, would like to see in them an independent fragment of the early tradition recording an authentic happening, but he makes no attempt to prove his theory, which would be convincing only if it were shown that Mark bore no animosity towards the family of Jesus, but that is not the case.

something of no consequence: they were deliberately mutilating the episode which vv. 20–1 introduced and made more brutal. In their substance and in their place in the text, are these two little verses then so daring and so shocking? We must admit that they are, as least as regards v. 21, which, moreover, suffered from this fact when the text was transmitted.[1] After much keen discussion in the past, critics are now unanimous that the expression οἱ παρ' αὐτοῦ could only refer here to the 'relatives' of Jesus, his family in the widest sense, including his mother and his brothers (cf. Mark 3.31). But there are still a few commentators[2] who assert, against all the evidence, in order to soften the tone of this verse, that the word ἔλεγον does not have οἱ παρ' αὐτοῦ as its subject but simply means 'it was said'. The family of Jesus, it is suggested, sought to put an end to his ministry on the basis of false reports, but realized their mistake when they went to visit their 'prodigal son' on the spot (vv. 31–5). In fact, the author of Mark really does mean that Jesus' family accused him of being mad and, seeing him installed at a distance with his disciples and followed by a great crowd, they set out on an expedition to take hold of him and bring him back. Accordingly, the move by the mother and brothers of Jesus in v. 31, their attempt to draw him outside and the use of ζητοῦσιν in v. 32, take on a rather disquieting meaning which is not to be found in Matthew and Luke.

The author of Mark denounces with some vigour the intrigues and insincerity of the mother and brothers of Jesus in 3.21,31–5. But he does worse than that if we look at the context in which he places this double pericope. It is interesting in the first place that he should have inserted this episode just after the institution of the Twelve (3.13–19) chosen by Jesus

---

[1] The 'Western' text, represented by D,W,it, is the result of a clumsy attempt to correct v. 21 in the light of v. 22. It is hard to understand that a critic as sound as E. Lohmeyer (*Ev. d. Mk.*, pp. 76–7) should give his preference to a variant so obviously late, whatever individualists like A. Pallis, *Notes on the Gospels according to St Mark and St Matthew*, 2nd edn (London 1932), ad loc. and P. L. Couchoud, 'Notes de critique verbale sur saint Marc et saint Matthieu', in *JTS*, vol. xxxiv (1933), pp. 113ff. may have thought about it.

[2] In particular, M. J. Lagrange, *Ev. Marc*, pp. 70–1; B. H. Streeter, *The Four Gospels, a Study of Origins* (London 1924), p. 189; A. E. J. Rawlinson, *Saint Mark*, pp. 41–2.

as his permanent collaborators. It would be impossible to lay more stress on the difference between the real friends of Jesus and his family, who do nothing but place obstacles in his way. The same comparison to the disadvantage of the family of Jesus is made, moreover, in chapter 6, where the visit to Nazareth immediately precedes the sending out of the Twelve as missionaries. This confirms, if there were any need to do so, that the author of Mark is campaigning in this part of his book against the family of Jesus, that is to say, above all, against James.

The author's polemical artifice is even more visible if we turn to the verses he inserted between the two parts of the episode relating to the family of Jesus (3.22–30). These contain the controversy between Jesus and the scribes on the subject of his powers of exorcism, which his opponents ascribe to collusion with the 'prince of the devils'. They have parallels in Matthew (12.24–32) and in Luke (11.15–22; 12.10–11) but, in those two Gospels, there is no connection between them and the apophthegm concerning the real family of Jesus. In Matt. 12, the apophthegm begins only at v. 46 and verses 33–45 are devoted to a series of sayings about the significance of what men say, the danger of asking for signs and the risk of relapse after exorcism; in short there is no shadow of a connection between 12.24–32 and 12.46ff. In Luke the distance separating the controvery in question and the apophthegm concerning the real brothers and mother of Jesus is far greater still, since the apophthegm occurs in 8.4–8. In Mark, on the other hand, the connection is suggested not only by the insertion of the controversy in the middle of the apophthegm but also by the relationship between 3.21 and 3.22. In the former of these two verses Jesus' family accuses him of being mad; in the latter, the scribes come from Jerusalem accuse him of 'having Beelzebub',[1] which is rendered in v. 30 by 'having an unclean spirit'. It is the same libellous charge that Jesus' most implacable enemies simply formulate a little more brutally than his family, since any mental disorder was ascribed in those days to possession by an evil spirit.

---

[1] Concerning this rather strange (and perhaps corrupted) name cf. Strack–Billerbeck, vol. I, pp. 631–4; W. Foerster, art. βεεζεβούλ in the *TWNT*, vol. I, pp. 605–6; V. Taylor, *St Mark*, pp. 238–9.

Surely then one is forced to think that the severe condemnation by Jesus in vv. 28–9 of blasphemers against the spirit that
is in him is directed, in the mind of the Evangelist, *at the family
of Jesus as well as at the scribes of v. 22*. It is all the more probable
since the little editorial note of v. 30 is conceived in terms that
can apply equally well to those who said ἐξέστη as to those who
proclaimed βεεζεβοὺλ ἔχει. If, then, the scribes who have come
from Jerusalem have committed a sin that can never be forgiven,
so has the family of Jesus, the author of Mark would have us
understand. What more could he have done to destroy the
claims of James and his party? We must therefore consider the
author of Mark, who is personally responsible for the curious
editorial touches we have just been observing, as the avowed
enemy of James, the Lord's brother, sole head of the church of
Jerusalem for many years, until his martyrdom in the year 62.[1]

This hostility, so clearly expressed by such daring means, can
only have emanated from a person of headstrong character,
original and audacious and little inclined to indulgence or
patience. This confirms the conclusions we reached in Chapter
1 and our impressions in the foregoing pages. When traces of
polemic appear in Mark, they are largely due to his own editorial work and reflect the animosities and impatience in his
own mind and in the minds of those in his own circle. They
enlighten us greatly as to the circumstances of Mark's birth:
we can say now that this Gospel was born in a milieu which
despised the Pharisees slightly without having lost hope of con-
verting them; where the scribes and the leaders of the Jerusalemite priesthood were feared and hated; where the Jerusalem
Temple was execrated; where certain Christians were criticized
for their legalistic scruples and their naive apocalyptic beliefs,
whereas the claims of a popular and emancipated Christianity
were upheld against a tendency to express the new faith in
intellectual and apologetic terms; where there was constant
emphasis on the martyrdom of Jesus, whereas certain Christians
preferred to gloss over this painful aspect of his ministry; where,
lastly, it was commonly felt that in spite of the great merits of

[1] An excellent account of the state of knowledge about the 'episcopate'
of James at Jerusalem and his martyrdom will be found in M. Goguel,
La naissance du christianisme (Paris 1946), pp. 124–53.

James and John, the sons of Zebedee and, above all, of Simon Peter, these men no longer had the monopoly of any special revelation and had not always been equal to the tasks Jesus had entrusted to them. These various opinions form a relatively coherent whole, cemented together by the outright condemnation of the authority of James, the Lord's brother. But they are simply the reverse of a coin whose obverse is made up of a certain number of positive beliefs and aspirations of which the Gospel likewise bears the mark and which we shall now endeavour to trace.

Chapter Three

THE CAUSES DEFENDED
BY MARK

The principal theological ideas contained in the Gospel according to Mark are expounded in the fullest commentaries on that book.[1] It is not our intention here to embark again on what has been so well done by several theologians of renown, but rather to endeavour, in the light of the conclusions reached in the foregoing chapters, to discern the major theological themes that run through this work of a not very speculative character. One may doubt whether the author of Mark did anything more than receive and pass on many of the religious ideas contained in the church tradition and in the stories he added. In any case it did not occur to him either to plumb their depths or to build them into a connected whole, so that his 'thought' is reduced to a rather heterogeneous collection of ideas drawn from various sources.

However, the Evangelist, following an emotional urge, seems to have paid very special attention to a few ideas whose practical consequences he felt to be decisive. These are above all ideas concerning the Christian mission, which he makes no attempt to expound systematically but which emerge at numerous points of his text. For these ideas he takes up arms, like a man who wishes to justify the existence and the practices of the communities he represents and to appeal to the other churches to change their way of life and their thinking in certain respects. He chooses his material in the light of these ideas, in order to illustrate them clearly, and he arranges his book around them,

---

[1] M. J. Lagrange, *Ev. Marc*, pp. cxliii–clxiv; A. E. J. Rawlinson, *St Mark*, pp. l–liv; V. Taylor, *St Mark*, pp. 114–29.

so that his plan takes on a special importance.[1] In short, these ideas form the living core of his work because he had them personally at heart and was expressing the profound beliefs and aspirations of the society in which he lived.

1

JESUS, BEARER OF THE GOSPEL

It seems paradoxical to describe a Gospel wholly devoted to an account of Jesus' ministry on earth as having a primarily ecclesiological purpose. However, it will be recalled that the Gospel according to Matthew is designed to provide the churches with the catechetical and disciplinary 'compendium' without which their life and teaching would be in danger of going astray.[2] Allowing for the obvious differences, it is our belief that the purpose of Mark's Gospel is the same. It is the author of Mark who first thought of giving the Christian communities a body of teaching in the shape of an account of Jesus' ministry on earth. The author of Matthew, in following his example, showed that he grasped his predecessor's intention and saw no objection to its principle, even if he thought the result had certain shortcomings. In this way he helps us to overcome our surprise at a process so little in keeping with our modern way of thought.

That does not suffice, however, to explain the choice of this form by the author of Mark, in which certain empirical factors must certainly have played a part. The Lord's teaching, which constituted the main part of the church tradition, had by his day mostly taken the shape of brief accounts of isolated episodes of Jesus' ministry on earth.[3] Led into searching the popular memory for stories about Jesus by his desire to combat certain tendencies he found in the church tradition, the Evangelist found himself confronted with material relating for the most

---

[1] Cf. pp. 73ff. above.
[2] Matthew is 'written for a church, that is to say a group in need of practical rules and concrete instructions . . . the charter of a society establishing itself to last', writes M. Goguel, *Introd. au N.T.*, vol. I, pp. 439–40 and X. Léon-Dufour quotes his opinion with approval in A. Robert–A. Feuillet, *Introd. à la Bible*, vol. II, p. 181.
[3] These are in particular the 'apophthegms' of R. Bultmann, *Gesch. d. syn. Trad.*, pp. 8–73.

part to the earthly life of Jesus. It was quite natural that he should give his book a semi-biographical form.

Nevertheless, that was not, in our opinion, the decisive reason for the choice of this literary genre, which at first sight would seem ill-suited to his purpose. His underlying reason is a theological one which had already exerted a great influence on ecclesiastical tradition: the crucified Christ was known to have risen from the dead, and, in spite of his glorification, to be still in the midst of his disciples and of all the people ready to listen to him. His past action and teaching were thus not always clearly distinguished from his present action and teaching.[1] In preserving and referring to the words he once spoke in Galilee and at Jerusalem, Christians did not feel that they were looking back to the past; they were working for the building of the Church in the present and for the strengthening of its communion with the risen Christ.

This semi-confusion between the past and the present of Jesus Christ was not overcome by the author of Mark, as has been realized by such critics as J. M. Robinson[2] and W. Marxsen.[3] For the first-mentioned, the overall structure of the Gospel and the numerous editorial touches are due to the parallelism the Evangelist saw between Jesus' former combat with Satan and the struggle carried on by the Church in the course of history at the prompting of the Holy Spirit.[4] According-ing to the second, the strange absence of a conclusion to the Gospel according to Mark constitutes, together with a number of other features of his work, an invitation to read his account as much as a prophecy of the approaching return of the Lord to Galilee as a reminder of the earthly life of Jesus of Nazareth.[5] Whatever one may think of the specific theories of these two

---

[1] Cf. for example the way in which Paul, in 1 Cor. 7.10ff., quotes in the present tense one of the Lord's commands which is certainly a saying of the historical Jesus, crucified more than twenty years before.

[2] J. M. Robinson, *Das Geschichtsverständnis des Markusevangeliums.*

[3] W. Marxsen, *Der Evangelist Markus, Studien zur Redaktionsgeschichte des Evangeliums.*

[4] Op. cit., in particular pp. 82ff.

[5] 'Thus one can practically say that Galilee identifies the now risen Christ with the earthly Christ, just as, on the other hand, the expected parousia—also in Galilee!—identifies him with the Christ who is to come again' (translated from op. cit. p. 146).

critics, both more or less drawn to the idea of a Marcan system,[1] they are right on one point, we believe: starting from the
current and implicit notion of the identity of the risen Christ
and the man Jesus, the author of Mark made a special effort to
develop and exploit this idea.[2]

It is commonly agreed that to achieve his end the Evangelist
took the course of christological embellishment, in the sense
that he gave the historical Jesus the titles by which Christians
referred to their heavenly Lord.[3] This suggestion seems not
improbable at first sight, considering the wide variety of
christological titles and ideas which the New Testament
shows us were current among the Christians of the first two
generations.[4] In our view, however, it is very questionable,
even if it be allowed that the Evangelist may have yielded
here and there to the pressure of a very general tendency to
speculate about the person of Jesus Christ. The author of Mark,

---

[1] It can scarcely be denied that they both approach Mark with the idea
of fitting his message into the framework of very modern theological
categories, that of J. M. Robinson being borrowed from O. Cullmann's
theology of the history of salvation and that of W. Marxsen from R.
Bultmann's existentialist theology. It would be naive to reproach them
with this—exegesis with no prior theological assumptions is impossible.
But who can fail to see the danger that lies in projecting a too elaborate
and abstract system of thought on to a work as closely linked to events
as Mark's Gospel?

[2] It is a significant detail that he is the New Testament writer who uses
the historic present by far the most: 151 times (of which 72 with the
verb λέγειν), whereas Matthew uses it 78 times, of which 59 with λέγειν;
Luke 4 to 6; John 162, for a text two-fifths as long again. (J. C. Hawkins, *Horae synopticae* 2nd edn, pp. 143–9; M. J. Lagrange, *Ev. Marc*,
pp. lxix–lxx.)

[3] This is basically, with some variations of detail, the theory of many
critics who believe Mark used a written document relating the life of
Jesus or the reminiscences of Peter (cf. pp. 19ff. above). It is also that of
W. Wrede, *Das Messiasgeheimnis* . . . (cf. for example pp. 145–6); of
M. Dibelius, *Formgeschichte des Evang.*, pp. 265–79; of R. Bultmann,
Gesch. d. syn. Trad., pp. 362ff. (in particular pp. 370–2) and of many
of their disciples. It is, lastly, that of an author like J. Héring, *Le
Royaume de Dieu et sa venue*, 2nd edn (Neuchâtel 1959), pp. 128–43,
in whose view Mark introduced the title and idea of 'Christ' into a
tradition that still spoke only of the 'Son of Man'.

[4] Cf. on this subject O. Cullmann, *Christologie du N.T.*, pp. 15–16.

as we have shown,[1] does not favour such speculation, or at least not when he scents in it an apologia or an intellectual game. Hence, if he had deliberately changed the titles by which Jesus was known in the material derived from tradition, it would have been in a downward, rather than in an upward direction.[2]

In fact, he must have preserved more or less intact the titles which the church tradition, on the one hand, and various popular story-tellers, on the other, gave Jesus in the documents and stories the Evangelist used. It would be strange, if he himself had intervened actively, that the only two titles frequently given to Jesus in the Gospel, namely 'Master'[3] and 'Son of Man'[4] should be precisely those very rarely applied to Christ in Christian usage of the first century.[5] At most one might think

---

[1] Cf. pp. 117ff. above.

[2] The author is definitely reducing the christological content when, after Peter's confession, he omits Jesus' praise of him for having recognized him as the Christ (cf. pp. 121–2 above).

[3] Mark uses διδάσκαλος twelve times to designate Jesus (4.38; 5.35; 9.17,38; 10.17,20,35; 12.14,19,32; 13.1; 14.14), to which must be added the three times he uses 'rabbi' (9.5; 11.21; 14.45) and the one time he uses 'rabboni' (10.51). In Matthew, διδάσκαλος is applied to Jesus only ten times and 'rabbi' twice ('rabboni' not at all), despite the emphasis laid on the teaching of Jesus. In Luke, 'rabbi' and 'rabboni' are not used at all and διδάσκαλος is used thirteen times. The frequency of titles is thus much greater in Mark, which is only three-fifths as long as Matthew or Luke. These two latter Evangelists must certainly have omitted these words in several cases when they came across them in their source material (cf. Mark 4.38 and par.; Mark 9.5 and par.).

[4] In Mark we find the expression ὁ υἱὸς τοῦ ἀνθρώπου fourteen times (2.10,28; 8.31,38; 9.9,12,31; 10.33,45; 13.26; 14.21,21,41,62). It is used a little more often in Matthew (thirty times) and in Luke as often as in Mark (twenty-five times). In all three cases one has the impression of respect for the vocabulary of tradition, particularly as the expression occurs in sayings of Jesus, whose wording authors hesitated to change. But it is still possible that Mark left out a 'Son of Man' here and there (cf. p. 171, n. 3 below).

[5] As we know, the terms διδάσκαλος (and the corresponding semitic titles) and ὁ υἱὸς τοῦ ἀνθρώπου are to be found nowhere in the New Testament apart from the Gospels (if we except the one use of ὁ υἱὸς τοῦ ἀνθρώπου in Acts 7.56), to designate Jesus. This fact is rather surprising and almost certainly due to the absence of these two titles from the religious language current in the first century of the Christian era, except perhaps from that of the very first church of Jerusalem.

that he sometimes preferred the former of these titles to another one, seemingly more suitable, because he considered it sufficiently neutral not to set his readers on a false trail of speculation about the person of the living Christ.[1] But nobody has thought for that reason of imputing to him the intention of campaigning in favour of a christology of the Master, any more than for a christology of the Son of Man.[2] As for claiming that the author of Mark was seeking to impose the title of Christ on the church tradition, together with the idea that Jesus had already been the Messiah in his life-time, this seems absolutely ruled out by the rare use of the term Χριστός in the Gospel[3] and also by the rather

---

[1] Perhaps this is the case in Mark 10.51, where the use of the word 'rabboni' by the blind beggar Bartimaeus, who had just called Jesus 'Son of David' (10.47–8) takes the edge off the christology of this title, which the Evangelist mistrusted.

[2] Thus Th. Preiss, 'Le Fils de l'Homme', in *Etudes théologiques et religieuses*, vol. XXVI (1951), no. 3 and vol. XXVIII (1953), no. 1, who resolutely rejects this idea on page 25 of his first fascicle; E. Percy, *Die Botschaft Jesu*, p. 286, in whose opinion Mark is preserving here a Palestinian term; O. Cullmann, *Christologie du N.T.*, p. 157, for whom the 'christology of the Son of Man is not that of the synoptic Gospels'; H. E. Toedt, *Der Menschensohn in der synoptischen Ueberlieferung* (Gütersloh 1959), pp. 252–4, for whom Mark simply made very partial use of the texts concerning the Son of Man he received via church tradition. The opposite theory is implicit in R. Bultmann, *Gesch. der synopt. Trad.*, 4th edn, p. 31, when he considers the sayings concerning the sufferings of the Son of Man as creations of the hellenistic community introduced into his Gospel by the author of Mark but unknown as yet to the *logia*. This does not prevent the celebrated critic from saying (ibid. p. 82) that the title of υἱὸς τοῦ ἀνθρώπου was lost in hellenistic Christianity, which must consequently have constructed important *logia* around a title that was no longer used. This scarcely helps to clarify the issue!

[3] It is used seven times (1.1; 8.29; 9.41; 12.35; 13.21; 14.61; 15.32), the first and third times without the article, which makes the title into a proper name as in Paul. The occasional use of the title 'Son of God' (1.11; 3.11; 5.7; 9.7; 14.61; 15.39; cf. 13.32 and perhaps 1.1 if one accepts the long text) does not add very much to this short list because it is a title whose imprecise meaning would have led Mark, inspired perhaps by Ps. 2.2,7, to prefer it to that of Christ, possibly not Greek enough for his liking (cf. 14.61; 15.32,39; perhaps 1.1). It is useful to remember that Matthew uses Χριστός seventeen times and υἱὸς τοῦ ἀνθρώπου twelve times, without mentioning the five times he refers to the 'Son' (κατ᾽ ἐξοχήν).

suspect character conferred on this word by the context whenever it is preceded by the definite article.[1]

One might also suppose that the projection of faith in the risen Christ on to the person of the man Jesus came about in Mark through the channel of ideas relating to the work of Christ rather than that of christological titles. As we have already shown,[2] the Evangelist attached great importance to remembrance of the suffering, death, and resurrection of the Master. This attitude would appear above all to serve a polemical purpose: the denunciation of the cowards who truncated the gospel in order to curry favour with the Jewish authorities, and of those same authorities who were responsible for the Jesus' death. But that does not rule out the possibility of an influence exerted on the Evangelist by a concept of the work of Jesus Christ that he then tried more or less consciously to weave into his book at the price of distorting the traditional material. Many critics agree with this theory, in three rather different forms: some maintain that Mark was influenced by Paul and borrowed more of less faithfully all his main ideas;[3] others, without denying a

---

[1] We have already stated (pp. 121–2 above) our views on 8.29 and its context as well as on 12.35ff. (pp. 117–9) and 13.21 (p. 120). In 14.61 and 15.32, the malevolence of those who give Jesus this title and the correction introduced by the nearby use of other titles (14.61–2; 15.39) show the reservations Mark had about the title of Christ. While this might be an echo of Jesus' own reserve in regard to this title (J. Héring, *Royaume de Dieu*, pp. 111–27; O. Cullmann, *Christol. du N.T.*, pp. 103–10), it is in any case only one of the manifestations of the refusal by the author of Mark to countenance any kind of christological speculation. It is therefore quite superfluous to have recourse, in order to explain it, to a 'Messianic secret' theory like that of W. Wrede, *Das Messiasgeheimnis* (cf. in particular pp. 115ff.), or of E. Percy, op. cit., pp. 286ff.

[2] Cf. pp. 122–5 above.

[3] Without going back earlier than the beginning of the twentieth century one can cite several critics of repute among the supporters of this theory: J. Weiss, *Das älteste Evangelium*, pp. 94–5; A. Loisy, *Les évangiles synopti- ques* (Ceffonds 1907–8), vol. I, pp. 116–17 and *L'Evangile selon Marc*, pp. 37–44; B. W. Bacon, *The Gospel of Mark* (New Haven 1925), pp. 221–71; C. G. Montefiore, *The Synoptic Gospels*, 2nd edn (London 1927), pp. xlv–xlvii, with a caution imitated by B. H. Branscomb, *The Gospel of Mark*, p. 191; W. Marxsen, *Der Ev. Markus*, pp. 145–7, who is much more positive; J. Schreiber, 'Die Christologie des Markus- evangeliums' in *Zeitschrift für Theologie und Kirche* (1961), pp. 154–83.

certain Paulinism in Mark, look instead for the origin of the
ideas characteristic of his Gospel in the preaching of Peter;[1]
others again ascribe the christology implicit in Mark to the echo
to be found in this book of the kerygma of the primitive hellenistic Church.[2]

The second of these theories, which belongs more to the
debate on the sources of Mark,[3] is too visibly inspired by apologetic motives to merit long discussion. It does not agree very
well either with what we can gather of Peter's theology from
other sources.[4] Lastly, despite what has sometimes been said,[5]
it is difficult to reconcile with the reserve the author of Mark
displays towards Peter.[6] The theory of Mark's Paulinism has

---

[1] This theory is quite often presented as the accompaniment to an
attenuated form of the preceding one, by critics who attribute the Gospel
according to Mark to John Mark of Jerusalem, the companion of
various apostles. Its best-known defender is M. J. Lagrange, *Ev. Marc*,
who considers 'Peter's catechesis' as the principal source of Mark
(pp. cviii–cxiii), rearranged by the Evangelist from the literary point
of view (pp. cxxi–cxxii), but entirely respected by him from the point
of view of facts and ideas (pp. cxxvi–clxiv). To him may be added W.
Grundmann, *Evang. nach Mk.*, pp. 15ff. (who is nevertheless drawn to
Marxsen's ideas) and X. Léon-Dufour, 'Les évangiles synoptiques',
in A. Robert and A. Feuillet, *Introd. à la Bible*, vol. II, pp. 213–8, who
says, for example, in regard to the way in which Mark systematizes
the facts of Jesus' life, in particular the 'messianic secret': 'It is no
doubt in Peter's experience that one must look for the origin of this
systematization.'

[2] This theory is defended in particular by M. Goguel, *Introd. au N.T.*,
vol. I, pp. 358–65 and W. Werner, *Der Einfluss paulinischer Theologie im
Markusevangelium* (Giessen 1923), as yet in a rather negative form, for
the purpose of refuting the theory of the Paulinism of Mark. It took
more definite shape with R. Bultmann, *Gesch. d. syn. Trad.*, p. 372;
A. E. J. Rawlinson, *St Mark*, pp. xliii–xlv; C. H. Dodd, *The Apostolic
Preaching and its Development*, pp. 38–43.

[3] Cf., pp. 21ff. above, what we have said on this subject.

[4] The comparisons made by J. Weiss, *Das älteste Evangelium*, pp. 95–7,
between Mark and I Peter are not very convincing and do nothing to
solve the problem of the authenticity of that Epistle. Nor does O.
Cullmann's theory, *Saint Pierre*, pp. 57–60, according to which Peter
was the first to recognize the theological significance of Jesus' death
and give him the title of 'Servant of God', allow us to conclude that
Mark's thinking depended directly on his in this respect, since the
Evangelist never calls Jesus παῖς or παῖς θεοῦ.

[5] Cf. M. J. Lagrange, *Ev. Marc*, pp. cxi–cxiii.

[6] Cf. pp. 125–30 above. We shall return later to the traditional identifica-

been refuted in such masterly fashion by M. Werner[1] that despite the timid and laboured rehabilitation attempted by B. W. Bacon,[2] there would be little need to pay attention to it if W. Marxsen had not taken it up again recently in a rather new form.[3] The essential (and almost only) argument is that, apart from Paul, the author of Mark is the only New Testament writer who uses the word εὐαγγέλιον quite frequently.[4] As in this critic's opinion the term derives from Eastern paganism and more specifically from the first forms of the imperial cult, he sees Paul as having borrowed the word from that cult and believes that the author of Mark could not have received it except from Paul, which he would not have done without a fairly close theological dependence on him. It is thus with the help of Pauline concepts, the critic suggests, that the author of Mark sorted out and recast the confused mass of the synoptic tradition. This reasoning does not seem convincing, for several reasons: the pagan origin of εὐαγγέλιον is highly doubtful; its introduction into the Christian vocabulary is difficult to place and it is not at all certain that Paul initiated its use without qualification;[5] lastly, this word is closely bound up with itinerant missionary preaching and its use reveals only an interest taken in the propagation of Christianity,[6] not the fact of belonging to a particular school of thought.

The third theory, according to which Mark recasts the synop-

---

tion of the author of Mark with John Mark of Jerusalem (pp. 246–9 and 251ff.).

[1] Op. cit. (Giessen 1923).　　　　[2] Op. cit. pp. 221–71.

[3] Op. cit., in particular pp. 83–92, 98–101, 145–7. There is nothing to be learned from J. C. Fenton ('Paul and Mark' in *Studies in the Gospels, Essays in Memory of R. H. Lightfoot*, ed. D. E. Nineham, pp. 89–112), who seeks to explain Mark by reference to the Epistles of Paul.

[4] Seven times in Mark, sixty times in Paul (Pastoral Epistles and Ephesians included), whose total length is almost three times that of Mark (32,349 words as compared with 11,242, according to R. Morgenthaler, *Statistik*, p. 164); four times in Matthew; twice in Acts; it is not used in Luke or John.

[5] On these two points R. Bultmann, *Theologie des N.T.*, 3rd edn, pp. 89–90, defends ideas that are incompatible with W. Marxsen's theory. With regard to the whole history of the word εὐαγγέλιον, reference should be made to the article on it by G. Friedrich (*TWNT*, vol. II, pp. 718–34), whose own theories, however, are sometimes questionable.

[6] Cf. pp. 183ff. below.

tic tradition in the light of the theology of the hellenistic Church as it existed before Paul and in his day, holds more probability. But with R. Bultmann it takes too systematic a form to be accepted without qualification. According to this critic, it was above all the 'myth of Christ' (cf. Phil. 2.6ff., Rom. 3.24ff.) that the author of Mark was seeking to illustrate with the help of miracle stories and apophthegms.[1] Consequently, the idea of the redeeming sacrifice and of the elevation of a divine being was the author's principal theological contribution to his work, where it served as a principle to guide the ordering of less 'mythological' material. But R. Bultmann himself admits that the idea of the death of Jesus as an expiation no doubt goes back to the earliest Church.[2] As for the two christological titles most characteristic, in his view, of the kerygma of the Church that had grown up in the midst of Greek culture, namely those of κύριος and υἱὸς τοῦ θεοῦ,[3] they are certainly to be found in Mark. But the first of them is much rarer in Mark than in any other New Testament book with the exception of the Epistle to Philemon and the Johannine epistles.[4] Moreover, κύριος is often applied to God when Mark uses it (12.11,29,30,36; 13.20; cf. 12.9); even where it appears to apply to Jesus there are places where it could apply to God (5.19; 13.35) or to any person (2.28; 11.3). Lastly, where the term definitely applies to Jesus, there is nothing messianic or supernatural in its meaning: 12.36,37 is suggested by Ps. 110 and is used for a purely polemical purpose;[5] in 7.28, the word in the vocative is

---

[1] R. Bultmann, *Gesch. d. syn. Trad.*, pp. 372–3.
[2] *Theol. des N.T.*, 3rd edn, pp. 48–9.   [3] Ibid., pp. 123–35.
[4] The word κύριος is found in Mark only eighteen times (according to R. Morgenthaler, *Statistik*, p. 115, who includes in this number several very doubtful cases), which means once in every six hundred and twenty-five words, roughly, whereas in Paul (if we count the Pastoral Epistles and Ephesians), it occurs about once every hundred and eighteen words (which allows us to ignore the exception constituted by the short Epistle to Philemon), in John it occurs once in every two hundred and ninety-six words (which reduces the importance of its almost complete absence from the Johannine Epistles) and in Revelation once in every four hundred and twenty-eight words, whereas this book is by far the most reserved in its use of κύριος of all the New Testament writings except Philemon, 1, 2 and 3 John, and Mark.
[5] It is quite legitimate to suppose, however, that the very surprising application to Jesus of the title 'Lord', which was already given to God

scarcely more than a specially respectful form of address justified by the fact that it is put in the mouth of an importunate woman seeking Jesus' help. Even if we allow that in 5.19 and 11.3, κύριος, used without qualification, definitely refers to Jesus, there is no proof that there either this term has its full christological meaning; in any case, it would be difficult to claim seriously, on the basis of these two verses, that Mark resorts here to the usage of the earliest Church of Greek culture, from which, nevertheless, R. Bultmann asserts he derives his christology.

As for the title of υἱὸς τοῦ θεοῦ, used seven or eight times by Mark,[1] it comes closer to the Evangelist's central ideas, since it is pronounced twice by God (1.11 and 9.7), twice by 'unclean spirits' rather well-informed about God's affairs (3.11 and 5.7), once by the High Priest (14.61), once by the centurion on guard at the foot of the cross (15.39) and possibly twice by Jesus himself (12.6; 13.32). But this title certainly goes back to the earliest Church[2] and is still for Mark simply a sort of less hermetic variant of the word Χριστός.[3] How then can one see in its use by Mark an indication of the influence exerted on the Evangelist by the kerygma of the first Church of Greek culture, in particular in the matter of christology?

Thus it is not to any pre-paulinism of the kind postulated by R. Bultmann[4] that the author of Mark owed the concept of the

---

in Judaism, was facilitated by the words of Ps. 110.1. Cf. O. Cullmann, *Christologie du N.T.*, pp. 113-4, 176-7.

[1] Cf. p. 143, note 3 above.

[2] Cf., for example, R. Bultmann, *Theol. d. N.T.*, 3rd edn, pp. 52-3; J. Bieneck, *Sohn Gottes als Christusbezeichnung der Synoptiker* (Zurich 1951), *passim*; O. Cullmann, *Christologie du N.T.*, pp. 234ff. These two last-mentioned authors trace the title in addition back to Jesus himself. It is not for us here to settle that difficult question.

[3] Cf. p. 144, n. 1 above. J. Bieneck, op. cit., pp. 45ff. and O. Cullmann, op. cit. pp. 238-44, lay great emphasis on the distinction they claim the synoptic Gospels make between the concepts of Christ and of Son of God. We confess to being unable to see on what this argument rests, contradicted as it is by passages like Mark 14.61 and Matt. 16.16 (and Mark 1.1 in its long version), unless it is on the desire to safeguard the originality and antiquity of the title 'Son of God'. But one can agree that the authors of the synoptic Gospels made the two titles practically interchangeable, without necessarily assigning the same meaning to them in the usage of the first Christians or of Jesus himself.

[4] Cf. his *Theol. d. N.T.*, 3rd edn, pp. 66-186.

work of Jesus Christ, which guided him in his organization of the
materials he used.

Must we then deny that the author of Mark imposed on these
traditions and stories a certain idea of the person and work of
Jesus that may be personal to him but which more probably
corresponds to the implicit christology of the Greek-speaking
communities for which he was writing? It would not seem so.
As we have already shown,[1] he borrows on the one hand from
the authorized trustees of church tradition a series of pericopes
where Jesus appears in the guise of a rabbi and a Messiah,
founder of a new Jewish sect, and on the other hand, from the
popular society of northern Palestine, reminiscences bordering
on legend and pagan religiosity, where Jesus appeared as the
amazing healer, at once beneficent and elusive, who had
broken away from the narrow-mindedness of the strict Jews
and aroused their animosity. The personal christological
contribution of the author of Mark, which forms the foundation
of his literary work, devoted primarily to welding these two
components together into a coherent whole, consisted in
merging these two images of the person and work of Jesus into a
portrait in a distinctively 'Marcan' style, whose outline we must
now endeavour to trace.

This man Jesus defies all definition, so deep is the mystery
surrounding his person and his relationship to God. To give
him a messianic title is almost blasphemy; it is in any case a way
of resisting him or imposing on him the will of others.[2] Vis-à-vis

[1] Cf. pp. 34ff. above.

[2] If we except the confession of the centurion (15.39), which we shall
discuss later (cf. p. 236 below) and the two passages where God speaks
(1.11; 9.7) which, moreover, are more an appeal to Jesus, the various
more or less christological confessions and forms of address in Mark
come, in the vast majority of cases, from people begging importunately
for help (7.28; 9.17; 10.17; 10.48,49,51), from ill-advised disciples
(8.29; 9.5,38; 10.35; 13.1; 14.45), from more or less malevolent adversaries (6.16; 12.14,19; 14.61; 15.2,18,26,32) or from 'unclean
spirits' (1.24; 3.11; 5.7). Many of these strange confessors, moreover,
find themselves harshly treated by Jesus, whether he orders them to hold
their peace (1.25; 3.12; 8.30), greets them with haughty silence
(9.6; 14.46; 15.2-3,19-20,33) or demolishes them in a few words
(5.8ff.; 8.32-3; 9.19ff.; 9.39ff.; 10.36ff.; 12.15-17,24-7; 13.2; 14.62).
'Who Jesus really is, only those who follow him can know. . . . No

Jesus, the only proper attitude is one of wondering awe,[1] unconditional obedience,[2] total and unreasoning confidence.[3] There is no reason why he should not be very like the historical Jesus, but it is clear that he is also the Christ of the Christian faith, he who was worshipped in the Church to which the Evangelist belonged.

This Jesus is accomplishing on God's behalf an eschatological mission for which he has received the Holy Spirit.[4] His essential function is to go from place to place proclaiming the 'Good News' of God (1.14,38). Whereas John the Baptist could content himself with the crying in the wilderness, calling on people to repent—people who were already prepared to listen to him thanks to the presence quite close at hand of the great religious centre of Israel[5]—Jesus goes out into the furthest villages, to

---

formula once taught and repeated by disciples can tell this', as E. Schweizer very rightly says (translated from *Erniedrigung und Erhöhung bei Jesus und seinen Nachfolgern* (Zurich 1955), p. 19).

[1] As in 1.27; 4.41; 7.37; 9.32; 10.32; 14.3; 16.8.

[2] As in 1.16–20; 2.14; 6.7–13; 8.34–5; 10.17–31.

[3] As in 1.40ff.; 2.3ff.; 4.40; 5.21–43; 6.1–6; 8.17–21; 9.14–29; 10.46–52; 11.22–5. The πίστις suggested in these texts, most of which are accounts of healings, has not the theological depth, of course, that Paul places at the centre of the Christian life. But it is worth noting that this word, relatively rare in Mark (it is used five times, as against eight in Matthew and eleven in Luke) is supplemented by the verb πιστεύειν, much more frequent in Mark (fourteen times) than in Matthew (eleven times) or Luke (nine times). Trust in God or in Jesus is indeed therefore one of the fundamental spiritual attitudes that man is called upon to adopt in confrontation with the mysterious 'Son of Man'.

[4] Cf. Mark 1.10ff.; 3.29–30. Excellent comments on these texts will be found in J. M. Robinson, *Das Geschichtsverständnis des Mk-Ev.*, pp. 20ff., 42ff.; M. A. Chevallier, *L'Esprit et le Messie dans le bas-judaïsme et le Nouveau Testament* (Paris 1958), pp. 57ff., 92–4.

[5] According to Mark, the people attracted by the preaching of John the Baptist were those of 'all the land of Judaea and those of Jerusalem' (1.5), that is to say all the people who lived in the vicinity of the capital and the Temple. Luke is content to say that John the Baptist 'came into all the country about Jordan' to make his proclamation, which suggests an itinerant ministry but says nothing of the origin of the people he attracted (3.3). Matthew is closer to Mark and specifies simply that the wilderness where John preached was that of Judaea (3.1), that his hearers were 'Jerusalem and all Judaea and all the region round about Jordan' (3.5). Thus, it would seem, he combined the indications in Mark with those of the *logia*, reproduced by Luke. As it

the outer fringe of Jewish Palestine (1.38,39; 5.1; 6.7; 7.24,31; 8.10,22,27; 9.30; 10.1), seeking the crowds hungry for the word of God. The two great envoys from God are both like heralds, charged with the same proclamation,[1] but in the case of Jesus the author of Mark believes that the work of 'town crier' is no more a mere preliminary, but is a part of God's eschatological plan. It is no longer a matter of a chosen individual leading others on to 'prepare the way of the Lord' (1.3); it is the Lord God himself coming nearer to the world (1.15) with every stage of the career of Jesus. That God himself is coming in this itinerant preaching must be believed (1.15), understood (8.17–21), and sung (11.9–10). The 'Good News', the εὐαγγέλιον is not the content of that preaching only, it is more the fact that it is taking place everywhere.[2] It is in this

is not very likely that Mark used an independent source (cf. pp. 54–6 above), one can allow that the double geographical indication in (1.5) is the Evangelist's own work, like that in 3.7–8: the former designates a crowd of Jews firmly attached to their religious institutions and the latter a heterogeneous assembly where there were certainly at least some half-Jews.

[1] The word κηρύσσειν that Mark uses more often than any other book in the New Testament (twelve times, as against only nine times in Matthew and Luke, four times in Rom., 1 Cor. and 2 Cor.) is applied twice by the Evangelist to John the Baptist (1.4,7) and three times to Jesus (1.14,38,39); without being a technical term (cf. 1.45; 5.20; 7.36), in the case of these two emissaries of God, as for the disciples of Jesus (3.14; 6.12), it is one of the words that describes their obedience to the mission God has entrusted to them (1.3; 1.38; 6.7). On the other hand, John the Baptist and Jesus both call men to μετάνοια by reason of the coming of God into the world (1.3–5; 1.15), as the Twelve were also to do (6.12).

[2] This explains why the Evangelist can begin his book with the words ἀρχὴ τοῦ εὐαγγελίου Ἰησοῦ Χριστοῦ. What he is going to relate is how Jesus brought to men the 'God whose kingdom is coming', much more than what he taught or what one ought to think about him. John the Baptist is the forerunner to the eschatological event of Jesus' itinerant preaching; it is thus natural that his ministry should be described as the 'beginning' of that preaching. Hence the brief opening remark is not an *incipit* giving to the word εὐαγγέλιον the sense of 'account of the earthly life of Jesus'. It is a remark designed to justify the passage about John the Baptist at the beginning of the book, where it serves to prevent an interpretation of Jesus' ministry as a simple pre-eschatological occurrence. (Cf. 1.2,7–8.)

Whatever the interpretation adopted, the construction of vv. 1–4 is

modest action repeated a hundred times over that men must recognize God, without asking for a sign (8.11–12) or proof (11.27–33) other than the ministry of John the Baptist: it is too late to prepare oneself or to hesitate (10.17–22). Where Jesus speaks, God sows his seed (4.3ff., 26ff.) and the harvest is bound to follow (4.28) soon (13.28–30): the only choice that remains to men is to be 'good ground' (4.20).

In choosing to come into the world in this strange way, God is in danger of being halted at any time by the Arch-enemy, vis-à-vis whom he has renounced his superiority. This explains how, straight after his baptism, Jesus encounters Satan, come to tempt him even before he has begun his ministry.[1] Later, on several occasions, 'unclean spirits' in the service of the 'prince of devils' (3.22) will rise up along his path to prevent him from

---

obscure: C. E. B. Cranfield, *St Mark*, pp. 34–5, gives a good list of the various solutions proposed. The least unsatisfactory seems to be to place vv.2–3 in parenthesis and to remove all punctuation at the end of v. 1, which then becomes the attribute of Ἰωάννης in v. 4. This is indeed the only construction that justifies the curious ἐγένετο with which v. 4 begins. This verb is so neutral (in spite of the efforts of E. Lohmeyer, *Ev. des Mk.*, p. 12, n. 4, to give it a stronger meaning by referring to 2 Peter, 2.1 and 1 John 2.18, passages where in fact it is only used in order to avoid a repetition) that Mark nearly always uses it in an impersonal form (καὶ ἐγένετο . . . and similar expressions), with a subject designating a thing or an event (cf. 1.32; 6.2; 9.7; 13.29), or as a copula (a use in which it sometimes takes on the appearance of an auxiliary verb, when the attribute of the subject is a participle: 9.7). When, exceptionally, the subject is a person and it is not reduced to the function of a copula (9.33), Mark gives it a weak meaning such as 'to be in a certain place'. In 1.4 ἐγένετο is placed too much to the fore to have such a neutral meaning; it cannot have the role of an auxiliary, since the participle that could depend on it, κηρύσσων (βαπτίζων is preceded by an article in the Vaticanus reading, which is certainly the right one: cf. the commentaries of M. J. Lagrange, E. Lohmeyer, V. Taylor, C. E. B. Cranfield, W. Grundmann, ad loc.), is too far away to suggest any relation between them; it is therefore used as a copula and we have to look for an attribute for Ἰωάννης: the only possible one is v. 1, whose link with v. 4 is thus confirmed.

Concerning the meaning and origin of the word εὐαγγέλιον, cf. G. Friedrich, art. εὐαγγέλιον in *TWNT*, vol. II, pp. 718–34 and H. Clavier, *L'accès au Royaume de Dieu* (Clermont-Ferrand and Paris 1943), pp. 91–103.

[1] Cf. the excellent comments on this episode by J. M. Robinson, *Das Geschichtsverständnis des Mk-Ev.*, pp. 25–6.

fulfilling his mission as bearer of the gospel.[1] Even when direct opposition fails, the 'unclean spirits' seek to make use of the crowd attracted by Jesus' reputation as a healer to turn him aside from his main function and confine him to mere miracle-working.[2] The very vigorous defensive reaction of Jesus when confronted by certain people possessed by devils (1.26; 3.11–12; 5.8–9; 9.25), by certain miracle-hungry crowds (1.35ff.,45; 3.9,13; 5.30–2; 7.24) and by certain sick people or their families, who are capable, in their gratitude, of overwhelming him with a vast influx of people animated by no spiritual desires,[3] can mean, in our view, only one thing: the

---

[1] It is while Jesus is teaching in the synagogue at Capernaum that he is violently attacked for the first time by a demoniac (1.21ff.); it is when he is landing 'on the other side of the lake' (in order to teach, it would seem) that a man with an unclean spirit bars his way and, although overcome by Jesus, succeeds in obliging him by a ruse to board his ship again immediately (5.1ff.), but Jesus wins the day by making him spread the news of his preaching throughout the whole region (5.18–20). It is again Jesus' preaching that is opposed by the 'dumb spirit', which resists the disciples at a time when they should have been able to take advantage of all their Master's teaching (9.14ff.; cf. 8.31ff.) but show by their helplessness that his efforts have been in vain (9.19). If everywhere he goes Jesus combines teaching and exorcism (1.39; cf.3.15 and 6.7,12), it is because he is everywhere opposed by evil spirits.

[2] The most characteristic example of this is Mark 3.7–12, because it is a summary due to the author and represents his own views. Jesus has had some difficulty in escaping from the self-interested and rather unhealthy enthusiasm of the enormous crowd of people who follow him everywhere in order to take advantage of his miracle-working (vv. 9–10). The 'unclean spirits' (they are certainly demoniacs, as shown by J. M. Robinson, op. cit. p. 34, n. 1, and H. J. Ebeling, *Das Messiasgeheimnis und die Botschaft des Marcus-Evangelisten*, p. 120, as opposed to O. Bauernfeind, *Die Worte der Dämonen im Markus-Evangelium*, pp. 56–63) add to the general excitement with their sensational declarations in order the better to force him to comply with the wishes of the crowd. By reducing them to silence and withdrawing into the mountains to choose the Twelve as additional 'heralds', Jesus is thus defending his ministry as God's messenger. The same manoeuvre on the part of the evil spirits can be detected in 1.33ff., thereby throwing more light on Jesus' reply (v. 38).

[3] In view of the gist of v. 45 and Jesus' successful manoeuvre in vv. 35–9, it is certainly in this way that the author of Mark understood the Master's anger once the leper was cured and the command given to him to say nothing (1.40–4). The injunction to discretion in 5.43 is made for the same purpose, if we are to judge by 5.21,24,25ff. Similarly that of

Evangelist is seeking to show that Jesus, when attacked or tempted by Satan, at once perceives the evil intentions of one who wishes to put a stop to the spread of the 'Good News' of God.[1]

This astonishing εὐαγγέλιον is the manifestation of the mercy of a God who does not wish to come among men as a judge.[2] As it is carried from place to place therefore, it is natural that it should be accompanied by acts of kindness which illustrate at once God's power and salvation.[3] Sometimes these acts take the form of the announcement of the forgiveness of sins (2.5,9–10,17), but mostly they are acts of healing in response to the trust placed in Jesus by sick people or those who are looking after them. Such gestures are often performed for the benefit

---

7.36 and the less imperative one of 8.26. A counter-proof is provided by texts like 5.18–20, where Jesus encourages the spreading throughout Decapolis of the news of the exorcism of the Gadarene because he himself is not staying in the area and so is in no danger of being hampered in his progress by the crowd; or again by 2.2ff.; 3.1–5; 5.25–34 and 9.14, where the healings in public are openly commented on by Jesus before the crowd already assembled and there is no command to say nothing about them. In short, the order to remain silent is given only where it is necessary in order to preserve Jesus' freedom for his preaching.

[1] If the author of Mark has any general theory here, it is therefore concerned much more with the unremitting struggle by Satan to prevent the spread of the εὐαγγέλιον than with any idea of a messianic secret, which would be refuted by half the texts.

[2] It is striking that in his summary of the preaching of John the Baptist the author of Mark, unlike those of Matthew and Luke, should have omitted everything announcing an approaching judgement (the axe: Matt. 3.10 and Luke 3.9; the fire: Matt. 3.11 and Luke 3.16; the separation of the wheat from the chaff: Matt. 3.12 and Luke 3.17), leaving in fact only the promise of the Holy Spirit (Mark 1.8). The rarity of the words derived from the root κριν- is one of the special features of Mark's vocabulary: κρίνειν, κρίσις, and κριτής are all missing, although they occur quite frequently in Matthew and Luke; κρίμα occurs only once and κατακρίνειν three times, in connection with the condemnation of Jesus.

[3] The words δύναμις (5.30; 6.2,5,14; 9.39) and σῴζειν (3.4; 5.23,28,34; 6.56; 10.52) are quite often used in connection with healings, whereas elsewhere in Mark they have a more religious sense; it would be impossible to emphasize better the metaphysical significance of these acts of Jesus, even though they are concerned with the healing of the body.

of sick people brought by the crowd (1.32,34; 3.10; 6.53–6) but, even in that case, a minimum of faith is required (6.5–6). In other cases, individuals take advantage of a favourable opportunity to wrest from Jesus a healing that he had not intended to perform (1.40–4; 5.25–34; cf. 4.35–41); this provokes the Master's anger, since he wants to be free to heal those he wishes, but he nevertheless yields to compassion. Elsewhere a healing is brought about following a request that does not seek to force Jesus' hand and that testifies to a lively and sincere faith (1.29–31; 2.2–12; 5.21–4,35–43; 7.24–30; 7.32–7; 8.22–6; 9.14–29; 10.46–52); in those cases it takes place in a house or in a place apart,[1] which fact emphasizes that these are acts of mercy and not mysterious manifestations of Jesus' supernatural glory.[2] When the time seems right, however,

---

[1] The only apparent exceptions are 2.2–12, 9.14–29 and 10.46–52. But they are only exceptions at first sight. In 2.2–12, it is not at all certain that the author of Mark thought that the crowd had come into the house, as in 3.20 or 6.31; the expression used in v. 2 suggests rather a comparison with 1.33 and gives the reader to understand that, this time, the exterior approaches to the door did not suffice to contain the crowd, which was milling in the surrounding streets so that the sick could not get through; the presence of 'certain of the scribes' and the fact that the crowd does not react until the paralytic comes out of the house carrying his bed suggest, on the contrary, that the healing was performed in the presence of a small number of people. In 9.14–29, the remark in 9.25a seems to indicate that Jesus hastened to drive out the evil spirit in order not to give the crowd time to assemble; it is no doubt an editorial addition, since it is in clumsy contradiction to 9.15 and 9.20, but it is all the more interesting to us on that account; lastly, it will be noted that it is a case of exorcism, which is normally, in Mark, a struggle conducted in public. In 10.46–52, the scene occurs when Jesus is leaving Jericho and possibly at some distance from the city, since the blind man, who was no doubt outside the gates (παρὰ τὴν ὁδόν), has to be called by messengers to come to the 'Son of David', who is already some distance away; besides, no publicity surrounds this healing, since Bartimaeus follows Jesus and no reaction is recorded on the part of the crowd.

[2] It is not certain that this distinction was made by the popular story-tellers from whom the author of Mark gleaned his stories. They no doubt combined the two ideas in all their tales of Jesus the great wonder-worker (cf. pp. 45ff. above). The Evangelist, without always removing the traces of this initial confusion, makes a clear distinction between the 'combat' miracles, designed to sweep away obstacles in the path of the gospel (exorcisms, certain public healings) and the 'mercy' miracles (private healings; gestures to help the crowd, whether

Jesus does not at all forbid the news of the healing being spread abroad, which shows once more how arbitrary any theory of a 'messianic secret' is bound to be.[1] Jesus even occasionally resorts to a public healing as a weapon (3.1–5; cf. 2.2–12), a gesture which differs little from his exorcisms, since his adversaries, in the eyes of the author of Mark, are veritable demons (3.22–30).

God shows his mercy even more in one last aspect of the mission he entrusted to Jesus as the author of Mark understood it: the Son of Man, come to 'serve', that is to say to impart to mankind the 'Good News' and to illustrate it by actively doing good, has also come 'to give his life a ransom for many' (10.45). We shall not express an opinion here on the much-disputed authenticity of this saying[2] but shall confine ourselves

---

it be exorcisms, healings or distributions of food). M. Dibelius, *Formgesch. des Evang.*, pp. 66–100 and 219–34, believes that from 'short stories' that were accounts of epiphanies (p. 91) Mark derived a 'book of secret epiphanies', combining them with theologically neutral 'paradigms' and imposing on the whole a 'messianic secret' theory and a 'parables' theory. One should rather speak of a theory of 'combat against the forces of evil' and a 'theory of divine mercy', in order to explain the use made by the author of Mark of the miracle stories. As for the 'parables' theory, we believe it pre-dated Mark and that he tried to correct it (cf. p. 160 below).

[1] Hence we do not accept W. Wrede's claim, supported by H. J. Ebeling, *Messiasgeheimnis*, p. 65, according to which, to understand Mark properly one must arrive at a global interpretation of his theory of a messianic secret. What is essential in order to read Mark aright is to perceive the unity and originality of his implicit theological ideas, which one can certainly not reduce to a messianic secret invented by W. Wrede in order to account for several aspects of this Gospel. W. Wrede has the merit of having attempted to see in Mark a connected whole, independently of the old structure postulated by the Tübingen school. But his hypothesis has aged in its turn and it is hard to see why, from generation to generation, it should impose itself on all the critics. One must therefore welcome, even if their conclusions are still somewhat vague, the attempts made to approach the examination of the motif of secrecy in Mark from a new angle: for example, that of G. H. Boobyer, 'The Secrecy Motif in St Mark's Gospel', in *New Testament Studies*, VI (1959–60), pp. 225–35.

[2] This is known to be a highly controversial subject. The critics' conclusions are usually dictated by their ideas about Jesus' consciousness of being the Messiah. Those who believe that Jesus assigned to himself the role of 'Ebed Yahweh' conclude that Mark 10.45 is authentic (cf. the

to discussing the part it plays in Mark. It must be admitted that the jump from the idea of service to that of redeeming death is very sudden and surprising in the middle of this one verse,[1] whose second part obviously refers to Isa. 53.10–12,[2] whereas the first part bears no relation to that text. Moreover, Luke 22.24–7, which contains a fairly close parallel to Mark 10.41–5, has nothing that recalls 10.45b. We must thus conclude that the author of Mark, if he did not invent this little *logion* himself,[3] at least took the initiative of placing it here as

---

reasoning of O. Cullmann, *Christologie du N.T.*, pp. 59–60 or of J. Jeremias, art. παῖς θεοῦ, *TWNT*, vol. v, pp. 799ff.). Those who deny that Jesus saw his ministry in this way deduce that Mark 10.45 is an invention of the Christian community. The least serious criticism by far is that of R. Bultmann who, firmly convinced that Jesus *cannot* have presented himself as the 'Servant of the Eternal' (*Theol. des N.T.*, pp. 32–3), is content, for the purpose of refuting the authenticity of Mark 10.45 to refer to W. Bousset, *Kyrios Christos*, 3rd edn (Göttingen 1926), pp. 7–8 (*Gesch. d. syn. Trad.*, p. 154; a single peremptory sentence to which the few other allusions to Mark 10.45 in this work refer back), but this author does not even agree with him, since he attributes the invention of the idea of redeeming death to the hellenistic Church, whereas R. Bultmann himself is obliged today to trace it back to the very earliest Church (*Theol. d. N.T.*, 3rd edn, pp. 48–50).

[1] As is rightly pointed out by J. Wellhausen, *Das Evangelium Marci*, 2nd edn, pp. 84–5, who speaks of μετάβασις εἰς ἄλλο γένος in connection with the transference from the idea of service to that of giving one's life as a ransom; C. G. Montefiore, *Synoptic Gospels*, vol. I, p. 253, who thinks that the first half of 10.45 is authentic but not the second; E. Klostermann, *Das Mk.-Ev.*, 3rd edn, p. 108, who sees in these two ideas 'images of a different order'. A Loisy, often cited in support of the theory of the sudden jump from the idea of service to that of giving life as a ransom (thus A. E. J. Rawlinson, *St Mark*, p. 147), merely stresses the different origin of the two ideas, which the 'editor' sets down together here in the 'language' of Paul, in order to comment on them after his own fashion, 10.35–40 (*Ev. selon Marc*, pp. 308–11).

[2] The allusion to Isa. 53.10–12, today recognized by almost all critics, is nowhere better demonstrated than in H. W. Wolff, *Jesaja 53 im Urchristentum*, 3rd edn (Berlin 1952), pp. 60–4.

[3] It could be maintained that this saying is too short, the Evangelist's hand too visible in vv. 41–5, and the term λύτρον too exceptional in Christian literature of the first century (it occurs elsewhere only in Matt. 20.28, where it comes from Mark 10.45, and non-composite words of the λυτρ- type are very rare in the New Testament outside Luke-Acts) for Mark 10.45b to be regarded as a separate *logion*. In this case it would simply be an editorial addition, which would be just as

an appendix to another (Mark 10.42–5a) which did not mention Jesus' sacrifice but where he thought he might add a reference to it because of the proximity of 10.38–9. Why did the author of Mark see fit to make this addition? It was in order, we suggest, to establish a connection between the 'service' of Jesus as a preacher and a healer, related principally in chapters 1—8, and his role as victim, which is the main subject of 8.31—10.45, where in any case it supplies the fabric, thanks to the three predictions of the passion and the resurrection (8.31; 9.31; 10.32–4). In the light of the juxtaposition in 10.45 of these two aspects of Jesus' ministry, each takes on its true value: the work of the preacher-healer is seen clearly as the humble road chosen by God for his coming into the world and not as the triumphal march of a man endowed with supernatural powers; the sacrifice freely accepted is revealed as the act of redemption willed by God and not as the moving downfall of a misunderstood victim. Once again, consequently, the author of Mark fits the materials he uses into the framework of a general conception of the ministry of Jesus which does not coincide with any that inspired the other books of the New Testament.

2
JESUS, HEAD OF THE CHURCH

This conception of Jesus' ministry, as we have seen, even if it does not run counter to that deriving from the earliest church tradition and popular memory, nevertheless reflects a certain image of the Christ worshipped in faith by the church to which the author of Mark belonged. One should even say, more precisely, that what this author saw with the eyes of a believer was not the person of Jesus alone: it was Jesus and his followers he was thinking of, on the basis of the bonds uniting their

---

interesting to us, since we are trying to reconstruct the ideas of the author of Mark. He might have based his addition on the account of the institution of the Lord's Supper, which came to him from church tradition (J. Jeremias, *Die Abendmahlsworte Jesu*, 2nd edn (1949), pp. 88–9), and contained (Mark 14.24) the idea of Jesus' dying to save others (ibid. pp. 107–11). In any event, it seems difficult to be very positive about the origin of Mark 10.45b; one can only say that this half-verse is neither Pauline nor even pre-Pauline, but definitely Palestinian (Ed. Lohse, '*Märtyrer und Gottesknecht*', *Untersuchungen zur urchristlichen Verkündigung vom Sühnetod Jesu Christi* (Göttingen 1955), pp. 116–29).

Lord to his Church. He could do so the better for refusing to speculate on the titles and person of Jesus, whom he thus avoided isolating from the rest of mankind. In stressing Jesus' mission, on the contrary, he was placing the accent on what the Master and his disciples had in common.[1] It was thus easier for him to see in Jesus the leader of a group of people who shared his destiny than would have been the case had he placed the Lord's person on a pedestal.

In Mark, Jesus is always the leader of a group of men, if we except the end of the Passion story after Peter's denial and the flight of all the disciples. Nowhere does the Evangelist dwell on any activity Jesus might have engaged in away from the presence of his followers. He summarizes as much as he can[2]

---

[1] In 8.35, for example, the Evangelist puts into the mouth of Jesus a phrase, 'for my sake and the gospel's', which seems to diminish the person of the Master and has embarrassed many readers of Mark from the first century onwards. The parallel texts in Matthew (16.25) and Luke (9.24) indeed keep only 'for my sake' and certain copyists (D, P45, 28, 700; a, b, i, n; syr. sin., eth., arm.; Origen; according to S. C. E. Legg, *Euang. sec. Marcum cum apparatu critico nouo* . . . (Oxford 1935), ad. loc.) keep only 'the gospel', whereas others (33, 579; ff.: S. C. E. Legg, ibid.) reproduce the text of the synoptic parallels and some versions evade the difficulty by speaking of 'my gospel' (syr. sin.) or of 'me and my gospel' (one Vulgate manuscript; syr. peshitto). In 10.29 there is an almost identical expression which is also left out by Matthew (19.29) and Luke (18.29) but has embarrassed copyists and translators less (only ℵ* leaves out 'for my sake'), thanks to the presence of a second ἕνεκεν before the word 'gospel', which takes away from the diminution of the person of Jesus. Certain modern commentators also seem disturbed by the idea that the author of Mark might have wanted to join 'the gospel' to Jesus as a separate object of devotion to which Christians must be faithful just as they are to their Master. Hence they attribute to the καί which links the two words the meaning of 'that is to say' (thus, most recently, W. Marxsen, *Der Ev. Mk.*, pp. 84–5 and W. Grundmann, *Ev. nach Mk.*, p. 176). But a comparison with 10.29 invalidates that interpretation and we are forced to admit that the 'gospel' cannot be reduced to the person of Jesus, or even of the risen Christ. The author of Mark means that it is not enough to believe that Jesus is the Messiah but that one must also follow him as he spreads the gospel, that is to say become oneself an Evangelist, whatever the cost. By recalling the mission entrusted to Jesus, Mark is seeking to wrest his readers away from vain speculation and is urging them to share personally in this mission (cf. pp. 120ff. above).

[2] The same cannot be said of Matthew and Luke, who devote much more space to the baptism (Matt. 3.13–17, which Luke does not amplify),

the accounts of the baptism (1.9–11), the temptation (1.12–13) and the first preaching by Jesus in Galilee (1.14–15) in order to hasten on to the formation of the little group of disciples (1.16–20). In the rest of his narrative, the author of Mark imposes on material that is sometimes rebellious his idea of a Jesus who never leaves his disciples except to go into retreat.[1] While the church tradition presented Jesus as a popular preacher understood only by the elect, but whose words were usually spoken *coram populo*, the author of Mark introduces the idea of teaching on two levels, of which public preaching—elementary much more than mysterious—is the first; the second level is constituted by explanations to the disciples in which the substance of the teaching at the first level is clarified and systematized.[2] By this means, the Evangelist brings the dis-

---

the temptation (Matt. 4.1–11; Luke 4.1–13) and Jesus' first preaching mission before the calling of the disciples (Matt. 4.12–17; Luke 4.14–44) and who, in addition, linger lovingly over the genealogy of Jesus (Matt. 1.1–17; Luke 3.23–9), his birth and his early years (Matt. 1.18—2.23; Luke 1.26–56 and 2.1–52).

[1] Thus, in Mark, 1.35; 6.46; 14.32,35,39 are the only texts where the author speaks of Jesus praying and also the only ones where he is said to have left his disciples and gone away alone. In Mark 6.7–13,30, true, it is a question of sending the Twelve out on a distant mission, but it is not certain that the Evangelist was intending to describe a single happening or that he saw Jesus as remaining alone (cf. 3.18, which juxtaposes the two tasks of the Twelve: to accompany Jesus and to go on mission, without suggesting at all that they are to be carried out alternately or successively; the Twelve are the companions of Jesus, who chooses among them those whom he sends out on mission in turn). In any case, the Evangelist relates nothing that Jesus does while his missionaries are away; he even feels the need to fill in with a scene that has nothing to do with the main action (whatever the opinion of M. Goguel, *Jesus*, 2nd edn, pp. 281ff., who wants to make the introduction of Herod in Mark 6.14ff. reflect a historical fact that was decisive for Jesus' ministry, whereas, in fact, it is simply a literary artifice).

[2] This in our view is the significance of the famous 'chapter of parables', (Mark 4.1–34). As is well-known, this grouping of texts, due to the Evangelist, raises very difficult problems since it contains two different explanations of Jesus' use of parables (4.10–12 and 4.33–4) and gives an interpretation of the parable of the Sower that is oddly placed (4.13–20, whereas the parable ends at 4.9) and is generally considered to be the work of the Christian Church, being so Greek in style and language and inclining as it does towards the allegorization of the parable. There is such a contrast between 4.10–12 and 4.33–4 that one hesitates

ciples into a number of pericopes where the tradition probably made no mention of them (7.17–23; 10.10–12; 10.23ff.; 13.3–4); similarly he arranges certain miracle stories received from popular story-tellers (8.17–21; 9.28–9). Elsewhere, the

---

to believe that the same author could put forward two such different theories so close together: the parables cannot really have been for him at once a means of hardening the hearts of the Jewish masses (10–12) and an elementary mode of teaching (33–4). It is generally agreed, therefore, that one of these explanations came from his source and was simply kept in the text, enveloped in his own personal ideas. But which of these two passages does represent his own ideas? Most critics opt for 10–12, which is regarded in this case as the Evangelist's invention or else as a *logion* which he did not properly understand; at the same time it is claimed that most of vv. 33–4 comes from the source, which ascribed to the parables their real purpose of images designed to enable the masses to grasp spiritual realities.

This is untenable, unless one accepts the messianic secret theory as axiomatic. The verses given pride of place by the Evangelist are 4.33–4, while vv. 10–12 are lost between the parable of the Sower and its explanation. Mark 4.33–4 is also the passage where the author speaks his usual language ἐλάλει τὸν λόγον: cf. 2.2; 8.32; κατ' ἰδίαν: cf. 6.31,32; 7.33; 9.2,28; 13.3), whereas in 4.10–12 certain essential terms appear for the only time in his work (κατὰ μόνας; τὸ μυστήριον) and the language is singularly involved (cf. the bizarre expressions οἱ περὶ αὐτὸν σὺν τοῖς δώδεκα; ἐκείνοις... τοῖς ἔξω; ἐν παραβολαῖς τὰ πάντα γίνεται). It seems obvious that 4.33–4 is an editorial summary serving, with 4.12, to frame the little collection of parables of 4.3–32. As for 4.10–12, it is the traditional explanation of the parable of the Sower, conceived as a series of 'images' (τὰς παραβολάς in v. 10; ἐν παραβολαῖς in v. 11, apply to this one 'parable'). The author did not dare to leave it out and was content to make it, with the help of v. 13, the germ of a 'parables theory' which he spelled out in vv. 33–4 and then in vv. 14–20 added for good measure his own explanation of the parable of the Sower, to which we shall return later (p. 189).

The bibliography relating to the parables is immense, ranging from A. Jülicher's highly significant work, *Die Gleichnisreden Jesu*, (1st edn. Tübingen 1899, 2nd edn 1910) to that of J. Jeremias, *Die Gleichnisse Jesu*, 3rd edn. (Göttingen 1954), via C. Dodd, *The Parables of the Kingdom*, 2nd edn (London 1936). It is enough here to say that in addition to the pages that the chief commentators devote to Mark 4.1–34, good comments in line with the classical theory concerning this passage will be found in Ch. Masson, *Les paraboles de Marc 4* (Neuchâtel-Paris 1945); E. Percy, Liknelseteorien; Mark 41.1f och kompositionen av Mark 4.1–34 in *Svensk exegetisk årsbok*, vol. III (1947), pp. 258–78; W. Marxsen, 'Redaktionsgeschichtliche Erklärung der sogenannten Parabeltheorie des Markus', in *Zeitschrift für Theologie und Kirche*, vol. LII (1955), pp. 255–71.

presence of the disciples is suggested almost implicitly by
editorial notes, placed usually at the beginning or end of a
pericope in such a way that the persons introduced play no
part in the scene itself, which clearly shows the artificial nature
of these texts (1.21a; 2.15–16; 3.20; 4.34; 5.31,37; 6.1; 8.34;
11.11,15a,19,27; 12.43). In other passages, lastly, the presence
of the disciples is simply suggested by the context in which the
author places the episode he is relating.[1] In short, in Mark
more than in any other of the Gospels, Jesus[2] is everywhere in
the company of his disciples.

It is likely that on this point Mark reflects the historic reality:
as a rabbi, Jesus certainly spent much of his time with his
pupils.[3] But the author of Mark accentuated this aspect of
Jesus' career, drawing his inspiration instinctively from the
situation of the Christian Church, where alone the risen Christ
manifests himself. Some of the features of Jesus' activity that
are frequently mentioned in Mark confirm this tendency: the
repeated references to the 'house' where he stays in the
different places on his route[4] suggest the private houses where

[1] Thus the sentence in 1.38 lets it be understood that the disciples are
present in 1.39–45; the reference to the house in 2.1 gives the same
impression regarding 2.1–12; 2.23ff. and 3.7 regarding 3.1–6; 4.35–41
and 5.31,37 regarding 5.1–20; 7.17ff. and 8.1ff. regarding 7.24–37; etc.

[2] Apart from the fact that Mark alone specifies that it was among the
functions of the Twelve to be with Jesus (3.14), it reports in much less
length than the other three Gospels the teaching of Jesus, which often
sets him apart from his followers and concentrates attention on him
alone.

[3] Among recent publications, nowhere is this point better made than by
H. Riesenfeld, *The Gospel tradition and its beginnings, a study in the limits of
'Formgeschichte'* (London 1957), pp. 23ff. It is perhaps worth noting
here that Mark, while devoting relatively little space to the sayings of
Jesus, presents him as a teacher (The words formed from the root
διδακ-, like διδάσκειν, διδάσκαλος, διδαχή, διδασκαλία, are more frequent
than in the other Gospels) surrounded by pupils (μαθητής is as frequent
as in Matthew and more frequent than in Luke, having regard to the
relative length of the Gospels). It is the historical truth which comes to
the surface here, although it does not altogether correspond to the
Evangelist's own ideas; but he has been made more aware of it perhaps
by the vocabulary of certain Christian circles of his day (cf. p. 181, n. 2
below).

[4] In 1.29; 2.1; 2.15 (?); 3.20; 7.17,24; 9.28,33; 10.10. The expression
κατ᾽ ἰδίαν (4.34; 6.31,32; 7.33; 9.2,28; 13.3) appears to refer in several
cases to a house.

Christians used to gather in the first century;[1] the allusions to
the meals the Master took with his followers evoke irresistibly,
because of their associations with the two stories of the multiplication of the loaves (6.35ff.; 8.1ff.) and the account of the last
supper (14.12ff.), the Christian Eucharist celebrated at the
'Lord's table';[2] the private character of certain healings
performed by Jesus recalls the way in which the churches took
care of their sick and strove after their recovery.[3] Even such
a detail as the method of preaching ascribed to Jesus in Mark is
reminiscent of that of certain Christian missionaries of the first
century;[4] there again the picture of Jesus' ministry on earth is

---

[1] Cf. for example Acts 2.2,46; 5.42; 8.3; etc.; Rom. 16.5; 1 Cor. 16.19;
Col. 4.15; Philem. 2.

[2] Thus in 1.31; 2.15–16; 3.20; 6.31; 7.2; 7.27–8 (?); 8.14ff. The expression 'Lord's table' is to be found in 1 Cor. 10.21.

[3] Concerning the private character of the healings in Mark, cf. p. 155
above. The importance attached by the churches of the first century to
the healing of their own sick is well enough known for it not to be
necessary here to do more than refer to texts like 1 Cor. 12.28 or Jas.
5.14–15.

[4] The necessarily itinerant nature of the mission described in 1.38 is
suggestive of the 'Hellenists' (Acts 8.4–40; 11.19–20) or of Paul (Acts
13—14 and 16—20; Rom. 15.19,23–25). The plan followed in depicting
Jesus' activity in Capernaum (Mark 1.21–34) is fairly comparable to
that used in Acts 13—14 and 16—19 to relate the missionary activity
of Paul: the preaching in the synagogue begins on the first Sabbath
following arrival in the town (Mark 1.21; Acts 13.14; 14.1; 16.12–13;
17.1–2,10; 18.4,19; 19.8); it lasts a certain time and meets with great
success (cf. the imperfects in Mark 1.21–2, even if τοῖς σάββασιν means
the day of the Sabbath and does not necessarily indicate that the
same thing is repeated week after week; Acts 13.42ff.; 16.12ff.; 17.2;
18.4; 19.8); the missionary encounters violent opposition in the
synagogue and, although he triumphs over it, he decides to stop preaching there and to move to another place (Mark 1.23–9; Acts 13.45ff.;
18.5–7; 19.9–10); in that place, which may be a private house, he
gathers together those he has won over, but he is besieged by a more or
less distraught crowd (Mark 1.29,32–4; Acts 14.5,19; 17.5ff.; 18.12ff.;
19.10ff.); sooner or later he prefers to leave the town to continue his
ministry elsewhere (Mark 1.35ff.; Acts 13.51; 14.6,20; 17.10,14).
Care should of course be taken not to force these parallels, which are
not all entirely convincing if taken alone. But the general outline is
just the same. It would be absurd to deny on this account the historicity
of the episodes related in Mark 1.21–39; it would seem that we should
consider only the grouping of them together as the work of the Evangelist, who was seeking by this means to give a typical picture of Jesus

probably not too distorted but it is seen through the prism of habits acquired by the communities that claimed him as their Lord after the resurrection.

True, the author of Mark knows that there are differences between the presence of Jesus among his disciples and that of the risen Christ in the Christian Church. In his day the life of the Church no longer knew the somewhat disorderly jubilation that the physical presence of the Son of Man had once made possible: fasting, unthinkable in those days (2.19), has recovered its meaning for the Church, on condition that it is made the occasion for commemorating the day when the Bridegroom left her.[1] It is not certain that the closest companions of Jesus during his life on earth will remain at the right hand of Christ in his glory (10.35–40) after he has laid down his human life. Moreover, the death that hangs over the Son of Man will not be shared by his followers[2] since, the Evangelist emphasizes, he is to give his life that others may live (10.45; 14.24). Lastly, such secrets as the disciples could not reveal while they were sharing the earthly life of Jesus become public property as soon as the Son of Man has risen from the dead (9.9), which shows that the author of Mark did not entirely identify the preaching of the Christian Church with the message of which the Master's followers were the bearers at the time when he lived as a simple man among them.[3]

---

ministry. The similarities it bears to the pictures in Acts 13—14 and 16—19 are of course not due to literary borrowing. They exist because the two works are describing the same reality, namely Christian missionary preaching, which, Mark is anxious to show, began with Jesus himself.

[1] Cf. p. 109, n. 1 above.

[2] In 10.33–4 it is first specified that the group formed by Jesus and his disciples are all going up to Jerusalem (10.33a), then that the Son of Man alone is to endure suffering and death before he rises again (10.33b,34). The Passion story lays strong emphasis on the solitude in which Jesus goes to his death (14.50–1,54,66–72).

[3] This is the only text in Mark where anybody is enjoined to temporary silence. It would seem completely arbitrary to extrapolate from this one verse and claim that other similar commands are also limited in time: Mark 8.30, for example, is a permanent prohibition to substitute christological theses for the true Word (cf. pp. 120ff. above). The strictly limited import of Mark 9.9 must be preserved: the reference to certain mysterious visions was not introduced into Christian preaching until

But these few reminders of the difference between the situation of the disciples of the man Jesus and that of the Christians grouped around the risen Christ are almost negligible in comparison with the very many passages where that difference disappears entirely. Although in the matter of fasting Mark notes a change in the state of affairs after Jesus has been 'taken away', he lays much greater stress on the fact that the great innovation goes back to the day when the Bridegroom came among his friends, that is to say to the beginning of the Master's earthly ministry (2.19–22). In regard to all the other religious duties he mentions, he makes no distinction between the attitude of the disciples and that of the post-resurrection Christians:

---

after Christ's resurrection. In our view, therefore, E. Sjöberg, *Der verborgene Menschensohn in den Evangelien* (Lund 1955), pp. 162–3 and H. Baltensweiler, *Die Verklärung Jesu* (Zurich 1959), pp. 120ff., are mistaken in seeing in this verse one of the expressions of a messianic secret theory whereby the Evangelist sought to account for the reserve displayed by Jesus towards the title of Messiah. It seems much more likely that Mark 9.9 is a naive remark in which the author of Mark was endeavouring merely to explain the somewhat tardy appearance of the story of the vision and of the words from heaven accompanying it which, as we have seen, originally went hand in hand with the account (Mark 1.9ff.) of the baptism of Jesus (cf. p. 56 above). It is difficult to go further and say whether the transfiguration was an appearance of the risen Christ, as has often been claimed, by critics ranging from J. Wellhausen (*Das Evang. Marci*, 2nd edn, p. 71) to M. Goguel (*La foi à la résurrection de Jésus dans le christianisme primitif* (Paris 1933), pp. 234ff.) and R. Bultmann (*Gesch. d. syn. Trad.*, pp. 278–80), or whether, as E. Meyer has asserted, for example (*Ursprung und Anfänge des Christentums* (Stuttgart-Berlin 1921), vol. 1, pp. 152–6), it was a vision that appeared to several disciples, in particular to Peter. Certainly, in preserving the record of this event, the church tradition had been concerned not with dating it or describing it exactly, but with its theological significance, and had drawn to that end on numerous Old Testament themes that have been well sorted out by H. Riesenfeld, *Jésus transfiguré, l'arrière-plan du récit évangélique de la Transfiguration de Notre Seigneur* (Copenhagen 1947). The author of Mark imposed in addition his own conception of the occurrence, in which he saw, according to G. Boobyer (*St Mark and the Transfiguration Story* (Edinburgh 1942)) a prefiguration of the parousia and, in our view, the identification of the earthly Jesus with the risen Christ, hence also of the situation of the disciples with that of the Church (cf. pp. 169–171 below). H. Baltensweiler's attempt, op. cit. pp. 87ff., to reconstruct the original happening is thus rather venturesome, while at the same time distinctly interesting.

the same laxity in the observance of the Sabbath (2.23ff.); the same freedom with regard to the rules of ritual purification (7.1ff.); the same habits of prayer, where restraint is combined with unconditional faith and a concern for the forgiveness of sins (12.40; 11.24–5). Even if Jesus could not promise certain of his companions that their privileged relations with him during his life on earth would continue after his death, he taught them how to remain in the front line (10.41–4; 9.35; 13.33–6), assured them, as he did all others who believed in him, that their sacrifices and vigilance would be rewarded (8.34–8; 10.28–31; 13.27), and taught them that acts of kindness done in his name to the humblest of God's creatures—to children, for example—would always be the way to communion with him and with God (9.37). Although Jesus went alone to his death, he foresaw, according to Mark, that his followers would not always be spared, since they would be called upon to drink of the same 'cup' and receive the same 'baptism' as he (10.38–9), to endure the same hatred (13.13), to be persecuted as members of his 'family' (10.30; cf. 3.35), to 'take up their cross' and to 'deny themselves' in order to follow him (8.34), to lose their lives for his cause, just as he had sacrificed his for the whole of mankind (8.35; cf. 10.45). Lastly, if the Christian message has been added to on various points by comparison with what was being preached during Jesus' lifetime, it must be strongly emphasized that for the author of Mark these are questions of detail which do not affect the immutability of the gospel brought to mankind by Jesus and his followers.[1] Indeed his christological reserve makes little of the step to be taken to incorporate into the pre-paschal preaching the news of the death and resurrection of Jesus. In his eyes there is no passage from an

---

[1] It is very striking that Mark should take the 'gospel', without any qualification, to mean both the preaching of Jesus (1.15) and the work to which the disciples must devote their lives (8.35; 10.29), whereas John and Luke avoid associating the word with Jesus (cf. however Acts 15.7 and 20.24) and that Matthew visibly dislikes speaking of 'the gospel' alone when he is relating the activities or words of Jesus (he always accompanies the word by some qualification or a demonstrative: Matt. 4.23; 9.35; 24.14; 26.13). Concerning the relationship between Jesus and the gospel in Mark, cf. pp. 149ff. above; concerning the way in which Mark sees the service the disciples owe to the gospel, cf. pp. 191ff. below.

'Evangelium Christi' to an 'Evangelium de Christo', but the same triumphant onward march of God's 'Good News', before and after the apparent defeat suffered by the man Jesus.

It would nevertheless be wrong to be misled by this christo-logical reserve into imagining that, for the author of Mark, Jesus is more or less completely wrapped up in a past to which the Church is linked solely by its own continuity and that he sees Jesus only as the 'illustrious founder of our great move-ment'. Altough Mark contains no account of the resurrection, nor of any christophany,[1] there are many specific references to Jesus' rapid victory over death. The Master is not a great man whose memory must be honoured after his death and whose spirit must be carefully kept alive among the members of the Christian communities until his triumphal coming again at the end of the world.[2] He is the man who, overwhelmed and put to death by a vast conspiracy, remained in the tomb where he was thought to have been buried for ever only 'three days' before he rose again (Mark 8.31; 9.31; 10.34). At a single blów, the disaster in which his followers had lost him was wiped out. But the author of Mark is anxious to show how difficult that

---

[1] Cf. our remarks on the subject, pp. 65–68 above.

[2] This seems to be the idea underlying Peter's speech in Acts 3.12–26 (cf. in particular vv. 20–1) and chapters 4—20 of the Book of Revelation (cf. in particular chapter 12, of which an excellent historical study with pertinent comments will be found in P. Prigent, *Apocalypse 12: histoire de l'exégèse* (Tübingen 1959)). It will be noted that, according to certain specialists, the Qumran community, who revered so highly the memory of the Teacher of Righteousness, expected his return at the end of the world as the Messiah of Aaron or as the only Messiah: this theory is defended in particular by J. Allegro, 'Further Messianic References in Qumran Literature', in *JBL*, vol. LXXV (1956), pp. 174–87, and by A. Dupont-Sommer, *Les écrits esséniens. . . .* , pp. 331–3. But the idea of any supernatural activity on the part of the Teacher of Righteousness between his death and his final reappearance does not seem to exist in Essene literature. (We do not accept the exegesis of the 'Commentary of Habakkuk', col. xi,ll. 2–8, which A. Dupont-Sommer, op. cit., p. 278, prefers to maintain in spite of all the objections, and which sees in this passage an allusion to the punishment inflicted by the Teacher on his enemies after they have put him to death.) In this case there is a distinct similarity between their messianic ideas and those of Acts 3.12–26 or of Rev. 12.

miraculous event was to interpret for people accustomed to the idea of the resurrection of all the dead on Judgement Day (12.18–27). He puts into the mouths of the three intimate disciples who had just witnessed the transfiguration a question so naive that the two other synoptic Gospels preferred not to reproduce it and Peter, James, and John dare not put it to Jesus: 'What does rising from the dead mean for the Son of Man?' (9.10). For the author of Mark, the disciples who ask this question are no doubt not very brilliant exponents of the Christian faith.[1] But does he answer it himself?

One hesitates at first to think so, for, as always, the theological ideas of the author of Mark are ill-formulated and expressed in inadequate language. It would seem nevertheless that this author sees in the resurrection of Jesus a precise meaning for the life of the Christian Church; that of a mysterious return to his own people at whose head he takes his former place. True, the two curious allusions in Mark 14.28 and 16.7 are more suggestive of solitary wanderings covered by an incognito lifted only occasionally for the benefit of a few disciples (cf. Luke 24.13–32 or John 21), but they are known for their obscurity and it is difficult to judge the precise part they play in the Gospel.[2] We shall see later why it is preferable not to pay too much attention to them.[3] On the other hand, the texts that speak of the second coming of the Son of Man in glory (Mark 8.38; 13.26; 14.62) seem to postulate an elevation of the risen Christ, since he is seen as coming with the angels and in the clouds of heaven. But this elevation is nowhere expressly mentioned in Mark. The announcement in 14.62a to the members of the Sanhedrin that they will see the Son of Man sitting on the right hand of power is only a prophecy concerning the Day of Judgement and not the near future, as it has become in Matt. 26.64 and Luke 22.69. For the author of Mark, the risen Christ will return to God's side only when the hour of Judgement has come.

In the meantime, however, he is not cut off from God. But,

---

[1] Cf. pp. 123ff. above.
[2] It is in any case going too far to make the whole interpretation of Mark depend on these two verses, as W. Marxsen does in *Der Ev. Markus*, pp. 47–59.
[3] Cf. p. 236 below.

according to the Evangelist, he is once more in a situation comparable to his situation before the crucifixion, except no doubt that his presence is no longer physical or tied to one place.[1] He lives with his people, inspires them, guides them, and guarantees their communion with God, thanks to the honour that his Father shows him henceforth before the face of all believers. This, we believe, is the meaning of the Marcan account of the transfiguration (9.2ff.). To be glorified beyond anything which man can imagine, Jesus does not need to be elevated to the Father at the price of complete separation from his followers. It is enough for him to leave behind the less intimate of his disciples and go up into a 'high mountain' with the others for a short retreat. There, God sends his greatest messengers to him, envelops him in the unendurable radiance of divine beings and himself testifies to him before the stunned disciples. After that, everything returns to normal quite quickly, in spite of Peter's idea that it would be good to perpetuate this supernatural encounter by making the three men present the

---

[1] Whatever the origin of this little story of Christ walking on the water (Mark 6.45–52), it no doubt gives an idea of how the Evangelist saw the presence of Jesus among his followers. The Lord sends the disciples where they have to go (v. 45), while keeping watch over them, even after night has fallen (vv. 47–8a); when he sees them in difficulties he goes towards them and seeks to smooth their way (v. 48); if their distress is too great he climbs into their boat and talks to them, whereupon they can sail ahead once more (vv. 49–51a). The reference to the bewilderment of the disciples is designed in part to bring home to the Evangelist's readers that the incident oversteps the bounds of the earthly ministry of Jesus and concerns them personally (vv. 51b–52). The same idea can be glimpsed behind 8.17–21, which in addition uses the same words as 6.52: συνιέναι (vv. 17,21); οἱ ἄρτοι (vv. 16,17,19); πεπωρωμένη ἡ καρδία (v. 17). It seems likely that it is the key to all the texts in Mark where the disciples' bewilderment is expressly mentioned: 4.13 and 7.17–18, which justify the introduction of a commentary in order to bring a difficult parable closer to the reader; 4.41, which emphasizes the inability of the human mind to grasp how a simple human presence, with its weaknesses, can be combined, in one person, with the power of the Almighty; 9.10, 9.32 and 10.38, which suggest that the disciples could not imagine in the abstract what would follow their Master's resurrection. In each of these cases, the reader of Mark is clearly encouraged to think that the situation or the words that so astonished the disciples are explained by the presence of the risen Christ in the midst of his people. On this point W. Wrede is right (*Messiasgeheimnis*, pp. 93–113).

lackeys of the three great servants of God, that is to say by forming a little closed circle dedicated to contemplation. Jesus finds himself alone again with his disciples and leads them back to the crowd below, with its wearisome incredulity (9.19), to take up again with them the humble ministry that Satan will do everything he can to hinder.[1]

Against this threat bound up with the very nature of the 'Good News' of God, the community would be helpless, moreover, if the risen Christ were not in its midst in order, at the slightest call, to put the Prince of the devils and his agents to flight (4.35–41; cf. 6.45–52 and 9.14–29). It is only under this leadership that it can dare to challenge Satan on his own ground (3.27). But if the Lord sits in its midst and bids it drive back the Devil as well as preach the gospel, it need no longer fear an unequal combat; it is sure of the victory because it is only the instrument of the indwelling Christ.[2]

Thus, it is at once the man Jesus and the risen Christ come back to his own people that the author of Mark places at the centre of his narrative. He is not unaware of the difference between them—in chronology, in their mode of being present, in the understanding the disciples may have had of the one and the other. But it is difficult to find passages in the Gospel

[1] It is indeed significant that as soon as he comes down from the mountain Jesus finds himself facing a mocking crowd and above all an 'unclean spirit' particularly well entrenched in a sick child (9.14–29). The author of Mark was probably seeking in this way to show that the glorified Christ of 9.2–8 had not withdrawn from the bitter struggle of the preceding chapters (right up to 8.33) but that he had come straight back to the front line of battle where he would remain until the last. The Evangelist thus lets it be understood that the risen Christ has taken up arms again in the midst of his own people. Cf. pp. 152ff. above.

[2] In Mark, the mission entrusted to the Twelve is formulated in the same terms as Jesus' own mission (cf. Mark 1.14–15,21–39, on the one hand, and 3.15 and 6.7,13, on the other) and is seen as a temporary 'seconding' which merely enlarges the area covered by the Master's preaching. In Matthew and Luke, the use of the word ἀπόστολοι at the time of the appointment of the Twelve (Matt. 10.2; Luke 6.13), and the very full instructions given to them (Matt. 10.5–42; Luke 9.3–5 and 10.2–16) emphasize the institutional aspect of the delegation of powers by Jesus, who is thus providing for the future of the Church. In Mark, on the contrary, one has the impression that the Lord is always in the midst of the fray and that he makes all those he chooses to employ at a given moment act in his name (cf. 8.35 and 10.28–31). Cf. pp. 181–3 below.

that concern one and not the other. It would seem that this confusion is deliberate, as the author's plan already suggests, combining as it does a semi-biographical presentation of Jesus' ministry with an exposition of the Master's real ecclesiological intentions.[1]

This deliberate merging of the Jesus of before the crucifixion with the Jesus of after the resurrection, in order to reform a Church that the author considered unfaithful, can also be detected in the use made in certain texts of the mysterious title 'Son of Man'. Many critics have stressed the profound difference existing between the three groups of texts where Mark uses the expression ὁ υἱὸς τοῦ ἀνθρώπου:[2] out of fourteen cases, two refer to a person present on earth possessing special authority (Mark 2.10,28), three apply to the eschatological envoy of God who will come to judge the world (8.38; 13.26; 14.62) and the nine others (8.31; 9.9,12,31; 10.33,45; 14.21,21, 41), to a personage destined to suffer, to die, and to rise again. It is obviously to this latter aspect of Jesus' ministry that the title applies best, in the Evangelist's eyes. Nevertheless, he felt obliged to retain a few of the sayings preserved by tradition in which 'Son of Man' was used in one of the other two senses.[3] Three of these texts interest us here because, having regard to their context, they suggest the presence of the risen Christ in the midst of his people.

In Mark 8.31–8 the author places quite close to one another a saying concerning the suffering of the Son of Man (8.31) and

[1] Cf. pp. 83–6 above.
[2] These three groups are to be found also in Matthew and Luke, a fact which enabled the latest critic to make a complete study of the question of the Son of Man in the synoptic Gospels (H. E. Toedt, *Der Menschensohn in der synoptischen Ueberlieferung* (Gütersloh 1959)) to found the plan of his work on this classical distinction.
[3] One must agree, with H. E. Toedt, op. cit. pp. 111–2, that in Mark 3.28 the Evangelist left out the reference to the Son of Man contained in the material derived from tradition. But it should also be regarded as probable that he knew and rejected certain sayings common to Matthew and Luke where the 'Son of Man' is presented as He who is coming, sayings of which many seem to be traceable back to Jesus (ibid. p. 60). The Evangelist's reserve in regard to the church tradition (cf. pp. 44f. and 84–5 above) and to christological speculation (cf. pp. 116ff. above) make these omissions perfectly explicable.

another concerning his coming in glory (8.38). Between them, he places several *logia*, whose chief feature in common is their uncompromising call to the public confession of the outlawed Son of Man. This call is addressed to the 'people', that is to say to the whole Christian Church, as well as to the disciples.[1] It is accordingly put into the mouth of the risen Christ as much as, if not more than, into the mouth of the man Jesus. It contains an invitation to 'come after' the Master, to 'follow' him, each 'taking up his cross' (v. 34), an invitation which must be understood in the literal sense.[2] Thus, in the time between his resurrection and his coming in glory, the Son of Man has come back to lead his people again from place to place in the service of the 'Good News' (v. 35).

In Mark 2.10, the Evangelist seems to have retained the reference to the 'Son of Man' because of the divine authority (ἐξουσία) Jesus attributed to himself in this *logion*. The title did not seem to him suitable to describe the humility of Jesus on earth (cf. Matt. 8.20 par., and 11.19 par., for which there is no equivalent in Mark). Without undertaking an exegesis of a

---

[1] The reference to the people in this context is surprising, so much so that Matthew and Luke omit it (Matt. 16.24: τοῖς μαθηταῖς αὐτοῦ, and Luke 9.23: πρὸς πάντας). It is certainly due to the author of Mark (V. Taylor, *St Mark*, p. 381) and reveals his desire to stress the universality of the call that follows (W. Grundmann, *Ev. nach Mk.*, p. 174).

[2] The author of Mark has no gift for abstract thinking, as can be seen from innumerable signs. For him, to 'follow Jesus' is certainly to follow his example. But it is first of all to follow in his footsteps, from place to place (cf. for example 1.18,20; 3.7; 5.24; 6.1; 11.9). To 'take up one's cross' means for him (whatever the original meaning of this *logion* may have been: cf. E. Dinkler, 'Jesu Wort vom Kreuztragen', in *Neutestamentliche Studien für Rudolf Bultmann* (Berlin 1954), pp. 110–29) not simply to 'accept suffering and risk death' but much more than that to 'accept to be judged by the Sanhedrin', to 'place oneself outside the law', like Jesus himself, that is to say to go headlong to one's death. But the presence and power of the risen Christ transforms the situation miraculously: the mission will succeed and the missionaries will not be put to death, whereas the cowards will perish, for want of the Lord's protection (v. 35). The realistic nature of the promise in v. 35 is emphasized by the down-to-earth wisdom of v. 36–7; and the Son of Man, when he comes again in glory, will simply be concluding publicly his work as the risen Christ at the head of his Church (v. 38).

much-debated verse,[1] one may point out that the sudden appearance of this title in the first controversy recorded by Mark was certainly designed to strike the readers of the Gospel, who were no doubt accustomed to hearing reproaches of the kind made here to Jesus by the scribes. To say 'Son of Man' was to remind Christians that he who claimed the divine prerogative of remitting sins had suffered for mankind and would be man's judge on the Last Day. The author of Mark was thus addressing Christians, over the heads of the scribes with whom Jesus was arguing, not in order to tell them a story but to explain to them their situation and to assure them that the presence of the risen Christ in their midst guaranteed the forgiveness of their sins and entitled them to announce the same forgiveness to others (cf. e.g. Matt. 18.18; John 20.23).

In Mark 2.28 it is likewise in a *logion* attributing exclusive authority to Jesus that the author of Mark has kept the expression 'Son of Man'.[2] And it is also in a controversy of the

---

[1] On this point see the commentaries, in particular that of V. Taylor, who devotes two excursuses to Mark 2.10 (pp. 199–201), and R. Bultmann, *Gesch. d. syn. Trad.*, pp. 12–14; H. E. Toedt, *Der Menschensohn i.d. synopt. Ueberlief.*, pp. 117–21.

[2] In 2.10 it was a question of the ἐξουσία of the Son of Man; here he is given the title of κύριος (. . . καὶ τοῦ σαββάτου). It has sometimes been claimed that 'Son of Man' here is a too literal translation of the Aramaic בַּר־נָשָׁא, used in this case, in the sense of 'man', as in the preceding verse: thus J. Wellhausen, *Ev. Marci*, p. 20; R. Bultmann, *Gesch. d. syn. Trad.*, pp. 58–9; M. Black, *An Aramaic Approach*, 2nd edn, pp. 246–7. But this theory does not withstand close scrutiny. If the translator had been faced twice with the same expression he would not have rendered it in two such different ways. If we suppose that the expression used in v. 27 was slightly different from that in v. 28 (בַּר־נָשׁ, for example), then we must assume that the original Aramaic played on the similarity of form and the difference of meaning, just as the Greek text does. This rather subtle play on words eluded Matthew and Luke and led them in their parallel texts (Matt. 12.1–8 and Luke 6.1–5) to omit Mark 2.27, which they considered less important. This theory seems much more rational than that which makes Mark 2.27 a second century interpolation (B. H. Branscomb, op. cit., p. 58, whose argument rests on its absence from Matthew and Luke and the Western text of Mark) or that which sees in Mark 2.28 a commentary from the pen of the author (A. Loisy, *Ev. selon Mc.*, p. 104; E. Klostermann, *Das Mk.-Ev.*, 3rd edn, p. 31). The latter found this saying already combined with v. 27, but it is impossible to say whether this combina-

kind that must have arisen between certain Pharisees and certain Christians in the earliest years of the Church. It is permissible for the disciples to break the rules of the Sabbath in case of need[1] because Jesus is in their midst and takes the responsibility of encouraging them to do so, just as David did for his men (vv. 25–6). Jesus, the 'Son of Man', died for all mankind (Mark 10.45) and will save from the cosmic disaster, on the Day of Judgement, those who have believed (Mark 13.24–7). Thus God has given him power over mankind, while reserving to himself power over the rest of creation (Mark 13.32). But the Sabbath does not belong to the part of creation that is external to mankind; it was created after man and because man was the noblest of God's creatures: cf. Gen. 1.1—2.4a.[2] It is therefore in the sphere entrusted by God to the Son of Man, who can do with it as he pleases for the benefit of his fellow-missionaries (Mark 2.27–8). The presence of this curious amplification in Mark can only be explained if it is addressed to Christians as convinced of the presence of the risen Christ among them as David's followers were of the presence of their leader.

Thus, Mark relates the life of Jesus in the company of his

---

tion can be traced back to Jesus (the authenticity of v. 28 is not claimed by many critics: on this point M. J. Lagrange is alone among the modern critics of Mark), to the Aramaic-speaking Christian community, or to the Greek-speaking church (cf. the cautious remarks of V. Taylor, *St Mark*, pp. 219–20). We shall not attempt to settle this difficult question but any solution is acceptable that does not destroy the connection between v. 27 and v. 28.

[1] This, it would seem, is what emerges from the reference to the hunger of David and his followers in v. 25. The author of Mark doubtless thought that Jesus and his companions were in a hurry to spread the 'Good News' and had no time to prepare a meal on the Sabbath day, so they picked ears of corn by the side of the road (cf. the curious ὁδὸν ποιεῖν of v. 23) in order to eat as they went along. In his opinion the Christian missionaries, led by the risen Christ, can do the same if it is to serve the cause of the gospel.

[2] The rabbinic parallels to Mark 2.27, listed by Strack–Billerbeck, vol. II, p. 5, and mentioned by almost all the commentators, are remote, as P. Billerbeck agrees (ibid.). E. Lohmeyer, *Ev. d. Mk.*, pp. 65–6, is accordingly right to look elsewhere and suggest an exegetical discussion on Gen. 1 and 2. But his hypothesis is weakened by the fact that he sees too great a break between v. 27 and v. 28.

disciples and sees the existence of the Church as a revival, after the resurrection, of this briefly interrupted companionship. The Master pursues his mission, in a greater radiance, with the helpers already chosen and those he wishes to add to their number. He remains the Head, the only Head, of his Church and has no need of a successor, since his presence among his followers is as real as before his crucifixion. The polemical significance of this idea of the presence of the risen Christ is obvious: anybody posing as the head of the universal Church or of a local church with a universal primacy sees his claims swept away at once. Around the time when Mark was written, the only Christian who claimed any role of this kind was James, the Lord's brother, and we have already seen[1] with what ferocity the Evangelist seeks to destroy his reputation. It is not surprising that an author as convinced of the speedy, active, and constant intervention of the risen Christ in the affairs of his Church should have reacted strongly against the Jerusalemite tendency to impose on Christianity a dynastic structure comparable to that which Islam was to adopt six centuries later. Conversely, it is natural that an enemy of James and his family should have been prompted to lay stress on the fact that Jesus did not leave his followers in the lurch but continued to lead them as he did before his crucifixion: what better way could there be of demonstrating that the post of head of the Church was not vacant?

Although Mark's reserve in regard to Peter is less marked than his hostility to James,[2] it too betrays the desire not to put a man at the head of the Christian community, whose leader and active protector Christ still is. By diminishing Peter's superiority over the other disciples and associating him as often as possible with Andrew and the sons of Zebedee, the author of Mark probably wished to emphasize that only one person was entitled to the highest place in the Christian Church, namely Jesus Christ. But that does not mean that he had an anarchistic or uncompromisingly egalitarian conception of Christian society. He recognized that the Lord needed permanent helpers, chosen by him and assigned to certain duties.[3]

---

[1] Cf. pp. 130ff. above.   [2] Cf. pp. 125ff. above.

[3] It would be wrong, for example, to interpret texts such as Mark 9.33ff., 10.13ff., 10.28ff., 10.35ff. as denying all authority in the Church. It is

These helpers were in the first place the three or four disciples closest to Jesus who were the first to be called and the most thoroughly initiated into his teaching and superhuman powers. It would seem that the author of Mark saw in them in the first place the guarantors of the church tradition, which earned them his respect, it is true, but also some impatience when he thought that they were seeking to take advantage of their position in order to gain personal privileges and restrict the Master's freedom.[1]

The 'aides de camp' of the bearer of God's 'Good News' were in the second place the 'Twelve', chosen by Jesus at the beginning of the second section of Mark's Gospel (Mark 3.13–19) and mentioned thereafter about ten times (4.10; 6.7; 9.35; 10.32; 11.11; 14.10,17,20,43; cf. also 10.41). There is no doubt that this group, whose antecedents and history are somewhat mysterious,[2] was known to the Evangelist through the tradition

---

simply a matter of recalling those who hold that authority to humility and a spirit of service and of condemning severely the usurpation of honours in heaven by those to whom the Church's ministry has been entrusted.

[1] Cf., for example, Mark 8.32–3 and 10.38–40. The brief allusion to the call to Levi (Mark 2.14), in terms very similar to those relating the calling of Peter, Andrew, James and John (Mark 1.16–20), shows moreover, as early as the first section of Mark, that certain of Jesus' disciples, although they did not play any outstanding part subsequently, were called almost as early as the closest companions and knew practically as much as they about the Master's ideas. Mark's identification of Levi with one of the Twelve, James, the son of Alphaeus (still supported by W. Grundmann, *Ev. nach Mk.*, p. 79), seems highly improbable.

[2] The existence in the Essene sect of a college of twelve members, plus (or among whom) three priests (I QS, col. vIII, ll.1–4), is an interesting parallel, but does not enlighten us very much about the origin of the Twelve, except to confirm the hypothesis that explains the formation of groups of twelve leaders by a desire to ensure the representation of the twelve tribes, that is to say of the whole of Israel (cf. Matt. 19.28; Luke 22.30). The historicity of the constitution of the group of Twelve by Jesus himself has often been questioned, either because it is claimed to be a post-paschal event (thus R. Schütz, *Apostel und Jünger* (Giessen 1921), p. 76; R. Bultmann, *Theol. d. N.T.*, 3rd edn, p. 38; E. Hirsch, *Frühgeschichte des Evangeliums*, vol. 1, 2nd edn (1951), p. 21) or because it is thought that chance had reduced the number of disciples to twelve by the end of Jesus' ministry on earth (M. Goguel, *Jesus*, 2nd edn, p. 272). These theories have no basis and are rightly rejected by most critics, since they cannot explain the presence of Judas in the group of

of the Church.[1] The author of Mark does not regard them with any special favour and even relates episodes which show the Twelve in a rather unfavourable light (9.33ff.; 10.41). But he has no objection to letting it be seen what an important part they sometimes played in the entourage of Jesus. Their function is sometimes to receive esoteric teaching (4.10; 10.32–4) or to partake with Jesus of a more or less ritual meal (14.17ff.; cf. also 3.20 and 6.30ff.). These two aspects of their ministry would seem to have been the most important in the eyes of the church tradition, which had grown up in the rather enclosed community of the earliest church of Jerusalem.

The author of Mark endeavoured for his part to place the accent on two other features of the role assigned by Jesus to the Twelve: to accompany Jesus everywhere he went; to go out

---

leaders. Sound remarks in support of the historicity of Jesus' own choice of the Twelve in Mark 3.14–19 will be found in the articles in *TWNT*, vol. II, pp. 325ff., by K. H. Rengstorf; V. Taylor, *St Mark*, pp. 229 and 619ff.; G. Bornkamm, *Jesus von Nazareth* (Stuttgart 1956), p. 138; W. Grundmann, *Ev. nach Mk.*, pp. 79–80. But the exact significance of that choice, the part played by the Twelve in the first events that followed the resurrection (cf. 1 Cor. 15.5; Luke 24.33ff.; Acts 1.13–14; Matt. 28.16–20), their precise role in the first church of Jerusalem (Acts 1.15—6.6), the later fate of the group and of most of its members —all these are still so many question-marks.

[1] Even if we agree with V. Taylor, op. cit. p. 620, that most of the references to the Twelve in Mark are in passages where the hand of the author can certainly be seen and that consequently some of them are his own addition, it has to be admitted that some of them go back to the church tradition. This is the case with 4.10, where it is hard to understand why several commentators think that the words σὺν τοῖς δώδεκα were added by the author of Mark (thus E. Lohmeyer, who is not very positive; V. Taylor, C. E. B. Cranfield, ad. loc.) whereas, if the passage has been retouched, it would seem clear that it is by introducing the vague expression οἱ περὶ αὐτὸν σύν . . . , which assimilates the audience of v. 10 to that of v. 34, reducing the esoteric (and even sectarian) character of vv. 10–12, received from the tradition (cf. p. 160, n. 2 above). Similarly, in 3.13–19, if it is certain that vv. 13–15 are the work of the author, it is just as certain that vv. 16–19 reproduce an existing list, probably a written one (cf. the strange repetition at the beginning of v. 16 of the first words of v. 14). It does not follow that the author of Mark used a 'Twelve' source together with a 'disciples' source, as claimed by E. Meyer, *Ursprunge und Anfänge des Christentums*, vol. 1 (Stuttgart-Berlin 1924), pp. 133ff., supported by E. Hirsch, *Frühgesch. d. Evang.*, vol. 1, 2nd edn, pp. 196–205 (cf. p. 23 above).

preaching far and near in order to extend his sphere of action as the bearer of God's Good News. That is in any case the two-fold definition of their function given in Mark before the list of their names and it has every likelihood of being an addition by the author himself.[1] As bodyguards of an itinerant Jesus (11.11) the Twelve did not fulfil their function with conspicuous success (14.26–50) and now they have to learn to go out with him towards all men and make themselves their servants (10.44), not to rule over the Christian community from a privileged place of residence (10.42–3). Chosen to spread the gospel as widely as possible (6.7–13), they must hasten from place to place to open the Church to as many as are drawn to it by their preaching (6.30–44), without ever being able to linger anywhere to live on what they have got (6.45). Then, and then only, will they have earned the title of ἀπόστολοι and will cease to be mere ἀποστελλόμενοι.[2]

---

[1] Cf. the preceding note. Matthew and Luke did not keep the exact equivalent of Mark 3.14–15 (Matt. 10.1; Luke 6.13), which is only required in the plan of Mark in order to introduce 3.19ff. and 6.7–13 in particular.

[2] This probably explains the curious process whereby Mark slips the word ἀπόστολος into his text (6.30). Instead of using it several times, as Luke does, or placing it at the head of the list of the Twelve, as in Matt. 10.2, he applies it incidentally to the emissaries of Jesus when they return after the completion of their mission and on the eve of the multiplication of the loaves, when the Master turns them with a single word into the foster-fathers of a whole people. Until then Mark had spoken only of the ἀποστέλλειν with which Jesus had sent them out on their journey (3.14; 6.7). Thus he had avoided the technical term, thereby stressing that it derived its meaning, not from the rabbinic Hebrew usage of שָׁלִיחַ to designate the duly authorized representa-tive of a person or group but from the verb שָׁלַח and its Greek translation ἀποστέλλειν, with its much wider meaning of 'to send out' (cf. on this point K. H. Rengstorf, art. ἀποστέλλω κτλ., in *TWNT*, vol. I, pp. 397ff.).

It might even be claimed that the Evangelist gave to the word ἀπόστολος the meaning it sometimes has in secular Greek (ibid. p. 407, ll. 11ff.) and in Josephus (*Ant.* xvii. 300 and perhaps i. 146; K. H. Rengs-torf, ibid. p. 413, ll. 10ff.)of 'expedition' or 'delegation', and used it to designate, not individuals, but the groups of two disciples whom Jesus sent out to preach (6.7). This idea is not as paradoxical as it might appear, considering the fluctuating meanings of the word ἀπόστολος in the Greek of the day, where it is in fact scarcely ever applied to indi-viduals (ibid. pp. 407 and 413), and its obscure and complicated history

It is obvious, indeed, that the author of Mark mistrusts the pride and exclusiveness of the Twelve, which prompt them to reserve certain ecclesiastical offices to themselves or at least reserve the right to choose the holders, to the great prejudice of the propagation of the gospel (9.35–40; cf. 10.28–31). This is why, no doubt, he avoids mentioning them alone (4.10, where the words οἱ περὶ αὐτὸν σύν . . . seem to be an editorial addition) or even to refer to them in passages where tradition would have encouraged him to do so.[1] It is perhaps for the same reason that he places so far apart the pericope relating the mission of the Twelve (6.7–13) and that where, after their return, he tells the story of the multiplication of the loaves (6.30–44) without repeating expressly that it took place in the presence of the Twelve, of whom it is obvious that he is thinking if we read carefully vv. 30–35,[2] he was not anxious to lay too much stress

in Christian language of the first century (cf. ibid. pp. 421ff.; K. Lake, in *Beginnings of Christianity*, 1, vol. 5, pp. 37–59; A. Fridrichsen, *The Apostle and his Message* (Upsala 1947); M. Goguel, *L'Eglise primitive* (Paris 1947), pp. 86–109; E. Schweizer, *Gemeinde und Gemeinde-Ordnung im Neuen Testament* (Zurich 1959), pp. 176ff.; etc.). If ἀπόστολος is used in a wrong sense in Mark 6.30 by comparison with its use by Paul and Luke, this would be an extra indication of Mark's complete independence vis-à-vis Paul (cf. pp. 125ff. above), who certainly applied this term or its Hebrew or Aramaic equivalent to an individual (cf. 1 Cor. 9.1–5; 15.7; 2 Cor. 11.5; 12.11–12; Gal. 1.17,19). We hesitate, however, to pronounce definitely in favour of this unusual interpretation.

[1] Since he groups in chapter 13 a number of *logia* relating to eschatology, it would have been quite natural that he should have added the separate *logion* in which Jesus promises the Twelve that they will sit beside him to judge Israel (Matt. 19.28b; Luke 22.30b). It is probable that he was familiar with this *logion*, as with so many others he rejected (cf. pp. 37–40 above). If he does not quote it and prefers to include the menacing parable of 13.33–7, which Matthew and Luke leave out, it is probably because he fears to place too much emphasis on the privileges of the Twelve.

[2] Besides, Luke (9.1–6 and 9.10ff.) prefers to bring the sending of the Twelve out on mission and the multiplication of the loaves closer together in order to remove the doubt created by the author of Mark as to the identity of the disciples who witnessed the miracle. Matthew, on the contrary, by placing elsewhere the sending forth of the Twelve (Matt. 10.1ff.), omits any mention of them in connection with the miracle of the loaves (Matt. 14.13–21). The number of baskets of food collected after the meal (Mark 6.43) could be construed in Mark as a disguised reminder of the presence of the Twelve. In the parallel texts it

on the role of a group which laid claim to certain liturgical privileges (cf. Acts 1.14; 6.1–6). In any event, his desire to refute the claims of the Twelve in this direction would seem to explain why in Mark 8.1–10 he gives a second account of a multiplication of loaves obviously modelled on the first.[1] The miraculous meal that Jesus has his disciples serve to the crowd (6.37,41; 8.6) must not be understood as a unique event establishing the glory and goodness of the earthly Jesus and even more the liturgical authority of the group who distributed the food. It must be interpreted as the overflowing of God's goodness

has become merely a rather exaggerated way of emphasizing the scale of the miracle.

[1] It might be a case of a second tradition duplicating the first, as has often been said (cf. for example A. Loisy, *Ev. selon Marc*, pp. 224–8, who puts his theory very clearly). As we showed earlier (pp. 45ff.), the Evangelist must have heard the story told by some popular Galilean story-teller, as he did almost all the miracle stories; it would not be surprising that another story-teller should have related a slightly different version of the same episode. In any case, the author of Mark certainly put considerable literary effort into the section of his book that runs from 6.14 to 8.29 in order to organize the very disparate material he used and to bring out the significance of the events recorded. It is to him that the very clear parallelism between 6.30—7.37 and 8.1–26 is due. The parallel transmission of two groups of stories so similar and yet so complicated in their sequence (to think only of all the journeys in chapters 6—8!) and so pregnant with theological meaning, can scarcely be imputed to popular memory. The author of Mark must have built this part of his work up around a nucleus of the first group (6.35–55, roughly) which he added to considerably and then repeated in a rather shorter form (8.1–26). For this second 'cycle' he used a variety of material gleaned from popular memory or tradition, but above all he composed freely (8.16–21) or copied the stories of the first group: 8.22–6 presents astonishing similarities to 7.32–7, as does 8.1–9 to 6.35–44. In addition, 8.1–9 has lost the picturesque or unnecessary details which clutter up 6.35–44: Jesus discovers the crowd's unfortunate situation of his own accord (8.2–3, contrast 6.35–6), which is at once more charitable and more dignified: the preliminary dialogue between Jesus and his disciples is shortened (8.4–5 as compared with 6.37–9); the seating of the people is simplified (8.6a as compared with 6.39–40); the reference to the remains of the fish is omitted (8.8 as compared with 6.43b). A good commentary on the parallelism between 6.30—7.37 and 8.1–26 is to be found in V. Taylor, *St Mark*, pp. 628–32. His preference for the doublet hypothesis does not convince us, however, because this critic looks too quickly for 'historical veracity' without considering sufficiently the intentions of the author of Mark.

towards many people of all kinds, which no rule of discipline precludes, and as an appeal to all the disciples to 'serve at table' for the Lord. It may even be wondered whether, in insisting somewhat on the twelve baskets of bread left over after the first miracle (6.43; 8.19) and on the seven baskets left after the second (8.8,20) the author is not suggesting a comparison with the Twelve and the Seven who had a leading role in the first church of Jerusalem (Acts 1.13 and 6.5). The Book of Acts expressly states that these two groups had at one time or another among their duties that of preparing community meals (Acts 6.1–4; cf. 4.32ff.). Is Mark pleading then for the rights of the Seven at the same time as for a Church open to all? There would seem to be nothing against this conclusion.[1]

But the author of Mark does not simply want to add one group to another in order to increase the Lord's following by a few members. What he has at heart is to check any too strict limitation of the Lord's entourage of people who accompany him and spread the Good News on his behalf. This explains why he favours the most general of the terms whereby tradition designated Jesus' companions, namely μαθητής.[2] It may seem

---

[1] It is also, with some slight differences, the opinion of A. Loisy, *Ev. selon Marc*; E. Klostermann, *Das Mk-Ev.*; J. Sundwall, *Die Zusammensetzung des Markus-evangeliums* (Abo 1934); W. Grundmann, *Ev. nach Mk.*, all ad. loc.

[2] Cf. p. 162, n. 3 above. Mark uses μαθητής to designate Jesus' disciples forty-two times, which is much more often than Luke (thirty-four times) and roughly as often as Matthew (sixty-nine times in a Gospel more than half as long again), whereas this latter Gospel endeavours to reproduce in full the sayings of Jesus preserved in the church tradition. Luke, on the other hand, uses the word twenty-eight times in Acts when referring to Christians, whereas this usage is unknown in the rest of the New Testament. It can even be said that the word is applied almost exclusively to Christians belonging to the intimate circles of the Seven and of Paul (9.36,38 are the only exceptions). Is it a usage pre-dating Luke —a title that certain Christians (Palestinians no doubt) gave themselves? With K. H. Rengstorf, art. μαθητής in *TWNT*, vol. IV, pp. 417ff. (especially pp. 462–3) and E. Haenchen, *Die Apostelgeschichte* (Gottingen 1961) (13th edn of the 3rd part of the Kritisch-exegetischer Kommentar über das Neue Testament begr. v. H. A. W. Meyer), p. 213, n. 2, we believe that is so. The author of Mark may thus have been encouraged to use the term μαθητής frequently because of its ambiguity, since, in certain Christian circles, it was applied equally to the pupils of

paradoxical that he should use this word so often when the
Master's teaching has such a small place in his book. It is
because the 'disciples' in his eyes are in the first place people
who *follow* Jesus everywhere (2.15 etc.), who are his natural
spokesmen (2.16; 10.13), who are plunged, thanks to his
presence in their midst, into a way of life that is contrary to the
most firmly established conventions (2.18,23; 7.2,5; cf. 10.28)
and who take on all sorts of material tasks on his behalf (3.9;
4.35–8; 6.37–9,41; 8.6,14–16; 9.5; 11.1–7; 14.12–16). Before
being the Lord's itinerant audience they are his attendants.
It is only secondarily that they appear as recipients of teaching
that the author of Mark regards as more thorough than that
dispensed to the people.[1] This places them on the same footing
as Peter, James, and John, or as the Twelve, as the guarantors
of the true tradition. As they do not form a closed group like
the last-mentioned,[2] the Evangelist is probably seeking to
justify in this way the liberties he takes with the official tradition
and to show that its use and propagation are not reserved to a
chosen few.

He is also seeking, most definitely, to underline the perfect
continuity that exists between the group of Jesus' followers
before the crucifixion and the men who, after the resurrection,
journey from place to place under the leadership of the living
Lord, whether they were won over to him before or after Good

---

the former rabbi Jesus and to believers in the risen Messiah. Cf. pp.
252ff. below.

[1] Cf. pp. 159ff. above. It is only from Mark 4.34 onwards, that is to say
from the seventh time the word μαθητής is used, that the theme of Jesus'
private teaching to his disciples appears. It is found thereafter in 7.17;
8.17ff.; 8.30–1; 9.28–9; 9.31–2; 10.10–16,23ff.; 11.22–5; 12.43–4.
It is thus relatively developed in the third, fourth, and fifth sections of
the book, but it is in the forefront in the fourth section only (8.30—
10.52).

[2] The 'disciples' are not recruited by an unsolicited personal call as the
Master's intimates are (Mark 1.16–20 and 2.14), or by choice from a
list of qualified candidates drawn up by a panel, like the Twelve
(Mark 3.13–19). They seem to choose themselves, by accepting the
sacrifices required and following in the steps of Jesus who makes no
attempt to restrict their number (Mark 2.15b; 8.34ff.; 9.38ff.; 10.51–2).
The story of the rich man is a resounding demonstration of the fact that
anybody could become a disciple, but the rigours of life with Jesus
sufficed to limit the candidates (Mark 10.17ff.).

Friday. There is no need, in order to be a 'disciple', to have belonged to the small phalanx of Jesus' first chosen companions. All that is necessary is to have the will to become an itinerant missionary in the service of the Good News and, to that end, to sacrifice fortune, family, and life itself; whoever does God's will by following Jesus (3.33–5); the madman of the country of the Gadarenes (5.18–20); whoever takes up his cross and preaches the gospel without shame or fear (8.34–9.1); whoever fights against Satan in the name of Jesus (9.38–40); whoever gives up all he possesses to follow Jesus from place to place (10.17–31); the blind man of Jericho (10.51–2)—all these are 'disciples' in the same sense as the first great actors in the gospel story, even if the term is not formally applied to them. Together with the most famous among the Twelve, they may rise to the highest rank in the 'Kingdom of God come in glory' (9.41; 10.29–31; 10.40). In the eyes of the Lord, all brave and active missionaries are equal.

3
THE PROGRESS OF THE MISSION

Around the risen Christ, who exercises his power in the midst of his people, the author of Mark thus sees different groups gather, whose essential function is to carry the Good News from place to place. As described by the author in numerous places throughout his book, they are 'missionary teams' and not guardians of the tradition or of a nascent hierarchy, as in the other canonical Gospels. Here he is seeking to counter the sectarianism and exclusiveness he believes he detects among certain Christians.[1] But does he not himself succumb to a similar temptation by reducing the Church to a few leaders whose devotion is boundless, but for whom the world is no more than a vast chequer-board and its people pawns in the great contest between Christ and his followers and Satan? By restricting the space devoted in his book to the teaching of Jesus, is he not preventing his readers from hearing the Master's call to each individual in his daily life, and is he not excluding all but missionaries from communion with the risen Christ?[2]

---

[1] Cf. pp. 108ff. above.

[2] Clearly it is the deficiency of Mark's Gospel in ethical teaching that caused the Gospels of Matthew and Luke to be preferred in the churches as early as the end of the first century.

By his great mistrust of christological speculation, is he not making it impossible to group around the one confession of faith all the believers who have not the exceptional spiritual force to break away from their social ties and go out into the highways and byways? By showing too much hostility or reserve towards the first leaders of the parent community of Jerusalem, is he not threatening to cut off the community for which he is writing from the main body of the Church and restrict its efforts to the evangelization of a few small towns?[1] In short, the Evangelist can be criticized for having little 'Church sense', for which missionary enthusiasm can never be a total substitute.

But the critic's task, when faced with a document such as Mark, is not to repeat the criticisms that may have been made by the early churchmen. It is to look for the explanation of the special features of the text he is examining and, in this case, to ask himself whether, though ill-suited to the needs of the churches of the year 100, this Gospel might not have been written to meet those of certain Christian communities of the middle of the first century. The ecclesiological themes in Mark can perhaps be explained by circumstances so different from those that prevailed later that it requires an effort of historical imagination to reconstruct them. In any event, it will be useful to examine the work again from this rather new angle in an attempt to grasp its ecclesiology more clearly. The most natural way of doing this is to follow the plan of Mark which, as we said earlier,[2] was dictated by the author's desire to expound the real intentions of Jesus in regard to his Church.

The first section (up to 3.12) is governed by the twofold idea of the call to the people, and especially to a few chosen men, and the break with the leaders of the Jewish nation. Just as the κηρύσσειν of John the Baptist draws to him the whole population of Judaea (1.4–5), the κηρύσσειν of Jesus (1.14,38–9) attracts enormous crowds (1.33,45; 2.2–4,13; 3.7–9), hungry for miracles and very difficult to handle (3.9!). These throngs are

---

[1] This risk did not exist if Mark came from the Christian community in Rome. But the Roman origin of the Gospel is far from certain, despite all the arguments that can be advanced in its favour. Cf. pp. 240ff. and pp. 248ff.

[2] Cf. pp. 84–5 above.

so dangerous that at first Jesus has to take refuge in flight (1.35ff.; 1.45). Then he returns and, having got the crowd under control, succeeds in drawing it away to the shores of the sea of Galilee, where it is easier for him to retain his freedom of action (3.9) and where he even begins to teach (2.13; cf. 4.2). The author emphasizes the very varied origins of the people thus gathered together (3.7–8): they have all left the country and community in which they formerly lived and attached themselves to Jesus. At the same time, Jesus has come into conflict with the chief leaders of the Jewish people: the scribes (2.6ff.; 2.16), the Pharisees (2.16,18,24; 3.6), the disciples of John the Baptist (2.18). Very soon the break with them becomes irreparable and the fate of Jesus is decided (3.6). At the end of this section, then, we find Jesus, who has deliberately put himself outside the law,[1] placed by the Evangelist face to face with a throng of uprooted and spiritually undiscerning people. Many disciples, among them some of the privileged custodians of the tradition (1.16–20), are already at the Master's side and the subject of bitter thrusts on the part of the leaders of Judaism (2.18,24), but as yet play no active part.

In presenting this picture, the author of Mark is obviously thinking of the first stage in the formation of Christian communities. The proclamation of God's message and the miracles that accompany it burst open the old social and religious framework, disturb the peace in the synagogues and drive the crowds into the streets and out along the roads. They thus provide Jesus Christ with the raw material, rebellious but essential,[2] with which to reconstitute his people, after the traditional leaders have been rejected. This molten mass that has to be reshaped and forged is the mass of the Israelites: passive listeners in the synagogues (1.22–27,39; 3.1–5), despised country

---

[1] The attitude of Jesus in 3.1–5 amounts to a provocation of the leaders of Jewry (E. Lohmeyer, *Ev. des Mk.*, pp. 68–9, rightly stresses the ironic and aggressive character of the question put by Jesus in v. 4. W. Grundmann, *Ev. nach Mk.*, p. 71, goes further: 'Jesus, warned by the Pharisees, defies them with an act. . . . This act can cause Jesus to be stoned. . . . ' (translation).

[2] The author of Mark obviously imagines that Satan is using the crowd to hinder Jesus' action. Cf. p. 153, n. 2 above.

people,[1] townspeople (1.33; 2.2), wretched pariahs (like the leper of Mark 1.40–5), rich 'publicans and sinners' (2.14–17). It is not merely a question of the Galileans, among who Jesus preached; it is the whole of Jewish Palestine (3.7–8), in short all the rank and file of Palestinian Judaism separated from their leaders by the call of the 'Son of Man'. These people are the potential Church and remain so throughout Mark, if we except the Passion story (cf. for example 11.18; 12.37). The author of Mark thus sees the Christian mission as a call to a religious revolution among the Jews of Palestine. There is nothing surprising in this, considering the hostility he shows to certain leaders of that nation.[2]

But the crowd swarming around Jesus (3.7–8) comes also from regions peopled with pagans, at least in part: Idumaea, Peraea, Phoenicia. The Evangelist, though he sees in the proclamation of the Good News a move on God's part to take the Jewish people in hand again, does not believe that the gospel should leave out other nations. Those on the borders of Jewish Palestine are in any case shaken by the mysterious coming of the Kingdom and uprooted from their traditional society, just as the Israelites are. Mentioned after the inhabitants of the areas populated by Jews, they are given second place and will not form the nucleus of the Church, but they too are virtually a

---

[1] The Evangelist pays quite striking attention to the coming of Jesus, or of the gospel, to the small towns and the countryside: cf. 1.5,38,45; 5.1ff.; 5.14; 6.7; 6.10 (which is easier to explain if it is a matter of a series of visits by the Twelve to small towns and country areas); 6.56; 7.24,31 (τὰ ὅρια is no doubt to be interpreted here as indicating that Jesus visits the area round the towns mentioned without entering them); 8.10 (id. for τὰ μέρη); 8.27; 11.1ff.; 11.11; 14.3–9. Even though one should not be too quick to identify the 'am-ha'arets of later rabbis, the 'country people', with the Palestinian peasants (cf. the texts collected in Strack–Billerbeck, vol. II, pp. 494–519, together with the preliminary remarks on page 494), it is probable that the Evangelist deliberately stresses the frequency of Jesus' excursions into the countryside. He wants to show that in his ministry the Master has not neglected the country people, the despised members of almost any civilization, the 'pagani' of all religions based on the study of a holy Book.

[2] Cf. pp. 94ff. above. This hostility towards the Jewish leaders is not 'anti-semitism', as T. A. Burkill believes: 'Anti-semitism in St Mark's Gospel', in *Novum Testamentum*, vol. III (1959), pp. 34–53; it is the reflection of the desire of an extremely radical Jewish reformer to rid Israel of its bad shepherds.

part of it.[1] This will become clearer still in the course of the third and fourth sections of Mark (6.14—10.52).

Thus it cannot be said that Mark's Church is a 'Jewish sect'. It is a movement which aims at seizing the religious government of Israel in God's name and winning over the neighbouring peoples at the same time. The means whereby this revolution is to be brought about are the proclamation of the Good News, verbal battle with Satan and his minions and the bringing of deliverance and compassion to the weak, especially the sick.

The second section of Mark (3.13—6.13) marks the end of the solitude of Jesus as he faces the crowd and the enormous work of preaching that still has to be accomplished. The few men set apart in 1.16–20 and 2.14 to follow the Master are replaced by a carefully chosen group (3.13–14), that of the Twelve (3.16–19), whose pre-eminent role in the Church the author is anxious to show. We have said enough about this rather mysterious body of men, so that we need not dwell on them here.[2] Their choice suffices to assure them of a privileged place beside the Master (3.14; 3.31–5), but there is already a feeling[3] that it is

---

[1] E. Lohmeyer, *Ev. des Mk.*, p. 72, has suggested seeing in the list of geographical names in Mark 3.7–8 the names of the regions where there were Christians at the time when Mark was written, but he is not very positive on this point—rightly so, in our opinion. This list is not a first attempt at church statistics, but a reference to the need for a mission to the Gentiles of these places in order to consolidate the initial results achieved by Jesus. On the question of the universalism of Mark, cf. pp. 194ff. below.

[2] Cf. pp. 176ff. above.

[3] It is indeed striking that this section devoted to the choice, training, and sending out on mission of the Twelve should mention them expressly only in its introduction (3.13–19) and its conclusion (6.7–13). Everywhere else, even in 4.10, they are replaced by much less sharply defined groups (3.32,34; 4.10,34–5; 5.31; 6.1), except for the three intimates of 5.37, who, moreover, are accompanied by the parents of the dead girl (5.40), whose faith (5.36) makes them 'disciples'. Thus the author of Mark does not simply relate how Jesus once prepared the Twelve for their ministry; he shows how the converts who are ready to become itinerant missionaries must learn at the feet of the risen Christ, while at the same time the mission goes on, before they in turn set forth to preach the gospel. Cf. the sound remarks on this rather bewildering mixture by J. M. Robinson, *Das Geschichtsverständnis des Mk.-Ev.*, pp. 94–5.

not a right that will be reserved to them for ever (10.35–40). Their authority as companions of Jesus appears to be bound up with the possession of the Holy Spirit, given to help all those sent forth by Christ to overcome the wiles of Satan.[1]

Having received special teaching from Jesus (4.33–4), they will learn the difficulties of the missionary struggle and the strength with which Jesus overcomes them (4.35—6.6) and then they will be ready to be sent forth in their turn, two by two, with precise instructions (6.7–13). Their sphere of action is not specified, but it is possible that the author of Mark limited it to the Jewish countries: in Decapolis, a largely non-Jewish region, another preacher is charged with proclaiming the gospel (5.17–20). In all this section, which might have been marked by a studious retreat and the christological initiation of a privileged few, the people are always present and always in the way (3.20,32; 4.1,33; 5.14,21,24,31,37–40; 6.2,13), even on the sea (4.37). They receive their share of the Master's teaching (4.1,33) and even sometimes glimpse his supernatural glory (5.14ff.; 5.25–34). In short, they enter step by step into the community of the faithful.

It is to the people, moreover, that the teaching given by Jesus in Mark 4.1–34 is in the first place addressed, as the

---

[1] The idea of a gift of the Holy Spirit to men is only to be found in embryo in Mark. This is indeed one of the strongest reasons for denying that any influence was exercised by Paul on the author of this Gospel. The Holy Spirit descends upon Jesus (Mark 1.10–11) and inspires him in his combat. Thus it is the presence of the risen Christ among his people that guarantees the presence of the Spirit in the Church. The 'baptism with the Holy Ghost' that Jesus administers to the people (Mark 1.8) consists in the healings and exorcisms of 3.10–12, which replace the baptism with water administered by John the Baptist to those same people (1.5). We must be careful not to think here of individual gestures separating the masses from a certain number of 'saints'; the author is thinking in terms of eschatological manifestations that have an impact on the crowd. On the other hand, anybody who takes up with Jesus the itinerant struggle with Satan, any missionary, is filled with the Holy Spirit, like Jesus himself (3.22–30), because he is the instrument through whom the Master acts (cf. pp. 112–3 above). He can therefore be very sure of receiving the help of the Spirit if he appears before a tribunal (Mark 13.11). It can be said that for Mark the Holy Spirit is inseparable from the proclamation of the 'Good News'; it is the strength of God which makes the gospel irresistible. Cf. E. Schweizer, art. πνεῦμα in *TWNT*, vol. VI, pp. 394–401.

Evangelist stresses (4.1–2,11–12,33). True, he has no illusions about the results the Master can expect when he addresses the crowd in the pictorial language they can understand: the vague glimmer that penetrates will not be enough to pluck them out of their spiritual torpor (4.11–12). But that is no reason for not 'speaking the word to them, as they were able to hear it' (4.33). The 'sowers' must pursue untiringly their thankless task instead of wrapping themselves up in vain sectarian pride.[1] The Master promises them that in spite of all the apparent disappointments and failures, the seed will finally germinate and spring up in the most amazing fashion. It is in order to make sure that the missionaries of his group learn this lesson that, of all the parables of Jesus that he knew, the author of Mark chose to reproduce here three parables about growth from seeds (4.3–9,26–32). This allowed him to bring out strongly the contrast between the small beginning—or even the failure that seems to follow the sowing—and the sure triumph that will follow. The explanation he gives of the parable of the Sower is on the same lines.[2] The few other *logia* he adds (4.21–5) have

---

[1] As we have shown above, p. 160, n. 2, the author of Mark reinterprets the parable of the Sower in order to rid it of the layer of sectarianism in which the church tradition has enveloped it (4.10–12) and restore to it the idea of spiritual conquest that he thought Jesus meant it to convey.

[2] This explanation must be his own, or at any rate that of the church to which he belonged. It therefore reflects his thinking quite faithfully. It is given, as we have said, in order to refute the predestinarian and sectarian interpretation of the parable of which a trace remains in 4.10–12. We are consequently entitled to see in it a glorification of the missionary branch of the Church, to the detriment of its narrow clique. Those who bring forth fruit (v. 20) are the Christians who have understood that the right way to receive the word is to propagate it in one's own turn as much as possible; in contrast to them, the people 'sown among thorns' (vv. 18–19) are those who are unfruitful and do not propagate the word for fear of jeopardizing their situation, their fortune, or their ambitions. It is not said of them that they lose their faith or deny it, but only that in them the word remains hemmed in, stifled and captive. They are the timid Christians denounced in 8.34—9.1; 13.9–13; the sectarians of 4.10–12; all those who have not understood that conquest is of the very essence of the gospel. The people 'sown on stony ground' (vv. 16–17), who do not differ greatly from those referred to in v. 15, (ὁμοίως, says v. 16), are the flash-in-the-pan sympathizers, the masses who fear persecution and know nothing of perseverance: the 'people', whose evangelization, though apparently successful, has to be undertaken all over again because their faith does not last. Lastly,

also a distinctly missionary flavour: it is obvious in the case of
vv. 21 and 22; for the very obscure verses 24–5 it would also
seem to be the case.[1] Duly enlightened as to the meaning of

---

v. 15 refers to the enemies of the mission—the leaders whom Satan
inspires and uses.

There is no reason to say that this interpretation by Mark loses sight
of the fact that 'despite failures, the amazing harvest is the supreme
lesson', as V. Taylor claims, *St Mark*, p. 258. The point of the parable
is perhaps blunted by the desire to contrast the enterprising Christians
with their timid brethren, but only the fantastic promise of an im-
measurable harvest can justify the former and accuse the latter. The
Evangelist has turned the edge of the parable slightly but he has not
been false to its meaning by losing himself in explanatory details, by
allegorizing it or by sacrificing eschatology to psychology (contrary to
the view of many authors, like F. Hauck, *Das Evangelium des Markus*
(Leipzig 1931), p. 51; E. Lohmeyer, *Ev. des Mk.*, pp. 84–5; Ch. Masson,
Les paraboles de Marc 4, pp. 35–9; J. Jeremias, *Die Gleichnisse Jesu*, pp.
65–7). He has given an ecclesiological explanation of it, as indeed the
partisans of the explanation contained in 4.10–12 had done before him.
1 In the mind of the author of Mark, vv. 21–3 are certainly designed to
lay emphasis on the missionary intention of vv. 14–20. The *logion* of
v. 24, despite the new introductory formula (καὶ ἔλεγεν αὐτοῖς) probably
carries on from vv. 21–3, which its opening recalls. Although its context
in Matthew (7.2) and Luke (6.38), which might be that of the *logia*,
adds to its eschatological form (the passive designates God and his
retributive judgement) the idea of the generosity that is demanded,
the author of Mark must have known this saying separately, and have
seen in the use of μέτρον and μετρέω an allusion to the greater or less
abundance of 'fruit' borne by Christians (v. 20), that is to say to the
intensity of their missionary effort. W. Grundmann, *Ev. nach Mk.*,
p. 97, classes this interpretation first out of three possible ones, but does
not choose between them.

V. 25 is found twice in Matthew and Luke: in the parallel to this
passage (Matt. 13.12; Luke 8.18) and at the end of the parable of the
talents or pounds (Matt. 25.29; Luke 19.26). It is a sure indication
both of its presence in the *logia* and of its acceptance by Matthew and
Luke as being also suitable to explain the parable of the Sower, in
accordance with the use Mark had made of this *logion*. In the second
context, Matthew and Luke have thus given the *logion* a meaning that
corresponds to their own interpretation of the parable and different
from that they gave to it on the basis of the *logia* in chapters 25 and 19
respectively. But in Mark 4.25, the source of Matt. 13.12 and of Luke
8.18, this saying is without doubt a borrowing by the author from the
church tradition (from the *logia*, if preferred) and more specifically
from some archetype of the parable of the talents, which this author
passed over along with so many others (cf. pp. 42–4 above). The

these few parables and the power of Jesus, the missionaries can go
forth to win people to the cause with the same weapons as their
Master (6.7,12–13): solemn call to repentance, based, of course, on
the Good News (cf. 1.14–15); power to drive out devils; gifts of
healing. Can we believe that the author of Mark was thinking
of the Christian missions of his day when he drew up this strangely 'activist' table of the journeys of the Twelve in the service
of their Master? One is entitled to hesitate when one thinks of
the place occupied by christological preaching in the missionary
discourses of Acts[1] and in the missionary activity of Paul
(1 Cor. 1.18—2.5; Gal. 3.1). And yet, as we have seen,[2] the
author of Mark was opposed to any 'discourse about Jesus
Christ' (8.30) and saw the disciples' task as the intrepid proclamation of God's Good News, claiming the outlaw Jesus as their
'pathfinder' (8.31ff.).

He had accordingly an idea of missionary preaching that
was different from that of the first church of Jerusalem, or of
Paul or of Luke. For him, it would seem, this preaching was in
two states: first a trumpet blast designed to overthrow the
established order, the κηρύσσειν; then, teaching addressed to
the crowd of people thus set in motion, followed by a commentary on it for the 'disciples', the διδάσκειν or διδαχή.[3] It would

Evangelist must therefore have attributed to this *logion* the meaning
it has kept in Matt. 25.29 and Luke 19.26 (but lost in Matt. 13.12 and
Luke 8.18, on account of the new interpretation of the parable to the
Sower in the other two synoptic Gospels): the disciple who has made
the word given into his keeping by the Master fructify will be richly
rewarded; he who has failed to do so will be stripped of everything on
the day of the parousia. Once again, it is a call to the mission that we
hear in these verses. Cf. the sound remarks on this subject by M. J.
Lagrange, *Ev. Marc*, pp. 114–5, and G. Dehn, *Le Fils de Dieu, Commentaire à l'évangile de S. Marc* (Paris 1936), p. 92 (the 2nd edn (Geneva
1957), p. 71, omits, mistakenly, the good exegesis of these verses).

[1] About which E. Haenchen, *Die Apostelgeschichte*, 3rd edn (Göttingen
1961), p. 73; J. M. Robinson, *Le Kérygme de l'Eglise et le Jésus de
l'histoire* (Geneva n.d.), p. 56, n. 1; J. Dupont, *Les sources du Livre des
Actes; état de la question*, s. 1 (1960), pp. 42–3, have recently said, in
spite of the great differences of opinion between them on the subject
of the sources of Acts, that this book derived from very early traditions,
especially in the matter of christology.

[2] Cf. pp. 116ff. and 141–4 above.

[3] The noun διδαχή, which occurs five times in Mark (1.22,27; 4.2;
11.18; 12.38), that is to say very much more often than in the rest of the
New Testament (except for 1 Tim., Tit. and the Epistles of John:

certainly be wrong to systematize too much the indications given here and there on this subject. But the verb κηρύσσειν is used chiefly in Mark 1,[1] whereas the terms διδάσκειν and διδαχή are fairly evenly distributed in chapters 1—12, which suggests that one opened the door to the others. Jesus (1.14,38,39), then the Twelve (3.14; 6.12), make their proclamation before beginning to teach (1.21,22,27; 2.13; 4.1–2; etc. . . . ; 6.30). The κηρύσσειν is seen as a resounding *act* which clears the ground for teaching and is accompanied by exorcisms and healings, much more than as preaching loaded with a religious content.[2] It suffices alone as long as the old framework has not been destroyed: Jesus himself encountered great difficulties when he sought to *teach* in the synagogues (1.21ff.; 6.2ff.) and found himself obliged to replace this premature διδάσκειν with the loud 'proclamation' and its consequences (1.39; 3.1–5). Teaching becomes possible, on the contrary, when the crowd has followed

---

cf. R. Morgenthaler, *Statistik*, pp. 88 and 164), designates in each case the teaching given to the people; the verb διδάσκειν, used sixteen times (1.21,22; 2.13; 4.1,2; 6.2,7,30,34; 8.31; 9.31; 10.1; 11.17; 12.14,35; 14.49) to designate the teaching of Jesus or of his disciples, that is to say with a frequency even more exceptional for the New Testament (except in Col. and 1 Tim.: ibid.), applies in fourteen of these passages to teaching addressed to the people.

1 Six times (1.4,7,14,38,39,45), in a total of twelve. Apart from Jesus and John the Baptist, the 'publishers' of the Good News mentioned in Mark are chiefly people who have been healed (1.45; 5.20; 7.36) and the Twelve (3.14; 6.12). The message they bear varies accordingly, but it always consists in publishing the facts accompanying the visitation of God.

2 Cf. the report presented to Jesus by the 'apostles' (6.30) on ὅσα ἐποίησαν καὶ ὅσα ἐδίδαξαν. This supposes that, for the Evangelist, the apostles had 'acted' before they 'taught', whereas their κηρύσσειν preceded their miracle-working (6.12–13); and that, moreover, they had had time to do more than simply announce the coming of God (cf. the second ὅσα, which the copyists have sometimes left out and which suggests a certain diversity in the teaching given). Luke sensed, moreover, that there was some kind of underlying meaning in this repetition and left out the second half so as not to give the impression that the Twelve had overstepped their instruction. But, like Mark, he includes κηρύσσειν in the disciples' action (ποιεῖν), together with the exorcisms and healings. Alone among the moderns, M. J. Lagrange, *Ev. Marc*, p. 165, seems to hesitate a little over the meaning of this verse that the other commentators pass over or interpret as though the word ἐδίδαξαν were not there. The perplexity of Lagrange ought to be shared, in our opinion.

Jesus out of the towns and he has been able to take it in hand
(2.13; 3.7–12 and 4.1ff.; 6.34; 10.1). The missionary method
advocated by the author of Mark is thus more radical than that
of Paul and seems designed to attract the crowd more rapidly,
even at the price of severe reactions on the part of the religious
and civic authorities (13.9ff.) and to the detriment of the
quality of the message delivered. This explains the space
devoted by the Evangelist to the exorcisms and healings that all
these good people are so hungry for.[1] The real preaching begins
afterwards, but it too is very gradual (4.33), so as not to
frighten away the crowd and run the risk of forming too small a
community. This διδαχή, in his mind, certainly comprises a
presentation of Jesus, the bearer of God's Good News: the
composition of Mark alone is proof of this. But is is chiefly
scriptural and moral,[2] made up of 'wisdom' (6.2) and vigorous
verbal attacks on the bad shepherds of Israel (11.17–18;
12.35–40). The christological teaching proper was designed, in
the author's mind, for smaller groups of future missionaries
(8.31ff.; 9.31) ready to sacrifice their lives.

[1] Cf. pp. 45ff. and 112–3 above. A curious detail confirms that in his
eyes the missionaries needed to act as healers in order to gain a wider
audience with the people: to heal the sick the Twelve were not content
with pronouncing words or laying on their hands; they anointed a
great number of sick people with oil (6.13). What was with Jesus a
supernatural act of mercy becomes with them a social service performed with the help of a common means of medication. It suggests the
European or American missionaries who won the favour of people
in Asia or Africa by giving them quinine. Matthew and Luke naturally
eliminated this feature, which was not dignified enough for their liking
(Matt. 10 has no parallel to Mark 6.12–13; Luke 9.6 omits the references to exorcisms and anointings with oil) and makes the healing of
the sick one of the powers conferred by Jesus on the Twelve (Matt.
10.1; Luke 9.1–2), which Mark precisely does not (cf. Mark 3.14–15;
6.7ff.). Why this difference? For the author of Mark, it is Christ, risen
and present, who continues to heal each patient treated by his disciples
(cf. the indication on this point contained in Mark 9.14ff.), whereas
Matthew and Luke consider these latter as independent miracle-
workers handling the 'name of Jesus' and other similar formulae with
dexterity (Acts 3.6; 8.7; 9.40; 13.10–11; etc. Acts 9.34 constitutes an
exception to be explained by the use of a tradition). We can thus say
that our Evangelist is closer on this point to 'James' than to the authors
of the two other synoptic Gospels (cf. Jas. 5.14).

[2] Cf. K. H. Rengstorf, art. διδασκω κτλ. in *TWNT*, vol. II, pp. 138ff.,
especially pp. 141–50 and 166–7.

The third section of Mark (6.14—8.29) is concerned precisely with the role the missionaries have to play in the midst of the new people formed thanks to their collaboration with the Master. It is often claimed that this section is seeking to establish the mission among the Gentiles as part of the earthly ministry of Jesus.[1] It is true that we see Jesus here making several journeys into the regions bordering on Galilee where the Gentiles were much more numerous than the Jews: the region of Tyre (7.24), Sidon (7.31), Decapolis (7.31), Dalmanutha (?: 8.10), Bethsaida (8.22), the area round Caesarea Philippi (8.27). In addition, he moves about a great deal on the 'sea of Galilee' which separated the Jews from the Gentiles to the east (6.32,45–53; 7.31; 8.10,13). The discussion on ritual purity (7.1–23) and the episode of the Syro-phoenician woman (7.24–30) are moreover visibly dominated by the question of the presence of Gentiles in the Christian Church, whereas the context suggests that there were non-Jews among the beneficiaries of the miracles of 7.32–7 and 8.1–9). Even if it be allowed that Jesus was active some of the time outside Jewish territory,[2] one is entitled to detect in these chapters a measure of literary artifice that reflects the problems of the early Christians.[3]

In any case, it is by no means evident that this section is the only one in Mark where the problem of the mission to the Gentiles is referred to. On the subject of Mark 3.7ff. we have

---

[1] Cf. for example K. L. Schmidt, *Rahmen d. Gesch. Jesu*, pp. 172ff.; A. E. J. Rawlinson, *St Mark*, pp. 86, 98; B. W. Bacon, *Gospel of Mark*, pp. 163–4; E. Lohmeyer, *Ev. des Mk.* pp. 121–2, 144; V. Taylor, *St Mark*, p. 633; G. H. Boobyer, 'The Miracles of the Loaves and the Gentiles in St Mark's Gospel', in *Scottish Journal of Theology*, VI (1953), pp. 77–87;. J. M. Robinson, *Geschichtsverst. d. Mk.-Ev.*, pp. 94ff.; J. Jeremias, *Jésus et les Païens* (Neuchâtel and Paris 1956), pp. 27–8.

[2] As, for instance, do F. Burkitt, *The Gospel History and its Transmission* (Edinburgh 1906), pp. 89ff.; B. H. Branscomb, *Gospel of Mark*, pp. 129ff.; M. Goguel, *Jésus*, 2nd edn, pp. 288ff.; H. Clavier, 'La multiplication des pains dans le ministère de Jésus', in *Studia Evangelica, Papers presented to the International Congress on 'The Four Gospels in 1957', held at Christ Church, Oxford,* 1957 (Texte und Untersuchungen, vol. LXXIII) (Berlin 1959), pp. 441–57, especially pp. 445ff.; W. Grundmann, *Ev. nach Mk.*, pp. 153, 156. The opposite thesis is defended in particular by V. Taylor, *St Mark*, pp. 632ff. and J. Jeremias, *Jésus et les Païens*, pp. 26ff.

[3] Cf. pp. 83ff. above.

already said that the presence of Gentiles in the crowd surrounding Jesus was certainly charged with meaning for the
Evangelist, who composed this summary. Jesus goes beyond the
boundaries of Jewish Palestine in 5.1–20 and in 8.27—9.29,
passages which do not belong to the third section; he is several
times on the 'Sea of Galilee' in chapters 3—5; he also leaves
the region more or less when he withdraws into the 'wilderness',
or to 'a solitary place' (1.12,35,45; 6.31–2; 8.4) or when he
retires towards the shores of the 'Sea of Galilee' (2.13; 3.7;
4.1; 5.21; 6.34; 7.31), or even whenever he takes refuge 'on
the mountain' (3.13; 6.46; 9.2–8). We cannot therefore
consider the third section of Mark as the only part of this
Gospel where the author shows Jesus as the initiator of the
mission to the Gentiles.

On the other hand, this section does not bring any very daring
message of religious universalism. Jesus keeps to quite small
areas in the vicinity of a lake pompously called a 'sea';[1] he
agrees only as an exceptional step to intervene in favour of
Gentiles (7.25ff.) and appears much more anxious to hide
himself away than to make any proclamation when he is in a
non-Jewish land (7.24). As for his daring words about the
Jewish rules regarding ritual purity, they are never presented
as intended to facilitate the evangelization of the Gentiles.
How discreet, we may say, since one can place more trust in

[1] This use of θάλασσα for the Lake of Tiberias corresponds to the use of
the Hebrew *yam* in the Old Testament and rabbinic literature (cf.
Strack–Billerbeck, vol. I, pp. 184–5). But in Greek it has a somewhat
comic flavour and is a flagrant semitism (J. Wellhausen, *Einleitung in die
drei ersten Evangelien* (Berlin 1905), p. 34, and M. Black, *Aramaic Approach* . . . , 2nd edn, p. 96). Its elimination by Luke is easily explained
by that author's literary pretensions. But one might wonder whether
Mark did not keep the word (which he uses without the complement
τῆς Γαλιλαίας except in 1.16 and 7.31) in order to suggest to his readers
the real sea, the Mediterranean on which so many missionaries were
sailing in the first century and on whose shores were situated so many
Greek-speaking churches. Considering the confusion that prevails in
Mark between the earthly Jesus and the risen Christ, an intention of this
kind is quite conceivable. It is interesting to note that the frequency of
the word θάλασσα is much greater in Mark (nineteen times) than in any
other New Testament book, except the Epistle of Jude and the Book of
Revelation; Matthew and John, who also use this word for the lake,
come far behind Mark in this respect (R. Morgenthaler, *Statistik*,
pp. 104 and 164).

sayings and stories on which the author of Mark has not im-
printed his own ideas and aspirations. True, but we must
hasten to add: how strangely discreet, on the part of an author
who confuses so completely the earthly Jesus and the risen
Christ. Are we to conclude that this intrepid defender of the
mission did not place the proclamation of the gospel to the
non-Jewish peoples among the nearest of his concerns? Could
this militant Christian have lent only half an ear to the problems
posed by the entry of the Gentiles into the Church, this latter
being for him synonymous with an Israel rid of its bad shepherds, to which numerous Gentiles attached themselves of
their own accord? That would seem to be the case.[1]

A sectarian Church careful to keep itself pure, the independent growth of vast missions among pagan peoples, whose
success threatened to submerge the central community—
these are the main features of the great crisis in which Paul
and the Christians of Jerusalem came so severely into conflict
and which, in our modern eyes, often sum up the whole
history of the first generation of Christians. But at the same
date an open and mobile Judaeo-Christian church could
quite well come into severe conflict with a static and closed
parent church without any question of Gentiles arising. Such
a church could assert its revolutionary convictions while
remaining in the framework of Judaism and taking a vaguely
liberal attitude to proselytism among non-Jews, as long as it
was not faced with the prospect of a Gentile Christian majority
in its midst, whereas the leaders of the Jerusalem community
were prone to take fright at anything that happened anywhere
in the Church, since they claimed a universal primacy. For
such a church the question was not a burning one, as it was for
the Jerusalem community or the churches founded by Paul and
his group. It is accordingly to a church of this kind that the
author of Mark must have belonged for him to adopt such a
non-militant attitude on this question so hotly debated in the
course of the first Christian generation.[2]

---

[1] Agreeing in this with G. D. Kilpatrick, 'The Gentile Mission in Mark
and Mark 13.9–11', in *Studies in the Gospels, Essays in Memory of R. H.
Lightfoot*, ed. D. E. Nineham, pp. 145ff.

[2] It could of course be maintained that this lukewarmness reflects a state
of things where the disputes about the admission of the Gentiles to the

If, in Mark 6.14—8.29 the accent is not laid on the mission among the Gentiles, it is placed, on the other hand, on the attitude the 'disciples' should adopt to the crowd that throngs around the little group they form with the Master. The two miracles of the loaves and their context give very clear indications on this point.[1] They first suggest that what is asked of the disciples is difficult and paradoxical (6.35–7,51–2; 8.1–4, 17–21). They then refer to the compassion which bids them not refuse the people the aid they are clamouring for without knowing very clearly in what form they want it (6.34; 8.2). Over and above the brief teaching that is always essential (6.34; the three days mentioned in 8.2), the disciples have to feed this shepherdless flock (6.37; 8.1–4) in spite of their meagre resources (6.37–8; 8.4–5). Both stories refer doubtless to the Eucharist (6.41; 8.6): it is thus a matter of admitting the people to full communion, without waiting to sort them out or to instruct them at length.[2] Would that not threaten to ruin

Church had ceased and the presence of Gentiles in the communities seemed perfectly natural (this is roughly the argument of J. M. Robinson, *Geschichtsverst. d. Mk.-Ev.*, pp. 94–100). But, if we remember the hard struggles of Paul, at least up to the year 60, and the cautious attitude of Acts in explaining the difficulties of incorporating Gentile Christians into the Church (around 80–5!), it is scarcely conceivable that the communities Mark was written for could have regarded the problem as a thing of the past. On the contrary, there are reasons to believe that they had not yet been faced with the problem in a pressing form when Mark was written (cf. pp. 248ff. below).

[1] Which it is surprising to see no commentator remarks on, since the place occupied in these stories by the disciples and by the people is distinctly greater than in most of the miracle stories.

[2] W. Grundmann, *Ev. nach Mk.*, pp. 133–4, puts this quite well. One might go a step further, moreover, and wonder whether the two miracles of the loaves do not constitute in the eyes of the author of Mark the image of what the true cult, celebrated in the presence of the risen Christ by a liberated Israel, should be. These assemblies in 'desert places', where the disciples of Jesus officiate before a crowd of pilgrims—do they not perhaps replace, in his mind, the feasts of the Temple of Jerusalem (cf. pp. 101–7 above)? Is this not the new sacrifice he wants to substitute for those of the Mosaic covenant: no fixed place of celebration, probable secrecy (cf. the insistence on the rapid dispersal of the crowd), sacrificial offerings taken from the daily food of the poor, orderliness of the whole ceremony (6.39–40,43; 8.6,8)? These 'desert assemblies' form a striking contrast with the frequent meetings of the Jerusalem conventicles (Mark 14.12–25 and par.; Acts 2.42,46), which recall,

the community life centred around the ritual meal (cf. Acts 2.42,46)? Most certainly, but it is here that the miracle happens: instead of chaos and failure, the folly of admitting such an enormous crowd of people to the community is crowned with brilliant success (6.42–4; 8.8–9,17–21) because the Master watches over it himself. But this unexpected triumph cannot be savoured by the disciples: they must move on forthwith to other spheres of action, row head into the wind, risk famine (6.45ff.; 8.9–10,14–16).

Thus it is a stirring call to courageous missionary enterprise and an open Church that Mark makes the core of the chapters where the two miracles of the loaves appear. This understood, the significance of chapter 7, which comes between the two stories, emerges more clearly. The ritual purity rules are denounced because, in addition to their hypocrisy (7.9ff.), their acceptance by the Christians would force these latter to remain in a closed circle from which less zealous Jews[1] and the

---

with all due allowance for the different circumstances, the *sociétés* of French Protestant bourgeois that used to meet in the eighteenth century. The opposition between the partisans of *assemblées* and *sociétés* at that time was very keen (cf. for example E. G. Léonard, *Histoire ecclésiastique des Réformés français au XVIIIe siècle* (Paris 1940)). Could there have existed a similar conflict between two schools of Palestinian Christians? The idea ought not to be rejected out of hand (cf. pp. 251ff. below).

[1] There has been much discussion about the parenthesis formed by vv. 3–4 in chapter 7 of Mark and it has been stressed that to claim that πάντες οἱ 'Ιουδαῖοι complied with the purification rules recommended by the Pharisees would be an exaggeration. In any case, it is argued, the rules in question were not yet, in the first century, part of the 'tradition of the Elders' (cf. in particular E. Lohmeyer, *Ev. des Mk.*, pp. 138–40). In any case the Qumran discoveries have shown that, even before the Christian era, one Jewish sect at least recognized the absolute authority of a certain number of ritual purity rules whose application they extended to all repentant and faithful Israel (cf. W. Grundmann, *Ev. nach Mk.*, pp. 147–8). The parenthesis of Mark 7.3–4 thus appears less improbable, however surprising it may be in its detailed aberration (Matthew omits it, which shows his embarrassment; Strack–Billerbeck, vol. II, pp. 13–14, are very short of rabbinic parallels; Jewish scholars, like C. G. Montefiore, *The Synoptic Gospels*, vol. I, pp. 133–45, emphasize its strangeness). Can we see in it an interpolation from the pen of an ill-advised Christian Gentile, as B. H. Branscomb suggests, *Gosp. of Mark*, p. xxxvi and as V. Taylor, *St Mark*, p. 335, half believes, while rejecting the much more definite hypothesis of B. W. Bacon, *The*

Gentiles would of necessity be excluded. The rules that count are those that will enable the community to open wide its doors and to live in peace, that is to say they are those of simple, natural morality which result in mutual tolerance and peaceful coexistence (7.17–23). The exorcism accorded to the Syrophoenician woman for her daughter (7.24–30) prolongs this line of thought by showing that the Church cannot close its doors to the Gentiles, provided they remain in their place and really place their trust in Jesus. But that, for the author of Mark, is only a particular case of the general principle that the Christian Church must always stand wide open. The healing of 7.32–7, which v. 31 necessitates locating in a pagan country, confirms the capacity of non-Jews to become bearers of the Good News.[1]

Beginnings of the Gospel Story (New Haven 1909), p. 86 (ibid., pp. 338–9)? This is not our view, which is that these verses are from the pen of the Evangelist.

All that is needed is to understand 'Ιουδαῖοι in the restricted sense of Judaeans (with H. B. Swete, *Gospel according to St Mark*, 3rd edn, p. 143), which is not at all an impossible interpretation for the expression βασιλεὺς τῶν 'Ιουδαίων in Mark 15.2,9,12,18,26, the only other place where the word occurs in Mark. Obviously we cannot extend this meaning of 'Ιουδαῖος to the other synoptic Gospels, where the national and religious meaning certainly predominates (cf. the arguments of W. Gutbrod, art. 'Ισραήλ κτλ. in *TWNT*, vol. III, pp. 376–7, who, however, does not distinguish between Mark and the other synoptic Gospels). But there is nothing surprising in it from the pen of a Christian who did not yet feel himself estranged from Judaism (cf. pp. 90–1 and 101ff. above) and had a distinct preference for Galilee and its inhabitants (cf. for example W. Marxsen, *Der Ev. Markus*, pp. 33ff.). From where he was writing, that is to say from Judaea, whence the scribes of Mark 7.1 also came, Judaea no doubt seemed much more ritualistic than the rest of Palestine. This explanation of 'Ιουδαῖοι in Mark 7.3 seems much more likely than that which sees in it an allusion to the Jews of the western diaspora, among whom it is suggested that the readers of Mark lived. This latter interpretation is to be found, nevertheless, in several recent commentaries, including those of A. E. J. Rawlinson, E. Lohmeyer and W. Grundmann, ad. loc.

Interesting comments on Mark 7.1ff. are to be found in S. Schulz, 'Markus und das Alte Testament', in *Zeitschrift f. Theol. u. Kirche* (1961), pp. 184–97.

[1] The meaning of this pericope is not confined to this one idea. It also shows Jesus ready to make himself totally unclean in order to heal a Gentile. The lesson was no doubt directed at 'disciples' whom the very

The fourth section of Mark (8.31—10.52, finds us at the end of Jesus' ministry in northern Palestine and of the disciples' missions and at the beginning of a narrative already oriented towards Jesus' martyrdom and interlaced with discourses addressed to the disciples alone. One accordingly expects to find fewer allusions to the Church's missionary functions and its identification with a liberated Israel. But in several places we come upon what might be regarded, in its different forms, as a 'missionary ethic'. One might even say that almost the whole of Mark's ethical teaching is concentrated in these chapters. The author is not seeking to transmit to his readers the moral doctrine of Jesus, as the church tradition would nevertheless have enabled him to do. He is appealing for recruits, showing what the Master requires of missionaries, in order, no doubt, to check excessive zeal, but at the same time in order to rally those whose devotion is weakening and to shame the cowards who fear for their lives or property.

It might be objected that the exhortation and warning with which the moral teaching of these chapters begins (8.34—9.1) have a much wider scope than that of a call for missionaries. They are indeed addressed to the 'people' as much as to the 'disciples' (8.34), which led Luke to address them πρὸς πάντας and then to give a purely symbolic meaning to the images that follow.[1] But Matthew understood that such harsh words could not be addressed to everybody alike[2] and so he eliminated the people (Matt. 16.24). Mark, moreover, always gives the words he uses a fairly literal meaning. If he speaks here of the 'gospel' (8.35), which the other synoptic Gospels do not mention in this context, it is because he is thinking of those who are propagating it; if he speaks of taking up one's cross or

---

thought of touching a non-Jew filled with apprehension. It is thus once more an appeal for missionary action free of all ritualistic encumbrances.

[1] By replacing the aorist ἐλθεῖν with a present, by inserting καθ' ἡμέραν after the order to 'take up the cross', Luke has in fact transformed into an everyday moral precept what for Mark was an initial break, followed by a forward progress in the steps of the Master.

[2] The difference between Matthew and Luke reappears in the use they make of the parallel form of this parable which came to them from the *logia*: Matthew places it in the speech to the missionaries (Matt. 10.38); Luke makes it part of a speech to the 'innumerable multitude' that followed Jesus (Luke 14.27).

losing one's life, it is because he is thinking of the outlaw existence that may bring those who lead it to pay the final penalty. If then he speaks of 'following Jesus', it is similarly because he is thinking of those who accompany him, before the crucifixion and after the resurrection to carry the Good News from place to place. If the Master is speaking here to the people as well as to the 'disciples' it is because his words are addressed to serving missionaries as well as to those who will emerge from the anonymous crowd to join them: 'If there are any candidates, here are the conditions.'

This being so, one may even ask whether the *logion* of Mark 8.34 has not been retouched by the author who, starting from a saying such as those of Matt. 10.38 and Luke 14.27, wanted to counteract a too passive idea of the way in which the Christian missionaries were to 'follow Jesus'. It would seem indeed that the expressions ὀπίσω μου ἐλθεῖν and ἀκολουθεῖν μοι, which appear at the beginning and end of this saying, can be traced back to the same semitic expression, the Hebrew הָלַךְ אַחֲרִי or its Aramaic equivalent,[1] the former being a much more literal translation and so clumsy as to be practically unknown in secular Greek. Was the author of Mark trying here to avoid a repetition, as appears to be the case in 1.17,20, where he alternates the two expressions, using them in the same sense? But in that case why would he have changed so unnecessarily the original *logion* which contained the expression only once? It looks as though he was trying to restore to the expression ἔρχεσθαι ὀπίσω 'Ιησοῦ the strong meaning he feared it was losing in the church tradition. In order to do this, he brought it closer to the verb ἀκολουθεῖν, which for him has always the concrete meaning of 'to accompany on a journey' (cf. 1.18; 2.14–15; 3.7; 5.24; 6.1; 8.34; 9.38; 10.21,28,32,52; 11.9; 14.13,54; 15.41). Indeed if the Evangelist applied this term so frequently to the followers of Jesus, it is because he saw Jesus as continually on the move;[2] he did not use it in the religious and figurative sense that is scarcely distinguishable from the *imitatio Christi*.[3] In Mark 8.34, the author thus says to people

---

[1] Cf. for example J. Wellhausen, *Einleitung in die drei ersten Evangelien*, p. 33; G. Kittel, art. ἀκολουθέω, in *TWNT*, vol. I, p. 211, ll.8–16.

[2] Cf. pp. 149ff. above.

[3] Cf. the embarrassed explanations of G. Kittel, loc. cit., pp. 213–15,

for whom ἔρχεσθαι ὀπίσω Ἰησοῦ meant to 'become the successors of Jesus',[1] that nobody can 'come after Jesus' who has not shared in the itinerant ministry of the risen Christ and does not go from place to place proclaiming the gospel without caring for his own fate. Any disciple who is not an active missionary is a coward who shall perish now (8.35a) and hereafter (8.38).

The account of the exorcism that the disciples failed to perform (9.14–29) is without any doubt tinged with the ideas of the author of Mark on the place of exorcisms and healings in missionary activity. It is an appeal for boldness in the use of methods considered dangerous by Christians more anxious to defend the principle than to engage in the reality.[2]

As regards the dialogue of 9.33–50, it is quite clear from the start that it is a discussion about the ministry of missionaries. As we said earlier,[3] this group of separate sayings must have pre-dated Mark. We find in it nevertheless the trace of a slight reserve vis-à-vis the Twelve and an opposition to christological monopoly in which the author of Mark must have recognized ideas very similar to his own. The rules of church discipline that have been inserted (9.42–8; cf. Matt. 18.6–9) take on, in proximity to the dialogue concerning the unknown exorcist, a new significance, which Matthew did not want to preserve: the cause of scandal, who has to be eliminated, is not the trouble-maker whose disorderly conduct shocks the community, it is he who does not receive with open arms the 'free-lance' exorcist or the helpful sympathizer. The author of Mark took pleasure in thus pleading for an open Church.[4]

---

which are valid for Matthew and above all for Luke, but not at all for Mark. H. Clavier, *L'accès au Royaume de Dieu*, pp. 97ff., although he makes no distinction either between the synoptic Gospels, has found a good definition for this 'ethic of the Kingdom' when he says, 'The conditions of admission to the Kingdom are followed by the conditions for remaining there and ... these imply apostleship' (translation).

[1] As he had succeeded John the Baptist (Mark 1.7; Matt. 3.11; John 1.15). It would have been like shutting Jesus up in his tomb, in the eyes of the author of Mark, to think of oneself as 'following' him in that sense.

[2] Cf. pp. 112–3 above.   [3] Cf. p. 38 above.

[4] The adaptation of a number of separate *logia* to the idea of the necessarily open character of the community seems to be developed further in Mark 9.49–50, if we compare these verses with the parallels in Matthew 5.13 and Luke 14.34–5. A saying designed to keep the Church

Mark 10.1–31 is certainly an arrangement of separate passages by the Evangelist. Its leitmotiv can easily be perceived: texts relating to the family and its setting (house, land, etc.). Here again it is tempting to interpret certain passages entering into the composition of Mark as examples of the moral teaching of Jesus transmitted by the Evangelist to his readers. But verses 10.28–31 are obviously designed to encourage the missionaries who have left all to follow Jesus. Where vv. 13–27 are concerned, everything depends on the meaning attributed here to the expression 'enter into the Kingdom of God' (9.47; 10.15,23–25; cf. 10.14 and 12.34), which one might compare to the phrase 'enter into life' (9.43,45). Both are found solely in these few texts in Mark. 'The Kingdom of God' (9.1; 14.25; 15.43) and 'eternal life' (10.17,30) may have in this Gospel their most classical, Pharisaic meaning of the new state of affairs that will be brought about one day by the resurrection and the judgement of God. But there is also in Mark, as in the rest of the Gospel tradition, a 'secret of the Kingdom of God' (4.11) which is revealed to some by the proclamation to all of the Good News of the coming of the Kingdom (1.15) and by Jesus' teaching to the people about that same Kingdom (4.26,30). This secret is quite simply that by following in the footsteps of Jesus one enters directly into the Kingdom of Heaven.[1] The rich man's mistake is not to obey

---

from losing all character (and hence from any admixture likely to bring that about) becomes, in the collection reproduced by Mark, thanks to the removal of its menacing conclusion and the substitution of a more encouraging exhortation, an invitation to preserve the stimulating elements in the community and to live in peace. This twofold appeal, preceded in 9.49 by an allusion to the divine judgement which relieves men of the necessity to keep a close watch themselves over the purity of the Church, is incompatible with a narrow concept of the community resulting in frequent recourse to excommunication. These two verses are among the most enigmatic of the New Testament and every commentator tries his hand at interpreting them—without mentioning the efforts to trace the form and meaning of the words of Jesus which serve as a basis for the *logia* concerning salt, recorded in all three synoptic Gospels (cf. for example O. Cullmann, 'Que signifie le sel dans la parabole de Jésus?', in *RHPR*, 37th year (1957), pp. 36–43).

[1] There is an immense volume of literature on the 'Kingdom of God' and its secret as conceived by Jesus and the early Christians which it is impossible to list here. It must suffice to mention a few important works

the Law in bourgeois fashion (10.19–20), but to be anxious about his eternal life while refusing the one guarantee that leaves no room for doubt: to take possession of the Kingdom (10.14,21) by passing straight through its open door and embarking without discussion (10.15) and without a backward look (9.43,45,47; 10.21) on an itinerant life in the company of Jesus. In other words, the grace of God offers men a short cut to eternal life: a ministry of itinerant preaching in the company of the risen Christ. To those who do not take that road, because they are too rich (10.22ff.) or too intelligent (12.34; cf. 10.21), the Jesus of Mark's Gospel does not promise perdition. But for them, as for anybody who does not seize the opportunity offered, there is no hope except in God's omnipotent mercy (10.26–7).

The missionary must therefore be capable, in order to secure the salvation that is offered to him, of leaving his family, his possessions, his home (10.21,28–31) and his work (1.16–20; 2.14). But there is one striking omission from the list in Mark 10.29–30: it is not said that a would-be companion of Jesus must leave his wife, an exception that Matt. 19.29 retains but that disappears in Luke 18.29. Is it by pure chance that the nearest passage to this contains Jesus' words forbidding husband and wife to leave one another (10.2–12)? In our view it is not. The words of Jesus are certainly addressed to the whole of Israel and have a universal value despite their Jewish complexion. But the Evangelist only reproduced them here because the problem of separated couples must have been acute in the itinerant missionary circles for which he was pleading. One might even suppose that the pericope of Mark 10.13–16

---

published in the last thirty years which give an idea of the debates about this basic theological concept of the New Testament and the solutions proposed: H. D. Wendland, *Die Eschatologie des Reiches Gottes bei Jesus* (Gütersloh 1931); R. Otto, *Reich Gottes und Menschensohn* (Munich 1934) [E.T. 1943]; J. Héring, *Le Royaume de Dieu et sa venue*, (1st edn Paris 1937, 2nd edn Neuchâtel 1959); H.C lavier, *L'accès au Royaume de Dieu* (Clermont-Ferrand and Paris 1943); W. G. Kuemmel, *Verheissung und Erfüllung*, 3rd edn (Zurich 1956); A. N. Wilder, *Eschatology and Ethics in the Teaching of Jesus*, 2nd edn (New York 1950); H. Roberts, *Jesus and the Kingdom of God* (London 1955); J. Bonsirven, *Le Règne de Dieu* (Paris 1957). Cf. also K. L. Schmidt, art. βασιλεύς κτλ. in *TWNT*, vol. I, pp. 573ff., especially pp. 582–92.

concerning the way Jesus received little children[1] attracted
the author of Mark because of the difficulties encountered by
married missionaries owing to the presence of young children.
He saw in it a command not to leave them, at least in their
tender years.

If we note that the teaching given by Jesus in Mark
10.35–45 to the sons of Zebedee and then to the Twelve is an
exhortation to service to the point of self-sacrifice, addressed to
church leaders in whom the Evangelist saw the first missionaries, we must accordingly conclude, in regard to this fourth
section of Mark, as suggested above, that in it the Evangelist
is formulating a set of moral precepts for itinerant missionaries.

The fifth section of Mark (11.1—13.37) opens up to the Christian mission prospects for the future: on the ruins of the existing
Jewish institutions the missionaries must continue to go about
proclaiming the gospel, until the glorious parousia of the Son

---

[1] It seems to be a question of children of up to twelve ($\pi\alpha\iota\delta\iota\alpha$), but the
accent appears to be placed on their youth, even if Luke goes too far in
replacing this word on one occasion by 'infants' ($\beta\rho\epsilon\phi\eta$) in his parallel
to this pericope (Luke 18.15). It will be noted that in 10.29–30 the
'children' who have to be left behind in order to become a missionary
are spoken of as $\tau\epsilon\kappa\nu\alpha$, a term with no age connotation, which can be
applied to adult or adolescent descendants. A special problem arises in
connection with the word $\pi\alpha\iota\delta\iota\sigma\nu$ in Mark 10.15, since it is not clear
whether it is in apposition to the subject or the object of the relative
clause introduced by δs. The meaning and exegetical tradition seem
to impose the first interpretation, which is also that of Matt. 18.3. But
the order of the sentence and the context—both altered by Matthew, it
should be pointed out—do not allow the second to be rejected. In that
case, we would have a comparison between the reception given to the
Kingdom by the hearers of the gospel message and the reception given
to a little child: the Kingdom is as weak, insignificant and demanding,
but also as full of promise for the future, as a child; when face to face
with it, one must be as ready to receive it as one is to welcome a child,
otherwise nothing will happen and one will not enter into the Kingdom,
one will not become a missionary. Those who have taken the decisive
step, therefore, the 'disciples', must be especially kind and patient to
children who are as helpless and dependent in the world as they themselves, the heralds of this unpretentious Kingdom (10.14b). By distorting the meaning of this *logion* in an effort to make it more understandable, Matthew has led all subsequent exegesis into an impasse;
the discretion of Luke, who changed little in the passage as he found it
in Mark, enables us perhaps to correct Matthew's mistake.

of Man, which is not more than a few decades away. We have already discussed at some length the cleansing of the Temple and the episode of the barren fig-tree in chapter 11.12–25.[1] Here we must stop for a moment to examine the parable of the husbandmen (12.1ff.), not in order to investigate its authenticity—a much debated question[2]—but because its significance for Mark is of capital importance to us if we are to grasp the Evangelist's conception of the Christian Church.

As the quotation from Isa. 5.1–2, with which the parable opens, indicates, Mark establishes a comparison between this text and the celebrated 'song of the vine' in which the prophet relates the disappointment of Yahweh at the unfruitfulness of his chosen people. This reminiscence at once establishes an important fact: the vine of Mark 12.1ff. is not barren, like that of Isa. 5; consequently it is not threatened with destruction like the latter. The disappointment of the owner of the vineyard is with the husbandmen, affected by an inexplicable collective madness—not even to be explained by a tense social situation[3]—involved in a passive attitude of rebellion whose tragic conclusion is in no doubt from v. 4 onwards. In spite of this significant difference, Matthew is prompted by the analogy between the texts of Isaiah and of Mark to understand the parable as an allegory of the rejection of Israel (cf. Matt. 21.43). He has been followed in this by numerous commentators, who identify the Jewish people either with the vine or with the husbandmen.[4] But this interpretation is unjust to Mark 12.1ff. for, if it is an allegory, it overlooks the very clear distinction made in the text between the vine and those who cultivate it.

---

[1] Cf. pp. 103–6 above.
[2] Among the most interesting contributions of recent years we may mention those of W. G. Kuemmel, 'Das Gleichnis von den bösen Weingärtnern (Mark 12.1–9)' in *Aux sources de la tradition chrétienne, Mélanges . . . Goguel* (Neuchâtel and Paris 1950), pp. 120–31; J. J. Vincent, 'The Parables of Jesus as Self-Revelation', in *Studia Evangelica . . .* (1957), pp. 79–99, especially pp. 85–8.
[3] Rightly mentioned by C. H. Dodd, *The Parables of the Kingdom*, rev. edn (London 1961), p. 97, and also by others, but it does not explain everything.
[4] Thus, for example, A. Loisy, *Ev. selon Marc*, pp. 334ff.; C. G. Montefiore, *Synopt. Gosp.*, vol. I, pp. 273–5; E. Lohmeyer, *Ev. des Mk.*, pp. 243–9; W. G. Kuemmel, loc. cit., pp. 127–8.

And if this passage is not a real allegory,[1] the context condemns it, for everything in it is designed to convey opposition between the 'high priests', the scribes and 'elders' to whom the parable is addressed and the 'multitude' of Jewish pilgrims, representing the whole of Israel.

With the vast majority of commentators[2] then, we are inclined to say that the parable of the husbandmen is a violent attack on the religious heads of the Jewish people and the announcement of the replacement of these criminal madmen by new husbandmen who will do their work properly. The Evangelist is obviously thinking of the new structures that the risen Christ will set up: the Twelve perhaps, but others too, who are yet to be raised to authority (cf. 10.35–45). Thus the Christian mission is marching on, not towards the constitution of another chosen people but towards the eschatological restoration of Israel, foreshadowed by the cult of 'desert assemblies' (Mark 6.35–44; 8.1–10) and by the flocking in of the Gentiles (3.8; 5.1–20; 7.24—9.29). This conclusion is amply confirmed

---

[1] V. Taylor, *St Mark*, p. 472, tries to see in it a partial allegory, only a few of whose features have a specific meaning; W. Grundmann, *Ev. nach Mk.*, pp. 238ff., is even more opposed to the allegorical interpretation and refers to the non-allegorized version of the parable to be found in the *Gospel according to Thomas*, which might represent a very early form of the tradition. Indeed, *logion* 65 of this apocryphal text (*L'évangile selon Thomas, texte copte établi et traduit* by A. Guillaumont, H. C. Puech, G. Quispel, W. Till and Yassa Abd Al Masih (Paris 1959), p. 39; cf. also J. Doresse, *L'évangile selon Thomas ou les paroles secrètes de Jésus* (Paris 1959), p. 104, which gives this *logion* as number 69), is very simple and straightforward and does not contain the reference to Isaiah that helps to make Mark 12.1ff., appear an allegory, so that the reference can perhaps be imputed to the author of Mark. Cf. the interesting remarks on the subject of this passage of the *Gospel according to Thomas* by O. Cullmann, 'Das Thomasevangelium und die Frage nach dem Alter der in ihm enthaltenen Tradition', in *Theologische Literaturzeitung*, vol. 85 (1960), cols. 321–34, especially col. 332.

[2] This is in particular the theory of G. Wohlenberg, *Das Evangelium des Markus* (Leipzig 1910), pp. 307–12; M. J. Lagrange, *Ev. Marc*, pp. 305–12; A. E. J. Rawlinson, *St Mark*, pp. 160–4; G. Dehn, *Fils de Dieu*, pp. 205–7; E. Klostermann, *Das Markus-Ev.*, pp. 120–3; F. Hauck, *Ev. d. Mk.*, pp. 141–2; B. H. Branscomb, *Gosp. of Mark*, pp. 209–11; W. Grundmann, *Ev. nach Markus*, pp. 237–42; C. E. B. Cranfield, *St Mark*, pp. 364–9. V. Taylor, preoccupied as he is with the question of authenticity, is completely ambiguous on this point, so that it is difficult to know in which group to classify him.

by what was said above[1] about the polemical content of the rest of chap. 12 of Mark.

The future towards which the Christian mission is heading is envisaged in chapter 13 from a different point of view: that of its chronology. We shall not attempt to trace the sources or make a detailed exegesis of the Marcan version of the 'synoptic apocalypse', which interests us here only as the well-developed conclusion placed by the Evangelist at the end of his exposition of the real ecclesiological intentions of Jesus.[2] The general intention of the author of Mark when writing this chapter is clear. Without ceasing his exhortations based on the unforeseeability of the date of the parousia (13.32–7) and his encouragements derived from the fact that it is close at hand,[3] he is seeking to arm Christians against the manifold temptations of apocalyptic. In the flaring passions and calculating self-interest aroused in this way he sees the source of the worst evils of the Church: timidity in proclaiming the gospel; a rooted attachment to certain so-called holy places. He endeavours accordingly to show his readers that the Master offers them a

---

[1] Cf. pp. 97–8 above.

[2] Cf. the few indications given above (pp. 38 and 84) on the points that are not dealt with here.

[3] The double *logion* of Mark 13.30–1 is clearly intended, as placed by the Evangelist, to obviate any misunderstanding about the long list in 13.5–29 of happenings that are still in the future. He wants it to be understood in the first place that he is not postponing the parousia *sine die* and secondly that he is not seeking to tone down the words of Jesus about the end of the world or to prefer to his prophecies the somewhat materialistic certainty of the solidity of the created world. To achieve this, he seems to have joined together and adapted two separate *logia*, whose meaning, origin, and initial form are seen by the commentators in a wide variety of ways (cf. for example V. Taylor, *St Mark*, pp. 521–2 and 642; G. R. Beasley-Murray, *A Comm. on Mark Thirteen* (London 1957), pp. 99–104; C. E. B. Cranfield, *St Mark*, p. 410; W. Grundmann, *Ev. nach Mk.*, pp. 270–1). These two verses do indeed bear a relation to two other separate *logia* preserved by the synoptic tradition (Mark 9.1 and par.; Matt. 5.17 and par.). We are therefore sceptical of all attempts to link either the first of them or both to any source of a certain length, from the hypothesis of T. Colani (*Jésus-Christ et les croyances messianiques de son temps*, 2nd edn (Strasbourg 1864), pp. 201ff.) to that which W. Marxsen (*Der Ev. Markus*, p. 109) borrowed from J. Sundwall (*Zusammensetzung d. Markus-Ev.*, p. 77).

much wider, and, above all, more active, future than certain other Christians would have them believe.[1]

How does he show this? By a series of tableaux, in which it is not certain that he saw a description of periods destined to follow one another, but in which it is much more likely that he was seeking to refute, one after another, several apocalyptic ideas that threatened to obstruct the future in the eyes of the faithful. Vv. 5–8 form a first tableau: it begins with a warning (v. 5b) and ends with two remarks which simultaneously recognize in the events referred to in the interval a part of the eschatological drama, but reduce them to the level of a mere curtain-raiser (vv. 7b and 8c). The author seems to fear that the Christians may launch out into some political venture under an ambitious leader (vv. 6–7) and so stresses that wars are disasters to the same degree as natural disasters (v. 8). Why in these circumstances should one look for a messianic significance? The deceivers of v. 6 are difficult to identify precisely.[2] They will come in Jesus' name, making claims of their own: a surprising combination which perhaps denotes an editorial interpolation, but which must have had a specific meaning for the Evangelist. The author is no doubt thinking of the heads of the Church, who boast of being Jesus' successors and of having assumed after his death his role of Davidic Messiah, at the risk of one day leading Christians to their destruction.[3] It is James and his group who are attacked here,[4]

---

[1] Cf. above pp. 112–3, 120ff. W. Marxsen, op. cit. pp. 112ff., brings out very well the intentions of the author of Mark in this chapter 13.

[2] Cf., for example, the embarrassed and not very convincing explanations of v. 6 in E. Lohmeyer, *Ev. des Mk.*, pp. 270–1; V. Taylor, *St Mark*, pp. 503–4; C. E. B. Cranfield, *St Mark*, p. 395. W. Grundmann, *Ev. nach Mk.*, p. 263, is clearer, but stops on the threshold of our explanation.

[3] Cf. Matthew's addition of the words ὁ Χριστός after the ΕΓΩ ΕΙΜΙ of the eschatological Redeemer (on this point see, for example, Bultmann, *Das Evangelium nach Johannes* (Göttingen 1941, with a 1957 supplement), p. 167, n. 2). Regarding the attraction that the Jewish revolutionary nationalism of the time long held for the Palestinian church of the first century, cf. S. G. F. Brandon, *The Fall of Jerusalem*, pp. 74ff., despite the exaggerations that detract a little from this.

[4] Cf. pp. 130ff. above. Are the four disciples whom Jesus is addressing here being exhorted to be wary of James? It is possible, if we remember that there was a period of fluctuation in the church of Jerusalem soon after

together with any resurgence of a political messianism in the midst of the Christian community.

The second tableau goes from v. 9 to v. 13. Like the preceding one, it begins with a warning (v. 9a); it ends with a call for perseverance, the only guarantee of salvation (v. 13b), in which we must see the equivalent of v. 8c, that is to say the announcement of a very long and painful eschatological drama. But the accent this time is on taking heed to oneself, and not to another. The four disciples are exhorted not to seek to avoid persecution by soft-pedalling the proclamation of the Good News and preparing their apologia with care. Persecution is inevitable, because it is the manifestation of men's hatred of the name of Jesus (v. 13a) and one of the sad signs of the exacerbation of the worst human passions at the approach of the End (v. 12). Faced with the 'revolutionary' κηρύσσειν,[1] all the religious and political authorities of Palestine[2] are bound to

it was founded, when the authority of Peter and of James coexisted. This obviously difficult confrontation, even if their attitude was fraternal, must certainly have been the subject of discussion in the Christian circles of the day.

[1] Despite E. Lohmeyer, *Ev. des Mk.*, p. 272, and J. Jeremias, *Jésus et les païens*, it would seem very doubtful that the reference here is to an apocalyptic proclamation equivalent to that of Rev. 14.6ff. and reserved to the last days. Nor is this interpretation necessary in the case of Mark 14.9, which these two authors understand in the same way. But it is not possible either to identify this κηρύσσειν with the preaching of a Paul or a Luke, as most of the commentators do, even when they admit that the *logion* may originally have had a different meaning (thus W. Marxsen, *Der ev. Marcus*, pp. 118–20). We must attribute to this act of the disciples here the meaning that Mark gives it elsewhere, of 'revolutionary proclamation' (cf. pp. 191ff. above).

[2] With J. Wellhausen, *Das Evang. Marci*, 2nd edn, p. 102; E. Meyer, *Ursprung und Anfänge des Christentums*, vol. I, p. 130; V. Taylor, *St Mark*, p. 506, and several others, we believe that the author of Mark is thinking here only of the authorities—Jewish, Roman and protected by Rome—existing in Palestine in his day (cf. Acts 4.24ff.). It is not necessary to think of the diaspora—not in any case of the distant diaspora. On the other hand, the punctuation between v. 9 and v. 10 has long been in dispute, since Matthew in his parallel text (24.14) writes εἰς μαρτύριον πᾶσιν τοῖς ἔθνεσιν, attaching these words to the *logion* parallel to Mark 13.10), while in his other version of the same *logion* (10.18), he writes εἰς μαρτύριον αὐτοῖς καὶ τοῖς ἔθνεσιν (attaching these words to the equivalent of Mark 13.9), while quite a number of manuscripts (W, Θ, 108, 124, 127, 131, 157) and several early versions (mss of the old latin, syr. sin.

react with the utmost energy (v. 9). Let the disciples not be betrayed into cowardly caution! The κηρύσσειν is necessary, for it is part of God's plan, which will always find its 'heralds' (v. 10). Those who evade this dangerous duty run the risk of not benefiting by the eschatological salvation offered them, even if they employ the respite thus afforded in devising polished confessions of faith, forgetting that the Holy Spirit would dictate the most appropriate replies to them, if need be, on the spot (v. 11). To wait passively for the end of the world, taking care not to cause scandal, is thus just as bad as to try to bring it closer by rallying round a descendant of David.[1]

The third tableau (13.14–23) constitutes a sharp attack on all apocalyptic geography and in particular on any attempt to locate the parousia in Jerusalem. We have already discussed

---

bo. etc.) join the words καὶ εἰς πάντα τὰ ἔθνη of Mark 13.10 to v. 9 and separate the two sentences between the words ἔθνη and πρῶτον. This fact, added to the rather strange construction of Mark 13.10, recently led G. D. Kilpatrick ('The Gentile Mission in Mark and Mark 13.9–11' in *Studies in the Gospel, Essays in Memory of R. H. Lightfoot*, ed. D. E. Nineham, pp. 145–58) to revert to and develop a hypothesis put forward in 1924 by F. Burkitt and to attach the first five words of Mark 13.10 to the preceding verse. In that case, the bringing of the missionaries before the various political authorities (non-Jewish for the most part) would have been considered by the author of Mark as a 'testimony', not only to the authorities in question but also to the nations they represent. The end of v. 10 could then be attached to v. 11. This hypothesis is a very attractive one, since it rids v. 10 of its appearance of being an ill-placed parenthesis, remarked on, with slight shades of difference, by all the commentators. After describing the fact of what is bound to happen to them (vv. 9–10a), the author of Mark reverts in vv. 10–11 to the warning issued at the beginning of v. 9 and tells the missionaries how they are to behave in the face of that fact. The πρῶτον can then have either the meaning of 'before the end' that is usually attributed to it or, preferably, that of 'above all', 'in the first place', proposed by M. J. Lagrange (*Ev. Marc*, p. 338). Our preference is for 'in the first place', so that the sentence would mean 'the urgent task that God requires to be given priority is the proclamation of the gospel'.

[1] E. Lohmeyer's remarks (*Ev. des Mk.*, pp. 272–3) on this verse are singularly unfortunate: 'If Mark inserted this saying, it was because he manifestly knew only the kind of proclamation of the gospel that took place before a court. . . . The community was still living as though in hiding, waiting quietly upon the coming of the Lord; only the woes of the day of judgement provoked them to an open proclamation.' In other words, πρῶτον is taken to mean 'right at the end'.

this passage[1] and revert to it only to stress some of its features. It contains a prediction of the fall of Jerusalem and of Judaea owing to some appalling disaster ordained by God—a disaster from which none of those who persist in their attachment to the Temple can hope to escape. The author of Mark certainly meant this as a thrust at the church of Jerusalem, so entrenched on its holy hill.[2] But more important is the fact that he did not intend to identify this divine judgement with the end of the world and that he stresses the fact that history will go on after the disaster (vv. 19–20). He even foresees that several attempts will be made to replace Jerusalem as the scene of the second coming by some other place and he firmly sets aside these impostures (vv. 21–2). The final warning is addressed to the four disciples (v. 23), no doubt to urge them to emerge from their passive waiting in Jerusalem and carry the gospel from place to place before they are obliged to do so by the predicted catastrophe.

Lastly, a fourth tableau (13.24–9) describes the events which are to follow the terrible days of trial announced in vv. 14–23. Whereas the first three tableaux showed, in Mark's eyes, more or less simultaneous situations, the author places himself further ahead in the future, just before the Day of Judgement (v. 29). But he does not seek here to stress the suddenness of the end. On the contrary, he emphasizes the progressive character of the parousia of the Son of Man ($\dot{\epsilon}\nu$ $\dot{\epsilon}\kappa\epsilon\dot{\iota}\nu\alpha\iota\varsigma$ $\tau\alpha\hat{\iota}\varsigma$ $\dot{\eta}\mu\dot{\epsilon}\rho\alpha\iota\varsigma$ ... $\ddot{\epsilon}\sigma\sigma\nu\tau\alpha\iota$ ... $\pi\dot{\iota}\pi\tau\sigma\nu\tau\epsilon\varsigma$ ... $\kappa\alpha\dot{\iota}$ $\tau\acute{\sigma}\tau\epsilon$ ... $\kappa\alpha\dot{\iota}$ $\tau\acute{\sigma}\tau\epsilon$. ...) and the fact that the sinners will be present at the grandiose spectacle (v. 26). The contrast between this description and the sayings grouped together in Luke 17.20–4, so close to it in various ways (cf. Luke 17.23 and Mark 13.21, for example), is striking and seems to show an active editorial intention on the part of the author of Mark in these verses 24–27.[3] The Evange-

---

[1] P. 104, n. 2 above.

[2] It has moreover been pointed out (cf., for example, E. Lohmeyer, *Ev. des Mk.*, p. 276; V. Taylor, *St Mark*, p. 513) that the sayings of vv. 15–16 reflect the point of view of a country-dweller, and not of a town-dweller interested in his fellow citizens. There is a certain indifference with regard to the fate of the capital and its inhabitants —Christian or not—in the way it is said: 'Get out yourselves, these people are heading for disaster'.

[3] These four verses are a real apocalyptic pronouncement whose features

list is seeking to give the parousia a chronological dimension that will make it measurable, since he is anxious that the coming of the Son of Man should itself be regarded as a sign of the approach of the end. This at least is the conclusion which, however surprising, we must come to when we turn to vv. 28–29: the ταῦτα of v. 29 refers back to the substance of vv. 24–7 or, possibly, to that of vv. 5–27, which in any case includes the parousia among the signs of the fulfilment of time.[1] Thus, the

_____

are borrowed from various books of the Old Testament. The authors who, from T. Colani (op. cit.) onwards, believe that the author of Mark used a Jewish 'little apocalypse' as the source for all or part of his chapter 13, all attribute vv. 24–7 to this hypothetical document. But this little set of sayings could equally well be the work of the Evangelist or of any Christian wishing to give a context to the words pronounced by Jesus before the Sanhedrin, according to Mark 14.62 and par. It matters little, after all; what interests us here is the context in which the Evangelist places these verses and the fairly slow chronological progression that he imposes—or respects—in the midst of this vast upheaval, whereas he has no special liking for apocalyptic (cf. pp. 116–7 above). It seems obvious that if he had wished he could have built up, on the basis of sayings of Jesus, Old Testament texts, and Jewish or Christian models, a real 'little apocalypse'; if he did not do so and was satisfied with a few separate tableaux, it is because his aim was to exhort and warn, even where his text borders on pure description. Cf. on this point the broad consensus between critics as different as F. Busch, *Zum Verständnis der synoptischen Eschatologie: Markus 13 neu untersucht* (Gütersloh 1938), pp. 44, 80; G. R. Beasley-Murray, *Jesus and the Future, an Examination of the Criticism of the Eschatological Discourse, Mark 13, with Special Reference to the Little Apocalypse Theory* (London 1954), pp. 212–6; W. Marxsen, *Der Ev. Marcus.*, p. 128.

[1] In speaking of ταῦτα πάντα in verse 30, the author of Mark seems to be seeking to distinguish between the restricted reference in v. 29 (to vv. 24–7 only?) and a reference to the whole series of events from v. 5 onward. Matthew eliminates this distinction in the parallel verses 24.33–4, where ταῦτα πάντα occurs twice: the reference to what precedes thus becomes more general and does not necessarily include the parousia. Luke achieves the same result by toning down the picture of the parousia considerably (Luke 21.25–7) and inserting immediately afterwards an allusion to the time when 'these things begin to come to pass' (21.28), which lessens the effect of the ensuing parable of the fig-tree and its conclusion, which is almost identical with that of Mark (Luke 21.29,31) except for the subject added to the last phrase. All commentators agree that if Mark is to be taken literally the parousia must be included among the signs of the end of the world but all, with a unanimity rarely equalled, reject this idea. Is this wise? 'Summer' for

answer to the question asked by the disciples in Mark 13.4 is
that the final crisis has already begun (tableaux 1—3 with their
triple βλέπετε) and that the only real sign of the imminence of
the end will be the parousia itself, by which time it will be too
late to wake up (13.36). The awakening must come here and
now, in immediate obedience to the call of the Master (cf.
1.16–20).

After this quick review of Mark's ecclesiology, it will be
seen that we can draw the same conclusion as after the review
of the christology of this Gospel. The author had no gift or
inclination for speculation, but he was the spokesman of an
enterprising movement which, having broken away from the
mother church of Jerusalem, had launched out into a large-
scale missionary venture among the common people in Palestine and in so doing felt that it was obeying the command of
the risen Christ and at the same time following his earthly
example.

---

the author of Mark perhaps represented the judgement and the
solemn inauguration of the Kingdom of God, which are not mentioned anywhere in vv. 24–7. If this were so, the celestial phenomena,
the parousia and the gathering together of the elect would certainly
appear to him as signs of the approach of the Kingdom. In that case,
what is the consensus of the commentators worth against the evidence
of the text?

Chapter Four

THE TWO EDITIONS OF THE
GOSPEL ACCORDING TO MARK

Up to this point we have been postulating, for simplicity's sake, that the canonical Mark, in the most satisfactory version that contemporary criticism is able to reconstitute,[1] was practically

---

[1] We shall not seek here to go into all the questions that arise in relation to the text of Mark, however important they may be. It can be said that, generally speaking, less retouching has been done to Mark than to the other canonical Gospels because it was used less. But conversely, the preponderant influence of Matthew and Luke led to the introduction into Mark of numerous variants designed to bring it into line with them and these are sometimes difficult to detect: for example, in 1.6, where only D and a few old latin manuscripts seem to have kept the original text, which is submerged everywhere else by a variant taken from Matt. 3.4 (cf. L. Vaganay, *Initiation à la critique textuelle néotestamentaire* (Paris 1934)). It is in any case around these two major features of the text of Mark that the debate concerning the Caesarean text of the Gospels has centred for the past half century (cf. B. M. Metzger, 'The Caesarean Text of the Gospels', in *JBL*, vol. 64 (1945), pp. 457–89; J. Duplacy, *Où en est la critique textuelle du Nouveau Testament?* (Paris 1959), pp. 41ff.).

Quite a full account of the textual criticism of Mark is to be found in M. J. Lagrange, *Ev. Marc*, pp. clxv–cxci. But these pages written in 1910 and scarcely amended since 1928 have become out of date since the discovery of the Chester Beatty papyri and the progress of the discussion on the Caesarean text. The chapter devoted to the text by V. Taylor in the introduction to his *St Mark*, pp. 33–43, is convenient but very brief. Other recent commentaries scarcely touch on the subject. This is also true of general works on the text of the New Testament, like L. Vaganay, op. cit., F. G. Kenyon, *Our Bible and the Ancient Manuscripts*, (London, 3rd edn by A. W. Adams, 1958), or V. Taylor, *The Text of the New Testament, A Short Introduction* (London 1961). Much detail about the textual problems is to be found in C. S. C. Williams, *Alterations to the Text of the Synoptic Gospels and Acts* (Oxford 1951), and in the edition of S. C. E. Legg, *Novum Testamentum graece*

identical with the original work that had inaugurated the literary genre of the Gospel in the first century and had been the main source of Matthew and Luke.[1] Now what we have to ask ourselves is whether this preliminary hypothesis is sound and, if not, what difference this makes to our ideas about the making of the Gospel according to Mark. It is not a question of refuting the arguments that led us to reject the theory of an early pre-Gospel or of extensive sources relating the whole of Jesus' ministry on earth,[2] but of putting the question whether, as early as the first century, before or after the writing of Matthew and Luke, there were two or more editions of Mark. By this we do not mean texts revised in regard to a few details[3] but a recasting of the work involving certain changes in its structure, with the addition or omission of fairly large passages. Without changing radically the significance of the work, such rewriting could have distorted it considerably and so oblige us to re-consider certain aspects of the analysis given in the foregoing chapters.

1
FROM THE CANONICAL GOSPEL
TO THE ORIGINAL WORK

There are three means of detecting the existence of one or more editions of Mark prior to the canonical version: observation of the sutures and literary anomalies of all kinds to be found in

---

secundum textum *Westcotto-Hortianum, Evangelium secundum Marcum* (Oxford 1935). Whatever the faults of this work, it is the only major critical edition of Mark where the P 45 variants are discussed.

[1] In particular we rejected the hypothesis of an original text of Mark extending beyond 16.8, since lost, but used by Matthew, Luke, or even the first chapters of Acts (cf. pp. 63ff. above.)

[2] Cf. pp. 21–8 above.

[3] As certain authors believe took place after the composition of Matthew and Luke (thus J. C. Hawkins, *Horae synopticae*, p. 152; J. Weiss, *Das älteste Evangelium*, p. 4 and *passim*) or after that of Luke and before that of Matthew (M. Goguel, *Introd. au N.T.*, vol. 1, pp. 297–308). Such small alterations are conceivable but they are of more interest to the historian of the text than to the literary critic, and indeed the manuscript tradition contains no indication of their existence. Such hypotheses as may be built up around corrections of this kind would thus seem to be valueless, unless they fit into a broader hypothesis demonstrating the necessary existence of two editions on literary grounds.

a book whose style is so unpolished; an examination of the other two synoptic Gospels and the way in which they made use of Mark; and a study of the general structure of the work and its internal economy, both literary and intellectual.

The first of these means is of little practical use. It allows us indeed to notice many points of undoubted exegetical interest, as we have seen in the course of the foregoing chapters and as good commentaries illustrate in abundance. But, if we have no overall hypothesis to guide our choice, how can we distinguish those features of the text (anacolutha, awkward parentheses, odd repetitions, clumsiness of style and vocabulary, etc.) which are to be ascribed to the author's servile reproduction of his source or to his lack of education, from those which point to a subsequent editor or are errors introduced by copyists? Even supposing that in some cases this distinction can be made, how could the few isolated phenomena that it would seem necessary to ascribe to a reviser of the text be interpreted without recourse to a hypothesis based on other less diffuse observations? In other words, sutures and literary anomalies can be a source of secondary indications to confirm a theory that has already been worked out; they can never serve to prove the existence of more than one edition of Mark.

The second means appears more promising, since the observations that are its point of departure are less diffuse and their significance is clarified by a knowledge of the methods of composition peculiar to the authors of Matthew and Luke. True, it too depends on a general assumption, namely that Mark preceded Matthew and Luke and that both the latter Gospels show a literary dependence on Mark. But that, expressed in those vague terms at least, is a very widely accepted idea, whose soundness we saw earlier[1] and which does not call forth the same objections as the hypotheses referred to above. It has often been claimed that Luke used an edition of Mark that differed from the canonical version and the same has sometimes been suggested of the edition of Mark that was the main source of Matthew. What are the merits of these two theories?

That Matthew was based on an edition of Mark different from the canonical version is, we believe, unlikely. Matthew is

[1] Cf. pp. 11ff. above.

too skilfully ordered a work with its regular alternation of
narrative and discourse and its arrangement of anecdotes and
isolated sayings in coherent groups for us to feel surprise that it
should depart from the plan of Mark in a number of respects.
What is striking, on the contrary, is that it should remain
faithful to an order which required in some places an illogical
arrangement of the source material.[1] From this it can be deduced that the version of Mark used had the same internal
structure as the one we know. Moreover, Matthew, who did
not hesitate to abridge the narratives of Mark in order to cut
out unnecessary detail, allows himself only very small cuts and
negligible improvements of style when he uses discourses put
into the mouth of Jesus by his predecessor or important
narrative passages like the Passion story.[2] Nothing then, but the
absence in Matthew of essential groups of sayings or narrative
passages to be found in the canonical Mark could suggest that
Matthew was using an earlier edition of Mark which did not
contain those passages. However, that is nowhere the case.[3]

[1] For example, Matthew is led by the presence of parables in Mark 4,
among them two 'parables of the Kingdom', to include several more of
these in his chap. 13, whereas the most natural place for them would
have been in his chap. 25. Similarly the attack on the Pharisees would
have been more naturally placed in Matthew in chap. 12 or 13, rather
than in chap. 23. But it is also a collection of sayings directed against
the scribes and Mark 12.37–40 afforded an opening for a discourse on
that subject, so that Matthew followed Mark, rather than his natural
inclination. It should be remembered too that Matthew, who liked
arranging his material according to subject, ought logically to have
placed the calling of Levi (Matthew, in his Gospel) next to the calling
of Peter, Andrew, James and John; if he does not do so (cf. Matt.
4.18–22 and 9.9) it is no doubt in order not to depart from Mark, where
the calling of Levi is represented as coming some time after the calling
of the other four (1.16–20).

[2] Cf. for example M. Goguel, *Introd. au N.T.*, vol. i, pp. 416–7. Thus
one can see that the account of the execution of John the Baptist is
reduced in Matt. 14.3–12 to less than half its length in Mark 6.17–29,
whereas the story of the passion is not abridged at all in Matthew, nor is
the synoptic apocalypse.

[3] In fact whenever Matthew omits an unimportant passage to be found in
Mark the reason is easily seen, so that it is unnecessary to suppose that
the passage in question was missing from the copy of Mark that was
used. The omission of the story of the healing of the man with the
unclean spirit in the synagogue at Capernaum (Mark 1.23–8) is
explained by the desire not to ascribe Jesus' prestige to his miracle

We are therefore entitled to say that, apart perhaps from a few unimportant details, the edition of Mark used by the author of Matthew was the same as the one we read today.[1]

Can we say the same of the edition of Mark used by the author of Luke? There is some justification for doing so. Luke, indeed, even more than Matthew, keeps to the main outline of the plan of Mark. The author certainly changed the place of a few quite important passages,[2] so that it might well be thought that his copy of Mark followed a different order from that of the canonical Mark, but that was not necessarily the

---

working but to his teaching alone. The parable of the seed that springs up of its own accord (Mark 4.26–9) is not really omitted, but replaced by that of the good seed and the tares (Matt. 13.24–30). The healings in Mark 7.32–7 and 8.22–6 are rejected as too laboured and replaced by a much more triumphant summary account of the success of Jesus as a healer (Matt. 15.29–31). The discussion on the subject of the unauthorized caster-out of devils is left out because it was likely to undermine the authority of the regular heads of the Church (Mark 9.38–40). The episode of the widow's mite (Mark 12.41–4), from which it was difficult to draw a moral and ecclesiastical lesson, is replaced by the passage on alms-giving (Matt. 6.2–4) and the anecdote of the tribute money (Matt. 17.24–7), both of which conveyed the same ideas in a form much easier to handle.

[1] That Matthew used a version of Mark longer than the canonical edition, as was sometimes claimed in the nineteenth century (H. Ewald, *Die drei ersten Evangelien* (Göttingen 1850, and 2nd edn 1871), pp. 77–8 and *passim*; H. Holtzmann, *Die synoptischen Evangelien* (Leipzig 1863), who, however, abandoned the hypothesis of a proto-Mark in 1878) is no longer maintained by anyone today. The theory that Matthew used an edition of Mark shorter than the canonical one has been more widely held, in forms coming close sometimes to the idea of a 'naive pre-Gospel', by critics from F. Schleiermacher ('Uber die Zeugnisse des Papias von unsern beiden ersten Evangelien', in *Theol. Studien und Kritiken*, vol. v, 1832, pp. 735–68) to W. Bussmann (*Synoptische Studien* (Halle 1925–31), vol. 1) and including E. Reuss (*Die Geschichte der heiligen Schriften des Neuen Testaments*, 6th edn (Brunswick), pp. 182ff.), C. Weizsaecker (*Untersuchungen über die evangelische Geschichte* (Gotha 1864), who later abandoned the idea of a proto-Mark), G. Meyer (*La question synoptique* (Paris 1877)) and W. W. Holdsworth (*Gospel Origins* (London 1913)).

[2] Luke 6.12–16 corresponds to Mark 3.13–19; Luke 8.19–21 to Mark 3.31–5; Luke 22.21–3 to Mark 14.18–21; Luke 22.52–62 to Mark 14.62–72. But in each of these cases Luke moves the passage by only a very few verses.

case.[1] Moreover, Luke omits a certain number of passages to be found in the canonical Mark without any apparent reason for doing so.[2] Some of them may have been missing from his copy of Mark, which may either have been mutilated or, more probably, have been a pre-canonical edition.

But it is impossible to construct a hypothesis on such isolated observations. They would need to be filled out with the help of many others drawn from areas which it is not for us to explore here. In endeavouring to do this, a number of scholars have arrived at a theory of a proto-Luke, which they rank ahead of the canonical Mark as the principal source of the canonical Luke.[3] This theory, though suggestive, is scarcely convincing,

---

[1] As we showed earlier (pp. 79–86), the plan of Mark was stricter than has often been thought and could not easily have been changed. For example, the exact place of Mark 3.13–19 and 3.31–5 was of the utmost significance in the eyes of the author (cf. pp. 132ff. above and *passim*) and is certainly not the result of a revision of his work.

[2] This is the case above all of the passages he does not replace elsewhere with a text from a different source (as Mark 1.16–20 is replaced by Luke 5.1–11). Thus Mark 4.26–9,33–4; Mark 6.45—8.26, (of which there is only a very partial equivalent in Luke); Mark 9.43–8; Mark 10.1–9,35–40; Mark 11.12–14,20–5; Mark 13.22–3; Mark 14.3–9, 55–61; 15.16–20,34–5. We shall come back to the texts of Mark 14—15. Where the others are concerned, the omissions from Luke present no serious problem except in the case of Mark 6—8, the end of chap. 9, the beginning of chap. 10, and the central part of chap. 11. Hence the importance attached to these few cases by the supporters of the theory that Luke used a proto-Mark generally supposed to be earlier than the Mark used by Matthew (in addition to the scholars mentioned in p. 219, n. 1 above, among those who hold this view are critics who believe that Luke alone used a proto-Mark, like V. H. Stanton, *The Gospels as Historical Documents*, 3 vols. (Cambridge 1903–20), vol. ii, pp. 142ff., E. Hirsch, *Frühgeschichte des Evangeliums*, 2 vols. (2nd edn, Tübingen 1951), vol. i, pp. xvii, 206 and vol. ii, pp. 3–26 and 290–1, and, to a lesser degree, M. Goguel, *Introd. au N.T.*, vol. i, pp. 297–308). But the big omission of Mark 6.45—8.26 is self-explanatory—for literary reasons (avoiding doublets and obscure teachings) and for theological reasons (Luke's refusal to antedate the beginning of the mission among the Gentiles). Those at the end of chap. 9 and the beginning of chap. 10 are probably due to Luke's dislike of wordiness (Mark 9.43ff.) and for exegetical arguments of a too rabbinical stamp (Mark 10.2–9 is omitted, in the same way as Mark 7.1ff.). The most embarrassing question is that of the omissions from chap. 11, to which we shall return (pp. 230–1 below).

[3] A theory quite often advanced in Germany before 1914 (cf. for example

in view of the extreme disorder of the two big sections of Luke (6.20—8.3 and 9.51—18.14) inserted between the two parts underlying which the plan of Mark is to be found. These two sections clearly contain a mass of material which Luke received in no special order and linked up superficially to the plan of Mark by placing them in the context of a journey in Galilee and a journey to Jerusalem.[1] They reveal no trace of a plan of their own, without which no proto-Luke could have existed. The chief source of Luke, then, is and remains a canonical or pre-canonical Mark.

On one point, however, the supporters of the proto-Luke theory have met with the approval of some of their opponents: when they admit the existence, at the origin of Luke 22—24, of a separate account of the passion relating all the events recounted in Mark 14—16 without being in any way based on those chapters or on the independent narrative that preceded them. It is indeed agreed that, whereas Matthew was content to follow Mark without any more than stylistic improvements and small additions which have no effect on the course of the tragedy (the condemnation of violence in Matt. 26.52–4; the suicide of Judas in Matt. 27.3–10; the message from Pilate's wife in Matt. 27.19; Pilate washing his hands in Matt. 27.24–5; the resurrection of 'saints' in Matt. 27.52–3; the watch set at the tomb in Matt. 27.62–6; the appearance of the

---

P. Feine, *Eine vorkanonische Ueberlieferung des Lukas in Evangelium und Apostelgeschichte* (Gotha 1891); B. Weiss, *Die Quellen des Lukasevangeliums* (Berlin 1907). It subsequently found its chief supporters in other countries: in England, B. H. Streeter, *The Four Gospels, a Study of Origins* (London 1924), in particular pp. 199ff.; V. Taylor, *Behind the Third Gospel* (Oxford 1926), and *The Formation of the Gospel Tradition* (London 1933, 2nd edn 1935), pp. 191–201; T. W. Manson, *The Sayings of Jesus*, 2nd edn (London 1949), pp. 26–8 and *passim*; in America, B. S. Easton, *The Gospel before the Gospels* (London 1928); F. C. Grant, *The Growth of the Gospels* (New York 1933) and *The Gospels, their Origin and Growth* (London 1957), especially pp. 46–8 and 118–19 (somewhat reserved, but quite favourable to the hypothesis); in Sweden, H. Sahlin *Der Messias und das Gottesvolk, Studien zur proto-lukanischen Theologie* (Uppsala 1945) (rather venturesome).

[1] Cf. the remarks on this subject of M. Goguel, *Introd. au N.T.*, vol. 1, pp. 502ff. and the rather brief ones of H. Conzelmann, *Die Mitte der Zeit, Studien zur Theologie des Lukas*, 3rd edn, pp. 53ff. [E.T. *The Theology of St Luke* (London 1960)].

angel in Matt. 28.2–4), Luke on the other hand gives an account that diverges from Mark on several important points: omission of the anointing at Bethany (Mark 14.3–9); substantial differences in regard to the Last Supper (Mark 14.22–5 and Luke 22.15–20); speech of farewell and warning after the meal and before the departure to the Mount of Olives (Luke 22.21–38, which has only a very partial equivalent in Mark 14.19–21 and 14.29–30); significant differences in regard to the scene at Gethsemane (Mark 14.26–42 and Luke 22.39–46); change in the place of the scene of Peter's denial (Mark 14.66–72 and Luke 22.56–62); omission of the appearance of Jesus by night before the Sanhedrin (Luke 22.66; cf. Mark 14.53); differences in the dialogue between Jesus and his Jewish judges (Mark 14.60–4 and Luke 22.67–71) after the elimination of the false witness against him (Mark 14.55–9); introduction of the appearance before Herod (Luke 23.4–16); etc. In short, to turn to figures, whereas in the other sections common to Mark and Luke there are more than 50% of the words common to both texts, in the case of the Passion story the percentage drops to 27%, despite the similarity of the two accounts.[1]

These facts can certainly be explained in several different ways: Luke's freedom vis-à-vis his source, Mark 14—16; use in several places of complementary traditions side by side with Mark 14—16, as is the case with Matthew; use by Luke of a separate Passion narrative to which he added by borrowing from Mark 14—16; exclusive use by Luke of a Passion story deriving from the same original as that of Mark, but which had evolved differently; etc. But of all these interpretations, the one which fits best what we know of Luke's literary habits[2] is the last; it ascribes to him no disdain of word-for-word reproduction or of the plan of his source material, nor any inclination to combine documents of different origin, whereas the two characteristics peculiar to him are timidity in recasting the documents he uses and a certain severity, which causes him to

---

[1] J. Hawkins, 'St Luke's Passion Narrative, considered with reference to the synoptic problem', in *Studies in the Synoptic Problem*, ed. W. Sanday (Oxford 1911), pp. 76–94.

[2] Cf. H. J. Cadbury, *The Style and Literary Method of Luke* (Cambridge, Mass. 1920).

eliminate any source he considers inferior to a parallel text. Faced with two complete Passion stories, Luke's task was not to combine them or to add here and there to the version he preferred features taken from the other, but to choose one or the other, even if, at a given point, he decided to insert a compact body of material from various sources.[1]

If in Luke 22—24 the author followed, with his usual numerous improvements of language and style, a document relating the passion a little differently from the canonical Mark, can we believe that he chose the separate narrative and rejected in its favour a whole section of the book on which he relied so much elsewhere? It is difficult to do so—the decision would have been an unnecessarily radical one. Are we then to assume that his edition of Mark differed from the canonical Mark where the Passion story was concerned? That seems at first sight more likely. However it is hard to see how a revision of the Passion story contained in the proto-Mark after Luke had used it could have introduced the anointing at Bethany, changed the order of events at the Last Supper, omitted Jesus' healing of the ear of the High Priest's servant, introduced the

---

[1] This composite passage, in which Luke might be thought to have grouped together the *logia* he had gleaned here and there and believed ought to be attached to the Passion story, could only be Luke 22.21–38. This short piece has all the characteristics of the literary genre of the 'farewell speech' as defined by J. Munck ('Discours d'adieu dans le N.T. et dans la littérature biblique', in *Aux sources de la tradition chrétienne*, pp. 155–70) and as Luke placed in the mouth of his great hero, the apostle Paul (Acts 20.18–35). It is quite clearly due to Luke and designed to give more force to the Passion story he had received from tradition. The theory of A. Wautier d'Aygalliers, *Les sources du récit de la Passion chez Luc* (Alençon 1920), (use of the Passion story of Mark in three successive recensions, with the addition of a few features borrowed from other sources), and that of V. Taylor, *Behind the third Gospel*, pp. 33–75 (use by Luke of a Passion story unknown elsewhere, with additions taken from Mark 14—16) do not seem readily compatible with Luke's tendency to choose among the sources available. The same objection can be made to H. Schuermann (*Quellenkritische Untersuchung des lukan. Abendmahlsberichtes.* . . . , 3 vols (Münster 1953–7)), who, despite his demonstration of Luke's use of a separate Passion story, makes several verses of Luke 22 come from Mark 14. F. Rehkopf (*Die lukanische Sonderquelle* (Tübingen 1959)), while he shows that these borrowings from Mark are doubtful, feels obliged, for not very convincing reasons, to postulate certain others in Luke 22—24.

appearance before the Sanhedrin, omitted the appearance before Herod, introduced the brutality of the Roman soldiers, omitted the dialogues with the women of Jerusalem and the thief, introduced Jesus' cry of anguish (Mark 15.34) and omitted his confident prayer to the Father (Luke 23.46), etc. Such a radical recasting would surely have had its counterpart in Mark 1—13, where, precisely, there is not a trace of it. Moreover, one wonders what purpose it could have served.

Only one course remains: to admit that the Mark used by Luke as his chief source contained no account of the Passion. An accidental mutilation as serious as this being highly unlikely, we would have to conclude that there was a first edition of Mark that stopped at the end of chapter 13. Such a hypothesis seems absurd at first sight, when one thinks of the importance of the death and resurrection of Jesus Christ for the Christian teaching and thought on which the New Testament is founded. In any case it runs counter to the mental habits of a generation of criticism which has so often said that the Gospels are Passion stories preceded by a long preface. Why have recourse to such a surprising notion to explain a phenomenon which, after all, is quite secondary? Does Mark not resist absolutely any attempt to take it to pieces in this way?

2

THE RELATION OF CHAPTERS 14—16
TO THE REMAINDER OF THE GOSPEL

No, we do not think so. A certain number of indications that can be gleaned from an examination of Mark's Gospel even support the above hypothesis and confirm that the original Mark, more or less identical with the canonical Mark from chapters 1 to 13, stopped at the end of the synoptic apocalypse. Let us now see what they are.

The first has to do with the plan of Mark. We have already emphasized the strangeness of the end of the canonical Mark, so clumsily written that it is hard to believe that it was written by the author of Mark's Gospel.[1] On the other hand, we have also shown[2] that chapter 13 is the culmination of the development that begins around 8.30. These last verses contain a solemn appeal to the disciples to watch, which a final sentence

[1] Cf. p. 68 above.   [2] Cf. pp. 207–8 above.

(v. 37) extends to all believers. This would be a simple and straightforward but at the same time entirely suitable conclusion to the foregoing chapters if the Passion story did not begin immediately afterwards. Chapters 14—16, then, seem to be a sort of appendix, comparable to John 21, about which the same questions can be asked. It might even be claimed that since John 21 ends with a conclusion designed to end the whole Gospel, while Mark 14—16 has no such conclusion, it is less arbitrary to doubt whether these three chapters belonged to the earliest version of Mark than it is to say that John 21 was not part of the fourth Gospel in its first form.

Besides, chapters 14—16 rather upset the balance of the plan of Mark we traced earlier.[1] Instead of a Jesus eternally present, they show us a Jesus who is going away; instead of a Master still in the midst of his followers, they show us a man abandoned, delivered alone into the hands of merciless enemies. In short, these chapters relate events of history instead of exhorting their readers to 'make history', as in Mark 1—13. Can it be said that this difference is natural and that the Passion story is the essential complement to the foregoing chapters, without which they would have no meaning? That would be to overlook the fact that the passion and the resurrection are referred to frequently in those chapters, especially in the section 8.31—10.52 and that there is no proof that the author thought an account of the passion necessary since he was concerned with the Good News and its propagation and did not in any case feel the need to tell the story of the resurrection. After the three prophecies of the passion (8.31; 9.31; 10.33-4) and the account of the transfiguration (9.2ff.), chapters 14—16 come as a repetition serving no real purpose from the viewpoint of the author of the original Mark. He did not start his book at the birth of the man Jesus; why then should he continue it up to the death of the Master, when he had thus shown so clearly that the work he had undertaken was not a biography? In these circumstances it is quite wrong to say that in Mark 'the Passion story . . . becomes the centre of gravity, the Easter story forms . . . the conclusion . . . of the life whose mystery is revealed to the mind from the start'.[2] No, the story of the

---

[1] Cf. pp. 79ff. above.

[2] 'Die Passionsgeschichte . . . gewinnt das Schwergewicht; die Oster-

resurrection does not even exist in Mark and the story of the passion is only a disturbing appendix. It is the fact of the passion and the resurrection which forms the hidden centre of gravity of the whole work and makes it unnecessary to relate the ineffable.

To those who counter this argument by pointing to the numerous allusions to the passion and the resurrection of Jesus in Mark 1—13, we would reply that the allusions to these two facts prove nothing in support of their theory and that there would need to be precise references to some feature or other of the narrative in Mark 14—16 to prove that these chapters were an integral part of the Gospel of Mark from the beginning. Anything to be found in chapters 1—13 which is incompatible with chapters 14—16 would, on the other hand, be an excellent argument in support of our hypothesis. Let us then look at these texts.

The allusion in 2.19–20 is rather too vague to be related to chapters 14—16. The threat in 3.6 comes far too early and from people who, according to chapters 14—16, played not the slightest part in the passion; if it proves anything in regard to those three chapters it is that they were not in the earliest version of Mark. The announcement of Jesus' betrayal by Judas when the list of the Twelve is given in 3.19 does not prepare the way for 14.10–11—it makes those verses unnecessary. The rather disdainful reference to the naive belief in the resurrection of John the Baptist (6.14) is more or less contrasted with the fact of the resurrection of Jesus and not with any particular apologetic detail in Mark 16.1–8. Was there not a risk that the account of how courageously John the Baptist

---

geschichte . . . bildet den Abschluss des . . . Lebens dessen Geheimnis den Geistern gleich zu Anfang kund wird . . .' (R. Bultmann, *Gesch. d. syn. Trad.*, p. 397). The famous statement by M. Kaehler (*Der sogenannte historische Jesus und der geschichtliche, biblische Christus*, 2nd edn revised (Munich 1956), p. 59, n. 1), that 'etwas herausfordernd könnte man die Evangelien Passionsgeschichten mit ausführlicher Einleitung nennen' no doubt fits the other canonical Gospels (except for Luke, perhaps); to apply it to Mark is quite wrong. It is accordingly regrettable that two good recent commentaries of Mark still speak of the account of the passion and resurrection as the climax to which the whole work is tending (V. Taylor, *St Mark*, p. 106; C. E. B. Cranfield, *St Mark*, p. 14).

stood up to Herod and faced his summary execution (6.17–29) would detract from the story of the passion in which Jesus remains silent and seems to be convicted more or less according to the rules? From a literary standpoint it would be easier to understand the presence of this passage (as an example of heroism for the messengers of God) in a Gospel lacking the Passion story than in the canonical Mark.

The allusions to the Eucharist in 6.41–2 and 8.7–8 refer to the liturgical practice of the day and not to Mark 14.12–25, with its paschal overtones and esoteric character. The allusion in Mark 9.9–10 to the Son of Man rising from the dead, those in 8.38 and 13.26–7 to his coming in glory have too many parallels to be taken as referring to Mark 14.62. The transfiguration (9.2–8) has links with the baptism and the mysterious life of the risen Christ among his followers, but not with chapters 14—16. The brief references to the death of Jesus (9.11–13; 10.38,45) have no connection with these three chapters except, possibly, an allusion to the cup of Mark 14.36—is it very conclusive evidence? The quite striking parallelism between Mark 11.1–6 and 14.12–16 does not mean that the first is a preparation for the second, but rather suggests the use of the same theme by two separate traditions, one of which found its place in the original Mark while the other was placed at the beginning of the Passion story finally added by the editor of the canonical Mark. The parable of Mark 12.1–12 alludes merely to the fact of the death of Jesus. As for the prophecy of the destruction of the Temple (13.1–2), we have already pointed out[1] that it is somewhat difficult to reconcile with 14.57–9 and 15.29; the presence of this passage would be easier to explain if Mark in its original form did not include chapters 14—16 than if it did.[2]

---

[1] Cf. above p. 105, n. 1, at end.

[2] Matthew and Luke sensed the difficulty so strongly that they glossed it over by changing the account of the trial of Jesus. According to Matthew, the false witnesses accuse Jesus of saying he was able to destroy the Temple and to build it again in three days (26.60–1). Luke makes no mention of this accusation, nor of the gibes of the passers-by on the same subject at the time of the crucifixion (Mark 15.29 and Matt. 27.40), but transfers the accusation to the trial of Stephen (Acts 6.14). Would he have done so if he had known the canonical Mark? It is doubtful. R. H. Lightfoot devotes a chapter of his interesting little book *The*

There remain the three great prophecies of the passion and the resurrection (8.31; 9.31; 10.33-4) which the critics vie with one another in quoting as the principal indications that the author of Mark included in chapters 1—13 to prepare the way for chapters 14—16. Let it be said first of all that they are oddly placed, if that is their purpose. Why should they be so close together, if they are designed to mark the progress of the whole story towards the cross? But since the Evangelist chose to place the mark of that tragedy on one section only of his book, why did he not prefer the last section, if indeed everything converges on chapters 14—16? His dramatic ends would have been better served if he had refrained from wandering off on to other subjects in chapters 11—13. Unless in fact he never sought to make the section 8.31—10.52 lead up to another part of his book—that is to say, if chapters 14—16 were added subsequently.

Without a doubt, the facts to which these brief prophecies refer are those related in Mark 14—16. It is even clearer in Mark 10.33-4 than in 8.31 and 9.31, considering the additional details that are given: a specific reference to Jesus being *condemned to death* by the chief priests and the scribes (cf. 14.53, 55,64), of his being delivered to the *Gentiles* (cf. 15.1), of *violence and abuse* inflicted by them (cf. 15.16-20)—all indications that are missing or less clear in 8.31 and 9.31. But the picture is still a very shadowy one and its features are only those known to all Christians from confessions of faith such as that to be found in 1 Cor. 15.3ff., except perhaps for the three kinds of violence and abuse enumerated in Mark 10.34a. Indeed two striking omissions prevent us from maintaining that this prophecy is modelled on Mark 14—16: there is no mention at all of Pilate and his judgement; there is no specific reference to the cross. This short passage is consequently far more lenient towards the Roman authorities than the account in Mark 14—16. We should not conclude too quickly that its purpose is to direct the reader's attention towards these latter

---

Gospel Message of St Mark, to demonstrating the close parallelism and correspondences of all kinds which he finds between Mark 13 and Mark 14—15; after reading his arguments one inclines strongly to the opposite view.

chapters. In fact, without being incompatible, the two coexist a little uneasily.

The difficulty grows when we look at a feature common to the three prophecies: the announcement of the resurrection μετὰ τρεῖς ἡμέρας. Is this expression compatible with Mark 15.42 and 16.2? It seems doubtful, whatever some may have said on the subject.[1] The meaning of the expression is no doubt not very precise, but it means first and foremost 'shortly after'. However, Matthew and Luke both felt the need to replace it by τῇ τρίτῃ ἡμέρᾳ in the parallel passages, which shows that the text of Mark raised a difficulty for them. Our Evangelist would certainly have felt the same and would have made the same correction if his book had included the Passion story. If he did not do so, it is because there were no chapters 14—16.

These arguments, it may be objected, however interesting, are not strong enough to prevail against the marked topographical and chronological coherence of chapters 11—13, where the reader follows a rapid progression of dramatic events closely dependent on one another. But, as K. L. Schmidt has rightly

---

[1] Cf. in particular the somewhat confused explanations of E. Klostermann, *Das Mk.-Ev.*, 3rd edn, pp. 82–3; V. Taylor, *St Mark*, p. 378; C. E. B. Cranfield, *St Mark*, pp. 278–9. Matt. 27.63–4 certainly connects the two expressions μετὰ τρεῖς ἡμέρας and ἕως τῆς τρίτης ἡμέρας, but does not make them equivalent, since the second is to be understood as 'the third day' after the conversation between the Jewish leaders and Pilate on the morning after the crucifixion (Matt. 27.62) while the second refers to a period beginning with the death of Jesus. True, in Matt. 27.63 the 'chief priests' and the Pharisees refer to the prophecies of Matt. 16.21; 17.23; 20.19. But they do so as people from outside who know little about them and want to take all due precautions by keeping a longer watch over the tomb. It cannot accordingly be said that they use an exact equivalent of the τῇ τρίτῃ ἡμέρᾳ of the three predictions. Besides, Matthew may have thought that they knew only the prediction of Matt. 12.40, where the meaning of 'three days and three nights' is perfectly clear, even if the expression was influenced by Jonah 2.1 and was not taken literally by the Evangelist himself.

Mark 8.31, 9.31 and 10.33,34 thus use a turn of phrase which it is very hard to reconcile with the chronology of Mark 15.16 (cf. Hos. 6.2 LXX, where ἐν τῇ ἡμέρᾳ τῇ τρίτῃ is the equivalent of μετὰ δύο ἡμέρας). It is all the more surprising since all the other confessional passages in the New Testament that refer to the resurrection say 'the third day', which is quite compatible with that chronology.

shown,[1] the chronological unity of chapters 11—13 is purely artificial and the only texts traditionally attached, prior to Mark, to the Passion story were the account of the entry into Jerusalem and a few sayings of Jesus directed against the city. The impression of continuity given by chapters 11ff. is due to the precise chronological references in chapter 11 and chapter 14 as well as to the accompanying topographical indications. Their combination suggests indeed a sort of regularity in Jesus' life for a few days, when he spent the day in Jerusalem and the night at Bethany (11.1,11,12; 14.3), going from one to the other by the Mount of Olives (11.1; 13.3; 14.26). That is exactly the impression the author of this 'montage' wished to give.

The Passion story, with its chronological continuity so exceptional in the gospel tradition,[2] thus finds itself, with several chapters added at the beginning, become the account of a week in Jerusalem firmly joined on to the rest of Mark. Did the author, so little interested in chronology even when the tradition supplied him with certain indications of time,[3] depart here from his usual practice? It is not impossible, but one may wonder whether this little literary operation is not the work of the editor who grafted chapters 14—16 on to the earlier Gospel. Luke indeed, which has no equivalent to Mark 14.1ff., contains none of the topographical references to be found in Mark 11.11—13.37 (except for the references to the Temple; Luke 19.45,47; 20.1; 21.5–6,37–8), nor any of the chronological indications in the same passages, making up for their absence by small references underlining the fact that Jesus spent his days in the Temple (Luke 19.47; 20.1; 21.37) and was in the habit of spending his nights on the Mount of Olives (Luke 21.37)—references which the author seems to have borrowed from his Passion story (Luke 22.39,53) to give a rather more solid framework to his chapters 19.45—22.6. Why

---

[1] *Der Rahmen der Geschichte Jesu*, pp. 274–303.

[2] K. L. Schmidt, ibid. pp. 303ff. Cf. V. Taylor, *St Mark*, pp. 524–6 and 649–64.

[3] Cf. for example the strange 'after six days' of Mark 9.2, a meaningless phrase left over from some indication in the tradition. The 'day in Capernaum' (Mark 1.21–35), whose sequence of events was perhaps invented by the author of Mark, stands out alone in a story that has no subsequent precise chronology.

should the author of Luke have replaced a framework that his Mark would have provided quite satisfactorily[1] by one that was less topographically and chronologically precise? It seems certain that we are confronted here with an addition made to Mark after that Gospel had been used by Luke, for the purpose of masking the suture between chapters 13 and 14—16.

Ought we to agree with M. Goguel[2] that the addition includes all the incidents of the 'Bethany cycle' (Mark 11.11–14,20–5; 14.3–9), whose introduction was accompanied by some retouching of the text of the synoptic apocalypse? That is very doubtful, since the insertion of the story of the cleansing of the Temple between two fragments of another narrative is quite consistent with the literary practice of the author of Mark (cf. 3.20–1,31–5 and 3.22–30; 5.21–4,35–43 and 5.25–34; 6.7–13,30 and 6.14–29; 8.1–10,16–21 and 8.11–15) in the first place, and in the second place Luke contains a near equivalent to the cursing of the fig-tree in the parable of the barren fig-tree (Luke 13.6–9), so that we are entitled to conclude that he knew Mark 11.13–14,20–5 and rejected the story in favour of the parable, which he felt to be more charged with spiritual meaning. We ought accordingly to limit the retouching of chapters 11 and 13 of the original Mark to the introduction of a few chronological and geographical particulars in Mark 11.11–12 and 13.3 and some additional details inserted by the same editor at the beginning of the Passion story (Mark 14.1–9, perhaps).

Was this retouching done for purely literary reasons? One might, it would seem, discern another purpose in them, although not very clearly—that of recasting the chronology of the passion for liturgical motives. It looks indeed as though the editor responsible for the changes was seeking to fit the events beginning with the entry into Jerusalem and ending with the visit of the women to the tomb into a week beginning on a

---

[1] Luke could not but look with favour on the references to Bethany and the Mount of Olives, places which were associated with the arrest of Jesus (Luke 22.39–40) and his ascension (Luke 24.50, if we allow the authenticity of the last four verses of Luke, about which there may be some doubt: cf. P. H. Menoud, 'Remarques sur les textes de l'Ascension dans Luc-Actes', in *Neutestamentliche Studien für Rudolf Bultmann* (Berlin 1954), pp. 148–56).

[2] *Introd. au N.T.*, vol. I, pp. 297–308.

Sunday (11.1–11) and ending on the following Sunday
(16.2–8). Why do something so arbitrary, calling for bizarre
reshufflings that have been the bane of commentators ever
since?[1] Probably in order to help to establish in the churches
for which he was writing a 'Holy Week' celebration beginning
on a Sunday with the commemoration of 'Palm Sunday'
and ending the following Sunday with the resurrection of

---

[1] Not the least surprising of these interferences is the case of Mark 11.11–
12, where the editor makes Jesus behave, on entering the Temple, like a
conscientious tourist (περιβλεψάμενος πάντα) in order to explain the
postponement of the attack on the vendors until the following day. The
effect is slightly comic: Jesus appears to behave like a naive little pro-
vincial, as H. Holtzmann, *Die Synoptiker* (Tübingen 1901), pp. 90, 161,
and C. G. Montefiore, *Synopt. Gosp.* vol. I, pp. 261–2, rightly point out,
although other commentators reject this interpretation without any
definite reason as not being serious enough.

    In 14.1 and 14.12 the editor has not been skilful and the result is a
certain obscurity. The latter verse is well-known for the at least apparent
contradiction between its first half ('the first day of unleavened bread'
= 15 Nisan in the Jewish calendar, except in a few exceptional texts
cited by Strack–Billerbeck, vol. II, pp. 812ff.) and the second half
('that thou mayest eat the Passover' = 14 Nisan). As for the former,
it is rather imprecise beneath its apparent exactitude (cf. for example
V. Taylor, *St Mark*, pp. 527–8). In both cases one senses the hand of an
editor unfamiliar with the Jewish calendar, which he doubtless knew
only from the customs of the diaspora, which were rather different
from those preserved in Palestine (eight days of unleavened bread
instead of seven, for example: Strack–Billerbeck, vol. II, pp. 814–15;
cf. J. Jeremias, *Abendsmahlworte Jesu*, 3rd edn (Göttingen 1960),
pp. 10ff.) [E.T. *The Eucharistic Words of Jesus* (London 1970)]. To
judge by the references to times in Mark 15.25,33,34 (cf. also 15.1,42),
which have no equivalent in the night scenes in chap. 14, and by the
strange allusion to the rising of the sun he saw fit to introduce in 16.2
alongside the reference to 'very early in the morning the first day of the
week' (this latter is of earlier date, having regard to the semitic use of
the cardinal μία for the ordinal, and must have meant 'well before
sunrise', but it was inconceivable apparently that a 'day' should
begin before 'daybreak'), the editor perhaps even placed the beginning
of the day at sun-rise, like the Romans. The first day of unleavened
bread would then be for him 14 Nisan, on the morning of which day the
Jews had to stop eating leavened food, the end of the afternoon of the
same day, with the Passover meal, marking the moment when they
began eating unleavened bread (cf. Strack–Billerbeck, vol. II, p. 813).
In any case, these difficulties bring out the fact that many of the
chronological details in the Passion story in the canonical Mark are
posterior to the rest.

Christ. An 'octave' of this kind might have comprised daily services corresponding to the events related in Mark 11—16. But that is still doubtful—except for the night of Thursday to Friday, marked by the celebration of the Eucharist, and the day of Friday, devoted to meditating on Jesus' martyrdom, if we can trust to the indications in Mark 14.12—15.47.[1] As this twofold commemoration covering a night and the following day—a Christian 'Passover' coinciding with the Jewish Passover—seems to have been the occasion for writing down the Passion story in its earliest form,[2] we may assume that it was the vehicle that carried the story through the first generation of the Church and that, conversely, growing familiarity with the story in slightly different forms[3] helped to make the celebration more widespread.

The work of the editor in joining together two documents known to the churches he was addressing[4] must have had a more restricted purpose: to fix the night from Thursday to

---

[1] In the canonical Mark, indeed, the day of Thursday is occupied entirely with preparations for the Last Supper (14.12–16) which took place in the evening of the same day (14.17–25), followed by the scene at Gethsemane (14.26–52) and the appearance of Jesus before the Sanhedrin (14.53ff.) the same night. The account of the Friday, with the appearance before Pilate and the crucifixion, is interspersed with references to times (15.1,25,33,34,42) whose potential liturgical significance is underlined by numerous commentators (cf. for example the most recent commentaries: V. Taylor, *St Mark*, p. 590; W. Grundmann, *Ev. nach Mk.*, pp. 312–13). The other days, on the contrary, are, except for the two Sundays, much less eventful or else composed of passages difficult to transpose into liturgy: Monday, the cleansing of the Temple (11.12–19); Tuesday, the arguments with the chief priests and the predictions of the future (11.20—13.37); Wednesday, the meal at Bethany, whose use in liturgy is indeed conceivable (14.1–11); Thursday, preparation of the Last Supper (14.12–16); Saturday, lastly, rest (16.1).

[2] Cf. pp. 59–63 above.

[3] This could explain the existence of several Passion stories which, while all going back to the same Jerusalem archetype, circulated at the same time among different churches: that of Mark–Matthew; that of Luke; that of John, in so far as it is independent of the others.

[4] Apart from juxtaposing the original Mark and the Passion story, the editor of the canonical Mark has been so discreet in his literary retouching that one is led to believe that he regarded both documents as 'canonical' texts rather than as sources which he was entitled to recast in a new mould. Cf. also pp. 246ff. below.

Friday and the day of Friday as the time for celebrations that
had hitherto been linked to the Jewish Passover and accordingly
held on different days of the week according to the year. It can
be readily understood that growing communities which were
recruiting more and more among non-Jews were beginning to
find it intolerable to have to depend each spring on the astro-
nomical calculations of the rabbis. And thus perhaps began a
liturgical emancipation movement of which the celebrated
dispute over the date of Easter which, at the end of the second
century, divided the more conservative Asian churches from the
principal churches of the day, was, after all, only the end result.[1]
It would remain to establish whether the choice of the night of
Thursday to Friday and the day of Friday for the commemoration of Jesus' martyrdom has a polemical significance and marks
the rejection of another tradition concerning the date of the
Last Supper and the arrest of the Master. That is not impossible, in view of the way the first Passion story must have
been condensed chronologically[2] and in view of the existence
of a few fragments of traditions placing those two events in the
night from Tuesday to Wednesday,[3] apparently for liturgical
reasons.

---

[1] On the subject of this quartodeciman dispute, see for example H.
Lietzmann, *Histoire de l'Eglise ancienne* (Fr. trans. by A. Jundt), vol. II,
(Paris 1937), pp. 132–5 [E.T. *The Beginnings of the Christian Church*
(London 1953)].

[2] Cf. on this subject the interesting remarks of M. Black, 'The Arrest and
Trial of Jesus and the Date of the Last Supper', in *New Testament
Essays, Studies in Memory of Thomas Walter Manson. . . .* ed. A. J. B.
Higgins (Manchester 1959), pp. 19–33. What this author says of the
Passion story in Mark would apply even better to the document so
lacking in chronological indications that the editor of the canonical
Mark added to Mark 1—13.

[3] It is to A. Jaubert (*La date de la Cène . . .*, pp. 79–102) that we owe the
recent reminder of the importance of texts such as the Syriac *Didascalia*
for the study of the chronology of the passion, even though her conclusions are open to question when they begin to look like returning to
the idea of the 'harmony of the four Gospels'. An indication of the
objections raised and the additional arguments advanced in the burning
discussion aroused by A. Jaubert's book may be gleaned from J.
Blinzler, 'Qumrankalender und Passionschronologie' in *ZNTW*,
vol. XLIX (1958), pp. 238ff. and A. Jaubert, 'Jésus et le calendrier de
Qumrân' in *New Testament Studies*, vol. VII (1960–1), pp. 1ff.

To these concordant pieces of evidence, which all tend to show that chapters 14—16 are later than the original Mark, an examination of the ideas expressed in the canonical Mark will enable us to add a few more, rather tenuous, indications, which nevertheless confirm our hypothesis in a way that leaves little room for doubt.

In the nature of the case, these chapters isolate Jesus from his disciples much more than chapters 1—13. Jesus goes alone to his crucifixion and this corresponds to Scripture (Mark 14.27,49), whose authority must impose on the disciples the recognition of the inevitability of the separation (Mark 14.29–31). Alone he will drink of the bitter cup (14.38) and deliver himself up to his executioners, while his followers flee (14.49–50). Nowhere is the accent placed on the call to 'follow Jesus', and the attempts of the anonymous young man (14.51–2), and then of Peter (14.54,66–72) to do so are mere bathos. Without seeking to squeeze too much from these texts,[1] one can say that they go even further in showing Jesus' isolation than was necessary for the progress of the story. Could the man who reproduced the *logion* in which Jesus says that his disciples will drink of the same 'cup' as he (10.38–9) and the one in which he calls them to 'bear their cross' and follow him (8.34), the author who so rarely separates the Master and his disciples, have told the story of the passion without slipping in some allusions to the disciples' sharing of Jesus' suffering and to the call to all men to do the same? It seems highly doubtful.

The christological reserve of Mark 1—13 has no counterpart in Mark 14—16. Retouched or not, in the canonical Mark Jesus' reply to the High Priest (14.62) is an acceptance of the titles of Christ and 'Son of the Blessed',[2] even if that acceptance

---

[1] As evidence of the total isolation of Jesus in Mark 15—16 one might also cite the terrible cry of 15.34: 'Why hast Thou forsaken me?', which is also the lament of a suffering man abandoned by all his fellows (Ps. 22.7–22).

[2] Unlike the case of the parallels in Matthew and Luke, where Jesus' reply to the High Priest is made more evasive, which leads some authors (in particular J. Héring, *Le Royaume de Dieu et sa venue*, 2nd edn, pp. 111–20) to maintain that Mark was revised at this point by the last editor. That is perhaps going rather far. Jesus' sayings about himself were not so readily corrected, as is demonstrated by the preservation in those sayings of the title 'Son of Man' and its disappearance everywhere

is qualified a little by the reference to the 'Son of Man' which immediately follows it. The centurion's confession (15.39), standing out so clearly and charged with meaning; the noble gesture of the woman who anoints Jesus' head (14.3ff.); the Master's at least partial approval of the title 'King of the Jews' thrust upon him by Pilate (15.2)—all these are passages in chapters 14—16 where the supernatural and messianic character of Jesus is strongly underlined, and where there is no reticence to be observed in regard to the use of the highest christological titles. Is the author who shows such willingness to glorify the person of Jesus the same as he who mutilated the tradition of Peter's messianic confession (8.27ff.), replacing its natural conclusion by a harsh call to missionary heroism,[1] and who reserved to God alone the right to speak of the Nazarene as his Son?[2] It scarcely seems possible to think so.

Furthermore, the resurrection of the crucified Christ has not exactly the same consequences in Mark 14—16 as in chapters 1—13. Coming forth from the tomb 'on the third day' and not 'after three days', the Master 'goeth before the disciples into Galilee' (Mark 14.28; 16.7), where they shall 'see' him (16.7). These two enigmatic verses, which have all the appearance of being superimposed on their respective contexts,[3] are interpre-

---

else. It would seem more probable that Luke 22.67–70 (a separate tradition from that of Mark) contains the key to the problem: the two sayings brought together in Mark 14.62—the answer to the question, 'Art thou the Christ?', and the attack contained in the allusion to the coming of the Son of Man—are independent here. What Luke left separate, the canonical Mark co-ordinated and Matthew, working on the text of the canonical Mark, sought to combine (hence his πλήν in 26.64), in accordance with the various authors' habitual literary practices. The attenuation of the 'I am' pronounced by Jesus which we observe in Luke and Matthew has nothing to do with the original form of any of these separate *logia*; its purpose is merely, without altering Jesus' words too much, to gloss over the absurdity that even a mildly sophisticated public would see in the pretension of a wretched prisoner to the messianic dignity.

[1] Cf. pp. 57–8 and 121ff. above.
[2] Cf. p. 143, n. 3 and p. 148 above.
[3] In the opinion of most commentators, Mark 14.28 breaks the continuity of ideas between the two verses on either side of it whose connection with one another is obvious (cf. the presence of the verb σκανδαλίζειν and the insistence on the πάντες in vv. 27 and 29). This

ted by Matthew, who reproduces them very faithfully (26.32; 28.7), as prophecies of the christophany on the 'mountain' where Jesus had appointed a meeting with the 'Eleven' and of which we learn only that it was in Galilee (Matt. 28.16ff.). But is that really the meaning the editor of the canonical Mark sought to give that saying when he used it to help dovetail the Passion story into Mark 1—13? Not necessarily, in spite of the ὄψεσθε in Mark 16.7 which, in the absence of any account of a christophany in Mark, appears to refer to the parousia, as in 14.62 and 13.26.[1] Conscious of the abrupt ending of the work resulting from the addition of Mark 14—16 to Mark 1—13, the editor is seeking, like his predecessor the Evangelist in Mark 13, to conclude by turning the reader's attention towards the future. In transforming the little ecclesiological treatise of Mark 1—13 into a partial biography of Jesus he had removed from the references to Galilee he found there the topical character they had originally, but he still felt from these pages that this was the sacred place from which the Good News had gone out. Jerusalem having lost its right to serve as the setting for the parousia (13.14ff.), Galilee was accordingly the obvious place to take over that role and to be the rallying place of the faithful around the Son of Man on the Last

---

verse is missing, moreover, in the Fayoum fragment (text in M. J. Lagrange, *Ev. selon saint Marc*, 7th edn, p. 383), but the significance of this fact is far from clear, having regard to the enigmatic nature of that document. Mark 16.7 has been the cause of innumerable arguments among critics on account of the difficulty of understanding the attitude of the women in 16.8 if they have just received the order in 16.7. We believe, with W. Marxsen, *Der Ev. Markus*, pp. 48–57 and contrary to H. von Campenhausen, *Das Ablauf der Osterereignisse und das leere Grab* (2nd edn, Heidelberg 1958), pp. 35ff. that it is indeed v. 7 which is an addition from the pen of the author of the canonical Mark. The text of Luke 24.6, with its allusion to the words pronounced by Jesus in Galilee, is no doubt a more accurate reflection of the original tradition and explains Mark's choice of this place to insert the reference to the Galilean parousia.

[1] Cf. E. Lohmeyer, *Ev. des Mk.*, pp. 355–6, whose reasoning W. Marxsen, op. cit., pp. 53–5, follows and amplifies. The reminder in Mark 16.7 of the announcement by Jesus of an appearance to the disciples in Galilee cannot be a reference to 14.28, where there is no question of seeing him. Surely it must be an allusion to 14.62 and 13.26, that is to say to the predictions of the parousia.

Day.[1] At the same time, the editor hoped to justify in his readers' eyes the rather excessive importance of the part played in Mark by this obscure district on the borders of Syria and Palestine.

He thus made a real effort to understand and to make understandable a document that was already difficult in his day. But he departed on two points from the ideas to be found in Mark 1—13 concerning what followed the resurrection; he situated the parousia geographically, despite the stern warning of 13.21–3; he believed in a separation of the risen Christ from his followers during the period between the crucifixion and the Second Coming—a separation interspersed with occasional encounters, perhaps, but which differs totally from the life together that the author of Mark 1—13 seems to be trying to describe for the same period.

The reason for this latter divergence is to be sought on the one hand in a cooling of missionary fervour on the part of the editor, whereas the Evangelist drew much of the ardour he displays in Mark 1—13 from the doctrine of the Good News. Chapters 14—16 contain no missionary command issued either by the Jesus of before the crucifixion or by the risen Christ, unlike the chapters of the other Gospels devoted to the passion and the resurrection (Matt. 28.19–20; Luke 24.46–8; John 17.18; 20.21–3). Verse 14.9 cannot be regarded as such a command. Whatever the original meaning of a saying whose authenticity can more easily be defended than is often admitted,[2] it is clear that in the context of the canonical Mark it takes on a new significance and applies to the preaching that is

---

[1] The verb προάγειν can apply to the act of walking at the head of a group (cf. Mark 10.32; 11.9) or to that of going ahead by another route (cf. Mark 6.45). As no tradition has preserved a record of the return of the disciples to Galilee led by Jesus and as 16.7 merely announces a meeting at a point to which they are all to go, the second meaning of a rendez-vous to which Jesus will go on ahead of his disciples is to be preferred. Most commentators see this rendez-vous as that of the Galilean christophanies (cf. V. Taylor, *St Mark*, pp. 607–8), but it is far more likely to be the great eschatological meeting suggested by E. Lohmeyer, *Ev. des Mk.*, pp. 355–6.

[2] Because of the numerous semitisms it contains and its typical form of Jesus' mode of expressing himself, according to J. Jeremias, *Jésus et les païens*, pp. 17–18, whose arguments are impressive.

laid as a duty upon the disciples, as in Mark 13.10. But here it is a mere passing allusion which lacks the imperative character of the verse of the 'little apocalypse'. Moreover, the word εὐαγγέλιον conveys a rather different shade of meaning from the one it has in chapters 1—13: it is an *evangelium de Christo*, comprising an account of certain facts of the life of the Master, instead of the salutary announcement of the visitation that God has begun in the world.[1] The editor saw in this saying—and consequently in the doubtless isolated story that was its vehicle —a link between the Passion story, with the accent it laid on the death of Jesus alluded to here, and the original Mark, with its emphasis on the κηρύσσειν and the εὐαγγέλιον. It is thus probably he who inserted them both here, locating them in addition in Bethany (Mark 14.3), in order to improve the geographical cohesion of the two documents he was using.[2]

The words εἰς ὅλον τὸν κόσμον of this verse 14.9 were certainly, as he interpreted them, an allusion to the universality of the Christian message. Without indeed being as concerned as the author of Mark 1—13 with missionary action, the editor was nonetheless a convinced universalist. The incident of the centurion's confession at the foot of the cross (15.39) with its obvious symbolism is sufficient proof of this. Through this spokesman the whole Church of the Gentiles confesses its faith in advance, at a time when the Jewish companions of the Master are in flight or in any case understand nothing of the events that are taking place around them, if we are to judge by the attitude of the women named in 15.40–1,47 and 16.1–8. It is the voice of a religious community formed chiefly of former Gentiles and now scattered throughout the world that reaches us through Mark 14.9 and 15.39. It rings very differently from that of chapters 1—13, where the mission is just beginning, where the missionaries' main efforts are directed towards

---

[1] Cf. pp. 149ff. above.

[2] The somewhat similar account in Luke 7.36 contains no indication of the place, whereas the name of Jesus' host is the same as in Mark 14.3ff. If it is a question of a doublet, as it may be, we are entitled to conclude that the reference to Bethany in Mark 14.3 is a later addition by the editor of the canonical Mark, rather than a sign of the Bethany origin of the story, as W. Grundmann, for example, *Ev. nach Mk.*, p. 276, would have it.

the Jews and the Gentiles are still playing a secondary part.[1]

And so we see that chapters 14—16 of Mark convey certain theological ideas that are scarcely compatible with the convictions of the author of Mark 1—13: the importance of christological confession sayings: the separation of the risen Christ from his followers; a change in the meaning of εὐαγγέλιον; a reduced universalism. Here too, then, we find reasons to think that the Passion story was a subsequent addition to a first version of Mark that ended at 13.37.

3
ORIGIN OF THE CANONICAL GOSPEL

If the canonical Mark is the 'second edition, revised and supplemented by a long appendix', of an earlier Gospel, can the theories usually advanced as to its date, its place of composition and the identity of its author still stand? Can one still say, with the majority of commentators, that it appeared shortly before (or shortly after) the year 70 in the church of Rome and that its author was John Mark of Jerusalem, the companion of Paul (Acts 12.25; 13.5–13; 15.37; Philem. 24), of Barnabas (Acts 12.25; 13.5–13; 15.37,39) and above all of Peter (1 Pet. 5.13; Papias, according to Eusebius, *H.E.*, III. 39,15)? With regard to the place, it would seem so, but the answer is probably in the negative as regards the date, which ought to be set later, and the identity of the editor, whom it is difficult to see as John Mark.

Where the place is concerned, the canonical Mark itself gives practically no indication, unless it be that it is clearly intended for the Greek-speaking communities whose literary demands were modest[2] and who were recruited primarily

---

[1] Cf. pp. 194ff. above.

[2] This can be seen from the total absence of literary artifice that characterizes the work and which the editor would have tried to remedy if he had felt the need to do so. In fact he did not even attempt to give any polish to his introduction or his conclusion, which proves that his readers were people lacking in any knowledge of rhetoric. Nobody seriously maintains that the canonical Mark is a translation from Aramaic, as C. C. Torrey (*Our Translated Gospels* (London n.d.) suggests, or from Latin, as P. L. Couchod ('L'évangile de Marc a-t-il été écrit en Latin?', in *RHR*, vol. xvci (July–Dec. 1926)) claims. The question of the influence of Latin is relevant at the level of the editor, who may

among the Gentiles, to judge by the unhesitating universalism that can be sensed underlying Mark 15.39 and 14.9. These characteristics are common to numerous churches in the second half of the first century. The few Latin words that are merely transliterated in Greek and not translated all belong to the current language of the Greek-speaking regions of the day, being introduced by daily contact with the Roman administration, army, coinage and techniques.[1] Their use is merely the sign of a certain indifference to the origin of words, of an author, that is to say, who has no time for purist rules and is happy to write as he would speak. One exception is worthy of note, however: the word κοδράντης (Mark 12.42), a transcription of the Latin *quadrans*, applies to a small copper coin that did not have currency in the Eastern part of the Roman Empire; here it serves to explain to the reader what the two λεπτά placed by the widow in the Temple treasury were worth. We may therefore regard it as a slight, but definite, indication of the Gospel having been written for Westerners.[2] Failing anything better, there exist a few references to the origins of the canonical Gospel of Mark in Christian authors of antiquity,

---

have been more or less bilingual, like so many Romans of his day. That of the influence of Aramaic is relevant at the level of the authors of Mark 1—13 and Mark 14—16 and the written or oral sources on which they drew (cf. p. 251 below).

[1] These words are the eight nouns δηνάριον, κεντυρίων, κῆνσος, κοδράντης, κράβαττος, λεγιών, ξέστης, σπεκουλάτωρ, and the expressions τὸ ἱκανὸν ποιεῖν (*satisfacere*) and ὅ ἐστιν (*hoc est*). All of these were current in the popular Greek of the first century, wherever it was spoken (cf. Blass–Debrunner, *Grammatik*, 10th edn, pp. 6–8).

[2] It is nevertheless worth noting the cautious remark of M. J. Lagrange, *Ev. Marc*, p. 331, that the λέπτον (mite) was not a recognized currency unit, so that it needed in any case to be explained and that the *quadrans* was well enough known in the East for Matt. 5.26 to refer to it without the author feeling any need to translate it into Eastern currency. But the λέπτον was common among the people (cf. the references to various inscriptions cited by W. Bauer, *Griechisch-Deutsches Wörterbuch* . . . . [E.T. Arndt-Gingrich (London-Chicago 1957)], under this word) and Luke used the word twice (Luke 12.59; 21.2) without explanation. It is accordingly in the West, rather than in the East, that the explanation in Mark 12.42 was necessary. It seems, moreover, to be correct, for it makes the λέπτον the equivalent of the rabbis' פְּרוּטָה, the smallest of the Jewish coins, worth half a *quadrans* (cf. G. Wohlenberg, *Ev. des Mk.*, p. 327, n. 23; Strack–Billerbeck, vol. II, p. 45).

from Papias to Chrysostom. Some of these texts say nothing about the place where the Gospel was composed and completed. A fragment of an anti-marcionite prologue found heading the Gospel of Mark in a manuscript of the old Latin version of the Greek Bible, which might go back to the second half of the second century,[1] places the composition of Mark 'in partibus Italiae'; Clement of Alexandria speaks of it being composed in Rome, at the request of the listeners to Peter.[2] John Chrysostom, on the contrary, places it in Egypt;[3] though his opinion may be of little value, at least it shows that the theory of the Gospel's composition in Rome was not universally held towards the end of the fourth century. Now current, this theory nevertheless lacks definite evidence, although no other place of composition is as well substantiated in antiquity.

But, as B. W. Bacon, the great modern defender of the Rome hypothesis,[4] asks, how could a work as undistinguished as Mark have circulated widely among the churches and enjoyed a measure of authority with them despite the competition of Matthew, Luke, and John and of its distant claim to descent from an apostolic source? The only plausible explanation is that it was covered by the prestige of a very important church which gave special credit to it, no doubt because the book was written by one of its members and for its own use. All things considered, this important church could only have been the

---

[1] Text published and annotated by D. De Bruyne, 'Les plus anciens prologues latins des évangiles', in *Revue bénédictine*, vol. XL (1928), pp. 193–214. The date of composition of these prologues is open to question; they are sometimes said to date only from the third century.

[2] In a passage of chapter 6 of the *Hypotyposes* quoted (or paraphrased) in two slightly different ways in Eusebius, *H.E.*, II. 15 and VI. 14, 5–7; in another passage of the same work, preserved in the Latin version in the fragment entitled 'Adumbrationes Clementis Alexandrini in epistolas canonicas', and published by O. Staehlin in vol. III, pp. 203–15 of his edition of the works of Clement in *Griechische christliche Schriftsteller* (Berlin 1905–9)—a passage in which Clement is commenting on 1 Pet. 5.13. Irenaeus, *Adv. Haer.*, III. 1,1 (Ed. Sagnard, 1952, in the series Sources chrétiennes, pp. 176–8) is vague on the subject of the place of composition.

[3] A text cited and commented on by V. Taylor, *St Mark*, p. 32.

[4] B. W. Bacon, *Is Mark a Roman Gospel?* (Cambridge, Mass. 1919) (Harvard Theological Studies, vol. VII).

church of Rome, as ancient tradition suggests;[1] and so it is in Rome that we will place the work of the editor who joined Mark 14—16 to the original Gospel by means of a little discreet retouching, consisting chiefly in a few chronological additions and probably also some brief explanatory remarks such as we find in 3.17; 7.11,34; 12.42; 15.16,42.[2]

As we saw earlier,[3] one of the ends served by thus combining two existing documents must have been to implant in the community concerned the celebration of Holy Week and in particular to establish a Thursday night and a Friday for the commemoration of the crucifixion. If we are right in this, it might stand in the way of placing the editor's work in Rome. According to H. Lietzmann, indeed, who refers on this point to a text of Irenaeus of Lyons, the celebration of Easter was introduced into Rome only under Bishop Soter, that is to say not long before A.D. 175.[4] But there it is a question of Easter Sunday only and it is quite possible that the celebration of the Friday was introduced much earlier and that its adoption signified a break with the Jewish liturgical year. If we reject this distinction, then the origin of the canonical Mark must no doubt be located elsewhere than in Rome. We do not believe, for our part, that the text of Irenaeus needs to be understood in the strictest sense. There is no reason why the church of the

---

[1] This is the opinion of almost all the commentators of the past half century, in particular A. Loisy, *Ev. selon Marc*, pp. 52–3; G. Wohlenberg, *Ev. des Mk.*, pp. 24–5; M. J. Lagrange, *Ev. Marc*, pp. xxx–xxxi and cvii (without enthusiasm); A. E. J. Rawlinson, *Gosp. acc. to St Mark*, p. xxx; B. H. Branscomb, *Gosp. of Mark*, pp. xv–xviii; V. Taylor, *St Mark*, p. 32; W. Grundmann, *Ev. nach Mk.*, pp. 18–19 (although he seems a little shaken by the arguments of W. Marxsen, *Der Ev. Markus*, *passim*, in favour of composition in Galilee); C. E. B. Cranfield, *St Mark*, pp. 8–9.

[2] The expression ὅ ἐστιν which introduces these brief remarks is probably a Latinism (cf. Blass–Debrunner, *Grammatik*, 10th edn, p. 88) modelled on the expressions *hoc est* and *id est*; it is in any case a familiar turn of phrase which good authors appear to avoid and which Mark is the only book of the New Testament to use.

[3] Cf. pp. 231ff. above.

[4] The passage from Irenaeus appears in Eusebius, *H.E.*, V. 24, 11–18. Cf. H. Lietzmann, *Hist. de l'Eglise ancienne*, vol. ii, pp. 134–5. The great historian's interpretation of this text is not supported by the slightest specific argument.

capital should not have been commemorating the passion and resurrection of Jesus for a long time in an annual celebration on a Friday in early spring before it decided to celebrate Easter Sunday. The canonical Mark may well have originated in Rome as has so often been said.

With regard to the date of this second edition of Mark, the theories current in contemporary criticism seem more open to question. It is usually agreed that Irenaeus and the anti-marcionite prologue[1] constitute good reasons for placing the composition of Mark after the death of Peter, which makes the earliest possible date 65. It cannot be put much later than 80, because of the use of Mark by Matthew, or by Luke, or by both, according to the critics.

In an attempt at greater precision, many critics look to the chronology of the Jewish war of 66–70, of which they believe there is an echo in Mark 13. Depending on their understanding of that chapter they opt either for a date earlier than 70 (J. Weiss, M. Goguel,[2] A. E. J. Rawlinson, V. Taylor, W. Marxsen, F. C. Grant,[3] W. Grundmann, C. E. B. Cranfield), for a date around 70 (C. G. Montefiore, S. G. F. Brandon,[4] the Table of Contents of the New Testament[5] by M. Goguel and H. Monnier) or for the years 75–80 (M. Goguel again,[6] B. H. Branscomb, A. Loisy, B. W. Bacon). The hypothesis we have advanced regarding the composition of the canonical Mark

---

[1] Cf. p. 242, notes 1 and 2 above.

[2] At least this is the theory he puts forward in his introduction to the synoptic Gospels in Goguel and Monnier, *Le Nouveau Testament, traduction nouvelle d'après les meilleurs textes*. . . . (Paris 1929), pp. 18–19, where the hypothesis of a second edition later than 70 is never mentioned (except perhaps in two vague and passing allusions, p. 19, n. 1 and p. 21).

[3] F. C. Grant, *The Gospels, their origin and their growth* (London 1957), p. 107.

[4] Who finds it possible, in a recent article, to fix with certainty upon the year 71 ('The Date of the Markan Gospel', in *N.T. Studies*, vol. 7 (1960–1), pp. 126–41).

[5] Loc. cit., p. 441.

[6] Thus in *Introd. au N.T.*, vol. 1, p. 375; *Jésus*, 2nd edn, p. 103. The hesitations of the great French critic suffice to show the complexity of the problem, on which he had nevertheless reached a conclusion as early as 1909 (*L'Ev. de Marc dans ses rapports avec ceux de Matthieu et de Luc*), but had been honest enough to change his mind on further reflection.

prevents us from attaching the slightest importance to the apocalypse of chap. 13 for the dating of the final work, which simply reproduces a much earlier text. We do not believe that the Jewish war of 66–70 has left any visible imprint on Mark, nor that it was the cause of its composition.[1] Thus for the dating of the final version of Mark's Gospel the year 70 and the fall of Jerusalem have not the vital importance that is often alleged.

As the tradition of the close of the second century, to which we are accordingly brought back, could only have tended to link the canonical Mark as closely as possible to its patron saint, the apostle Peter, a *terminus a quo* set at the year 65, to take account of the probable date of Peter's death,[2] is an extreme early limit; it is on the face of it more probable that Mark came into being in its final form ten to twenty years later.

We have also shown that Luke did not know the final edition of Mark, whereas Matthew used it as his principal source. Now Luke-Acts, we believe,[3] was written in the vicinity of the Aegean sea about the years 80–5. Even if we take into account the slow circulation of books in the first century A.D., it seems

---

[1] Cf. what was said above, pp. 208ff., about the significance of Mark 13, in which Luke thought he saw a prediction of the disaster of 70 (cf. Luke 21.20) and about which the vast majority of commentators have thought the same, without any good reason. Cf. also what was said above, p. 206, of the parable of Mark 12.1–9 and its meaning for the author of the original Gospel. In any case these texts appeared in the original version and were merely taken over in the canonical Mark, whose composition they accordingly cannot explain.

Some critics connect not only the composition of Mark 13, but that of the whole of the canonical Mark, with the troubles caused in the Christian Church by the war of 66–70: thus, a short while ago, S. G. F. Brandon, *The Fall of Jerusalem*, pp. 185–205; W. Marxsen, *Der Ev. Markus*, pp. 112–28 and *passim*. For the first-mentioned, Mark is a defensive reaction after the war; for the second, an exhortation contemporary with the events. Neither of these two interesting attempts succeeds in explaining convincingly the origin of Mark because their authors have not penetrated sufficiently to the core of the work and felt the overriding passion that animates it. It is this passion, and not the outward circumstances from which the Church suffered, that explain why Mark came into being.

[2] Which we, with O. Cullmann (*Saint Pierre*, pp. 61–137) and many others, place in Rome during Nero's persecution (64).

[3] Cf. E. Trocmé, *Le Livre des Actes et l'histoire*, pp. 70–5, where we defend these ideas, which, moreover, we are by no means alone in holding.

doubtful that the cultured doctor Luke could have been unaware for two or three years of a work sponsored by the great
church of Rome and which was precisely a document of the
type that Luke-Acts was designed to replace (Luke 1.1-4).
Conversely, the timid editor who joined Mark 14—16 on to
Mark 1—13 would probably have taken more liberties with his
sources if he had had access to the great work written 'to
Theophilus' and had not been discouraged by it from his own
modest undertaking. As he did not keep himself as well-informed as Luke, and as Luke's work may not have enjoyed the
patronage of an important church immediately, some years
may have elapsed before it came into his hands. In other words,
the publication of the canonical Mark might have coincided
with that of Luke-Acts or even have been slightly later. We
cannot go beyond 85, however, in order to leave time for Mark
to reach the circles in which Matthew emerged and to become
well enough established to serve as the foundation for this new
Gospel composed a few years before the end of the first century,
we believe, in a church that had not succumbed to the attractions of Luke-Acts. The relative success of Mark and the total
failure of Luke in the 'Matthaean' church are to be explained,
respectively, the one by the prestige of the Roman community
and the other by ignorance or hostility resulting from the anti-
paulinism of that same church.[1]

After what we have said of the reasonably official origin and
the late date of the canonical Mark, it is clear that the identity
of the editor of this final version is of little interest. The work
was undertaken by an anonymous ecclesiastic of the Roman
community, using two documents already known in his circles.
One of them, of a liturgical nature, which served perhaps for
the annual commemoration of our Lord's passion, came from

---

[1] In other words, it seems that the church which produced 'Matthew'
held the church of Rome in esteem but had no esteem for anything that
emerged from the communities that clung to the legacy of Paul. It
must either have been unaware of the existence of Luke-Acts or else
have turned away in hostility from a work so obviously inspired by the
desire to do justice to the memory of the Apostle of the Gentiles.
Matthew did not, then, use Luke, although it would have been possible
chronologically. On the subject of the anti-paulinism of the community from which Matthew emerged, cf. S. G. F. Brandon, *The Fall
of Jerusalem*, pp. 217-43.

Jerusalem[1] and was attributed to Mark. Without having necessarily been its author, Mark may have translated, supplemented, and circulated it.[2] From this small document, the name was transferred to the canonical Mark, thus placing it under quasi-apostolic patronage and giving it indirectly a share in the reflected authority of Peter, with whom tradition

[1] Cf. pp. 59–63 above.

[2] It is probably to Mark that we owe two not very liturgical features of the Passion story—the reference to Alexander and Rufus, the sons of Simon of Cyrene (15.21), and the picturesque adventure of the young nudist (14.51-2). These two details, left out by Matthew and not mentioned in Luke's account of the passion add a charmingly naive touch. The first assumes that the author was writing for people who knew Alexander and Rufus, obscure members of their community or visitors to them whom we can no longer identify (there are references to Christians called Alexander in 1 Tim. 1.20 and 2 Tim. 4.14 and to one called Rufus in Rom. 16.13, but these names were very common). The second looks as though it might be auto-biographical—the signature, so to speak, of the witness presenting the story to his Greek-speaking readers; there seems no reason to doubt the authenticity of this little incident and it is tempting to see in it one of the youthful memories of John Mark of Jerusalem, an early Christian convert (cf. Acts 12.12,25).

Being the nephew of the Cypriot Barnabas (Acts 4.36; Col. 4.10), with whom he collaborated at Antioch and in Cyprus (Acts 12.25; 13.5,13; 15.29), attached at times to a group of missionaries led by Paul (Acts 13.5,13; Col. 4.10; 2 Tim. 4.11; Philem. 24), Mark must have spoken Greek even better than Aramaic. As a native of Jerusalem (Acts 12.12,25), a former clandestine witness of Jesus' arrest and certainly in close touch with Peter (Acts 12.12; 1 Pet. 5.13; Papias, etc.) he was the ideal person to translate and edit for Greek-speaking Christians the Jerusalem Passion story of which Peter was, if not its author, at least its principal guarantor. Mark 14—16 has preserved this translation for us, mistakes and all (14.3; 14.41: cf. M. Black, *The Aramaic Approach*, 2nd edn, pp. 159–62). The important part played by Peter in this story may be due to additions to an earlier shorter account (as has often been said, without any convincing proof, from R. Bultmann onwards, *Gesch. d. syn. Trad.*, pp. 297–308), but these additions go back to before Mark. Mark's work is difficult to date but it cannot be placed before 45 (approximate date of the beginning of Mark's missionary activity: cf. Acts 12.25; 13.5) or after 75–80. It could be situated in Rome shortly after the death of Peter (in accordance with the tradition preserved by Irenaeus and in the anti-marcionite prologue, where it is applied to the Gospel as a whole), that is to say between 65 and 70, at the time when the Christian community was binding up its wounds after the persecution suffered under Nero.

associated John Mark of Jerusalem. The name of the editor who combined this 'Passion according to Saint Mark' with Mark 1—13 will never be known. We are greatly indebted to him, however—less, perhaps, for having preserved the Passion story (which would have been transmitted in any case, considering its wide circulation in its various versions) than for having saved the much more mysterious text which he made the body of the canonical Mark. Without him, the original Mark would have come to us only through the work of Luke, that greatly distorting mirror in which it is very difficult to distinguish the author's sources. Where does this text, so fortunately preserved almost intact, come from and what does it tell us of the community in which it was composed?

4
THE ORIGIN OF THE GOSPEL IN ITS
EARLIEST FORM
(Mark 1—13)

As we have already remarked several times,[1] the thoughts and feelings of 'the author of Mark' (that is to say the writer who composed Mark 1—13, who is of markedly greater worth than the narrator and translator of Mark 14—16 and than the timid editor who combined the two documents to form the canonical Mark) were bound up with Palestine. That is not due solely to the fact that it was the country where Jesus and the first Christians lived, the place where the ecclesiastical tradition and the miracle stories which are the raw material of his book grew up. To compare Mark with Luke, still so Greek despite the abundant Palestinian documentation, is instructive here. To take only one example, that of the geographical references, to which both are inclined to give a theological significance,[2] it can be said that Luke has of Palestine the simplified picture

---

[1] Cf. pp. 48ff., 88ff., and 184ff. above.

[2] Cf. on this point the rather venturesome but highly suggestive research carried out by E. Lohmeyer, *Galiläa und Jerusalem*; R. H. Lightfoot, *Locality and Doctrine in the Gospels* (London 1938); H. Conzelmann, *Die Mitte der Zeit*, in particular pp. 12–86; W. Marxsen, *Der Ev. Markus*, in particular pp. 33–77; G. H. Boobyer, 'Galilee and Galileans in St Mark's Gospel', in *Bull. of the John Rylands Library*, vol. 35 (1953), pp. 334–48.

that one would expect of the man from outside, however well-informed,[1] whereas the author of Mark is much more conscious of the diversity, and even the tensions existing between regions and groups, despite the minuteness of the country.[2] This is the outlook of a Palestinian by birth or adoption.

But a Palestinian writer, even though Jewish, could have left out of account his personal point of view if writing for people for whom Palestine meant nothing, except perhaps a distant Eastern district with strange customs which was of interest only because of the presence of Jews in all the great cities of the civilized world.[3] The best example of this de-provincialization is perhaps the work of the historian Flavius Josephus. It is enough to bring him to mind to realize that the author of the original Mark was thinking, when he composed his book, of readers for whom Palestine was a close and living reality. Who else could have understood the allusions to so many obscure little towns on the shores of Lake Tiberias, itself pompously called a 'sea', to bizarre customs and complex rabbinical arguments, to undistinguished princelings of north-eastern Palestine and their followers? The original Mark was written by a man of Palestine for Palestinians who, even though they might not live there, were attached to their country by strong ties.

To these indications we can add a few more. A Jew himself, the writer was addressing readers of whom the great majority were Jews too, urging them to put on the armour of the gospel

---

[1] Palestine for him is first and foremost Jerusalem, its Temple and the surrounding area; it is also the country of the Jews, where Jesus did his work on earth and from where, in God's own time, the mission will go out into the Gentile world. Apart from the Romans, the only inhabitants who are not Jews are in his eyes the Samaritans, the official heretics.

[2] He hints that Jesus' enemies in Galilee are urged on by Jerusalem (3.22; 7.1) and shows the authorities in the capital as exploiters and conspirators whom the pilgrims hamper in the accomplishment of their designs. He knows that Palestine and the surrounding regions are not inhabited by Jews alone (cf. 7.24ff.). He distinguishes between Judaea and the rest of the Jewish lands (Mark 1.5; 3.7, etc.) and designates it alone for destruction (Mark 13.14).

[3] Just as today people are interested in Israel wherever there are Jewish communities, or indeed as they are interested in Kabylia wherever groups of Kabyle workers have settled.

and wrest Israel from its bad shepherds, at the same time opening the door wide to their Gentile neighbours. It is in particular against the religious authorities of Jerusalem, and especially the scribes, that he directs his furious attack, as though seeking to defend the provinces against the capital. By his plan,[1] by the editorial touches whereby he extends the action from the shores of Lake Tiberias, where he had collected much of his documentation,[2] to all the neighbouring regions, by the threat he announces to be hanging over Jerusalem and the whole of Judaea, our author concentrates attention on the part of Palestine situated north and north-east of Samaria.[3] One cannot assert for this reason that the original Mark was composed in that area, but it was certainly composed by a man or for a group with a special interest in the whole of the region of which Galilee forms the core.[4] The circles from which the

---

[1] Which concentrated all Jesus' activity in Jerusalem in the last section (chaps. 11—13) and located all four preceding sections in Galilee or its vicinity.

[2] Cf. pp. 52–4 above.

[3] The absence in Mark of any reference to Samaria and the Samaritans, whereas all the other parts of Palestine are mentioned, is a surprising feature (Matthew who inherited this silence on the subject feels the need to explain it: Matt. 10.5). It is hard to see why our Evangelist did not refer to this part of the country in passages such as 3.7–8 or 10.1. It seems doubtful that he could have basically detested the Samaritans in particular, since his hostility to the Temple of Jerusalem would have drawn him to them. One hesitates to ascribe his silence to the fear of being considered an accomplice of heretics, since one or two references to these people and their country would not have done him any harm and he was obviously not a man to be pettily cautious. Perhaps he thought it best not to include Samaria among the mission fields he was proposing to his readers. Did he see in it a barren land where the Good News produced bitter fruit, as in Judaea? Or did he regard it as the preserve of missionaries who did not belong to his own group? It is difficult to say, but his silence probably conceals some kind of bitterness. Is it the result of a disappointment suffered by himself or by somebody close to him? It is clear in any case that the evangelization of Samaria had encountered unforeseen difficulties (Simon Magus: cf. Acts 8.9–13,18–24) and provoked certain rivalries among Christian missionaries (Acts 8.5–8,12,14–17,25; John 4.37–8).

[4] This, with some qualifications, is the conclusion of all the authors cited on p. 248, n. 2. J. Schreiber, 'Die Christologie des Markusevangeliums', in *Zeitschr. f. Theologie u. Kirche* (1961), pp. 154–83, speaks of Tyre, Sidon, or Decapolis.

original Mark emerged were persuaded that the religious revolution in Israel had its roots in Galilee and not in Jerusalem.

Are these conclusions compatible with the language in which the work was written? It is indeed clear that the original Mark, which corresponds almost word for word with the canonical Mark 1—13, is no more a translation from an Aramaic original than is the later Gospel. If we except the sayings of Jesus, which are obviously translated, we can only say that the earliest version of the Gospel was written in the Greek which a Jew speaking Aramaic might have used, and that certain of the stories about Jesus it contains came to the Evangelist in their Aramaic form.[1] Can we allow that a book addressed to Jews who had ties with north-eastern Palestine could, in the first century of our era, have been written in Greek? The first language of these regions was still Aramaic, even though Greek-speaking colonies had settled in various places and many people, both Jews and Gentiles, knew Greek more or less.[2] However, Greek was the language with the greatest cultural prestige and it would be enough to explain the author's preference for it that the circles among whom the book was written should have been composed largely of Greek-speaking Jews and that in addition the author should have wished his appeal to make a certain impact on the world outside Palestine.

The author of the first Mark, a Greek-speaking Palestinian Jew, was also a Christian and it is not without interest, despite appearances, to look for a moment at that side of his personality. As we were examining his ideas earlier, we could observe that he was neither an ordinary Christian nor a peaceable Christian. The ideas he expresses or hints at on the subject of the person and the work of Jesus, the Gospel and Satan's resistance to it, the orientation, the urgency, and the method of missionary conquest, Christian ethics and the Christian cult, history and eschatology, differ considerably—sometimes radically—from those of other Christian writers of the first century and seem not always compatible with those of the very earliest

---

[1] This conclusion is borrowed from M. Black, *Aramaic Approach*, pp. 206–7.

[2] Cf. on this subject, for example, G. Dalman, *Jesus-Jeschua, die drei Sprachen Jesu . . .* (Leipzig 1922), pp. 1–6; S. Liebermann, *Greek in Jewish Palestine* (New York 1942).

Church, in so far as we know what its ideas were.[1] Our Evangelist does not fit very well into the old pattern that opposes a
conservative Jewish Christianity to a radical Gentile Christianity, but neither does it fit readily into the substitute patterns
suggested.[2] It is preferable to admit, with some recent authors,[3]
that a close study of Mark forces us to revise our ideas on the
formation of Christian thought during the first forty years of
the history of the Church.

However, the ideas of the original Gospel of Mark are too
little developed and clarified, too closely bound up with anecdotes and allusive 'sayings of Jesus' for it to be possible to
detect and locate them without paying the greatest attention
to the polemical side of the work. The Evangelist was filled
with violent hostility towards the scribes and the Temple of
Jerusalem as well as to all the authorities that controlled the
Temple. He detested James, our Lord's brother, and had
reservations in regard to Peter and the Twelve, whose authority,
nevertheless, he recognized in some measure. He had no particular ties with Paul and his horizon did not extend far beyond
the boundaries of Palestine. He represents, thus, a section of

---

[1] It is thus not surprising that despite the apparently inoffensive character
of Mark, there should have been heretics in the second century who used
its reserved christology and other special features in support of their
own ideas. Irenaeus, *Adv. Haer.*, III. 11, 7, is doubtless not inventing
when he reproaches 'those who separate Jesus from the Christ' with
preferring Mark to the other Gospels. But this one sentence does not
enable us to identify the heretics he is denouncing in this way (cf. A.
Benoit, *Saint Irénée, introduction à l'étude de sa théologie* (Paris 1960),
p. 113).

[2] Among the recent theories seeking to explain the formation and
development of Christian theology in the first century can be mentioned those of R. Bultmann (in particular in his *Theologie des N.T.*,
2nd edn, pp. 66ff.), who places between the thinking of Paul and that
of the primitive Church a sort of hellenistic and syncretistic pre-
paulinism which influenced Paul, deutero-paulinism and early catho-
licism; M. Werner (*Die Entstehung des christlichen Dogmas* (Berne–
Leipzig 1941, 2nd edn 1953), who believes in a growing hellenization
of Christian thinking as eschatological expectations began to lose their
urgency; J. Munck (*Paulus und die Heilsgeschichte* (Aarhus-Copenhagen
1954)), who presses to the point of paradox the theory of the total
similarity of views of Paul and the leaders of the church of Jerusalem.

[3] Thus E. Lohmeyer, *Galiläa und Jerusalem*; J. M. Robinson, *Geschichtsverständnis des Mk.-Ev.*; W. Marxsen, *Der Ev. Markus.*

opinion that remained on the fringe of the great currents that thrust Christianity on towards its universal destiny without losing the ties that bound it to the Jewish past and to the teaching of Jesus. It is solely on account of having produced, thanks to the genius of one man, a literary work of enduring influence that the group in question deserves perhaps to be saved from the oblivion to which its insignificant numbers and want of missionary success would normally have condemned it for ever. In the circumstances, then, it would be a rather vain task, considering the numerous and vast areas of obscurity that almost entirely surround the history of the origins of the Christian Church, to seek to identify the author of the original Mark and the community in which it was composed.

At this point, then, we would drop our enquiries into these two points if the Book of Acts did not introduce us to a group whose polemical outlook and theological ideas showed striking resemblances to those we have detected in Mark: the group of the Seven (Acts 6—8; cf. Acts 11.19–21; 22.20). This is not the place to go into all the numerous questions that arise concerning the antecedents and origin of these few men and the part they and the circles they represented played in the first church of Jerusalem.[1] But the little we know of them shows them as very close to the author of the original Mark. Their appearance, in the Book of Acts, coincides with serious quarrels in the church of Jerusalem that had been hitherto so united (Acts 6.1), leading up to a limitation of the powers of the Twelve (Acts 6.2–6), who subsequently seem little inclined to

---

[1] Among the numerous recent studies devoted to the Seven and their milieu special mention may be made of the book by M. Simon, *St Stephen and the Hellenists in the Primitive Church* (London–New York–Toronto 1958); various articles by O. Cullmann, in particular that which appeared in the collective volume, *Les Manuscrits de la Mer Morte, Colloque de Strasbourg* (1955) (Paris 1957), pp. 61ff., under the title 'Secte de Qumran, Hellénistes des Actes et Quatrième Evangile' and that in *New Testament Studies*, vol. v (1959), pp. 157–73, entitled 'L'opposition contre le temple de Jérusalem, motif commun de la théologie johannique et du monde ambiant'; C. Spicq, 'L'épitre aux Hébreux, Apollos, Jean-Baptiste, les Hellénistes et Qumran', in *Revue de Qumran*, vol. III (1959), pp. 365ff.; P. Geoltrain, 'Esséniens et Hellénistes', in *Theologische Zeitschrift*, vol. xv (1959), pp. 241ff.

take the part of the Seven and their people in the face of persecution (Acts 8.1). In the following years the relations between this group and the leaders of the first church of Jerusalem do not seem to have greatly improved, since Peter and John go into Samaria to reap what Philip has sown (8.5–25), Peter goes to Caesarea (chap. 10) without bothering to meet Philip, who was no doubt established there (Acts 8.40 and 21.8–9), and the Christians living in Jerusalem who shared these ideas appear, shortly before the year 60, to have lived on the fringe of the great Church headed by James.[1]

The Seven of Acts 6.5 are Jews by birth, except for one, who is a proselyte from Antioch. They all have Greek names and Luke calls the section of the community whose clamourings their election was designed to calm down 'Grecians', a word which in his vocabulary[2] means 'Greek-speaking'. Moreover it is often among Greek-speaking Jews that these men are active (Acts 6.8–10; 11.19). They are not universalists: if Philip turns to the Samaritans and to an Ethiopian eunuch (Acts 8.5–39), even here it is only a question of heretic Jews and a proselyte, at least in intention. Circumstances alone seem to have prompted some of them to address themselves to Gentiles, in distant Antioch (11.20–1). Their sphere of action is limited, moreover, to Palestine, Phoenicia, Cyprus and their farthest outpost, Antioch, 250 miles from Galilee (Acts 8.5ff.; 8.26,40; 11.19–21). Their missionary method relies largely on wonder-working (Acts 6.8; 8.6–8,13), appeals to the people (6.8; 8.6) and provocative speaking (Acts 6.10–11,13–14; 7.2–53). In all these fields they practice exactly what the original Mark teaches.

We know little of their theological ideas since, except for Stephen's not very clear speech in Acts 7.2–53, we can glean

---

[1] The 'old disciple', to whom, according to Acts 21.16, the Christians of Caesarea—a community led by Philip, one of the Seven—took Paul after escorting him right to Jerusalem, was a Cypriot called Mnason, who welcomed Paul to his house before the latter had announced his arrival to the church (the Western variant attenuates this by making Mnason live in a place that Paul passed through on his way; this is clearly a later correction).

[2] We leave aside here the question of the origin of the term used in Acts 6.1, 9.29 and 11.20 (cf. the works enumerated on p. 253, n. 1). In any case, for Luke it meant Greek-speaking people.

only a few isolated features from the accounts of their doings to be found in the same book.[1] However, there too some suggestive comparisons can be made. The Temple of Jerusalem is denounced as contrary to God's will and doomed to destruction (Acts 6.14; 7.44–50) without the principle of the cult of sacrifice being challenged. The leaders of the Jewish people are attacked as eternal rebels who, in the steps of Aaron (7.40–1) and of Solomon (7.47–50) have for centuries been 'resisting the Holy Ghost' (7.51–9), but the claim that they are the chosen people does not seem to be rejected. The idea that a nomadic life is part of the destiny of Israel (cf. the stress laid on the wanderings of Moses in 7.20–44) is combined with the recognition of Palestine as the Holy Land (Acts 7.5,17,45). The law given by God has not been kept by the leaders of Israel (7.53), who showed their determination to disobey even before they received it (7.39); thus even the most venerable customs can be changed (6.11,13–14). All this is rather reminiscent of Mark 7.1ff. and 10.2–9.

The christology of this group seems somewhat rudimentary. An allusion to a 'prophet like unto Moses' applies perhaps to John the Baptist; the title of 'the Just One' given to Jesus is singularly flat and can scarcely be regarded as christological. The invocation of 'Lord Jesus' (7.59) has nothing distinctive about it and its equivalent is to be found in almost all the books of the New Testament. As for the vision of the 'Son of Man standing on the right hand of God' (7.56), it echoes the words that all the Gospels attribute to Jesus on the subject of the parousia of the Son of Man; this title belongs to the common store of evangelical tradition and is only used here in order to threaten the martyr's enemies with speedy retribution. Consequently, the followers of the Seven used the common christological titles, but, to judge by Stephen's speech, the group is little interested in christological speculations, which have no place at all in this very long passage. What rouses people's passions is the destiny of the people of Israel, the imminent triumph of the Just One risen from the dead over the bad shepherds who had thought they were rid of his interference for ever (cf. Acts 7.35, where the word λυτρωτής recalls per-

---

[1] Stephen's ideas, as they emerge from the speech in Acts 7, are well discussed by M. Simon, *St Stephen*, pp. 39–77.

haps the λύτρον of Mark 10.45)—a triumph that will open the
eyes of the hoodwinked nation. Their meditation nevertheless
dwells readily on the unmerited suffering that Jesus accepted
out of humility (7.52; 8.32–5). On these few points comparisons can be made with the ideas of Mark; in any case there
is no conflict.

The doctrine of the Holy Ghost professed by the Seven also
presents some analogies with that of the author of the original
Mark. This is the more striking since that doctrine is revealed
to us in documents transmitted by Luke, whose ideas on the
subject were quite different and who certainly did not accentuate features that he must have thought bizarre. For the Seven,
the Holy Ghost is the force that inspires the disciple bearing
witness or defending his faith or his person to utter irresistible
words (6.10; 6.15 probably; 7.55; 8.29–39). It is also the spirit
of prophecy given to certain believers (cf. Stephen's prophetic
speech in chap. 7; the resemblance of the Philip of Acts 8.26–40
to the Elijah of 1 Kings 18; Acts 21.9–14). But it is not a gift to
be received by every believer, and on this point there is a
serious difference between the 'apostles of Jerusalem' and the
Philip of Acts 8.14–17, whose position is similar to that of the
author of Mark.

In short, the Seven and the circles they influenced behave
exactly as our Evangelist wished and think as he does on all the
points where we can discern their ideas at all clearly. It is
accordingly among them that the original Mark was written
and found its first readers. The difficult situation in which they
found themselves vis-à-vis official Judaism and also in the
Palestinian church can accordingly explain certain surprising
features of the Gospel: the violence of certain polemical passages, the passion that sweeps it along, its curiously limited
horizon, the mixture of respect and freedom in its attitude to
the Jerusalem tradition. It even explains why the book was
written, its plan and its primary intention. Harshly persecuted
by the Jewish authorities, the Seven and their group have fled
out of reach of their mortal enemies but they have kept, in
their refuges not far from the land of the Jews, the mentality of
emigrés preparing to return in triumph and looking for the
best mode of attack for their religious religious revolution. Expelled
from Samaria by their rivals from Jerusalem, they thought to

find revenge in Galilee and the neighbouring areas, where they walked with the risen Christ in the steps of the earthly Jesus.

Fact or fable? A little of each, no doubt. And so we shall not look in the original Mark for much information about the history of the Seven and their group, apart from the few general features outlined above. On the other hand, we shall look in the Gospel for enlightenment on the religious ideas of these first Greek-speaking Christians, which have been so mysterious hitherto that they lent themselves to the most conflicting—and sometimes the most arbitrary—reconstructions. We shall look in it too for information about the thought and life of the Christian adversaries of the Seven. Thus we shall see that the church of Jerusalem began very early, as can be guessed from the account in Acts 1—5, to take on the aspect of a closed and somewhat sectarian community, probably with some Essene features and more concerned with theological debates with the scribes of the synagogues and the preservation of order, purity, and sound doctrine inside the Church than with conquest or heroism. While we can judge this attitude less severely than the author of the original Mark, since we no doubt owe to it the preservation of the sayings of Jesus whose essence was subsequently reproduced in Matthew and Luke, we can nevertheless glean from his criticism of the Jerusalemites quite a number of details about the mother-church.

It is customary, when one is studying an anonymous work like Mark—in particular the original Mark—to find an author for it. Let us respect that custom—vain though it may be to do so, considering our ignorance of the personality and career of any of the few first century Christians who might come to mind. The author to whom we propose attributing the original Mark could be Philip, the evangelizer of Samaria and the only one of the Seven, apart from Stephen, of whom we know a little, although the information we have about him is limited to what we find in one chapter of Acts (chap. 8) and a few verses in another (21.8ff.), if we except the quite probable tradition that after the year 70 he lived at Hierapolis.[1] As a person he

---

[1] According to Eusebius, *H.E.*, III. 39, 9, who quotes Papias, Philip the Evangelist and his prophetess daughters settled at Hierapolis in the province of Asia after the fall of Jerusalem.

had both originality and enterprise. Having settled in Caesarea
some time after fleeing from Jerusalem (Acts 8.40), he was still
living there with his family (Acts 21.8–9) shortly before 60.
From this convenient base where the Jewish authorities were
not very likely to trouble him, considering the mixed population and the fact that there was a Roman Procurator in the
town, one may suppose that he made missionary expeditions
across northern Palestine and into the surrounding countries.
To justify his audacious activity and to attract collaboration
and help one can readily believe that he might have written his
'account of the true ecclesiological intentions of Jesus'. That
could be regarded as the literary aspect of his ministry of
εὐαγγελιστής that Acts 21.8 attributes to him.[1]

Written by an author somewhat suspect to Christians of all
affiliations on account of his break with the church of Jerusalem,
devoid of literary interest and very deficient where the teaching
of Jesus was concerned, the original Mark cannot have spread
very far beyond the circles for which it was intended. Its
influence was therefore slight for many years. This makes it
even more difficult to date, particularly in the absence of any
definite *terminus a quo*. It was not before having gained some
experience of the life of an itinerant missionary that the author
of Mark 1—13 wrote his book. The earliest date that can be
contemplated thus depends on the date (unknown but ob-

---

[1] A number of critics have already maintained that Philip the Evangelist
was the author of a document used by one or other of the canonical
Gospels or at least the narrator from whom some of the stories they
contain derived. According to A. Harnack, *Lukas der Arzt, der Verfasser
des dritten Evangeliums und der Apostelgeschichte* (Leipzig 1906, Beiträge zur
Einleitung in das Neue Testament 1), the special source used by Luke
apart from Mark and the *logia* came from Philip; according to H.
Ewald, *Die Bücher des Neuen Bundes übersetzt und erklärt* (Göttingen 1850,
2nd edn 1971), pp. 57ff., the oldest Gospel, written in a very semitic-
flavoured Greek, and used in the three synoptic Gospels, was the work of
Philip the Evangelist. It is not our intention here to revive these very
outdated hypotheses, any more than that of E. Reuss (cf. for example,
La Bible, Nouveau Testament, vol. 1: *Histoire évangélique* (Paris 1876),
pp. 88–9), according to whom the Proto-Mark did not contain the
Passion story (nor 1.1–20, nor 6.47—8.26). But, considering the
authority of the scholars in question, we derive encouragement from
them to submit to criticism ideas which coincide with theirs on certain
points.

viously early) of the persecution that drove him from Jerusalem. We cannot, however, make it earlier than 40, the date by which the threat to the Christians from the collusions between the Pharisees and Herod Agrippa (d. A.D. 44) was beginning to justify their strange association in Mark 3.6 and 12.13 and when the emotion roused by Caligula's plan to have his statue set up in the Temple (in 39–41) explains the wording of Mark 13.14. The latest possible date is still more uncertain. But we may suppose that it was at Caesarea, during his two-year stay when Paul was a prisoner there, that Luke discovered the original version of Mark. This would mean that it was written at latest in 57, before which date no critic places the beginning of Luke's stay. In short, Mark 1—13 must have been written in Palestine around the year 50 of our Christian era.

CONCLUSION

Having reached the end of this enquiry, the reader will perhaps be surprised to have found only a few brief allusions to the question that must be uppermost in the mind of any sensible person who opens the Gospel according to Mark: what does this little book, in which Jesus is in the centre of the stage from beginning to end, tell us about him? Have we, indeed, merely skirted round a problem whose historical face is sheer and whose theological face is marked by numerous precipices?

Perhaps, it is true, the vast bibliography and the complexity of the elements of the problem have caused us to hang back for the time being. This will not be held against us, we trust, since the present study provides certain materials that can be used for the work that remains to be written. In order to understand Jesus properly, we believe, it is essential to have as accurate a knowledge as possible of the primitive Christian community, its internal and external difficulties, its ideas and customs. Whatever one may think of its fidelity to the crucified Master, it is this community which, having heard and loved him, has made him known to us. For the historian as for the theologian, this community is for ever associated with him—it would be naive or disingenuous to argue the contrary. If then, this study has helped even a little to throw light on the history and thought of the first Christians, it has at the same time, we believe, helped to bring Jesus closer.

On the other hand, if our conclusions regarding the formation of the canonical Mark and its two component parts are correct, we have in the steps of other critics, but in rather a new way, freed the documents concerning the Master's ministry in Jerusalem from the ties that bound them to Holy Week and made new hypotheses possible concerning the course of the passion events, of which chapters 14—16 seem to us to give a stylized account, but a very early one and one that is usefully paralleled by that of Luke, whose independence we have stressed. We have elucidated the plan of the original work in greater detail than earlier critics and shown once again in the process that its historical foundation is very slender. Our conjecture as to the origin of the miracle stories and their significance is more satisfactory than any of the previous ones. With regard to the transmission of the sayings of Jesus, we have shown how closely it was bound up with the Jerusalem community and marked by that community's ideas. By setting a fairly early date for the composition of the original Mark we have at once brought the emergence of the Gospel as a literary genre closer to the time when Jesus lived on earth, and made it more difficult to discern, as is still sometimes attempted, a straightforward biography of the Galilean behind any of the canonical Gospels. Lastly, we have concluded for or against the authenticity of a number of important sayings attributed to Jesus.

These results, we are ready to admit, have not the value of a synthesis with Jesus himself as the subject of study. But perhaps our failure to tackle 'the problem of Jesus' will be found more excusable if it is agreed to accept this book as an approach that has led to certain discoveries, partial but precise, which, we are convinced, will clear the way to a better view of the target. It will be for us to show, in due course, whether our cautious circling around the problem today has indeed prepared the ground for a frontal attack. This we hope to do one day, conscious though we are of the difficulty of the undertaking.

BIBLIOGRAPHY*

1
WORKS OF REFERENCE

ABEL, F. M., *Grammaire du grec biblique*, Paris 1927.

BAILLY, M. A., *Dictionnaire grec-français*, Paris n.d. 1894.

BAUER, W., *Griechisch-deutsches Wörterbuch zu den Schriften des Neuen Testaments und der übrigen urchristlichen Literatur*, 4th edn, Berlin 1952; 5th edn, 1958. [E. T. Arndt-Gingrich, London-Chicago 1957.]

BLACK, M., *An Aramaic approach to the Gospels and Acts*, 2nd edn, Oxford 1954.

BLASS, F., *Grammatik des neutestamentlichen Griechisch; bearbeitet von* A. Debrunner, 10th edn, Göttingen 1959. [E. T. rev. R. W. Funk, Cambridge 1961.]

Dictionnaire de le Bible, Supplément . . .; commencé sous la direction de L. Pirot *et* A. Robert, *continué sous celle de* H. Cazelles. Paris 1928 – A to P only.

*Dictionnaire encyclopédique de la Bible: les choses, les hommes, lesf aits, les doctrines . . .; publié sous la direction d'*Alexandre Westphal; 2 vols, Paris 1932 and Valence n.d. [1935].

DUPLACY, J., *Ou en est la critique textuelle du Nouveau Testament?* Paris 1959.

FEINE, P. and BEHM, J., *Einleitung in das Neue Testament*, 11th edn, Heidelberg 1956.

GOGUEL, M., *Introduction au Nouveau Testament*, 4 parts in 5 vols, Paris 1922–6.

GROLLENBERG, L. H., *Atlas de la Bible; traduit et adapté du néerlandais par* R. Beaupère, Brussels 1955.

HENNECKE, E., *Neutestamentliche Apokryphen in deutscher Uebersetzung . . .; hgg. von* W. Schneemelcher, vol 1, 3rd edn, Tübingen 1959.

HOSKYNS, E. and DAVEY, F. N., *The riddle of the New Testament*, London 1947.

* Works published before 1919 have been mentioned only if they have been particularly useful.

Introduction à la Bible; sous la direction de A. Robert *et* A. Feuillet, vol 2 (Nouveau Testament), Tournai 1959.

KENYON, F. G., *Handbook to the Textual Criticism of the New Testament*, 2nd edn, London 1926.

——, *Our Bible and the ancient manuscripts*; rev. A. W. Adams, 5th edn, London 1958.

KNOPF, R., LIETZMANN, H., and WEINEL, H., *Einführung in das Neue Testament*, 5th edn, Berlin 1949.

LEGG, S. C. E., *Nouum Testamentum graece secundum textum Westcotto-Hortianum, Euangelium secundum Marcum cum apparatu critico nouo plenissimo* . . . , Oxford 1935.

LEMAIRE, P. and BALDI, D., *Atlas biblique: histoire et géographie de la Bible*, Louvain 1960.

McNEILE, A. H., *An introduction to the study of the New Testament* . . . : rev. C. S. C. Williams, 2nd edn, Oxford 1953.

MICHAELIS, W., *Einleitung in das Neue Testament: die Entstehung, Sammlung und Ueberlieferung der Schriften des Neuen Testaments*, 3rd edn, Berne 1960.

MORGENTHALER, R., *Statistik des neutestamentlichen Wortschatzes*, Zurich-Frankfurt 1958.

MOULTON, J. H. and GEDEN, A. S., *A Concordance to the Greek Testament*, 3rd edn, Edinburgh 1926.

——, and HOWARD, W. F., *A Grammar of New Testament Greek*, vol 1, 3rd edn, Edinburgh 1908; vol 2, 1928.

——, and MILLIGAN, G., *The Vocabulary of the Greek Testament illustrated from the Papyri and other non-literary Sources*, London 1930.

Nouveau Testament, Le: traduction nouvelle d'après les meilleurs textes, avec introductions et notes, sous la direction de M. Goguel *et* H. Monnier, Paris 1929.

Novum Testamentum graece cum apparatu critico curavit Eb. Nestle . . . , 24th edn; ed. K. ALAND, Stuttgart 1960.

PERNOT, H., *Etudes sur la langue des évangiles*, Paris 1927.

RADERMACHER, L., *Neutestamentliche Grammatik: das Griechisch des Neuen Testaments im Zusammenhang mit der Volkssprache*, 2nd edn, Tübingen 1925.

RESCH, A., *Ausserkanonische Paralleltexte zu den Evangelien*, 3 vols, Leipzig 1893–7.

Reallexikon für Antike und Christentum: Sachwörterbuch zur Auseinandersetzung des Christentums mit der antiken Welt . . . , hgg. von Theodor Klauser, Stuttgart 1950.

SCHMOLLER, A., *Concordantiae Novi Testamenti graeci*, 10th edn, Stuttgart 1953.

STRACK, H. L. and BILLERBECK, P., *Kommentar zum N.T. aus Talmud und Midrasch*, 6 vols, Munich 1922–61.

Theologisches Wörterbuch zum Neuen Testament: bear. von G. Kittel, hgg. von G. Friedrich, Stuttgart 1933–73.

TISCHENDORF, C., *Novum Testamentum graece . . . editio octava critica maior*, Leipzig 1869.

VAGANAY, L., *Initiation à la critique textuelle néotestamentaire*, Paris 1934.

Vocabulaire biblique; publié sous la direction de J. J. von Allmen, 2nd edn, Neuchâtel-Paris 1956.

WESTCOTT, B. F. and HORT, F. J. A., *The New Testament in the Original Greek, Introduction and Appendix*, Cambridge 1882.

WIKENHAUSER, A., *Einleitung in das Neue Testament*, 2nd edn, Freiburg-im-Breisgau 1956.

WRIGHT, G. E. and FILSON, F. V., *Westminster Historical Atlas to the Bible*, new edn, London 1958.

2

THE SYNOPTIC TRADITION AND THE LITERARY RELATIONSHIPS OF THE GOSPELS

ALBERTZ, M., *Die synoptischen Streitgespräche, ein Beitrag zur Formengeschichte des Urchristentums*, Berlin 1921.

BERTRAM, G., *Die Leidensgeschichte Jesu und der Christuskult, eine formgeschichtliche Untersuchung*, Göttingen 1922.

BORNKAMM, G., BARTH, G., and HELD, H. J., *Ueberlieferung und Auslegung im Matthäus-Evangelium*, Neukirchen 1959.

BULTMANN, R., *Die Geschichte der synoptischen Tradition*, 4th edn, Göttingen 1958. [E. T. J. Marsh, *The History of the Synoptic Tradition*, Oxford 1963.]

BUSSMANN, W., *Synoptische Studien*, 3 vols, Halle 1925–31.

BUTLER, B. C., *The originality of St Matthew*, Cambridge 1951.

CADBURY, H. J., *The Style and Literary Method of Luke*, Cambridge, Mass., 1919–20.

CERFAUX, L., *Recueil Lucien Cerfaux: études d'exégèse et d'histoire religieuse . . .*, 2 vols, Gembloux 1954.

CONZELMANN, H., *Die Mitte der Zeit: Studien zur Theologie des Lukas*, 3rd edn, Tübingen 1960. [E. T. G. Buswell, *The Theology of St Luke*, London 1960.]

DIBELIUS, M., *Botschaft und Geschichte: gesammelte Aufsätze* . . . , vol. I, *Zur Evangelienforschung* . . . ; hgg. von G. Bornkamm, Tübingen 1953.

——, *Die Formgeschichte des Evangeliums* . . . hgg. von G. Bornkamm, 3rd edn, Tübingen 1959. [E. T. *From Tradition to Gospel*, 1935.]

DODD, C. H., *The Apostolic Preaching and its Developments*, London 1936.

——, *New Testament Studies*, Manchester 1952.

——, *The Parables of the Kingdom*, London 1935; rev. edn, 1961.

EASTON, B. S., *The Gospel before the Gospels*, New York 1928.

FARRER, A. M., *St Matthew and St Mark*, London 1954.

FASCHER, E., *Die formgeschichtliche Methode: eine Darstellung und Kritik, zugleich ein Beitrag zur Geschichte des synoptischen Problems*, Giessen 1924.

FIEBIG, P., *Der Erzählungsstil der Evangelien*, Leipzig 1925.

FINEGAN, J., *Die Ueberlieferung der Leidens- und Auferstehungsgeschichte Jesu*, Giessen 1934.

Formation, La, des évangiles: problème synoptique et Formgeschichte . . . , n.p. 1957.

FRIDRICHSEN, A., *Le problème du miracle dans le christianisme primitif*, Strasbourg 1925.

GOGUEL, M., *L'évangile de Marc dans ses rapports avec ceux de Matthieu et de Luc*, Paris 1909.

GRANT, F. C., *The Gospels, their Origin, and their Growth*, London 1957.

HAWKINS, J. C., *Horae Synopticae*, 2nd edn, Oxford 1909.

HIRSCH, E., *Frühgeschichte des Evangeliums*, Tübingen 1940–1, 2 vols; vol. I slightly augmented, 1951.

HUBY, J. and LÉON-DUFOUR, X., *L'Evangile et les évangiles*, Paris 1954.

HUCK, A., *Synopse der drei ersten Evangelien* . . . *völlig neu bearbeitet von* H. Lietzmann, 10th edn, Tübingen 1950.

JEREMIAS, J., *Die Abendmahlsworte Jesu*, 3rd edn, Göttingen 1960; [E. T. *The Eucharistic Words of Jesus*, London 1970].

——, *Die Gleichnisse Jesu*, Zurich 1947; 5th edn, Göttingen 1958; [E.T. *The Parables of Jesus*, London 1963].

JÜLICHER, A., *Die Gleichnisreden Jesu*, Tübingen 1899; 2nd edn, 1910.

KALLAS, J., *The Significance of the Synoptic Miracles*, London 1961.

KILPATRICK, G. D., *The Origins of the Gospel according to St Matthew*, Oxford 1946.

KNOX, W. L., *The Sources of the Synoptic Gospels* . . . ed. H. Chadwick, 2 vols, Cambridge 1953–7.

KOESTER, H., *Synoptische Ueberlieferung bei den apostolischen Vätern*, Berlin 1957.

LÉON-DUFOUR, X., *Concordance des évangiles synoptiques*, Paris-Tournai 1956.

LEVIE, J., *L'évangile araméen de saint Matthieu est-il la source de l'évangile de saint Marc?* Paris-Tournai 1954.

LIGHTFOOT, R. H., *History and Interpretation in the Gospels*, London 1935.

——, *Locality and Doctrine in the Gospels*, London 1938.

MANSON, T. W., *The Sayings of Jesus, as recorded in the Gospels according to St Matthew and St Luke; arranged with Introduction and Commentary*, London 1949.

MORGENTHALER, R., *Die lukanische Geschichtsschreibung als Zeugnis*, 2 vols, Zurich 1949.

NEPPER-CHRISTENSEN, P., *Das Matthäusevangelium: ein judenchrisliches Evangelium?* Aarhus 1958.

PERELS, O., *Die Wunderüberlieferung der Synoptiker in ihrem Verhältnis zur Wortüberlieferung*, Stuttgart 1934.

REHKOPF, F., *Die lukanische Sonderquelle: ihr Umfang und Sprachgebrauch*, Tübingen 1959.

RIESENFELD, H., *The Gospel tradition and its Beginnings: a Study in the Limits of 'Formgeschichte'*, London 1957.

——, *Jésus transfiguré: l'arrière-plan du récit évangélique de la Transfiguration de Notre Seigneur*, Copenhagen 1947.

RICHARDSON, A., *The Miracle Stories of the Gospels*, London 1941.

SCHMIDT, K. L., *Der Rahmen der Geschichte Jesu: literarkritische Untersuchungen zur ältesten Jesusüberlieferung*, Berlin 1919.

SCHUERMANN, H., *Quellenkritische Untersuchung des lukanischen Abendmahlsberichtes Lk*, 22.7–38, 3 vols, Münster 1953–7.

SOLAGES, B. de, *Synopse grecque des évangiles: méthode nouvelle pour résoudre le problème synoptique*, Leiden-Toulouse 1959.

STANTON, V. H., *The Gospels as Historical Documents*, 3 vols, Cambridge 1903–20.

STENDAHL, K., *The School of St Matthew and its Use of the Old Testament*, Lund 1954.

STREETER, B. H., *The Four Gospels: a Study of Origins*, London 1924.

Studia Evangelica: Papers presented to the International Congress on ' The Four Gospels in 1957' held at . . . Oxford . . . , Berlin 1959.

Studies in the Gospels: Essays in Memory of R. H. Lightfoot; ed. D. E. Nineham, Oxford 1957.

Studies in the Synoptic Problem; ed. W. Sanday, Oxford 1911.

Synoptische Studien für A. Wikenhauser dargebracht, Munich 1953.

TAYLOR, R. O. P., *The Groundwork of the Gospels*, Oxford 1946.

TAYLOR, V., *Behind the Third Gospel*, Oxford 1926.

——, *The Formation of the Gospel Tradition*, London 1933, 2nd edn 1935.

TORREY, C. C., *Our Translated Gospels*, London n.d.

VANNUTELLI, P., *De evangeliorum origine*, Rome 1923.

——, *Quaestiones de synopticis evangeliis*, Rome 1933.

VAGANAY, L., *Le problème synoptique: une hypothèse de travail*, Tournai 1954.

WELLHAUSEN, J., *Einleitung in die drei ersten Evangelien*, Berlin 1905; 2nd edn 1911.

WAUTIER d'AYGALLIERS, A., *Les sources du récit de la Passion chez Luc*, Alençon 1920.

3
STUDIES IN ST MARK'S GOSPEL

ALFARIC, P., *La plus ancienne vie de Jésus, l'Evangile selon Marc: traduction nouvelle avec introduction et notes*, Paris 1929.

BACON, B. W., *Is Mark a Roman Gospel?* Cambridge, Mass. 1919.

——, *The Gospel of Mark: its Composition and Date*, New Haven 1925.

BAUERNFEIND, O., *Die Worte der Dämonen im Markus-Evangelium*, Stuttgart 1927.

BEACH, C., *The Gospel of Mark: its Making and Meaning*, New York 1959.

BEASLEY-MURRAY, G. R., *Jesus and the Future: an Examination of the Criticism of the Eschatological Discourse, Mark 13, with special Reference to the Little Apocalypse Theory*, London 1954.

BOOBYER, G. H., *St Mark and the Transfiguration Story*, Edinburgh 1942.

BURKILL, T. A., *Mysterious Revelation: an Examination of the Philosophy of St Mark's Gospel*, Ithaca, N.Y. 1963.

BUSCH, F., *Zum Verständnis der synoptischen Eschatologie: Markus 13 neu untersucht*, Gütersloh 1938.

CADOUX, A. T., *The Sources of the Second Gospel*, London 1935.

CARRINGTON, P., *The Primitive Christian Calendar: a Study in the Making of the Marcan Gospel*, vol. 1: *Introduction and Text*, Cambridge 1952.

CRUM, J. M. C., *St Mark's Gospel: Two Stages of its Making*, Cambridge 1936.

DOUDNA, J. C., *The Greek of the Gospel of Mark*, Philadelphia 1961.

EBELING, H. J., *Das Messiasgeheimnis und die Botschaft des Marcus-Evangelisten*, Berlin 1939.

FARRER, A. M., *A Study in St Mark*, London 1951.

GRANT, F. C., *The Earliest Gospel*, New York 1943.

GUY, H. A., *The Origin of the Gospel of Mark*, New York 1954.

HARTMANN, G., *Der Aufbau des Markusevangeliums*, Münster 1936.

LIGHTFOOT, R. H., *The Gospel Message of St Mark*, Oxford 1950.

MARXSEN, W., *Der Evangelist Markus: Studien zur Redaktionsgeschichte des Evangeliums*, Göttingen 1956; 2nd edn 1960.

MASSON, Ch., *Les paraboles de Marc IV; avec une introduction à l'explication des évangiles*, Neuchâtel-Paris 1945.

PARKER, P., *The Gospel before Mark*, Chicago 1953.

ROBINSON, J. M., *Das Geschichtsverständnis des Markus-Evangeliums*, Zurich 1956.

SUNDWALL, J. *Die Zusammensetzung des Markusevangeliums*, Abo 1934.

THIEL, R., *Drei Markus-Evangelien*, Berlin 1938.

WEISS, J., *Das älteste Evangelium: ein Beitrag zum Verständnis des Markus-Evangeliums und der ältesten evangelischen Ueberlieferung*. Göttingen 1903.

WENDLING, E., *Die Entstehung des Marcusevangeliums: philologische Untersuchungen*, Tübingen 1908.

——, *Ur-Marcus: Versuch einer Wiederherstellung der ältesten Mitteilungen über das Leben Jesu*, Tübingen 1905.

WERNER, M., *Der Einfluss paulinischer Theologie im Markusevangelium*, Giessen 1923.

WREDE, W., *Das Messiasgeheimnis in den Evangelien, zugleich ein Beitrag zum Verständnis des Markusevangeliums*, Göttingen 1901; 2nd edn 1913.

ZERWICK, M., *Untersuchungen zum Markus-Stil: ein Beitrag zur stilistischen Durcharbeitung des Neuen Testaments*, Rome 1937.

4
COMMENTARIES ON ST MARK'S GOSPEL

ALLEN, W. C., *The Gospel according to St Mark*, London 1915.

BACON, B. W., *The Beginnings of Gospel Story*, New Haven 1909.

BEASLEY-MURRAY, G. R., *A Commentary on Mark Thirteen*, London 1957.

BRANSCOMB, B. H., *The Gospel of Mark*, London 1937 (The Moffatt New Testament Commentary).

CARRINGTON, P., *According to Mark: a running Commentary on the oldest Gospel*, Cambridge 1960.

CRANFIELD, C. E. B., *The Gospel according to St Mark*, Cambridge 1959 (The Cambridge Greek Testament Commentary).

DEHN, G., *Le Fils de Dieu: Commentaire à l'évangile de Marc*, Fr. trans., Paris 1936, 2nd edn, Geneva, n.d.

GOULD, E. P., *The Gospel according to St Mark*, Edinburgh 1896 (The International Critical Commentary).

GRUNDMANN, W., *Das Evangelium nach Markus*, Berlin 1959 (Theologischer Handkommentar zum N.T., II, 2nd edn).

HAUCK, F., *Das Evangelium des Markus*, Leipzig 1931 (Theologischer Handkommentar zum N.T., II).

HOLTZMANN, H. J., *Die Synoptiker*, 3rd edn, Tübingen and Leipzig 1901 (Handkommentar zum N.T., I.1).

HUBY, J., *L'Evangile selon saint Marc*, 2nd edn, Paris 1953 (The Holy Bible translated into French under the direction of the Ecole biblique de Jérusalem, commonly called the Jerusalem Bible).

JOHNSON, S. E., *A Commentary on the Gospel according to St Mark*, New York 1960 (Harper's N.T. Comm.).

KLOSTERMANN, E., *Das Markusevangelium*, 3rd edn, Tübingen 1936; 4th edn, 1950 (Handbuch zum N.T., 3).

LAGRANGE, M. J., *Evangile selon saint Marc*, 4th edn, Paris 1929; 7th edn 1942 (Etudes bibliques).

LOHMEYER, E., *Das Evangelium des Markus*, Göttingen 1937; new edn revised by G. Sass 1951 (Kritisch-exegetischer Kommentar über das Neue Testament, I.2, 10th edn and following).

LOISY, A., *Les évangiles synoptiques*, Ceffonds 1907.

——, *L'évangile selon Marc*, Paris 1912.

MERX, A., *Die Evangelien des Markus und Lukas nach der syrischen, im Sinaikloster gefundenen Palimpsesthandschrift erläutert*, Berlin 1905 (Die vier kanonischen Evangelien nach ihrem ältesten bekannten Texte, II.2).

MONTEFIORE, C. G., *The Synoptic Gospels: edited with an Introduction and a Commentary*, 2nd edn, London 1927.

PALLIS, A., *Notes on St Mark and St Matthew*, London 1932.

RAWLINSON, A. E. J., *The Gospel according to St Mark*, London 1925 (Westminster Commentaries).

SCHLATTER, A., *Die Evangelien nach Markus und Lukas*, new impression, Stuttgart 1947 (Erläuterungen zum N.T.).

——, *Markus, der Evangelist für die Griechen*, Stuttgart 1935.

SCHMID, J., *Das Evangelium nach Markus*, Regensburg 1954 (Regensburger Neues Testament).

SCHNIEWIND, J., *Das Evangelium nach Markus*, Göttingen 1934; 8th edn 1956 (Das Neue Testament deutsch, 2).

SWETE, H. B., *The Gospel according to St Mark*, 3rd edn, London 1909 (Macmillan New Testament Commentaries).

TAYLOR, V., *The Gospel according to St Mark*, London 1952.

WEISS, J., *Die Schriften des Neuen Testaments*, vol. I, 3rd edn, rev. by Bousset, Göttingen 1917.

WELLHAUSEN, J., *Das Evangelium Marci übersetzt und erklärt*, 2nd edn, Berlin 1909.

WOHLENBERG, G., *Das Evangelium des Markus*, Leipzig 1910 (Kommentar zum N.T. . . . ; hgg. von Th. Zahn, II).

5
OTHER WORKS CITED

ALFARIC, P., *Pour comprendre la vie de Jésus: examen critique de l'évangile selon Marc*, Paris 1929.

BALTENSWEILER, H., *Die Verklärung Jesu: historisches Ereignis und synoptische Berichte*, Zurich 1959.

BEILNER, W., *Christus und die Pharisäer: exegetische Untersuchung über Grund und Verlauf der Auseinandersetzungen*, Vienna 1959.

BENOIT, A., *Saint Irénée: introduction à l'étude de sa théologie*, Paris 1960.

BIENECK, J., *Sohn Gottes als Christusbezeichnung der Synoptiker*, Zurich 1951.

BLINZLER, J., *Der Prozess Jesu . . .*, 3rd edn, Regensburg 1960.

BONSIRVEN, J., *Le Règne de Dieu*, Paris 1957.

BORNKAMM, G., *Jesus von Nazareth*, Stuttgart 1956.

BOUSSET, W., *Kyrios Christos*, 3rd edn, Göttingen 1926.

BRANDON, S. G. F., *The Fall of Jerusalem and the Christian Church*, London 1951; 2nd edn 1957.

BULTMANN, R., *Das Evangelium des Johannes*, Göttingen 1941 (Krit.-Ex. Komm., II, 10th edn); 15th edn, enlarged 1957.

——, *Theologie des Neuen Testaments*, 3rd edn, Tübingen 1958; [E.T. K. Grobel, 2 vols, New York 1951–5].

CAMPENHAUSEN, H. v., *Der Ablauf der Osterereignisse und das leere Grab*, 2nd edn, Heidelberg 1958.

CHEVALLIER, M. A., *L'Esprit et le Messie dans le Bas-Judaïsme et le Nouveau Testament*, Paris 1958.

CLAVIER, H., *L'accès au Royaume de Dieu*, Clermont-Ferrand and Paris 1943.

COUCHOUD, P. L., *Jésus, le Dieu fait homme*, Paris 1937.

CULLMANN, O., *Christologie du Nouveau Testament*, Neuchâtel-Paris 1958; [E.T. S. C. Guthrie and C. A. M. Hall, Philadelphia 1959].

——, *Dieu et César: le procès de Jésus: saint Paul et l'autorité; l'Apocalypse et l'Etat totalitaire*, Neuchâtel-Paris 1956.

——, *Saint Pierre, disciple, apôtre, martyr: histoire et théologie*, Neuchâtel-Paris 1952; [E.T. F. V. Filson, 2nd edn rev., London 1962].

——, *La tradition: problème exégétique, historique et théologique*, Neuchâtel-Paris 1953.

DALMAN, G., *Jesus-Jeschua: die drei Sprachen Jesu: Jesus in der Synagoge, auf dem Berge, beim Passahmahl, am Kreuz*, Leipzig 1922; [E.T. 1929].

——, *Les itinéraires de Jésus: topographie des Evangiles*, French tr., J. Marty, Paris 1930.

DANIÉLOU, J., *Les manuscrits de la Mer Morte et les origines du christianisme*, Paris 1957.

DAUBE, D., *The New Testament and Rabbinic Judaism*, London 1956.

DIBELIUS, M., *Aufsätze zur Apostelgeschichte*, hgg. von H. Greeven, Göttingen 1951; [E.T. M. Ling, London 1956].

——, and KÜMMEL, W., *Jesus*, 3rd edn, Berlin 1960.

DODD, C. H., *According to the Scriptures: the Sub-structure of New Testament Theology*, London 1952.

——, *The Interpretation of the Fourth Gospel*, Cambridge 1953.

DORESSE, J., *L'évangile selon Thomas, ou les paroles secrètes de Jésus*, Paris 1959.

DREWS, A., *Das Markusevangelium als Zeugnis gegen die Geschichtlichkeit Jesu*, Jena 1921; 2nd edn 1924.

DUPONT, J., *Les sources du Livre des Actes: état de la question*, n.p. 1960: [E.T. K. Pond, London 1964].

DUPONT-SOMMER, A., *Les écrits esséniens découverts près de la Mer Morte*, Paris 1959; [E.T. G. Vermes, Oxford 1961].

ELLIOTT-BINNS, L. E., *Galilean Christianity*, London 1956.

Evangile (L') selon Thomas; texte copte établi et traduit par A. GUILLAU-MONT, H. CH. PUECH, G. QUISPEL, W. TILL and YASSAH ABD AL MASIH, Paris 1959.

FLEMINGTON, W. F., *The New Testament Doctrine of Baptism*, London 1948.

FRIDRICHSEN, A., *The Apostle and His Message*, Uppsala 1947.

GOGUEL, M., *L'Eglise primitive*, Paris 1947.

——, *Jésus*, 2nd edn, Paris 1950; [E.T. O. Wyon, *The Life of Jesus*, New York 1933].

——, *La naissance du christianisme*, Paris 1946; [E.T. H. C. Snape, London 1953].

GRAESSER, E., *Das Problem der Parusieverzögerung in den synoptischen Evangelien und in der Apostelgeschichte*, Berlin 1957.

GUIGNEBERT, Ch., *Le monde juif vers le temps de Jésus*, Paris 1935.

——, *Jésus*, Paris 1933; [E.T. New York 1935].

HAENCHEN, E., *Die Apostelgeschichte*, 4th edn, Göttingen 1961 (Krit. exeget. Kommentar über das N.T., III, 13th edn).

HERFORD, R. T., *Les Pharisiens*, French tr., Paris 1928.

HÉRING, J., *La première épitre de saint Paul aux Corinthiens*, Neuchâtel-Paris 1949 (Commentaire du N.T., VII; [E.T. A. W. Heathcote and P. J. Alcock, London 1962].

——, *Le Royaume de Dieu et sa venue, étude sur l'espérance de Jésus et de l'apôtre Paul*, Paris 1937; 2nd edn, Neuchâtel, 1959.

ISAAC, J., *Jésus et Israël*, Paris 1948; 2nd edn 1959.

JACOB, E., *Théologie de l'Ancien Testament*, Neuchâtel-Paris 1955.

JAUBERT, A., *La date de la Cène: calendrier biblique et liturgie chrétienne*, Paris 1957.

JEREMIAS, J., *Jerusalem zur Zeit Jesu*, 2nd edn, Göttingen 1958; [E.T. *Jerusalem in the Time of Jesus*, London 1969].

——, [French tr., *Jésus et les païens*, Neuchâtel and Paris 1956].

KÄHLER, M., *Der sogenannte historische Jesus und der geschichtliche, biblische Christus*; 2nd edn rev. by E. Wolf, Munich 1956.

KÜMMEL, W. G., *Verheissung und Erfüllung, Untersuchungen zur eschatologischen Verkündigung Jesu*, 3rd edn, Zurich 1956; [E.T. D. M. Barton, *Promise and Fulfilment* (Studies in Biblical Theology xxiii) Napierville 1957].

LAKE, K., and JACKSON, F. J., *The beginnings of Christianity, I: The Acts of the Apostles*; ed. F. J. Jackson and K. Lake, 5 vols, London 1920–33.

LÉONARD, E. G., *Histoire ecclésiastique des Réformés français au xviiie siècle*, Paris 1940.

LIEBERMANN, S., *Greek in Jewish Palestine*, New York 1942.

LIETZMANN, H., *Histoire de l'Eglise ancienne*; French tr., d'A. Jundt, 4 vols, Paris 1936–49; [E.T. B. L. Woolf, *The Beginnings of the Christian Church*, London 1953].

LODS, A., *Histoire de la littérature hébraïque et juive depuis les origines jusqu'à la ruine de l'Etat juif* (135 *après Jésus-Christ*), Paris 1950.

——, *Les prophètes d'Israël et les débuts du judaïsme*, Paris 1935; [E.T. 1937].

LOHMEYER, E., *Evangelium und Kultus*, Göttingen 1942.

——, *Galiläa und Jerusalem*, Göttingen 1936.

——, *Gottesknecht und Davidsohn*, Copenhagen 1945.

LOHSE, E., *Märtyrer und Gottesknecht, Untersuchungen zur urchristlichen Verkündigung vom Sühnetod Jesu Christi*, Göttingen 1955.

LOISY, A., *Histoire et mythe à propos de Jésus-Christ*, Paris 1937.

MANSON, W., *Jesus the Messiah*, London 1943; 2nd edn 1952.

MENOUD, Ph., *L'Evangile de Jean d'après les recherches récentes*, 2nd edn, Neuchâtel and Paris 1947.

MEYER, E., *Ursprung und Anfänge des Christentums*, 3 vols, Stuttgart-Berlin 1921–4.

MICHEL, O., *Der Brief an die Römer*, Göttingen 1955 (Krit.-exeget. Komm. über das N.T., iv, 10th edn).

MUNCK, J., *Paulus und die Heilsgeschichte*, Aarhus-Copenhagen 1954; [E.T. by author, *Paul and the Salvation of Mankind*, London 1959].

NEHER, A., *L'essence du prophétisme*, Paris 1955.

OTTO, R., *Reich Gottes und Menschensohn*, Munich 1934; [E.T. *The Kingdom of God and the Son of Man*, London 1943].

PERCY, E., *Die Botschaft Jesus: eine traditionskritische une exegetische Untersuchung*, Lund 1953.

PREISS, Th., *Le Fils de l'Homme: fragments d'un cours sur la christologie du Nouveau Testament*, 2 vols, Montpellier 1951–3.

PRIGENT, P., *Apocalypse 12 : histoire de l'exégèse*, Tübingen 1959.

RASCHKE, M. H., *Die Werkstatt der Markusevangelisten: eine neue Evangelientheorie*, Jena 1924.

REITZENSTEIN, R., *Das iranische Erlösungsmysterium*, Bonn 1921.

ROBERTS, H., *Jesus and the Kingdom of God*, London 1955.

ROBINSON, J. M., *A new quest of the Historical Jesus*, London 1959; German tr., *Kerygma und historischer Jesus*, Zurich-Stuttgart 1960; French tr., *Le kérygme de l'Église et le Jésus de l'histoire*, Geneva 1961.

SCHOEPS, H. J., *Theologie und Geschichte des Judenchristentums*, Tübingen 1949.

SCHÜRER, E., *Geschichte des jüdischen Volkes im Zeitalter Jesu Christi*, 3rd–4th edn, Leipzig 1909.

SCHÜTZ, R., *Apostel und Jünger*, Giessen 1921.

SCHWEITZER, A., *Geschichte der Leben-Jesu-Forschung*, 2nd edn, Tübingen 1913; [E.T. *The Quest of the historical Jesus*, London 1911].

SCHWEIZER, E., *Erniedrigung und Erhöhung bei Jesus und seinen Nachfolgern*, Zurich 1955; [E.T. *Lordship and Discipleship*, London 1960].

——, *Gemeinde und Gemeindeordnung im Neuen Testament*, Zurich 1959; [E.T. London 1961].

SIMON, M., *St Stephen and the Hellenists in the Primitive Church*, London-New York-Toronto 1958.

——, *Les sectes juives au temps de Jésus*, Paris 1960.

SJOEBERG, E., *Der verborgene Menschensohn in den Evangelien*, Lund 1955.

TAYLOR, V., *The Text of the New Testament : a Short Introduction*, London 1961.

TEEPLE, H. M., *The Mosaic Eschatological Prophet*, Philadelphia 1957.

TOEDT, H. E., *Der Menschensohn in der synoptischen Ueberlieferung*, Gütersloh 1959.

TROCMÉ, E., *Le 'Livre des Actes' et l'histoire*, Paris 1957.

VAGANAY, L., *L'Evangile de Pierre*, Paris 1932.

VAN DER WOUDE, A. S., *Die messianischen Vorstellungen der Gemeinde von Qumran*, Assen 1957.

VUILLEUMIER, R., *La tradition cultuelle d'Israël dans la prophétie d'Amos et d'Osée*, Neuchâtel-Paris 1960.

WENDLAND, H. D., *Die Eschatologie des Reiches Gottes bei Jesus*, Gütersloh 1931.

WERNER, M., *Die Entstehung des christlichen Dogmas*, Berne-Leipzig 1941; 2nd edn 1953.

WILDER, A. N., *Eschatology and Ethics in the Teaching of Jesus*, 2nd edn, New York 1950.

WILLIAMS, C. S. C., *Alterations to the Text of the Synoptic Gospels and Acts*, Oxford 1951.

WINTER, P., *On the Trial of Jesus*, Berlin 1960.

WOLFF, H. W., *Jesaja 53 im Urchristentum*, Bethel-bei-Bielefeld 1942; 3rd edn, Berlin 1952.

6

PERIODICALS AND COLLECTIVE WORKS
TO WHICH OCCASIONAL REFERENCE
HAS BEEN MADE

Aux sources de la tradition chrétienne; Mélanges offerts à M. Maurice Goguel à l'occasion de son soixante-dixième anniversaire. Neuchâtel and Paris 1950.

Biblica, Commentarii ad rem biblicam scientifice investigandam . . . ; editi a Pontificio Instituto Biblico, Rome.

Biblische Zeitschrift, Freiburg-im-Breisgau, then Paderborn.

Bulletin of the John Rylands Library, Manchester.

Ephemerides theologicae Lovanienses . . . : Commentarii de re theologica et canonica, Louvain and Gembloux.

Etudes théologiques et religieuses, Montpellier.

ΕΥΧΑΡΙΣΤΗΡΙΟΝ: Studien zur Religion und Literatur des Alten und Neuen Testaments H. Gunkel zum 60. Geburtstag . . . dargebracht, 2 vols, Göttingen 1923.

Evangile (L') de Jean: études et problèmes, n.p./n.d. [1958] (Recherches bibliques publiées sous le patronage du Colloquium Biblicum Lovaniense, III).

Expository Times, Edinburgh.

Harvard Theological Review (The), Cambridge, Mass.

Journal of Biblical Literature, Philadelphia.

Journal of Ecclesiastical History, London.

Journal of Theological Studies, Oxford and London.

Neutestamentliche Studien für Rudolf Bultmann zu seinem siebzigsten Geburtstag am 20. August 1954, Berlin 1954 (Beihefte zur Zeitschrift für die neutestamentliche Wissenchaft, 21).

New Testament Essays: studies in memory of Thomas Walter Manson . . . , ed. A. J. B. Higgins . . . , Manchester 1959.

New Testament Studies: an International Journal published . . . under the auspices of Studiorum Novi Testamenti Societas, Cambridge.

Novum Testamentum: an International Quarterly for New Testament and Related Studies . . . , Leiden.

Recherches de science religieuse, Paris.

Revue bénédictine, Maredsous, Belgium.

Revue biblique, publiée par l'Ecole Pratique d'Etudes Bibliques . . . de Jérusalem, Paris.

Revue de l'histoire des religions (Annales du Musée Guimet), Paris.

Revue de Qumrân, Paris.

Revue d'histoire et de philosophie religieuses, publiée par la Faculté de Théologie Protestante de l'Université de Strasbourg, Paris.

Scottish Journal of Theology, Edinburgh and London.

Sitzungsberichte der Berliner Akademie der Wissenschaften, Philosophisch-historische Klasse, Berlin.

Sitzungsberichte der Heidelberger Akademie der Wissenschaften, Philosophisch-historische Klasse, Heidelberg.

Studia theologica, cura ordinum theologorum Scandinavicorum edita, Lund.

Svensk exegetisk årsbok, Uppsala.

Theologische Literaturzeitung, Monatschrift für das gesamte Gebiet der Theologie und Religionswissenschaft, Berlin.

Theologische Rundschau, Tübingen.

Theologische Studien und Kritiken: eine Zeitschrift für das gesammte Gebiet der Theologie, Hamburg, then Gotha.

Theologische Zeitschrift, herausgegeben von der Theologischen Fakultät der Universität Basel, Basle.

Vigiliae christianae: Review of Early Christian Life and Language, Amsterdam.

Zeitschrift für die neutestamentliche Wissenschaft und die Kunde der älteren Kirche, Giessen, then Berlin.

Zeitschrift für systematische Theologie, Göttingen.

Zeitschrift für Theologie und Kirche, Tübingen.

SOME RECENT BOOKS
ON THE GOSPEL OF MARK
1963–74

MONOGRAPHS ABOUT THE GOSPEL OF MARK

BELO, F., *Lecture matérialiste de l'Evangile de Marc*, Paris 1974.

BEST, E., *The Temptation and the Passion: the Markan Soteriology*, Cambridge 1965.

BOWMAN, J., *The Gospel of Mark, the New Christian Jewish Passover Haggadah*, Leiden 1965.

BURKILL, T. A., *New Light on the Earliest Gospel: Seven Markan Studies*, Ithaca-London 1972.

HARTMAN, L., *Prophecy Interpreted, the Formation of Some Jewish Apocalyptic Texts and of the Eschatological Discourse Mark 13 Par.*, Lund 1966.

HOOKER, M. D., *The Son of Man in Mark*, London 1967.

HORSTMANN, M., *Studien zur markinischen Christologie*, Münster 1969.

KERTELGE, K., *Die Wunder Jesu im Markusevangelium*, Munich 1970.

LAMBRECHT, J., *Die Redaktion der Markus-Apokalypse*, Rome 1967.

LINDSEY, R. L., *A Hebrew Translation of the Gospel of Mark . . . with English Introduction*, Jerusalem n.d. [1969?].

MASSON, Ch., *L'Evangile de Marc et l'Eglise de Rome*, Neuchâtel 1968.

MAUSER, U., *Christ in the Wilderness: the Wilderness Theme in the Second Gospel and its Basis in the Biblical Tradition*, London 1963.

MINETTE DE TILLESSE, G., *Le secret messianique dans l'Evangile de Marc*, Paris 1968.

NEIRYNCK, F., *Duality in Mark: Contributions to the Study of the Markan Redaction*, Louvain 1972.

PESCH, R., *Naherwartungen, Tradition und Redaktion in Mk 13*, Düsseldorf 1968.

QUESNELL, Q., *The Mind of Mark: Interpretation and Method through the Exegesis of Mark 6.52*, Rome 1969.

RIGAUX, B., *Témoignage de l'évangile de Marc*, n.p. [Paris-Bruges], n.d. [1965].

SMITH, M., *Clement of Alexandria and a Secret Gospel of Mark*, Cambridge, Mass. 1973.

SUHL, A., *Die Funktion der alttestamentlichen Zitate und Anspielungen im Markusevangelium*, Gütersloh 1965.

SCHREIBER, J., *Theologie des Vertrauens: eine redaktionsgeschichtliche Untersuchung des Markusevangeliums*, Hamburg 1967.

TAGAWA, K., *Miracles et Evangile: la pensée personnelle de l'évangéliste Marc*, Paris 1966.

TREVIJANO, R., *Comienzo del Evangelio: estudio sobre el prologo de San Marcos*, Burgos 1971.

WEINACHT, H., *Die Menschwerdung des Sohnes Gottes im Markusevangelium*, Tübingen 1972.

COMMENTARIES ON THE GOSPEL OF MARK
(Not including new editions of earlier works)

GROB, R., *Einführung in das Markus-Evangelium*, Zürich-Stuttgart 1965.

HAENCHEN, E., *Der Weg Jesu, eine Erklärung des Markus-Evangeliums und der kanonischen Parallelen*, Berlin 1966.

NINEHAM, D. E., *The Gospel of St Mark*, Harmondsworth 1963.

RADEMAKERS, J., *La Gonne nouvelle de Jésus selon saint Marc*, 2 vols., Brussels 1974.

SCHWEIZER, E., *Das Evangelium nach Markus*, Göttingen 1967.

SCHNACKENBURG, R., *Das Evangelium nach Markus*, Düsseldorf 1966.

INDEX OF AUTHORS

Only modern authors are included in this index

INDEX OF MARCAN
REFERENCES